Capital, Class and Techn
in Contemporary Ameri

Nick Heffernan

CAPITAL, CLASS AND TECHNOLOGY IN CONTEMPORARY AMERICAN CULTURE

Projecting Post-Fordism

Pluto Press
LONDON • STERLING, VIRGINIA

First published 2000 by
Pluto Press
345 Archway Road, London N6 5AA
and 22883 Quicksilver Drive, Sterling, VA 20166–2012, USA

www.plutobooks.com

British Library Cataloguing in Publication Data
A catalogue record for this book is available from the British Library.

Library of Congress Cataloging in Publication Data
Heffernan, Nick.
Capital, class, and technology in contemporary American culture : projecting post-
Fordism / Nick Heffernan.
    p. cm.
Includes bibliographical references.
  ISBN 0–7453–1105–9 (hbk) — ISBN 0–7453–1104–0 (pbk.)
  1. United States—Social conditions—1980– 2. Social change—United
States. 3. Capitalism—United States. 4. Postmodernism—Social
aspects—United States. I. Title.
  HN59.2 .H44 2001
  306'.0973—dc21

                                                              00–009740

ISBN 0 7453 1105 9 hardback
ISBN 0 7453 1104 0 paperback

09   08   07   06   05   04   03   02   01   00
10   9   8   7   6   5   4   3   2   1

Designed and produced for Pluto Press by Chase Publishing Services
Typeset from disk by Stanford DTP Services, Northampton
Printed in the European Union by TJ International, Padstow

Contents

Introduction   1

Part 1   Late Capitalism, Fordism, Post-Fordism

1. Postmodernism and Late Capitalism   13
2. Class and Consensus, Ideology and Technology   29

Part 2   Putting 'IT' to Work: Post-Fordism, Information Technology and the Eclipse of Production

3. Making 'IT': *The Soul of a New Machine*   39
4. Faking 'IT': *True Stories*   72
5. Playing with 'IT': *Microserfs*   88

Part 3   Impotence and Omnipotence: The Cybernetic Discourse of Capitalism

6. Cybernetics, Systems Theory and the End of Ideology   105
7. Imaginary Resolutions: William Gibson's Cyberspace Trilogy   119
8. Artificial Intelligence and Class Consciousness: *Blade Runner*   148

Part 4   Capital, Class, Cosmopolitanism

9. Fordism, Post-Fordism and the Production of World Space   165
10. National Allegory and the Romance of Uneven Development: *The Names*   179
11. Blindness and Insight in the World System: *Until the End of the World*   205
Conclusion: Questioning Fordism and Post-Fordism   212

Notes   216
Bibliography   230
Index   245

Introduction

My purpose in this book is to explore the ways in which the stories we generate and tell ourselves, through literary fiction, film, journalism and social and cultural theory, register and represent change. The kind of change I'm particularly interested in might best be called structural – historic transformations of the ways our lives are organised and shaped economically, socially and culturally. It is my view that for the last twenty years or so the question of structural change has been asked most persistently, embracingly and, at times, confusingly through the terms postmodernism and postmodernity. Broadly speaking, I understand postmodernism to refer to a range of more or less novel aesthetic styles, cultural attitudes and philosophical or political positions which to varying degrees are expressions of and responses to historical change. Postmodernity, on the other hand, can perhaps best be understood as a description of that wider historical condition and experience of change out of which the various expressive postmodernisms arise.[1] Amongst all the disagreement, debate and polemic that surround these terms it is possible to identify at least one consistent proposition: that the postmodern is not a cultural matter alone, that it bears some kind of relation to the transformations wrought by, and within, contemporary capitalism, and that to inquire into the postmodern is also necessarily to inquire into the nature of Western capitalist societies as they have developed since, roughly, 1945.

It is perhaps no surprise, then, that some of the most influential theorisations of the postmodern have come from the political left, nor that the debate about postmodernism has become a vehicle for the interrogation, contestation and reappraisal of many of the categories and assumptions of left politics in general and Marxism in particular.[2] Two of the earliest American formulations of postmodernism, at least in the sense which predominates in the present debate about cultural change, came from the left cultural critics Irving Howe and C. Wright Mills. In his essay 'Mass Society and Post-Modern Fiction' (1956), Howe used the term to denote the proximity of 'enormous changes in human history' which, he claimed, were set to undermine the collective assumption that 'the social relations of men in the world of capitalism were established, familiar, knowable' (Howe, 1963: pp. 96, 80). Similarly, Mills in *The Sociological Imagination* (1959), argued that Western societies were in the throes of 'an epochal kind of transition' in which 'the Modern Age is being succeeded by a post-modern period'. We were ill-equipped to come to terms with this transition because the 'post-modern period' according to Mills, was defined precisely by a crisis in historical understanding due to the fact that 'our major orientations – liberalism and socialism – have virtually collapsed as adequate explanations of our world and of ourselves' (Mills, 1983: p. 184). The most influential recent theorisation of postmodernism has come from the Marxist critic Fredric Jameson for whom the term likewise suggests the arrival of radically new cultural and social forms associated with the 'systemic modification of capitalism', specifically with the onset of what he calls the 'historically original' stage of late capitalism (Jameson, 1991: pp. xii, 3).

But the connection between postmodernism and the structural transformation of capitalism is present even in the thinking of overtly anti- or post-Marxists for whom the notion of 'postindustrial society' rather than late capitalism or mass society serves as a reference point. Thus for Daniel Bell and Jean Baudrillard the transformation consists in the displacement of industrial production by consumption and image-manipulation; while for Jean-François Lyotard it is bound up with the effects and imperatives of new technologies, with the 'computerisation' of society, and the new importance of scientific knowledge and information, rather than industrial hardware, as means of production (Bell, 1973 and 1976; Baudrillard, 1975 and 1981; Lyotard, 1984).

One problem raised by all these formulations is the extent to which postmodernism should be understood as marking a decisive historical break in the cultural and social development of the capitalist West. Jameson, for instance, argues that the very 'case for its existence depends on the hypothesis of some radical break or *coupure*, generally traced back to the end of the 1950s or the early 1960s' (Jameson, 1991: p. 1). Bell, on the other hand, sees postmodernism as the logical extension of classical bourgeois individualism allied to antinomian and hedonistic impulses set in motion by the modernist art and culture of the late nineteenth century and the nascent consumer capitalism of the 1920s respectively (Bell, 1976). While Jameson has conceded that arguments for a break or a continuity are essentially groundless – he sees them as the opening gambits of competing stories about our recent history which are neither 'empirically justifiable' nor 'philosophically arguable' (Jameson, 1991: p. xiii) – it is nonetheless the case that they do raise certain conceptual problems for our understanding of the periodisation and dynamics of cultural change. For example, as Perry Anderson has observed, Jameson's strategy of basing his notion of postmodernism on Ernest Mandel's monumental account of late capitalism sits somewhat uneasily with his own claims for the centrality of a radical break occurring somewhere around 1960 (Anderson, 1998: pp. 78–9). For, according to Mandel (1978), epochal change in the capitalist mode of production occurs between 1940 and 1945. Jameson's point of historical rupture does not therefore straightforwardly accord with Mandel's description of historical transformation, a difficulty that is not entirely resolved by Jameson's claims about the non-synchronous relationship between economic and socio-cultural change (Jameson, 1991: p. xix). The implications of this are pursued in Chapter 1 below.

Wary of these difficulties, other commentators have sought to understand the cultural change denoted by postmodernism and postmodernity less as an epochal transformation of the entire capitalist mode of production and more in terms of a limited structural recomposition of social and economic relationships within late capitalism. Mike Davis (1985), Scott Lash and John Urry (1987), David Harvey (1989) and Stuart Hall (1989) all see postmodernism as, in some respects at least, bound up with the economic and social crises that have beset the capitalist West since the late 1960s when the sustained economic boom of the post-Second World War period climaxed and entered a decline. In particular, it is argued that certain widely identified characteristics of the postmodern can be traced in some way to the break-up of certain social and cultural arrangements that had underpinned the long boom as a shift occurs towards new relationships and structures, through which a resolution of the economic crisis is sought.

One way of looking at this transformation within late capitalism is by using the notions of Fordism and post-Fordism. Broadly speaking again, Fordism refers to the way in which economic, social and even cultural life was organised in the United States and Western Europe for the duration of the long postwar boom between 1945 and the early 1970s. The principal feature of this period was the establishment of a durable balance between the mass production of standardised goods on the one hand, and the mass consumption of such goods on the other. Crudely put, this balance (or 'equilibrium' as economists are wont to call it) worked to offset capitalism's inherent tendency towards crises of overproduction and underconsumption. Such crises, of which the Great Depression of the 1930s is the most recent and notable manifestation, had repeatedly ravaged capitalist societies and derived from the fact that wealth, or purchasing power, was not sufficiently widely distributed across the population always to ensure that there would be an adequate market for ever increasing volumes of industrially produced goods. Periodically, production – driven by the desire of owners and employers for constantly rising profits – so drastically outstripped the ability of purchasers to absorb and consume goods as to seriously disrupt the cycle of profitability, causing widespread failure of over-extended firms and the social blight of unemployment and deepening immiseration.

The apparent elimination of such crises in the post-1945 period by the establishment of a new equilibrium between the spheres of production and consumption rested on a particular reconfiguration of class relationships, what has sometimes been called the 'capital–labour accord' (Bowles and Gintis, 1982: p. 55). The market's ability to absorb ever expanding rates of production was secured by an extension and deepening of the purchasing power of the population at large. Capital, in the form of owners and employers, granted – indeed in many cases guaranteed – workers a steadily rising standard of living through regular increases in wages. In return, organised labour conceded to employers' demands for tougher discipline and extended managerial power in the workplace, held to be the keys to improved productivity and higher profits. Typically this involved workers submitting to stricter supervision and bureaucratisation (or 'scientific management') of tasks, accepting the constant technological restructuring of the workplace (increasingly involving the replacement of workers by automated machinery), and restricting expressions of protest and discontent to narrowly prescribed official channels ('no strike' pledges became a feature of the deals American labour unions struck with employers in the postwar period). Of course this class compromise, or trade-off between rising productivity and rising wages, did not materialise entire overnight, nor did it descend like a prefabricated model upon American capitalism in order to provide for a new epoch of stability and prosperity. It represented the always relatively fluid and precarious outcome of a whole series of conflicts, struggles and negotiations between workers and employers that remained continually in process. Nonetheless, the balance between production and consumption that it produced meant that increasing numbers of the working population were now able to consume (or at least aspire to consume) the very goods that they helped manufacture and were thus presented with the prospect of entering into a charmed circle of prosperity and growth.

The state, too, played its part in the equation by underwriting this balance of class forces. The social welfare apparatus, perfected and consolidated in the post-1945 period, guaranteed a minimum level of subsistence or purchasing power for workers, while heavy government subsidies to whole sectors of production (most importantly the armaments and aerospace industries) guaranteed markets, and hence profits, for employers. For 25 years this close relationship between the liberal democratic state and the capitalist accumulation process appeared to deliver stable growth and widening prosperity free from the cyclical crises that had dogged capitalist society in earlier periods. Forged in the United States in the mid-1940s, the Fordist model was exported to Europe and even beyond (a very distinct kind of Fordism developed in Japan, for instance) via Marshall aid and under the aegis of American global military and financial supremacy, so that the period since the Second World War, in the capitalist world at least, can in many respects be understood as Fordist in character.

Post-Fordism refers to the disintegration of this world in the recurrent economic and social crises that have beset Western capitalist societies since the early 1970s, and to the various patterns according to which its elements might be recomposed in the periods of restructuring which have ensued. While there is considerable agreement about what is meant by Fordism, post-Fordism is a much more disputed category. I'll give a fuller account of both terms in Chapter 1 below, but it is perhaps worth stating at this point that post-Fordism is best seen not as any fully achieved entity but as a projection of, or metaphor for, the processes and effects of social and economic restructuring within contemporary capitalist societies, the final form of which cannot be specified. There are many versions of post-Fordism on offer in this period of flux in which the notion of 'restructuring' has become a commonplace. None of these can be considered completely authoritative; indeed some versions contain strong elements of prescription which betray a more than accidental connection to the interests of particular social groups. For example, there is what we might call a managerial or employers' post-Fordism which stresses the importance of a new 'flexibility' in labour practices and relations. This, while partly describing what is presently occurring, is also an expression of employers' concerns perpetually to lower wage costs and have compliant workers. The description thus seeks in part to legitimate the further extension of what is being described.

Similarly there is what we might call a professional middle-class or culturalist post-Fordism which emphasises decentralisation, demassification and the demise of Fordist standardisation, particularly in the field of consumption, as key features of 'new times'. Pointing to the rise of new kinds of individualism, self-definition and identity formation, this description reflects the interests, experience and world views of those professional groups, often located in the cultural industries or involved with the dissemination of new microelectronic technologies, which receive their rewards for constructing and propagating new forms of consumption or 'lifestyle'. To propose a settled definition of post-Fordism is therefore not only empirically unjustifiable, it also involves certain ideological risks concerning precisely *whose* post-Fordism is being described. I will use the term not to denote any particular social and economic configuration but to point to what might be seen as a projected and highly contested social space in which various competing understandings and descriptions of change circulate and toward which the current processes of restructuring can be seen as tending. Clearly, though, given that it marks a sharp departure from Fordist arrangements, post-Fordism implies significant changes in patterns of work, production and consumption, in the balance of class forces, and in the conditions that circumscribe action and shape identity that are wide ranging in their effects and not limited purely to the economic sphere.

Indeed, one of the advantages of using the notions of Fordism and post-Fordism to investigate contemporary cultural change is that their reach extends across the economic, the social and the cultural without necessarily implying that the latter categories merely reflect processes that occur in the former. They suggest, rather, the interaction and interpenetration of economy, society and culture. As Stuart Hall has argued, 'the metaphor of post-Fordism ... is not committed to any prior determining position for the economy. But it does insist ... that shifts of this order in economic life must be taken seriously in any analysis of our present circumstances' (Hall, 1989: p. 119).

This returns us to the question of the relationship between post-Fordism and postmodernism as two of the most powerful descriptions of structural change in current use. I would not want to suggest any direct correspondence between the two either in terms of periodisation or putative content, though David Harvey has attempted to argue as much in his bold account of contemporary cultural change (Harvey, 1989).[3] Nor is it my objective to arrive at a conceptualisation or definition of the postmodern. However, I will in the following chapters claim that *some* of the cultural shifts and characteristics associated with postmodernism and postmodernity can be understood, indeed can most profitably be understood, in relation to the crisis of Fordism and the complex of responses to it that goes under the name post-Fordism.

It is important to state here that this relation is not a causal one. Many aspects of postmodernism can be traced back well into the period of Fordism and before. For example, if we consider the observation, central to many accounts of postmodernity, that culture has been taken over by the market and its imperatives then we must acknowledge that this development can be situated as far back as the 1920s when the importance of mass consumption, and hence cultural images of the 'good life', to economic growth was first widely established.[4] Thus such 'postmodern' characteristics as the mobilisation of desire as an economic force, or the saturation of social and subjective life with fantasy images that call into question distinctions between surface and depth or the real and the represented, must be understood as relatively continuous and long-term social processes which aroused comment and concern well before the turn towards post-Fordism or the emergence of so-called postmodernist claims about the 'society of the spectacle' or 'hyperreality'.[5]

Other features associated with postmodernity must also be seen in terms of the historical continuity of capitalist development. The diminishing importance of labour, production and even social class as orienting categories derives not simply from the unchallenged supremacy of consumption in contemporary social life, but also from the logic of modern capitalist production itself, in which automation – the replacement of living labour by dead labour as Marx put it – has been the method preferred by employers seeking to discipline workers and boost profits. What is often presented as a specifically postmodern sense of being profoundly distanced or detached from living contact with the material substratum of human life, from a direct and unmediated relationship with the natural or physical world out of which our means of subsistence are produced, has in fact been noted by analysts of 'modern life' since the late-nineteenth century, though the idea received particular attention during the 1950s, the first fully Fordist decade in the United States.[6] Similarly, stories about the dissolution of classes and class consciousness (usually meaning the *working* class and *working-class* consciousness) which are often part and parcel of postmodern positions or descriptions of postmodernity, are only extensions of earlier arguments that surrounded the scientific rationalisation of industrial labour in the 1910s and '20s and were intensified with the further automation and bureaucratisation of work in the full Fordism of the 1950s.[7] And related claims that postmodernity brings with it an unprecedented dispersal and unlocatability of power were also anticipated and rehearsed during the 1950s.[8]

Yet there *are* significantly new conditions that have emerged from the economic crises of the 1970s and '80s and the shift from Fordism to post-Fordism. Perhaps the most fundamental of these flow from the break-up of the class compromise that underpinned the postwar boom and allowed commentators to characterise this period as one of relative social consensus and political placidity. The drive to return to the high levels of profitability enjoyed during the heyday of Fordist growth has entailed an attack upon the perceived 'rigidities' of labour markets and industrial relations, and upon the share of social wealth enjoyed by wage-earners, that manifests itself in deeply altered patterns of production and consumption. The years since the early 1970s have witnessed huge breakdowns and shifts in the regional and global distribution of production in which the export of many kinds of industrial activity out of the advanced capitalist countries has perhaps been the principal feature.

For some commentators this is simply confirmation of the move towards a 'postindustrial' or 'informational' economic order presented as an evolutionary step in the human mastery of nature that takes Western societies beyond the era of heavy industrial manufacturing (Bell, 1973 and 1980a; Naisbitt, 1982; Stonier, 1983; Drucker, 1993). For others it constitutes a deliberate strategy of de-industrialisation by which owners and employers struggle to remove production from those areas in which organised labour had attained considerable power. It thus must be understood as a political and ideological offensive waged upon the capital–labour accord institutionalised under Fordism with the objective of recomposing its terms in favour of the owning and employing classes (Bluestone and Harrison, 1982; Clark, 1989; Hayes, 1990). This redistribution of production, and the redistribution of power and wealth that is its consequence, has in many respects been facilitated by new information or microelectronic technologies which, while constituting new branches of production and sources of profit in themselves, also bring with them new experiences and understandings of time and space, and new conduits and images of power. Thus the process of fragmentation that is often associated with both post-Fordism and postmodernism can be seen to have economic, social, and subjective or experiential dimensions.

This redistribution of production has been accompanied by a recomposition of Fordist patterns of consumption. On the one hand, there has been a prolonged contest over the past twenty years to reduce the 'citizen wage' or the amount of social wealth allocated to the working class through the welfare apparatus (Bowles and Gintis, 1982: p. 53). On the other hand, the search for higher rates of profitability has shifted the emphasis from Fordist forms of standardised mass consumption to new forms of customised or 'niche' consumption which revolve around notions of difference and distinction and imply new kinds of status gradation and social exclusion. The new information technologies have made the servicing of these more volatile markets practically feasible, but their construction has depended greatly on the leadership of particular social groups, in particular fractions of the new middle class to whom has fallen the duty of pioneering and communicating a whole series of rapidly changing taste cultures and lifestyle options (Lash and Urry, 1987: pp. 285–96; Pfeil, 1990: pp. 107–18). It is possible to argue, then, that there is occurring a partial displacement of broad, standardised, Fordist mass consumption underwritten by the state by new forms of symbolic and differential consumption propagated by relatively narrow elites or groups advantageously placed with regard to the new microelectronic technologies and the communications media.

These developments, inconclusive as they still are, can be linked to what is often described as a postmodern loss of faith in grand narratives of progress and collective emancipation. That is, with the breakdown of the Fordist formula for continuous growth, with the political crisis of liberal democracy which in many ways had come to rest upon the economic growth formula for legitimation, and with the kinds of restructuring touched on above, there is no longer quite the material basis to justify popular assent to such narratives as there once might have been (Bellah *et al.*, 1992; Woodiwiss, 1993). Fewer among us in the affluent West can any longer comfortably assume that the story of our lives (or if not our own, then our offsprings') will mirror in microcosm a larger social story of steadily increasing wealth, widening opportunity and upward social mobility. New times are insecure times for, as Anthony Giddens, Barry Smart and, perhaps most forcefully, Christopher Lasch have argued, the idea of progress upon which modern Western capitalism has rested now looks both intellectually and practically unsustainable (Giddens, 1984: pp. 228–37; Smart, 1992: pp. 19–27; Lasch, 1991 and 1996).[9]

However, certain forms of grand narrative persist. In particular, the attempt to dismantle the capital–labour accord has been accompanied by a return of militantly triumphalist celebrations of the free market and deifications of market forces that in some ways recall the 'end-of-ideology' episode of the 1950s. Then, the miraculous recovery of American capitalism out of the ruins of the Great Depression and the upheaval of the Second World War, and the widening circle of prosperity that Fordism ushered in, were held to have rendered any ideological opposition to it obsolete.[10] But what distinguishes the current crop of claims about the redundancy of political and social alternatives to or critiques of capitalism is its hostility to certain tenets of social democracy which the old end-of-ideology argument, while resolutely pro-market and anti-socialist, generally accepted. And while 1950s' end-of-ideology positions reflected the anti-communist preoccupations of the Cold War, the current celebration of the market as a universal principle has coincided with the collapse of communism in Eastern Europe and the apparent triumph of capitalism on a global scale, giving rise to such grand narrative theorisations of the omnipotence of the market as Francis Fukuyama's 'The End of History?' (1989).

Also at the global level, the crisis of Fordism has been expressed in a new degree of international integration of economic activity. The aforementioned dispersal of industrial production from the West to other parts of the world has been part of the transformation of what Immanuel Wallerstein calls the 'capitalist world system' which has led commentators to speak of a fully integrated, supranational global economy (Reich, 1990; Chandler, 1990); of a new international division of labour (Harris, 1987; Lipietz, 1987a); and of a new international competition in which multinational corporations and global currents of credit and information are more important as actors than are traditional nation states (Aglietta, 1982; Schiller, 1984; Brenner, 1998). One consequence of this has been what we might call the deterritorialisation or unmapping of Fordist world space which has accompanied the wavering of American military and economic world dominance since the end of the Vietnam War (Calleo, 1982; Chase-Dunn, 1989; Block, 1977). Yet this condition of spatial and geographical volatility does not spell the end of grand narratives of empire, as I argue in Part 4 of this book.

These are some of the sharp changes bound up with the notion of post-Fordism and frequently invoked in attempts to historicise postmodernism. This book does not set out to provide an exhaustive account or theorisation of such changes or do any more than to offer occasional, unsystematised suggestions about the historical and social underpinnings of postmodernism. What it *does* set out to do, however, is to examine a number of stories or cultural texts which take contemporary economic and social change as their central problem, as a spur to narrative and a challenge to representation. By reading and attempting to understand these stories through the framing concepts of Fordism and post-Fordism I'm seeking to produce insights into what is at stake in much of the economic and social restructuring of the past two decades. I also hope to illuminate the processes and modes by which crisis and social, economic and cultural changes are registered, symbolically represented, and pressed into narrative form. In light of the recent importance that has been attributed to narrative forms for our understanding of historical processes, it could be said that I approach my selected texts as histories of the present which engage with what I have described as the project of post-Fordism to project in turn their own versions, accounts and evaluations of new times.[11]

In as much as they engage in direct fashion with the current dissolution and recomposition of Fordism these stories are complex meditations upon the role and meaning of capital, class and technology in social and subjective life. They also, and not incidentally, raise and address many of the questions associated with postmodernism: To what extent is critical resistance to the imperatives of capital any longer possible or desirable? How can individuals reach an understanding of their position within the social structure when that structure is as volatile and complex as the contemporary world system? What of the integrity of self in a universe increasingly saturated with media images and microtechnologies whose function is to penetrate our inner lives and influence us in particular directions? These questions will be explored in the process of reading my chosen texts' representations of crisis and change. And while I will not attempt fully to account for or answer them, I will suggest that they can helpfully be understood in terms of the concerns and experiences of a particular social class, one which takes a leading role in the production and management of culture as well as in the technological and ideological reorganisation of Fordist class relationships and institutions. The exploration of economic, social and cultural change on the one hand, and the consideration of postmodernism as a cultural style on the other will therefore come together most closely in my discussion of the historical construction, social position, values and ideology of this class – the professional–managerial class.

Because the stories I have chosen to examine all overtly address themselves to the question of economic and social change I feel it unnecessary at this point to offer any detailed theorisation of the relationship between texts and history. The social and historical nature of the stories we consume and tell ourselves I take as a given. But they are not simple reflections of historical processes. Stories, texts, cultural images of all kinds are symbolic and imaginative *transformations* of materials that are thoroughly historical, social and political in character. Though not entirely determined by the historical moment of their production, texts are nonetheless significantly inhabited and influenced by the concerns, anxieties, ideologies and contradictions of that moment; indeed the principal function of the act of storytelling is the organisation of such materials into significant patterns. Among these concerns, and of primary importance to me in this book, is the question of social class. My readings will suggest that social class is not merely the hobbyhorse of market researchers, sociologists and diehard Marxists but is in fact a deep preoccupation of our individual and collective inner lives, a constituent of what Fredric Jameson calls the 'political unconscious' of capitalist societies which manifests itself in the form of the stories and images that circulate in our culture (Jameson, 1981 and 1979: p. 139).

More specifically, my interest here is in narrative manifestations of what at times I refer to as the political unconscious of the professional–managerial class. By this I mean a set of concerns, anxieties, values and views of the world which characterise this social class and come into play in the symbolic representation of its relationship to social, economic and cultural change. In particular, the figure of the professional and the codes of professionalism emerge in the chapters that follow as central means through which this relationship is negotiated and attitudes toward it expressed. The prevalence of stories that feature professionals as central characters and revolve around explorations of professional ethics and values suggests that the crisis of Fordism and the projection of various post-Fordisms is crucially bound up with the way professionals function in society, the way they understand themselves, and the way they are viewed in the culture at large.

My considerations of such questions as these emerge out of a focus on some of the specific features of the crisis of Fordism and of attempted resolutions of or responses to this crisis, especially those that emphasise the role of new technologies. Part 2 looks at stories that foreground the role of information technologies, computers in particular, and engage with the images, ideas and ideologies that have surrounded them both in the culture of Fordism and in the shift to post-Fordism. Part 3 examines the place of cybernetics and artificial intelligence in the understanding and management of capitalism and capitalist class relations, arguing that stories such as William Gibson's cyberspace trilogy or Ridley Scott's film, *Blade Runner*, must be understood as serious interventions into the debate about the social role of such technologies in a period of economic restructuring. Part 4 explores the process of contemporary globalisation as a symptom of and response to the crisis of Fordism in the West, a process that has been almost entirely dependent for its realisation upon the technologies discussed in the two earlier sections. The stories analysed here seek to find ways of representing this process and its effects, thereby dramatising some of its meanings and implications. However, before considering these cultural representations of crisis and transformation within contemporary capitalism, I will offer an account of the historical development of Fordism and the importance within it, and for whatever follows it, of the professional–managerial class and its privileged relationship to the innovative technologies that have become increasingly important to economic, social and cultural management.

Part 1

Late Capitalism, Fordism, Post-Fordism

1

Postmodernism and Late Capitalism

The usefulness of the terms postmodernism and postmodernity as descriptions of cultural change consists in their remarkably broad range of reference. Applied to cultural and aesthetic styles, to philosophical and political positions, as well as to modes of social and economic organisation, these terms both suggest and demand that change in any one of these areas be understood in relation to the others. Among theorists of postmodernism, Fredric Jameson has been the most insistent on the necessity of taking such a holistic or totalising view of the question. For Jameson postmodernism is much more than 'a purely cultural affair'; the question must refer to the whole mode of production and to the possibilities for understanding the nature of contemporary capitalism. Thus 'every position on postmodernism in culture – whether apologia or stigmatisation – is also at one and the same time, and *necessarily*, an implicitly or explicitly political stance on the nature of multinational capitalism today' (Jameson, 1991: p. 3, author's emphasis).

However, as Jameson's critics have not been slow to point out, the developed account of contemporary capitalism implicitly demanded by his framing of the postmodernism question is largely absent from his writing on the subject. The burden of explanation in this area falls upon Ernest Mandel's landmark work of modern Marxist political economy, *Late Capitalism* (first published in German in 1972), which Jameson uses to underpin his more culturalist description of postmodernism. To employ a stock metaphor of Marxist social theory, Mandel's work provides a base upon which Jameson's more 'superstructural' reading of contemporary history rests. In many respects, then, the relationship between the emergence of what Jameson calls a new 'cultural dominant' out of the ruins of aesthetic high modernism on the one hand and the structural transformation of Western capitalism since 1940 described by Mandel on the other is left largely untheorised. I want to begin by exploring this gap with a view to sketching a provisional economic–historical framework in which questions about some of the social, cultural and political changes implied by postmodernism might be better situated.

Periodisation and the 'Break'

As we saw in the introduction, Jameson explicitly formulates his notion of postmodernism in terms of an historically identifiable break situated around 1960. Not only does this break inaugurate a new mode of cultural production brought about by a massive shift in the relationship between economic 'base' and socio-cultural 'superstructure' which calls that traditional Marxian dualism into question, it also signifies the onset of 'a whole new type of society' (Jameson, 1991: p. 3). Rejecting both conservative and liberal narratives of the end of modernity which terminate in the arrival of a pluralistic, post-industrial information society which is no longer consonant with Marx's theory of the laws of capitalist development and hence immune to its critique, Jameson invokes Mandel's *Late Capitalism* as the only attempt within the Marxist tradition both to accept the 'historic originality' of this new society and to seek to account for it in terms of Marx's founding theory of the historical development of the capitalist mode of production.

One question that Jameson's use of Mandel raises is: How far does his notion of the postmodern break accord with Mandel's version of the development of post-1940 capitalism? To what extent do Jameson's cultural and Mandel's economic logics mesh? While this is not a matter of seeking out neat or mechanical correspondences between the two accounts, the difficulty of establishing a convincing 'fit' between postmodernism and late capitalism has been forcefully raised in objection to certain aspects of Jameson's thesis and offers a useful way into the gap referred to above.

In one of the earliest challenges to Jameson on his own ground (that is, in terms of a broadly Marxist historical understanding of the political economy of the United States and Western Europe since the Second World War), Mike Davis proposed that any break in Mandel's account of late capitalism should be located around the point of the economic slump of 1973–4 and not, as Jameson would have it, in the boom years of the late 1950s or early 1960s. Thus the 1960s cannot be characterised as the 'opening of a new epoch' in which the new cultural dominant of postmodernism expresses the arrival of 'third stage' capitalism in its highest and purest incarnation. Rather, for Davis, the 1960s is a *'fin-de-siècle* decade' marking the summit of the postwar economic boom and still dominated by the functional aesthetic of high modernism, particularly in the realm of architecture which Jameson himself takes to be the key indicator of cultural–economic shifts (Davis, 1985: pp. 107–8).

Davis's objection is not simply that Jameson has misread Mandel and therefore misunderstood the meaning of the 1960s, but that his conflation of postmodernism with the onset of a purer, fully global stage of capitalism concedes too much. In 'subsuming' and 'homogenising' the disparate and contradictory features of contemporary culture under the master concept of postmodernism, Jameson virtually announces the triumph of capitalism and effectively abandons the possibility of meaningful agency for social and political change. For Davis, the transformation in sensibility that postmodernism undoubtedly represents can better be read as a symptom of the *crisis* of contemporary capitalism, specific to the period following the slump of 1973–4, and expressive of the inherent instability and 'morbidity' of the structures of capitalist accumulation, rather than of their unassailable expansion. Thus the architectural postmodernism of the late 1970s and 1980s should be read as nothing more than the crystallisation of the limited *zeitgeist* of Reaganomics, the playfully commodified fantasy of its forms being the objective correlative of the speculative adventurism then accompanying the decline of productive capital investment in the face of a 'hypertrophic expansion of the financial services sector' (Davis, 1985: pp. 107, 109).

While this rush of capitals from the productive to the speculative sphere is a symptom of the instability of capitalist accumulation in the United States and globally since the oil crisis and slump of the mid-1970s, Davis warned that this should give little cause for political optimism on the left as the American labour movement occupied an increasingly enfeebled position within this process. Consequently, the restructuring of the relations of production that has accompanied this massive disinvestment in the manufacturing base of American capitalism has so far been largely carried out on capital's terms. This includes, Davis suggested, a partial regression to *precapitalist* models of productive relations. Postmodernism therefore signifies 'not some new stage in capitalist production, but a return to a sort of primitive accumulation' (the return of domestic production and sweatshop conditions, for example) based on the super-exploitation of a new urban proletariat (Davis, 1985: p. 110). This group finds itself inhabiting an increasingly class-polarised and degraded cityscape, the abandonment of modernist ideals of urban reform being another key component in Davis's notion of the postmodern condition, one that he subsequently explored in his brilliant study of Los Angeles, *City of Quartz* (1989).

Davis's emphasis on the human costs of restructuring and his situating of postmodernism within a debate about the importance of crises within the capitalist accumulation process counterbalances the tendency of Jameson's writing to suggest an inexorably smooth extension of capitalist commodity relations without either resistance or highly differentiated and locally specific effects. The notion of *crisis* is particularly important and will be returned to below. However, in other respects, Davis's reading of the formal significance of postmodernism, its architecture in particular, out-Jamesons Jameson. The claim that such buildings as Philip Johnson's AT&T in New York enact, in their apotheosis of the commodity form, the final eclipse of both use value and the principles of capitalist productivism (Davis, 1985: p. 108) takes Jameson's argument about commodification to levels that even post-Marxist proponents of 'hyperreality' such as Jean Baudrillard might not shrink from endorsing. In resisting Jameson's epochal reading of postmodernism for conceding too much to the spontaneous coherence of capitalism, Davis, despite a concern to confine postmodernism to the play of purely conjunctural forces, produces in fact an epochal reading of his own in which deeper shifts in the relations of production appear to be leading in pre- and post-capitalist directions simultaneously.

I dwell on this debate between two of the most prominent Marxist critics currently engaged in the attempt to describe and theorise the nature of contemporary social and cultural change to illustrate the fact that the terms of the relationship between a theory of postmodernism and postmodernity and a posited new stage of capitalism are of some political importance and by no means easily resolved. In order to pursue more effectively the implications of this debate it is necessary to return to the ground of the disagreement between Jameson and Davis, Ernest Mandel's *Late Capitalism*, and examine its claims about the distinctive nature of post-Second World War economy and society in the West.

Late Capitalism: A New Stage of Capital?

Late Capitalism is a massively ambitious attempt to provide the first integrated historical and theoretical account of the development of the capitalist mode of production since Marx's *Capital* itself. Its focus is on twentieth-century capitalism and on the period since 1940 in particular. Mandel's purpose is to demonstrate that, despite the huge scope and rapid pace of change which revolutionised the organisation of social and economic life in that century, the history of the development of capitalism in that period nevertheless conforms to the fundamental laws of motion of this mode of production as outlined by Marx.

Mandel is therefore keen to emphasise the continued validity of Marxism for any analysis and understanding of the contemporary period. In this sense, he claims, 'the era of late capitalism is not a new epoch of capitalist development. It is merely a further development of the monopoly capitalist epoch' (Mandel, 1978: p. 9). However, in practice Mandel applies a tripartite schema to the history of the capitalist mode of production which implies the existence of distinct stages of capitalist development, of which late capitalism, dating roughly from 1940, is the third and latest. (The previous two are the stage of 'freely competitive capitalism' described by Marx, and the age of 'classical imperialism' proposed by Lenin.) Moreover, his characterisation of capitalism as a form based on 'an inherent tendency towards ruptures', and his application of Soviet economist N. D. Kondratieff's theory of 'long waves' of capitalist development to this tendency, suggests an historical dynamic dominated by breaks, crises and structural transformations (Mandel, 1978: p. 27). As the theory of long waves is central to Mandel's definition and periodisation of late capitalism as a distinct phase of the capitalist mode of production, and therefore to the historical reading of the postmodern break, I will focus first on this aspect of his work.

According to Marx, the course of capitalist accumulation is cyclical. Competition between independent firms, far from guaranteeing a smooth and even pace of accumulation, allows only a pattern of successive expansions and contractions of production. A period of expansion in which the conditions for capitalist production are propitious (availability of relatively cheap labour power and raw materials, effective technologies, and hungry markets are among the conditions required here) will typically lead to a crisis of overproduction in which it becomes increasingly difficult for firms to realise (that is, transform into money payment and, hence, profit) the surplus value embodied in their commodities by selling them on the market. Frequently, such a crisis is expressed in terms of a disequilibrium between what Marx defined as the two fundamental sites of capitalist production: Department I (the sphere of production of capital goods or means of production), and Department II (the sphere of production of wage goods or means of consumption).

The feverish intensity of production in both departments, driven by the prospect of high profits and the competitive urge to beggar-thy-neighbour, comes to outstrip the capacity of the market to absorb and socially validate this production. The capitalists of Department II, unable to shift their commodities, reduce output. They decrease their demand for new means of production from the capitalists of Department I who, however, are still geared to producing for an expanding market. A crisis of overproduction ensues in which the limits of capitalist production are expressed in terms of mounting inventories of unsold capital goods and commodities. The period of expansion peaks and becomes a downward spiral as the prospects for profitable investment of already accumulated capital become increasingly bleak. The crisis of overproduction becomes a crisis of overaccumulation when a falling rate of profit signals that the mass of accumulated capital cannot be valorised or reproduce itself on an expanded scale. Acceleration in the tempo of accumulation gives way to deceleration and underinvestment, and the only way the process can be turned around (given that capitalist production takes place exclusively for profitable exchange rather than for use or need) is for a massive devaluation of overaccumulated capitals to occur, in order that the decks may be cleared and the rate of profit revitalised.

Traditionally, it has been the function of the slump or recession (in the absence of war and/or the rapid penetration of capital into hitherto inaccessible regions or spheres) to provide this crucial cleansing service. Marx saw this process occurring every seven to ten years, and the validity of the classical industrial or business cycle as he described it is generally accepted even by orthodox economists (hence the obsession of free-marketeers and Keynesians alike with the problem of equilibrium). Mandel's innovation, however, is to situate the classical cycle within an expanded cyclical framework of accumulation which conforms roughly to a 50-year span. For Mandel, this is 'no metaphysical superimposition' but an historically verifiable pattern which, he claims, can be traced by observing the long-term fluctuations of the rate of profit and the corresponding transformations in the rhythms of capital accumulation: 'The history of capitalism on the international plane thus appears not only as a succession of cyclical movements every seven to ten years, but also as a succession of longer periods, of approximately fifty years, of which we have experienced four up till now' (Mandel, 1978: p. 120).

While denying that there is any 'built-in periodicity' to his notion of the long wave, Mandel argues that, over seven- to ten-year cycles, repeated periods of underinvestment will set free a large pool of idle (in productive terms) capital – what he calls a 'historical reserve fund of capital' – which at a certain point will be injected into the production process on such a scale as to provide for a fundamental renewal of productive technology. Such a 'revolution in technology as a whole' stands at the beginning and sets the terms of each new long wave of accumulation, and the vast infusion of capital which precipitates it is triggered by '*a sudden increase in the rate of profit*' (Mandel, 1978: p. 114, author's emphasis). Among the factors likely to cause such an increase are: a rapid fall in the cost of the elements of production; a massive penetration of capital into regions and spheres previously beyond its reach; an abbreviation of the turnover time of capital (that is, the period from initial investment to the realisation of money profits on that investment) due to new methods of distribution and marketing; and, perhaps most importantly, a radical defeat of the working class which drastically improves the conditions for the exploitation of labour power and the extraction of surplus value.

The 'spring tide' of accumulation which follows upon such a technological revolution will, however, have the self-cancelling effect of generalising its potential and finally exhausting it. The long wave can therefore be subdivided into an initial period of accelerated accumulation, distinguished by an increasing rate of profit and of growth, and a period of decelerating accumulation in which the consolidation of the new productive forces leads to slower growth, reduced profits and finally to acute difficulties in the valorisation of capital and to a halt in its self-expanding reproduction. This latter period, though, is marked by the steady release of capital from the accumulation process into a state of readiness for rapid re-entry when the rate of profit, for a combination of the reasons noted above, takes a sudden upturn. This would provide for a further revolutionising of the productive forces and the cycle would be ready to begin again on a higher level.

The four long waves Mandel identifies in the history of the capitalist mode of production are as follows:

1. The period from 1793 to 1847, based on the spread of the handcrafted or manufactured steam engine.

2. The period from 1847 to 1893, characterised by the technology of the machine-made steam engine.
3. The period from 1893 to 1940/45, based on the generalisation of electric and combustion technology.
4. The period from 1940/45 to the present, based on innovations in micro-electronics and information processing, cybernetics, automation and nuclear energy.

Late capitalism in this sense coincides with 'the long wave of the third technological revolution' whose preconditions were supplied by the combined effects of the Great Depression of the 1930s, the victory of fascism over the working-class movements of Europe, and the Second World War itself (Mandel, 1978: p. 121). The crisis of chronic overproduction which, for Mandel, had beset the industrialised countries since 1914 and became institutionalised in the 1930s released underinvested capital and devalued existing stocks of fixed and circulating capital to such an extent that they would not constitute a significant barrier to the rapid and total renewal of installations and investments when the rate of profit began to rise again. Similarly, the long depression, in conjunction with the defeat of the European working class by fascism, effectively reconstituted the reserve army of industrial labour, enabling employers to drive down the cost of labour power and increase the rates of exploitation and surplus value. Finally, the outbreak of the Second World War revitalised large-scale industrial production and stimulated a new burst of (militarised) technological innovation (with research and development costs being for the first time almost completely underwritten by the state), while the formation of a highly disciplined yet relatively high-wage labour force sowed the seeds of the massive growth in working-class consumption on which the postwar boom was to rest. Moreover, the decimation of Europe's industrial infrastructure created the space for the vital expansion of unscathed American capital during the postwar reconstruction process. The outcome of the war determined that while late capitalism would be thoroughly global or multinational in character, it would be so under the hegemony of American capital, military leadership and the imperious sway of the dollar.

What then constitutes the 'historic originality' of late capitalism, as Jameson understands it? The overall shape of Mandel's analysis appears to suggest that the structures of late capitalist accumulation can be seen, after the shock of 1929–39, as tending to suspend or liberate capital from the periodic crises which hitherto were an integral part of its operations, thereby institutionalising an evenly rising rate of accumulation. In this sense late capitalism could be understood as a system aimed at suppressing the operations of the law of value, central to which is Marx's theory of the tendency of the rate of profit to fall over the long term. Historically, this has required that the penetration of capital into areas previously outside its scope proceeds apace in order to sustain a rising curve of accumulation, and that, within this dynamic, there is 'ensured a certain adequation between transformations of conditions of production and transformations of conditions of consumption' in order that a threatening disequilibrium between the two departments of production does not arise (Lipietz, 1987a: p. 32). Mandel of course seeks to demonstrate that any suspension of the law of value without the simultaneous abolition of capitalist relations of production is inconceivable. Strategies aimed at postponing a crisis of one sort invariably unleash contradictions that trigger crisis tendencies of another sort, and Mandel is adamant that over the broad span of late capitalism there is an observable tendency for the rate of profit to fall. However, this does not mean that capital has not achieved certain notable success in securing long periods of apparently uninterrupted and rapid growth, or that the forms and structures through which such growth has been realised do not display a high degree of historical novelty.

Certainly the prodigious expansion of commodity relations, which Jameson takes as the central feature of postmodernism, is the definitive characteristic of late capitalism and for Mandel represents a qualitative transformation in capitalism's spatial logic of 'uneven and combined development'. Accumulation in the competitive and imperialist stages was predicated on crucial differences in the levels of industrial development between vast regions and blocs of the globe, giving rise to the master metaphor of metropolitan 'centre' and underdeveloped 'periphery' to describe the effects of this logic. But the far-reaching expansion of commodity relations since 1945 has done much to problematise such distinctions.[1] The spatial logic of late capitalism by contrast tends to produce difference *within* as well as between regions and spheres; hence the recent and rapid industrialisation of many regions of the periphery or third world, the return (noted by Mike Davis earlier) of 'pre-capitalist' forms of production to the metropolitan countries, and the diversification of monopolistic corporations into wildly disparate sectors of activity.

Extended commodification has brought with it the industrialisation of agriculture (or the 'commodification of nature' as Jameson refers to it, with particular reference to the impact of the 'green revolution' on the third world) and the phenomenon of neo-colonialism linked to the now global reach of capital (Jameson, 1988c: pp. 185–6). It has also led within the so-called developed countries themselves to the huge growth of the services sector which Mandel argues is a central feature of late capitalism. Just as the former process has detached third world agricultural workers from the land to sell their labour power on the market, so the latter, in mechanising the domestic and recreational spheres of first world citizens, has released whole new sectors of the population (particularly women) into the labour market. In this way an ongoing recomposition of the reserve army of labour is achieved concurrent with the continual expansion of commodity production, thereby maintaining conditions favourable to employers for the exploitation of labour and the extraction of surplus value.

It is helpful, I think, to read the proliferation of service industries in the 'advanced' countries in terms of the spatial and temporal 'fixes' by which, according to David Harvey, capitalism typically overcomes its geographical and sectoral limits (Harvey, 1982 and 1989). For Mandel, service industries and occupations function to mediate between the sites of production and consumption and their increasing mechanisation has the effect of abbreviating the circuit (and therefore accelerating the turnover time) of capital. New modes of storage, distribution, merchandising and marketing in this sense reproduce the temporal logic of accelerated innovation which characterises the third technological revolution. Moreover, they point us in the direction of the issue of the 'consumer' or 'post-industrial society' which certain American commentators have taken as a signal that the capitalism described by Marx has been superseded.

However, it should be clear from the above account that the proliferation of service industries by no means implies a departure from capitalist production. As Mandel argues:

Far from representing a post-industrial society, late capitalism ... constitutes *generalised universal industrialisation* for the first time in history. Mechanisation, standardisation, overspecialisation and parcellisation of labour, which in the past determined only the realm of commodity production in actual industry, now penetrate into all areas of social life. (Mandel, 1978: p. 137, author's emphasis)

Consumerism, the 'move from a market economy to a marketing society' as Manuel Castells has put it, has important implications for the working class. It represents the full-blown industrialisation of the sphere of reproduction of wage earners' conditions of existence, that is, of the domestic and private lives of the mass of the population (Castells, 1980: p. 63). The significant gains in productivity unleashed by the advances of the third technological revolution result in a problem of over-capitalisation. Idle surplus capitals seek valorisation in new areas, areas outside industry proper in as much as they do not create new social value. This is the dynamic underlying the revolution in service industries. However, if these new domains of capital accumulation are to be successfully exploited, what is required is 'an advanced differentiation of consumption, and especially the consumption of the wage earners and the working class'; hence the centrality of mass consumption to postwar capitalism (Mandel, 1978: p. 389).

Late capitalism therefore has at its heart a particular balance between transformations in the conditions of production and of consumption which works to lessen the possibility of a traditional crisis of disequilibrium. This is historically achieved via the full integration of the working class and the labour movement into the structures of accumulation and their conscription as junior partners in the reproduction of capitalist social relations. The characteristic structural forms of post-Second World War capitalism – nationally recognised labour unions, the collective bargaining system and the social security apparatus – are the institutional manifestations of these developments.[2] The fact that these structures work in some senses to guarantee, as Michel Aglietta points out, 'the regular development of the mode of consumption' does not necessarily mean that the working class no longer exists or that it is no longer antagonistically positioned *vis-à-vis* capital within the accumulation process (Aglietta, 1979: p. 382). Indeed, as Mandel illustrates, the establishment of the new mode of consumption – in which a greater share of social surplus goes towards supporting a minimum standard of living for wage earners – puts extra pressure on capital to sustain the rate of exploitation by minimising labour costs through the continual improvement of the productivity of labour. On the other hand, wage earners respond to this by pressing for an even greater share of the value so produced to be allocated to them in the form of wages and benefits. If anything, then, the struggle over surplus value is intensified in late capitalism, though its focus is shifted from issues such as the length of the working day (the great concern of nineteenth-century workers) to the problem of the organisation and design of the labour process itself. Workers' claims for a greater share of social surplus cause capitalists to deflect the responsibility for guaranteeing basic levels of consumption on to the public sector through expanded welfare provision. This contributes to what

James O'Connor has called 'the fiscal crisis of the state'. Here the modern capitalist state's twin functions of accumulation and political legitimation are brought into conflict, as its role as guarantor of corporate profits runs up against popular expectations of regular increases in basic living standards (O'Connor, 1973).

The increased involvement of the state can be observed in a number of other features characteristic of late capitalism. For example, the institutionalisation after 1945 of what Mandel calls the 'permanent arms economy', providing guaranteed profits for capital investment, devolves entirely upon the state. So heavily does the state underwrite the production of military commodities that Mandel identifies this sector as a new and distinct department of production – Department III, producing means of destruction. Like the extension of the mode of consumption in late capitalism, the permanent arms economy serves as a profitable outlet for otherwise overaccumulated capital and thus works to defer the onset of crisis tendencies characteristic of earlier forms of capitalism. Moreover, the role that state-funded military research and development plays in intensifying the general rate of technological innovation and the upgrading of productive forces has been crucial to the long wave of accelerated accumulation after 1945.

The state in late capitalism therefore not only plays the central role in the allocation of surplus value and social capital through military expenditure and the creation of the welfare system, it also intervenes directly to alleviate the crisis tendencies of the traditional industrial cycle. It does so principally through fiscal and monetary policy, by issuing massive quantities of credit both directly, through government bonds and contracts, and indirectly, through the underwriting capacities of a central national bank. The proliferation of public and private debt on an unprecedented scale lies behind the steadily rising accumulation of the early phase of late capitalism. Large-scale credit allows accelerated expansion to continue beyond the limits of private and corporate property and profit, thus reducing the chances of any damaging slowdown or stagnation in the development of the forces of production. Just as importantly, credit guarantees liquidity (that is, means of payment) which, were it not available, would probably result in an old-fashioned crisis of realisation. The 'hypertrophic expansion of the services sector' identified by Mike Davis is clearly a part of this development but cannot be taken in isolation from the rise of advertising, marketing and the wholesale mass-mediatisation of modern capitalist societies. This reflects the institutionalisation of debt-based consumption and the industrialisation of the cultural apparatus which is increasingly linked to the promotion and dissemination of commodities through notions of lifestyle, taste and identity. With the issuing of ever more units of money to represent the same amount of total social value, inflation takes on the role played by cyclical recession in previous stages of capitalism, that of securing the devaluation of overaccumulated capitals and commodities. But inflation, according to Mandel and Aglietta, *conceals* this process, allowing corporations to fix higher prices and to pass the costs of amortisation (the replacement of obsolete means of production) and realisation (marketing, advertising and the like) on to the consumer, thereby reducing the share of surplus value eaten away by wage increases.

Yet there is an ever present danger that this structurally essential 'creeping inflation' will mutate into 'galloping inflation', bringing with it the *destruction* of profits as well as the desired erosion of wage values and thereby threatening the process of commodity production as a whole. Hence the crucial role of the state in regulating the money supply of the most powerful industrial nations. The fact that in late capitalism the state must take on the role of 'ideal total capitalist' in order to mitigate the contradictions provoked by the operations of many actual capitalists should make us wary of theories of a purely 'administrative', 'distributive' or 'managerialist' state no longer structured by class antagonisms arising from the production of surplus value and the realisation of private profit. Private corporations increasingly look to the state to guarantee profits and favourable conditions for expanded accumulation. However, the enlarged role of the state is at the same time a symptom of capital's increasing *difficulty* in securing smooth accumulation. Moreover, Mandel notes that such evidently political state intervention on behalf of capital carries with it the risk of alienating wage earners and thus of delegitimating the structures and institutions of liberal democracy.[3]

Limits to Late Capitalism

These considerations return us to the notion of crisis and to Mandel's insistence that the structural transformations made within late capitalism cannot ultimately succeed in eliminating the tendency of the capitalist mode of production toward crisis. Traditional crises of overproduction and underconsumption may have been deferred or made less likely by accelerated accumulation, expanded commodity consumption, credit mechanisms and structural inflation. But these have given rise to the recent phenomenon of 'stagflation', a combination of over-capacity and rising costs in which prices and unemployment increase simultaneously. This endangers the stability of the long wave of accelerating accumulation and, in the purview of orthodox economic theory, should be a logical impossibility.[4] The end of full employment and the return of diminishing profitability mark a sharpening of the social struggle over the allocation of surplus value and the end of whatever social consensus accompanied the expansionary phase.

For Mandel, this eventuality was inscribed in the very terms of late capitalism's 'take-off'. The fact that the nature of the third technological revolution determined that surplus profits (that is, profits above the average rate of profit and, from the point of view of a large corporation, the only profits worth seeking) were to be exclusively gleaned from technological rents (that is, advantages gained from monopolising certain technical advances in the forces of production) meant that there would be an inevitable tendency toward the automation of the production process. Human labour – the sole source of new value in Marxist theory – would be steadily driven out by machinery or 'dead' labour, as the logic of late capitalist mass production demanded that commodities be constantly reduced in value in order for them to be consumed *en masse*.[5] Such an increase in the ratio of dead to living labour would not carry deleterious implications for profitability as long as automation guaranteed substantial increases in the productivity of living labour. But, as the innovations of the third technological revolution became generalised over the long term and their impact on productivity weakened, there would be an inevitable increase in what Marx called the organic composition of capital.

In other words, the proportion of new value added by human labour in the production process would begin to decline in relation to the value already embedded in the machinery of production. Such a shift in value ratios would be expressed in the tendency of the rate of profit to fall. The only way to counteract this tendency is for capital to intensify the rate of exploitation of living labour. This has to be done by increasing the production of *relative* surplus value, that is, by improving the productivity of labour (the production of *absolute* surplus value through direct wage cuts or an extension of the working day being politically difficult in advanced capitalist societies). This of course requires further automation and mechanisation of the labour process and raises the probability of an eventual increase in the organic composition of capital. Consequently, the virtuous circle of automation and improved productivity mutates into the vicious circle of increased organic composition and declining profitability. Thus the production and extraction of relative surplus value becomes one of the most politically charged and contested features of late capitalism.

Accumulation, then, tends to cancel the basis of its own success, and the expansionary phase of the long wave gives way to a period of stagnation. The first signs of crisis appear in the monetary and financial spheres when difficulties in valorisation provoke intensified international competition. This brings pressure to bear on the international monetary system as the global role of the dominant world currency, the dollar, as the medium of international exchange, comes into conflict with its domestic role as inflationary buffer to the American industrial cycle. At this point, Mandel argues, the credit and financial apparatus floats free of the industrial cycle which in turn becomes synchronised across the major capitalist countries, interlocking their economies. Stagnation deepens on a global scale as no single major economy is able to claw its way out of trouble by offloading its devalued commodities on to a booming competitor (see also Block, 1977, Aglietta, 1982 and Brenner, 1998). The dollar crisis of 1966–7 which marked the imminent collapse of the international monetary order established at Bretton Woods would thus indicate that a turning point had been reached in the expansionary wave of late capitalism. At this point Mandel raises the question of 'whether a new long wave can be predicted from the second half of the 1960s onwards – the ebb after the flow' (Mandel, 1978: p. 146). Given the concerns of this chapter, it would also seem to raise the question of how cultural change might relate to such a development.

With respect to this last point, it is worth noting that Mandel's account would appear to support Mike Davis's argument that postmodernism be understood in terms of a *crisis within* the structures of late capitalist accumulation, rather than Jameson's suggestion that postmodernism marks the *arrival* of late capitalism in the cultural sphere. Yet this same account also suggests that this crisis is not a traditional one of simple overcapitalisation and that the 1960s cannot be dismissed in economic terms as a decadent *fin-de-siècle* moment. Rather it suggests that the decade be theorised as a watershed, a period of economic and cultural transition that prefigures the global slump of the 1970s and the epoch of restructuring that succeeded it. Postmodernism might then helpfully be understood in terms of a crisis *within* late capitalism, as bearing some important relation to the various strategies by which capital seeks to resolve the economic crisis and re-establish conditions of accelerating accumulation.[6]

This would necessitate the development of a theory of crisis capable of registering and illuminating the social and cultural, as well as economic, ramifications of transformations in the accumulation process. However, Mandel himself has been criticised for employing an overly mechanistic theory of crisis in

Late Capitalism in which the organic composition of capital rises and the rate of profit falls automatically, responding to the inevitable technical development of the forces of production (Davis, 1978; Rowthorn, 1980). This allows little scope for the agency of social classes or groups to shape the process and over-emphasises the repressive–dominative aspects of capitalist power at the expense of underplaying the extent to which the conditions for accumulation rest on complex discourses, ideologies and mechanisms of control, consent and dissent. If the relationship between contemporary cultural change and late capitalism is to be explored in terms of transformation and crisis within the structures of capital accumulation, then perhaps the best analytical framework is provided by the theory of capitalist regulation.

Regimes of Accumulation and Modes of Regulation: Fordism

The notion of historically specific regimes of accumulation which produce and operate in accord with characteristic modes of social and economic regulation derives from Antonio Gramsci's original insights into what he called 'Americanism and Fordism' (Gramsci, 1971: pp. 277–318). For Gramsci, an Italian communist writing in the 1920s, these terms denoted what he saw as 'the passage from the old economic individualism' to a new kind of industrial society, one foreshadowed by Henry Ford's massive, scientifically managed auto production plants in Detroit. Ford's strikingly large-scale and highly rationalised methods of mass production expressed for Gramsci early twentieth-century capital's 'inherent necessity to achieve the organisation of a planned economy' (Gramsci, 1971: p. 279). The question for Gramsci was whether or not the new structures of production prefigured in Ford's factories constituted the onset of a new historical epoch, and what the implications of this would be for the forms of working-class resistance and struggle that would necessarily accompany such a transition. Yet even at such an early date, Gramsci was prepared to conceive of Fordism 'as the ultimate stage in the process of progressive attempts by industry to overcome the law of the tendency of the rate of profit to fall' (Gramsci, 1971: p. 280). In this Gramsci was prescient for, as both Mandel and the theorists of the regulation school have shown, such attempts have come particularly to characterise the period of rapid accumulation in the industrialised West since 1945.[7]

There is, then, considerable formal and historical correspondence between Mandel's stage of late capitalism and the notion of Fordism developed since Gramsci. And there are, I would argue, distinct theoretical advantages to be gained by viewing late capitalism from the perspective of the regulation school. Firstly, as Michael Rustin has pointed out, the regulation model represents a decisive and successful break with the 'simple economism' that has often vitiated Marxist theory. It thus allows for a full appreciation and analysis of the economic *and social* complexity of contemporary capitalism (Rustin, 1989b: p. 54). Secondly, it focuses attention as much on the question of the reproduction of capitalist social relations as on the production process itself. This gives a greater role to more nuanced conceptions of ideology and scope for consideration of the differences which impinge upon modern class relations (gender, race, region and so on) as well the processes by which these are mediated (the technical organisation of work and of social life).

Finally, like the Gramscian notion of hegemony with which it is closely bound up, regulation theory grants a constitutive role to cultural and political processes, calling attention to the continually negotiated and thus always contested nature of social formations. The regulation approach and its paradigm of Fordism, then, place the class struggle – especially the wage relation and its constantly shifting configurations – at the heart of the accumulation process. By avoiding the traps of both technological determinism and mechanistic explanations of economic crisis it allows us, in the words of Manuel Castells, to 'consider ... capital as a social relationship and not as a mass of money or material means of production' (Castells, 1980: p. 25). Economic crises can therefore be approached as social and historical processes with specific political and cultural dimensions.

Consumption and the Wage Relation

The new forms of industrial organisation that Gramsci observed developing in America in the 1910s and '20s represented the beginnings of a shift from the old regime of *extensive* accumulation to a new regime of *intensive* accumulation. In essence, this transition consisted in a radical deepening of capitalist relations within the industrialised countries themselves. The old imperial circuits of capital ceased to be the principal basis of accumulation and the development of internal markets became the primary source of accelerated profitability. According to Michel Aglietta, whose account I am following here, this necessitated the production of a massive domestic pool of commodified labour power, of individuals prepared (or compelled for lack of an alternative) to sell their time to an employer in exchange for cash payment by which they might maintain themselves and their families. It also required the corresponding establishment of a universal mode of consumption through which the new labour force could, with its wages, acquire the commodities necessary to reproduce itself. The combined effect of these developments was progressively to eliminate virtually all enclaves of non-capitalist production and exchange that remained in the leading industrial societies.

With the generalisation of this intensive regime of accumulation throughout the capitalist West after 1945, the *wage relation* – the point at which workers exchange their labour for cash payment with which they must purchase the goods and services necessary to their maintenance – becomes the fulcrum of capitalist development. However, the expansion of the reach of wage labour has the effect of reducing the reserve army of labour (that is, the unemployed or those engaged in non-capitalist forms of production), making it difficult for employers to increase surplus value *absolutely*, by driving down wages or lengthening the working day, as was customary in the extensive mode of accumulation. Such strategies not only antagonise workers, thus endangering the stability of the wage relation, they also adversely affect workers' purchasing power and thus undermine the system of consumption. Within the intensive regime of accumulation, then, employers must increase surplus value *relatively*, by heightening the productivity of labour through technological innovation and constant refinement of the production process.

Consequently, control of the terms and conditions under which the wage relation develops becomes an imperative for successful accumulation. The need for productivity and the need to supervise closely and discipline labour at the point of production thus become intertwined. Both objectives are pursued, as we shall see in the following chapters, through the increasing subjection of labour to technological and bureaucratic imperatives. In this respect, as David Noble (1979) has implied, there is a clear line of descent from F. W. Taylor's theories of scientific management, which so impressed Henry Ford in the 1910s, to the robot or cyborg worker discussed in Part 3 of this book; and from Ford's notorious sociology department, which sought to rationalise his workers' domestic and personal lives, to more modern ideologies and techniques of 'human resource' management.

Aglietta defines the intensive regime of accumulation as one in which

> The capitalist class seeks overall management of the production of wage labour by the close articulation of the relations of production with the commodity relations in which the wage earners produce their means of consumption. Fordism is thus the principle of *an articulation between the processes of production and modes of consumption*, which constitutes the mass that is the specific content of the universalisation of wage labour. (Aglietta, 1979: p. 117, author's emphasis)

The attempt to manage this articulation successfully gives rise to a mode of regulation whose reach, in that it is principally concerned with the containment of the class struggle, is as much social and cultural as it is strictly economic. The structural forms characteristic of Fordism – the scientifically managed production process, the bureaucratised corporation, the mass labour union, the mechanisms of collective wage bargaining, and the social security apparatus – can therefore be understood as historically novel institutional channels for managing the potentially explosive class antagonisms of the wage relation. As such, they should be seen as manifestations of struggle rather than simple instruments of capital's domination or labour's capitulation. Similarly, mass consumption, 'which appeared to have resolved the contradictions of capitalism and abolished its crises' (Aglietta, 1979: p. 161), should be regarded as a key arena of struggle in late capitalist societies rather than as the sign of the extinction of the working class as an oppositional force as it was for the theorists of the Frankfurt School.

Indeed consumerism, while forming the basis of the expansionary long wave, also stands at the limit of the intensive regime of accumulation. For although smooth reproduction of the relations of production is in many respects guaranteed by the development of the mode of consumption, this same development raises the historical level of needs which workers seek to consolidate and institutionalise in the structural forms of Fordism. A struggle over the meaning of consumption arises, with 'capitalist' consumption for industrial profit pitted against 'worker' consumption to satisfy (and to raise) the level of basic needs (O'Connor, 1986: p. 180). This has the effect of 'reinforcing the antagonism of the wage relation and generalising this to the conditions guaranteeing the continuity of the maintenance cycle of labour power' (Aglietta, 1979: p. 165).

In other words, a guaranteed minimum 'social consumption norm' or basic standard of living becomes essential for the reproduction of a mass labour force and, hence, for intensive accumulation. However, this also forms a base on which wage earners can consolidate their material power and seek its extension in terms of an ever rising level of needs, with the result that '*the socialisation of consumption* becomes a decisive terrain and battle ground of the class struggle' (Aglietta, 1979: p. 165, author's emphasis). Thus the capital–labour accord that so many American commentators placed at the heart of the post-Second World War period of prosperity, consumerism and political consensus actually represented the emergence of new forms of social conflict and new channels for the class struggle. Moreover, the establishment of a basic consumption norm involved the extension of unproductive labour within the economy as more effort was devoted to the presentation and selling of commodities and to the maintenance of a vast system of private and public credit which facilitated expanded consumption (O'Connor, 1975 and 1986: p. 179). The costs of collective consumption thus began to eat into the proportion of surplus value available for the extended reproduction of capital. The structural forms of Fordism thus gradually became barriers to the continued success of intensive accumulation.

Crises of Accumulation: Post-Fordism

David Gordon, Richard Edwards and Michael Reich have summarised the historical construction and development of the Fordist regime as follows:

> A new social structure of accumulation emerged from the class conflict and political realignment of the dozen or so years following 1935. The outcome was a set of institutions governing accumulation quite unlike what had existed before ... The postwar boom grew out of that integrated complex of law, institutions and customary arrangements that we have labelled the 'postwar accord'. This social structure of accumulation was rooted in ... diverse (simple, technical, bureaucratic) systems of control of the labour process, class conflict channelled into the governmental arena, an extensive economic role for government, and the maintenance of a hegemonic military posture to protect the opportunity for American corporations to invest abroad. These institutions and arrangements have all begun to decay. (Gordon, Edwards and Reich, 1982: pp. 169, 180)

Between 1950 and the early 1970s, gross national product in the United States increased six-fold from $208.5 billion to $1,397.4 billion (Mandel, 1980: table 10). The total productivity of American labour increased almost twice as fast per year as it had at any other time since the beginning of the industrial revolution (Gordon *et al.*, 1982: table 6.1). The annual rate of increase in the rate of profit remained steady at between 5 and 6 per cent (Harvey, 1989: fig. 2.4). The annual rate of economic growth averaged over 5 per cent and exports grew at approaching 9 per cent per annum (Harvey, 1989: fig. 2.1, table 2.1). Real wages increased steadily, average weekly earnings rising from $200 per week in 1950 to $350 per week in 1970–1 (Harvey, 1989: fig. 2.2). The annual rate of inflation never rose above 6 per cent and averaged somewhat less than 3 per cent (Mandel, 1980: table 9). This gives some idea of the success of the Fordist boom period.

From 1973 to 1985, on the other hand, the average rate of growth in the American economy halved, the annual increase in the rate of profit dropped to 3 per cent, and real wages fell by about 15 per cent to an average of $300 per week (Harvey, 1989: figs. 2.1, 2.4, 2.2). Inflation persistently broke the 10 per cent barrier and permanent structural unemployment along with direct wage reductions were widely offered and pursued as the only practical remedies (Mandel, 1980:

pp. 87–90). This strongly suggests that the Fordist regime and its corresponding regulatory mechanisms had entered into a period of sustained crisis, the resolution of which would require the construction of a new social structure of accumulation (Gordon *et al.*, 1982: p. 241). It is to this that the notion of post-Fordism refers.

For Michel Aglietta, 'the crisis of Fordism is first of all the crisis of a mode of labour organisation ... expressed in the intensification of class struggles at the point of production; but this crisis extends to the sum total of relations of production and exchange' (Aglietta, 1979: p. 162). It is therefore to be seen not as a mechanical breakdown in the system of capitalist accumulation, but as the exposure, through struggles over the meanings of work, leisure and consumption, of the limits of a particular social formation. As Mike Davis has put it, 'the historical era defined by the equation of Americanism with democratic capitalism – that is, by the progressive expansion of bourgeois democracy and mass consumption under the aegis of the United States – is approaching its terminus' (Davis, 1986: p. 182). The economic crisis is thus equally a social crisis whose resolution demands a thorough reorganisation of the social relations of production, consumption, distribution and management, and whose outcome depends on the balance of social, political and economic forces leading into, and recast by, the restructuring period (Gordon *et al.*, 1982: pp. 242–3; Castells, 1980: p. 12). This raises the important question of the agency and ideologies of particular classes in both Fordism and post-Fordism.

Class and Consensus, Ideology and Technology

If we return to Gramsci's original notion of Fordism as an expression of the 'necessity to achieve the organisation of a planned economy' and to surpass 'the old economic individualism' in so doing, then we can see that its roots lie in the shift from freely competitive or *laissez-faire* capitalism to monopoly or corporate capitalism, a shift which is commonly identified with the Progressive era in American history. Martin Sklar has described this shift as follows:

> The movement for corporate capitalism reconstructed American society during the years 1890–1916. In effecting a reorganisation of property ownership and the market, and in attaining a revision of the law and of government–market relations, this movement established the fundamental conditions of what many historians regard as the mass-culture society and also as the organisational or bureaucratic society with its concomitant rise of a professional, managerial, and technical middle class. (Sklar, 1988: p. 441)

Also described by Warren Susman as the 'organisation revolution' and by Scott Lash and John Urry as the shift from 'unorganised' to 'organised' capitalism, it is clear that this shift contains in embryo the lineaments of Fordist regulation. It would take the purgative of depression and war, the impetus of the third technological revolution, and the dramatic extension of domestic popular consumption after 1945 for full Fordism and the long wave of rising accumulation to get underway (Susman, 1984: p. xx; Lash and Urry, 1987). But some consideration of this earlier period is important to an understanding of the social dynamics of Fordism in full swing.

Fordism's Progressive Inheritance

Sklar and other historians (Wiebe, 1967; Weinstein, 1969) have described how the shift from *laissez-faire* was engineered by a loose coalition of business interests, labour organisations and, perhaps most significantly for the concerns of this book, reformers drawn from the new middle class mentioned by Sklar above. Despite their differing positions within American society, these groups were linked in so far as they all 'viewed the problem of the relationship between capital and labour as central to the political and economic stability of the emerging system of large corporations' (Weinstein, 1969: p. 9). Many leaders of the vast corporations that emerged during the Progressive era felt that limited social reform was necessary in order to transcend the destructively volatile nature of the normal business cycle, and what Marx had called the 'anarchy of competition'. They sought reforms that would enable corporations to exert greater control over markets and prices and bring stability and predictability to economic activity so that their increasingly large investments could be protected and future growth planned on a rational basis (Chandler, 1962). Thus many influential capitalists came to accept that a degree of state regulation of business practices and ostensibly cooperative, rather than overtly confrontational, relations with labour at the point of production were integral to the achievement of greater economic stability, the long-term growth and protection of profits, and, not incidentally, the extension of corporate capital's social power.[1]

Labour leaders, on the other hand, were prepared to cooperate with capitalists in the reorganisation of social and economic life in return for a share in the envisaged prosperity of the new corporate order, as well as for the increased respect they felt labour would acquire from such cooperation. This was the period, according to Robert Wiebe, which saw 'the development of a new business unionism'. Wiebe notes the 'irony of America's first truly self-conscious wage-earners locating themselves by business values in a business system' (Wiebe, 1967: p. 125).[2] Thus the pattern was set for the post-Second World War system of collective bargaining exemplified, in Mike Davis's view, by the 'Treaty of Detroit' signed between the United Auto Workers and General Motors in 1950, the first major deal to link guaranteed long-term pay increases to a no-strike pledge. The magazine of American business, *Fortune*, summed up this important instance of the Fordist capital–labour accord thus: 'GM may have paid a billion a year for peace ... It got a bargain' (quoted in Davis, 1986: p. 52).

But the reformers drawn from what Wiebe called the new middle class were differently motivated (Wiebe, 1967: pp. 111–32). Their concern for the ordering of economic and social life derived from a conviction that the conflicts generated by *laissez-faire*, class conflict in particular, were wasteful of resources, prevented the efficient operation of industry and society, and were symptomatic of a debilitating irrationality within the capitalist system. Members of this new class identified themselves, through their special skills and professional expertise, with the ostensibly 'objective' and 'universal' values of science and reason, rather than with what they felt to be the narrow, sectional and class-determined perspectives of capitalists and organised labour alike (Wiebe, 1967: p. 147). They claimed, then, to stand above and beyond class interests and for the general good of society as a whole. Class antagonisms were viewed as irruptions of irrational conflict within an imperfectly organised system which could be treated as technical problems and were therefore amenable to technical solutions. New middle-class professionals and experts thus conceived reform as the means by which social organisation could be perfected according to the 'universal' principles of science, reason and efficiency which, properly applied, would bring prosperity and social peace.

As James Weinstein has argued, one of the principal products of this tripartite Progressive coalition of corporate capitalists, labour leaders and new middle-class reformers was the concept of consensus (Weinstein, 1969: p. 3). And it was this notion of consensus that re-emerged powerfully after the shock of depression and world war as a term through which the renascent American capitalism of the post-1945 period was understood and to which its remarkable success was attributed.[3] Curiously enough, though, consensus was now linked to the idea of revolution, a term by which commentators of the late 1940s and the 1950s sought to convey the depth of the social and economic transformations that distinguished post-1945 capitalism from the crisis-ridden and socially polarised capitalism of the depression years. In 1949 Daniel Bell proclaimed that the United States had undergone a 'non-Marxist revolution' in which class conflict had finally been eliminated not by overthrowing capitalism but by providing all social groups with a stake in it – a consequence of its perfected organisation and operation (Bell, 1949).

In *The Twentieth Century Capitalist Revolution* (1955), Adolph Berle also argued that cooperation between the corporations, political leaders and organised labour made postwar capitalism 'a far more effective, far more sensitive, and ... far more appealing organisation of affairs than was ever described under the aegis of *laissez-faire*' (Berle, 1955: p. 4). And a volume published in 1952 by *Fortune* magazine celebrated capitalism's new vigour with similar arguments about the centrality of consensus and employed a similar title – *USA: The Permanent Revolution*. 'Fifty years ago', the editors of *Fortune* collectively declared, 'American capitalism seemed to be what Marx predicted it would be and what all the muck-rakers said it was – the inhuman offspring of greed and irresponsibility'. But the postwar period had seen 'the formation of a kind of capitalism that neither Karl Marx nor Adam Smith ever dreamed of', thanks largely to the cooperative stance of organised labour. 'The anti-proletarian and non-ideological character of American labour', the editors continued approvingly, facilitated its incorporation into a broad social consensus led by businessmen, politicians and experts of various hues which, it was argued, underpinned the remarkable revitalisation and stability of modern American capitalism (Davenport *et al.*, 1952: pp. 62, 64, 90).

The regulation school's concept of Fordism can in this respect be seen as an alternative theorisation of what came to be called consensus capitalism. The paradigm of Fordism enables us to understand terms such as consensus and 'the end of ideology', through which the period of the long boom was often characterised, as denoting less the historical obsolescence of the class struggle and the suspension of ideological conflict than the channelling of these latter into the structural forms which became crucial to the expanded reproduction of capital. Rather than dismissing class conflict as residual and marginal to social processes, as accounts of consensus would have it, the concept of Fordism emphasises its centrality to post-1945 capitalism in so far as the structural regulation of production and consumption, the welfare apparatus, the collective bargaining system and so on are nothing less than the manifestation of such conflict in institutional form.

Returning to the transformations wrought during the Progressive era, we encounter a second feature of that period which, like the concept of consensus, becomes central to post-1945 American capitalism and to questions of Fordism and post-Fordism: the role of what Martin Sklar referred to as the new 'professional, managerial and technical middle class'. As many historians have already argued, the emergence of this new middle class is one of the most important features of the Progressive era and the shift from *laissez-faire* to monopoly capitalism (B. and J. Ehrenreich, 1979; Susman, 1984: pp. xx–xxii, 46, 238; Wiebe, 1967: pp. 111–13). Richard Hofstadter has neatly encapsulated this new social group's emergence thus:

> From 1870 to 1910, while the whole population of the United States increased two and one third times (from approximately 39.9 million to 92.4 million), the old middle class – business entrepreneurs and independent professional men – grew somewhat more than two times; the working class, including farm labour, grew a little more than three times; the numbers of farmers and farm tenants doubled. But the middle class (technicians, salaried professionals, clerical workers, sales people, public service workers) grew almost eight times, rising from 756,000

to 5,609,000 people ... The new middle class had risen from 33% of the entire middle class in 1870 to 63% in 1910. (Hofstadter, 1955: pp. 215–16)

The new and the old middle classes were separated by their respective relationships to property. Whereas the old middle class was a largely entrepreneurial, property-holding bourgeoisie central to the competitive period of what Daniel Bell called 'family capitalism' (Bell, 1988: chapter 2), the new middle class, central to the subsequent period of bureaucratic corporate capitalism, was essentially propertyless. In 1932 Adolph Berle and Gardiner Means argued that twentieth-century capitalism was characterised by a newly emerged split between ownership on the one hand and control on the other, revealing a major shift in the distribution of power within the corporate system. The sheer scale of the modern corporation, they observed, required that individual owners had to delegate control of its operations to a cadre of professional managers, engineers and technicians appointed according to expertise rather than capital assets or social status (Berle and Means, 1932). The social position of this group depended not on the ownership and inheritance of wealth or property but on the possession of educational qualifications, technical skills and professional credentials. While *ownership* of the productive apparatus of American capitalism remained in the hands of what could still be described as a capitalist class, *control* was increasingly put at the disposal of these new professional strata which held to values and visions that were significantly different from those of their employers.

The new middle class was also gaining influence in the United States outside business. Fields such as medicine, education, administration and social work were rationalised and professionalised as they expanded in response to the demands of an increasingly complex, urbanising, corporate society. Despite the apparent distance between such humanistic or caring professions on the one hand and the scientific, technical and managerial professionals of the industrial and business worlds on the other, 'a common consciousness of unique skills and functions', according to Robert Wiebe, 'characterised all members of the class'. Moreover, 'similar spirit, similar experiences, even roughly similar aspirations' – including a commitment to what Wiebe calls 'bureaucratic thought' – 'drew them together far more often than chance alone could have explained' (Wiebe, 1967: pp. 112, 113, 153). The new middle class as a whole was therefore defined, and defined itself, not by the possession of material capital but rather by cultural capital – skill, expertise and educational attainment. Of course, these things cannot automatically be transmitted to one's descendants in the same way that wealth and property can; they have to be renewed by each generation through individual effort. Thus, socially mobile and without the ballast of family property, the maintenance of class position became a highly precarious matter for members of the new professional middle class.

But it would be a mistake to view this new class simply as the passive product of the shift from corporate to monopoly capitalism. It was very much, as E. P. Thompson said of the English working class, 'present at its own creation'. Its agency was crucial in leading and effecting this shift, even as the conditions for its own existence were created by it, and its distinctive world views and ideologies were central to the explanation and legitimation of social and economic change in this period, particularly through the central tenets of Progressive reform. As Barbara and John Ehrenreich have argued, the members of this new professional-managerial class or PMC consciously grasped the roles which they had to play. They understood that their own self-interest was bound up in reforming capitalism, and they articulated their understanding far more persistently and clearly than did the capitalist class itself. The role of the emerging PMC as they saw it, was to *mediate* the basic class conflict of capitalist society and create a 'rational' and reproducible social order. (B. and J. Ehrenreich, 1979: p. 19, authors' emphasis)

Thus 'an extremely powerful professional–managerial or service class transformed the basic structuring of class relations' in the United States (Urry, 1986: p. 43). By intervening in the capital–labour relationship and articulating notions of consensus grounded in what it claimed were the objectivity and universality of its own technical expertise and 'scientific' principles, this class rapidly increased its influence and importance in corporate America. As the Ehrenreichs note, 'Every effort to mediate class conflict and rationalise capitalism served to create new institutionalised roles for reformers – i.e., to expand the PMC' (B. and J. Ehrenreich, 1979: p. 20).

This, of course, raises the question of the political and ideological valency of the professional–managerial class, in as much as we can schematically understand it to have opened up and occupied a social position 'between labour and capital' (Walker, 1979). Berle and Means had concluded in 1932 that this new class could not be identified entirely with the capitalist class as the interests of control were different from and often radically opposed to those of ownership (Berle and Means, 1932: p. 122). Indeed, as the Ehrenreichs note, there was a certain continuity between aspects of Progressive thought and the early American Socialist Party, just as there was a close relationship between middle-class radicalism and the New Left of the 1960s (B. and J. Ehrenreich, 1979: pp. 25, 30). But neither can the professional–managerial class be identified with the working class, for, though wage earners rather than property owners, 'the professional–managerial workers exist, as a mass grouping in monopoly capitalist society, only by virtue of the expropriation of the skills and culture once indigenous to the working class' (B. and J. Ehrenreich, 1979: p. 17). There is a sense, then, in which James O'Connor's claim that 'large-scale capital "created" the salariat [i.e. the professional–managerial class] in part to manage the production relations and productive forces and in part to solve the realisation crisis tendencies which in an earlier time haunted American capitalism' is accurate, though its functionalism and attribution of intentionality to an abstraction called 'large-scale capital' are perhaps questionable (O'Connor, 1986: p. 179). But his claim does point to the way in which the PMC's social role has involved supervising the working class well beyond the limits of the production process.[4] In this sense the professional–managerial class '"serves" capital as ownership and control become divorced; but as its own forms of intra-class organisation develop ... it gradually comes to make itself a separate class, a class-in-struggle, opposed in part to both capital and labour' (Urry, 1986: p. 46).

Fordism, Professionalism, Post-Fordism

It is to these forms of self-organisation, to its characteristic discourses and ideologies, and to what the Ehrenreichs call its 'common "culture" or lifestyle' that we must look the better to understand the political valency of the professional–managerial class (B. and J. Ehrenreich, 1979: p. 29).[5] The key form here is the *profession* and the key discourse that of *professionalism*; it has been through these that the class's understanding of its social objectivity, the disinterested nature or ideological 'neutrality' of its expertise, and its autonomy from both capital and labour have been articulated. Indeed, notions of autonomy and independence have always been central to what Burton Bledstein calls 'the culture of professionalism' (Bledstein, 1976: p. 178). In this respect, as Alvin Gouldner has pointed out, professionalism is an *ideology* through which professionals pursue their interests in competition with other classes and press their claims to social leadership (Gouldner, 1979: p. 19). It is, paradoxically, an ideology built upon claims to classlessness, purporting to embody the universal, collective interest and often centring, as we have seen, on notions such as consensus or community. This appeal to classlessness and focus on the 'irrational' nature of class conflict makes it a particularly attractive and influential discourse so that, as Terence Johnson notes, 'professionalism as an ideology' is remarkably 'pervasive' and 'not restricted to groups who have undergone professionalisation' (Johnson, 1972: p. 59).

The pervasiveness of professionalism as an ideology in the United States can be attributed to the massive expansion of professional–managerial positions in the post-Second World War period. While it had constituted itself as a class in the Progressive era, the PMC came fully into its own with the long boom and the proliferation of the state apparatus, the growth in higher education, the full extension of bureaucratic control from the production process to the spheres of distribution and demand manipulation, and the industrialisation of culture through the electronic mass media (B. and J. Ehrenreich, 1979: p. 25). By 1970 the ratio of professional engineers to craft workers in the manufacturing sector was nine times what it had been in 1900 (Gordon, Edwards and Reich, 1982: p. 237, table 6.1). In 1977 professional, managerial and technical posts comprised 23.8 per cent of the labour force, illustrating what Mike Davis calls the 'hypertrophy of occupational positions in the United States associated with the supervision of labour, the organisation of capital, and the implementation of the sales effort' (Davis, 1986: p. 213). And by 1980 it was possible to observe the peculiar demographic composition of this burgeoning class, which was dominated by 25–35-year-old members of the postwar baby-boom generation. This suggests the remarkable rate at which the children of blue-collar families had been recruited into the expanding professional strata, apparently confirming Daniel Bell's 1956 prediction of the comprehensive *embourgeoisement* of the working class (Pfeil, 1990: p. 99; B. and J. Ehrenreich, 1979: pp. 30–31; Bell, 1988: p. 268).[6]

Indeed, the period of full Fordism was so identified with the expansion of the professional–managerial class that the figure of the professional or the manager became absolutely central to the most influential studies of and debates about what we might call American Fordist culture from the 1950s onwards. In books such as David Riesman's *The Lonely Crowd* (1950), C. Wright Mills's *White Collar* (1951), William Whyte's *The Organisation Man* (1960), Vance Packard's *The Pyramid Climbers* (1962) and Robert Bellah's *Habits of the Heart* (1985), the very notion of American social character itself is inseparable from the figure of the white-collar professional or expert.[7] This figure also came to be identified with new psychological or personality types, new modes of experience, and the prevalence of new forms of bureaucratic, managerial and therapeutic authority that commentators felt had displaced direct class oppression and traditional religious, patriarchal or Oedipal forms of authority (Rieff, 1966; Lasch 1977a, 1979; Pfeil, 1990).

Many of these issues will be pursued in the following chapters. For now I simply want to stress the extent to which both the shift from *laissez-faire* to monopoly capitalism in the Progressive era and the consolidation of the Fordist regime in the post-1945 period cannot be understood without close attention to the social agency and ideologies of the professional–managerial class. The period of what we might call high Fordism between the late 1940s and the mid-1970s, and what other commentators defined at various times during the period as the capitalism of 'consensus', 'affluence' or 'plenty', was often seen as marking the point at which the professional–managerial class at last became the universal class, not only by virtue of its espousal of 'universalist' principles but in terms of sheer numbers, subsuming other classes (and hence eliminating class conflict) as a result of its dramatic growth. In *The Affluent Society* (1958) J. K. Galbraith saw this universalisation as both desirable, from the perspective of social harmony and progress, and inevitable, given the technological and scientific direction of capitalist development in the United States in the post-war period. Noting that what he called the 'New Class' of professionals, due to the technical, administrative and managerial requirements of advanced capitalism, was now millions strong, he maintained that 'the further and rapid expansion of this class should be a major, and perhaps next to peaceful survival itself, *the* major social goal of the society'. Education – the acquisition of cultural capital – would be the means to this end, becoming in itself 'the basic index of social progress'. But the real motor of expansion would be technological innovation, particularly the automation of the production process to which the role of the new class was intimately linked (Galbraith, 1969: pp. 276, 277, author's emphasis). Throughout the 1960s Galbraith continued to identify the expansion of the professional–managerial class with the rational 'salvation' of American capitalism, arguing that 'an economy where organised intelligence is the decisive factor of production ... brings into existence, to serve its intellectual and scientific needs, the community that, hopefully, will reject its monopoly of social purpose' (Galbraith, 1967: pp. 85, 391).

Galbraith's optimism that an expanding professional–managerial class would ultimately use its knowledge and control of the sophisticated technical structure of advanced capitalism to direct the system away from profit at any cost and toward rational and humane ends is very much in the Progressive tradition. This hope that professionals, technicians and experts can be 'more than simply lackeys of the capitalist class' (Weinstein, 1969: p. xi) continues to animate more recent calls for the universalisation of the PMC as an antidote to social and economic crisis, such as the one with which Barbara Ehrenreich concludes her otherwise highly critical survey of middle-class consciousness and culture, *Fear of Falling* (1989). Whatever its chances of coming to fruition, this vision is based in an appreciation of the close connections between the values and agency of the professional–managerial class on the one hand and the economic and social uses of technology on the other.

This particular relationship has been, and continues to be, of central importance to the organisation and reorganisation of the productive and social relations of modern capitalism. Constituted precisely through the possession of scientific or humanistic knowledge and claims to technical and intellectual expertise, the professional–managerial class can broadly be understood as the class whose leading role is the application of technique to social process. Technology (which I take to include organisational routines and structures, specialist knowledges and discourses, and media of communication, just as much as the 'hard' materials of engineering)[8] thus becomes an important vehicle for both action and reflection for this class, through which its social power is exerted and its views of the world articulated. Indeed, as John Urry (1986) and David Noble (1979) have suggested, the historical consolidation of the professional–managerial class was intimately bound up with the emergence of new techniques and technologies of production engineering and Taylorist discourses of scientific management in the first two decades of the twentieth century. These proved to be means by which professionals could appropriate power from capital on the one hand and workers on the other, thereby acquiring responsibility for the organisation and supervision of the technical division of labour and presenting themselves as 'objective' mediators of class conflict, essential to general social peace and prosperity. Scientific management was thus understood and propagated by this class not simply as a technique but as the centrepiece of a comprehensive world view, a model for the management of society as a whole in which all areas of productive and social life could be subjected to rationalisation and modernisation according to expert knowledge.[9]

The example of scientific management illustrates well the complexity and ambivalence of the professional–managerial class's privileged relationship to technology. While Taylorist scientific management and its offshoots can be understood as a rationale for deskilling and disciplining industrial workers by expropriating their knowledge and subjecting them to the logic of machine processes and bureaucratic work routines, it can equally be seen as an attack on the prerogatives and power of the owning class to use methods of overt coercion at the workplace. Technology here is thus *at one and the same time* a vehicle by which professionals service capitalists to the detriment of the working class as well as by which they restrict the direct power of capitalists in the workplace and articulate critiques of the capitalist system. Indeed, the notion of 'technocracy' – the rule of skilled and qualified professional elites – embraced by such trenchant critics of early twentieth-century capitalism as Thorstein Veblen was closely wedded to the ideas of scientific management and furnished many of the central tenets not only of the Progressive movement but also of American socialism in this period (B. and J. Ehrenreich, 1979: pp. 23–5).[10]

More recent generations of technology, such as the automated machinery on which Fordist mass production came to rest and the advanced information technologies on which the move to more flexible post-Fordist forms of production is based, have given rise to similarly complex processes and discourses of domination and liberation in which the relationship between technology, ideology and the figure of the professional is central. The terms of this relationship are particularly important and volatile at points of economic crisis when the transformation of the production process and a concomitant recomposition of the social relations of production are seen as necessary for the resolution of accumulation problems. I have been suggesting that the exhaustion of the Fordist postwar boom marks such a point. I will now turn my attention to some of the ways in which the relationship between capital, class and technology has been represented in various narrative projections of the shift from Fordism to post-Fordism.

Part 2

Putting 'IT' to Work: Post-Fordism, Information Technology and the Eclipse of Production

3

Making 'IT': *The Soul of a New Machine*

> Stories about technology ... play a distinctive role in our understanding of
> ourselves and our common history. Technology, the hardest of material artefacts,
> is thoroughly cultural from the outset: an expression and creation of the very
> outlooks and aspirations we pretend it merely demonstrates ... Media of
> communication are not merely instruments of will and purpose but definite forms
> of life: organisms ... that reproduce in miniature the contradictions of our thought,
> action and social relations.
>
> James Carey, Communication as Culture (1989: p. 9)

The microelectronics industry and its principal instrument and symbol, the
computer, have come to occupy a privileged position in the culture and imagination
of contemporary capitalism. We might find one explanation for this in Ernest
Mandel's account of how the post-1945 long wave of accelerating accumulation
was grounded in a third technological revolution whose core innovations issued in,
firstly, the widespread introduction of numerically controlled (that is, computerised)
continuous process production methods in industry and, secondly, the application
of electronic data-processing machines (computers) to commercial tasks in the
private sector. So important does Mandel deem the computer's role in revitalising the
rate of profit that he confers watershed status on the year 1954, during which the
first generation of commercially designed and privately purchased computers took
up their positions in the front line of the American economy, declaring that 'we can
thus date the end of the reconstruction period after the end of the Second World
War and the start of the boom unleashed by the third technological revolution from
that year' (Mandel, 1978: p. 194).

But even as the long boom of the 1950s and '60s gave way to the productivity
crises of the 1970s and '80s, the computer's imagined capacity for bringing about
economic salvation and dynamic social transformation only intensified. With
national and regional economies pinning hopes of recovery on the establishment of
indigenous versions of Silicon Valley and its charmed circle of industrial 'synergies'
(Morgan and Sayer, 1988: p. 39); with employers embracing automation as a cure-
all for sticky labour costs and product rigidity; and with the social geography of
production being reconceived in terms of an opposition between the outmoded
products and labour practices of the heavy industrial 'rustbelt' and the high-tech
products and flexible labour relations of the 'Sunbelt', the computer became a
cultural signifier of considerable power. Again, we might turn to Marxist economic
theory for an explanation of the conditions underlying this intensified faith in the
healing properties of microelectronic technology.

As I suggested in Part 1, the crisis of capitalism whose symptoms first became
evident in the mid-1970s can be understood as the crisis of a particular historical
configuration of the forces and relations of production and consumption. This broad
arrangement constitutes a regime of accumulation. It is manifested in the multiple

and specific institutional and organisational structures, or mode of social regulation, which arise to mediate and ultimately contain the potentially explosive class antagonisms of these relations, at the centre of which is the wage relation, the point at which workers sell their labour power to employers in exchange for means of subsistence. Fordism is the term that describes the productive balance of mass production and mass consumption that, broadly speaking, characterised the United States and Western Europe between 1945 and the late 1970s. The Fordist regime provided the social framework for the negotiation not only of economic forces and relationships in that period, but for political and cultural ones too. Indeed, Peter Wollen has claimed that the terms of the Fordist equation – mass production plus mass consumption with basic welfare provision producing inexorably rising standards of living – were so pervasive as to constitute a distinct 'world view', while Anthony Woodiwiss has persuasively argued that they formed the basis of the ideology of 'social modernism' which has dominated America's political, social and cultural attitudes for the last half-century (Wollen, 1991: p. 43; Woodiwiss, 1993).

Yet, as Fordist structures arose principally to manage the tensions and contradictions of the wage relation, it is not surprising that the limits of Fordism initially were exposed in relation to the production process itself. Here, according to Michel Aglietta, the problem of radically restructuring the prevailing patterns of production and work organisation in order to overcome the growing rigidity of the historic Fordist compromise with labour would have to be faced.

> Capital can escape from its contemporary organic crisis only by generating a new cohesion, a Neo-Fordism ... This transformation is only possible by a generalisation of a new mode of work organisation in which the principle of mechanisation is subordinated to the principle of information, with fragmented work giving way to the semi-autonomous work group and the procedure of hierarchical directives to the overall constraint of production itself. (Aglietta, 1979: p. 385)

The key word in this observation is 'information', and the key shift Aglietta anticipated was the shift from mechanisation to informatisation. In other words, the revitalisation of the profitability of capitalist production would depend on the effective deployment of computer and information technologies. Here we find an explanation of the place these technologies have been accorded in what we might call the capitalist imagination. Indeed, whole discourses and ideologies of 'postindustrial', 'information' or 'post-capitalist' society have arisen around them. These have in common a belief – or perhaps it might better be identified as a *desire* to believe – that the primacy of microelectronics means that the term 'capitalism' no longer applies to the Western economies, or if it does that it is certainly no longer the kind of capitalism analysed and critiqued by Marx – one driven by industrial production, the exploitation of labour, and class struggle – but rather one based on the clean and class-neutral categories of scientific innovation, knowledge and information. Daniel Bell is perhaps the founding father of this position, but the expansion and popularisation of the notion of the information society and its variants in the period since 1973 suggest that these perspectives are part of the construction and propagation of what might be called a post-Fordist world view or social vision (Bell, 1973, 1980a, 1980b; Naisbitt, 1982; Handy, 1990; Drucker, 1993; Neef, 1998).

As I noted in the introduction to this book, these perspectives at certain points overlap with the debate about postmodernism and postmodernity, most notably perhaps in Jean-François Lyotard's intervention into this debate in terms of postindustrialism and the general 'computerisation of society' (Lyotard, 1984: p. 67; Kumar, 1995). But before I pursue these questions, I want to bring discussion back to the role of information technologies in the resolution of the crisis of Fordism. Herbert Schiller has argued that the cultural resonance of IT since the 1970s derives from its function as capital's principal crisis-management tool:

> Industrial crisis, domestic and international, is the environment in which the new information technologies are being invented and deployed. Their employment is designed to overcome, or, at the very least, alleviate crisis ... This is the meaning of the mad scramble into electronics, the push toward privatisation in the economy at large, the reverence for computerisation, however mindless. (Schiller, 1984: p. 47)

IT serves a dual purpose in this view: as the quintessentially innovative and clean industry it promises in itself a return to the rapidly rising productivity and unblemished prosperity of the American 1950s and early '60s; and, as the technical nervous system of a global mass communications capability, it offers a new level of ideological penetration for American corporate world views and commodities, promising a return to the global ideological hegemony also associated with the Pax Americana of the 1950s and early '60s. IT, then, has been embraced for its magical capacity both to banish recession and precipitate what Herbert Schiller has called a 'new technology consensus' (Schiller, 1984: p. 5) strong enough to marginalise as technophobic and backward-looking those who would argue that the social and economic crises of the last two decades are systemic in nature, rather than contingencies which can be 'innovated' out of existence. In this respect IT has been enlisted as a powerful riposte to what Jürgen Habermas identifies as the crises of legitimation and motivation that, he has argued, tend inevitably to accompany economic crisis in advanced capitalist societies, and has been instrumental in the emergence, according to Mike Davis, of a 'new Americanism without Fordism' (Habermas, 1975: pp. 46–9; Davis, 1986: p. 182).

Along similar lines, David Harvey has contextualised the primacy of IT in terms of the transition out of the moribund structures of Fordist production and social organisation towards a new regime of 'flexible accumulation'. Harvey sees computerisation both embodying and facilitating more widely the switch from the geographically concentrated mass production of standardised commodities characteristic of Fordism to the dispersed, short-run production, niche marketing and just-in-time delivery of customised commodities that is increasingly the norm in advanced capitalist societies (Harvey, 1989: p. 124). Like Lyotard, but from a substantially different political perspective, Harvey relates capital's turn from Fordism to the question of cultural postmodernity, seeing beneath the transition towards flexible specialisation in production the appearance of a new kind of social space:

> In the social space created by all this flux and uncertainty, a series of novel experiments in the realms of industrial organisation as well as in political and social life have begun to take shape. These experiments may represent the early

stirrings of the passage to an entirely new regime of accumulation, coupled with a quite different system of social and political regulation. (Harvey, 1989: p. 145)

Tracy Kidder's book of popular reportage, *The Soul of a New Machine* (1981), David Byrne's film, *True Stories* (1986) and Douglas Coupland's novel, *Microserfs* (1995), address themselves overtly to the questions raised by this proximity of information technologies to the reorganisation of certain aspects of political and social life. In doing so, of course, they perpetuate the image of the computer as 'the defining technology and principal technological metaphor of our time' (Bolter, 1986: p. 40). But they also interrogate this status, and open up the space for a critical evaluation of the effects of IT not only on economic and social life, but on the private enclaves of character and subjectivity too.

Informating the Crisis

By 1980 the 'hesitant, uneven and inflationary recovery' of the late 1970s had foundered and the American durable commodities sector was experiencing contraction of a 'special severity' presaging the deepest recession to hit the Western industrialised economies since the war (Mandel, 1980: pp. 209–10). According to Morgan and Sayer, it is at precisely such times that the ideology of 'high-tech' comes into its own, giving rise to a general appetite for certain kinds of public narrative in which 'there is a potent union of popular mythologies of science ("whizz-kids" and white-coated scientists making "breakthroughs") and of free enterprise (heroic thrusting entrepreneurs, unfettered by corporate or bureaucratic ties)' (Morgan and Sayer, 1988: pp. 38–9). Published in 1981, just as the recession bit hardest, Tracy Kidder's *The Soul of a New Machine* both exploited and anatomised these images and ideologies of high-tech. Ostensibly a piece of journalism (in which category it received a Pulitzer Prize), Kidder's book is in fact an artful reworking of the traditional American success myth transposed from Horatio Alger's nineteenth-century settings to the silicon suburbs of New England's nascent information economy.

In accordance with Morgan and Sayer's characterisation of the ideology of high-tech, Kidder's book sets out as a rattling narrative of technical wizardry and entrepreneurial daring. This is established in the opening chapter, entitled 'How to Make a Lot of Money', which relates the brief (until then) and astonishingly lucrative history of the American minicomputer industry, in particular that of the Data General Corporation and its enigmatic and buccaneering chief, Edson de Castro. Indeed, the first computer we meet in a story about computers is de Castro's very first design, now ensconced in the foyer of his company's New England headquarters and programmed to display the continually updated fiscal history of the company. Kidder notes of the figures on the screen that 'anyone could see that they started small and got big fast', concluding that 'the computer in the case was telling an old familiar story – the international, materialistic fairy tale come true' (*Soul*: p. 11).

Yet however much Kidder implies that this is just an old-fashioned and thoroughly American tale of enterprise rewarded, he also carefully plots his story around the issues of historical shifts and socio-economic change. Driving out to Data General's headquarters through Stanford Silicon Valley (New England's high-tech nerve centre whose 'configurations', according to David Harvey, 'are quite new and special to the era of flexible specialisation' [Harvey, 1989: p. 160]) he ventures the following meditation, inspired by the view from the car window:

> The highway traverses some of the ghost country of rural Massachusetts. Like Troy, this region contains the evidence of successive sackings: in the pine and hardwood forests ... many cellar holes and overgrown stone walls that farmers left behind when they went west; riverside textile mills ... their windows broken now, their machinery crumbling to rust and the business gone to Asia and down south. However, on many roads that stand back behind the highway's scenery stand not woods and relics, but brand new neighborhoods, apartment houses and shopping centers. The roads around them fill up with cars before nine and after five. They are going to and from commercial buildings that wear on their doors and walls descriptions of new enterprise. Digital Equipment, Data General – there on the edge of the woods, those names seemed like prophecies to me, before I realised that the new order they implied had arrived already. (*Soul*: pp. 8–9)

The question of a whole new economic and, by implication, social order – one significantly inhabited by the ghost of earlier histories and modes of production – is dwelt upon here. But the precise nature of the change is not easy to articulate. From the outset of his story Kidder rejects the technological determinist notion of a 'computer revolution' in which the very presence of new technology is sufficient in itself to refashion the pattern of social relationships and the distribution of power. Rather, Kidder judges, 'the technology had served as a prop to the status quo' (*Soul*: p. 241). However, if the computer in some sense *is* a key to understanding whatever new order may already have emerged from the ghost of earlier social and economic formations, where can we begin to look for the locus of such change, and how are we to estimate the scope of its effects? Interestingly, like the regulation theorists, Kidder turns his attention to the production process itself in the search for clues, feeling that 'a more likely place to look for radical change was inside the industry actually producing computers' (*Soul*: p. 12).

Kidder's book recounts the story of Data General's Eclipse Group, a collection of around thirty young computer engineers whose task is to produce a new machine capable of restoring the corporation's endangered market position. In the intensely competitive environment of the minicomputer industry, with its frenetic pace of innovation and drastically compressed rates of obsolescence,[1] Data General has little more than a year to get this new machine from drawing board to market if it is not permanently to lose much of its business to a machine about to be unveiled by its major rival. Kidder tells us that 'the task of guarding against this sort of crisis fell mainly to engineers rather than to executives, as engineers would provide most of the ideas for new products' (*Soul*: p. 27). And the image of crisis becomes, through a series of linked metaphors, the dominant motif for both the business of computer design and for the narrative itself. The book's prologue consists of an account of the Eclipse Group's charismatic leader, Tom West, negotiating a storm at sea (West's sailing companions dub him 'a good man in a storm'); and clearly the sea-storm is an apt metaphor for an industry whose 'short product cycles lend to many projects an atmosphere of crisis, so that computer engineering, which is arduous enough in itself, often becomes intense' (*Soul*: p. 104).

As we have seen both Michel Aglietta and David Harvey observe, the heightened pitch of competition and the peculiar volatility of capital in a time of crisis demand organisational flexibility and innovation, and Kidder particularly concerns himself with the novel features of the Eclipse group as a corporate organism. Immediately striking, and signalled already in Kidder's observation that this industry tends to privilege engineers over executives, is the difference between the organisational ethos prevailing at Data General and that which characterised the archetypal American corporations of the long boom period in the classic accounts of Alfred D. Chandler, William H. Whyte, and David Riesman (Chandler, 1962; Whyte, 1960; Riesman, 1961). For it appears that Data General functions to a large extent as a constellation of relatively autonomous, dehierarchised work groups in the manner suggested by Michel Aglietta and quoted earlier. The Eclipse Group's informality of dress and manners, the absence of titles and hierarchical distinctions, the eccentric and individually determined hours and habits of work, and the apparently complete control over design and production enjoyed by its members could not be more at odds with the bureaucratic, grey-flannel world of William H. Whyte's 'organisation man', or indeed with the gigantic formality and rigidity of a 'mainframe' organisation such as IBM.

The very space in which the Eclipse Group works reflects this apparent ad hoc egalitarianism; the doorless and officeless 'maze' of cubicles offers no legible correlation of cubicle size or location to seniority or authority (*Soul*: p. 50). Power, too, appears to be distributed on a radically different basis to that which we associate with the archetypal bureaucratic corporation. Kidder describes how, finding no filing cabinet, group records, or even a list of group members, the newly appointed secretary 'went from one engineer to another, asking "Do you have *any* idea who you work for?"' (*Soul*: p. 57). He also remarks of EGO, the group's previous and aborted project for a new machine, that those working on it were 'nominally working for West, but [were] in fact amenable to no-one's control' (*Soul*: p. 30). Indeed, the significantly named EGO was conceived and built in a purely independent and quasi-secretive manner by the group in piqued response to what they felt was de Castro's inclination to pass 'sexy' new projects to Data General's purpose-built R&D facility in North Carolina. And again, of the process of building the new machine – finally to be called Eagle – Kidder observes that 'control seemed to be nowhere and everywhere at once' (*Soul*: p. 159).

This conception of power and authority being reconfigured, or dispersed, into 'maze-like' or 'decentred' patterns is characteristic of many influential postmodern positions or descriptions of postmodernity. Once again we are referred to the connections between new technologies and systemic social and cultural change. In particular, Mark Poster's claim that IT brings with it new patterns of 'institutional routine', social relations and subjectivity or selfhood is worth exploring here. For Poster (whose claims are in many respects supported by the more empirical and anthropological work of researchers such as Sherry Turkle), these new, IT-influenced forms are characterised by dispersal and 'electronic intertextuality' as opposed to the traditional qualities of 'solidity' and 'rationality'. As a result, he contends that the Marxist term 'mode of production' should be displaced by the notion of 'mode of information' as a fundamental concept of social analysis, and that 'modern' positions should be dropped in favour of 'postmodern' positions in the investigation of contemporary modes of living and working (Poster, 1990: pp. 6, 8,

14, 18; Turkle, 1984 and 1995). Leaving aside the merits of Poster's recommendations for the time being, it is worth noting for now the way in which the structural innovations embodied by the Eclipse Group appear to correspond to what has been described as an increasingly influential and timely 'postmodern' model of organisation. This is defined as 'an "autonomy" model which is self-referential, processual ... and which acts automatically, i.e. independently of external (human) control'. In this respect, the postmodern organisation rejects the model 'of the omniscient rational subject' and diverges from the 'modern' or 'control' model of organisation which, by contrast, is 'conceived as the expression of human rationality' (Cooper and Burrell, 1988: p. 104).

In many ways such a model sounds liberating, or at the very least more humane and responsive to the contingencies of a complex world, and there is a significant body of commentary that sees in the model of the decentralised 'network' organisation hopeful political implications. Not only are IT and the computer industry deemed to be catalysts for this 'greening' of the relations of work and of corporate organisation, but the computer itself seems to stand as a privileged model or metaphor for the ideal organisational or social configuration, one typically based on the notion of rapid, flexible and dehierarchised communication. This almost irresistible tendency to conceive of human and social relationships in terms of technological models is foregrounded in *The Soul of a New Machine*. For example, in the early stages of the as yet unnamed Eagle project, Tom West infiltrates Data General's competitor, DEC, to sneak an illicit glimpse of the insides of that company's rival to Eagle, the VAX:

> Looking into the VAX, West had imagined he saw a diagram of DEC's corporate organisation. He felt that VAX was too complicated. He did not like, for instance, the system by which various parts of the machine communicated with each other; for his taste there was too much protocol involved. He decided that VAX embodied flaws in DEC's corporate organisation. The machine expressed that phenomenally successful company's cautious, bureaucratic style. (*Soul*: p. 32)

The idea of an expressive continuity between technology and forms of social organisation, even of human subjectivity itself (a notion at its most influential in the debate surrounding cybernetics and artificial intelligence explored in Part 3 of this book), is a particular consequence of the microelectronics revolution. For the most part, earlier, mechanised forms of technology had lent themselves to an interpretation which polarised the qualities of humans and machines (however, see Seltzer, 1992). The abiding popular representation of the antagonistic relationship between worker and machine under Fordist structures of production remains Charlie Chaplin's film, *Modern Times* (1936). Yet, as William Kuhns has noted, the steady displacement of 'the mechanised conception of technology' by 'the media or information-control interpretation' suggested by IT 'leads to a conception of organic continuity between man and his technologies' (Kuhns, 1971: p. 9). Thus the popularisation from the 1960s onwards of Marshall McLuhan's notion of technology as the 'extensions of man' rather than his antithesis. And while electrified technological utopias are not unique to the era of postindustrial society (Edward Bellamy's version, *Looking Backward*, dates from 1888), the arrival of IT seems, to some at least, to have made them newly possible, if not inevitable.

Computers, Communications, Community

Computer technology has, then, become a crucial accessory to many recent reconceptions of community; and we must note that community itself is now a key and contested notion in discussions of contemporary or postmodern American culture, a fact attested to by the debate provoked by Robert Bellah's *Habits of the Heart* in the mid-1980s and the subsequent revival, culminating in the Clinton presidency's public endorsement, of communitarian approaches to social analysis in the 1990s (Bellah *et al.*, 1985 and 1992; Reynolds and Norman, 1988; Bell, 1993; Etzioni, 1994; Clinton 1996; Tam, 1998). In this respect it could be argued that much of the allure of *The Soul of a New Machine* resides in its vivid yet nuanced description of a working community operating at its intellectual limits, in the process not simply building a sophisticated machine but also, as one chapter heading puts it, 'building a team'. The machine itself is far from incidental to this sense of community of purpose. Both Kidder and the engineers themselves are inclined to think that the very complexity of the machine, the fact that no one person among them can fully understand how it works let alone aspire to technical command of all its components, demands a cooperative and collective approach to conception and construction. Though work on Eagle is segmented to some degree, roles nevertheless appear to be extremely fluid and multifaceted. The Eclipse Group is thus far removed from the fragmentation of tasks and the strict separation of mental from manual labour characteristic of the 'scientifically managed' classic Fordist enterprise. Team members are given to declaring how the machine 'goes beyond' any one amongst them, and Kidder too is struck by the fact that 'none of them dared to understand in detail how all the parts worked and fit together' (*Soul*: p. 151).

Implicit in such comments is a conception of community as an essentially provisional and loose voluntary association whose relationships are seen to operate in terms of an internal principle of accidental configuration rather than an exterior or determining principle of structuration. Applying the lexicon of postmodernism, the Eclipse Group exemplifies the kind of community which subsists without recourse to any overarching principle of legitimation, or what Jean-François Lyotard has called 'grand' or 'totalising narrative'. Indeed, in *The Postmodern Condition*, Lyotard famously claimed that it was precisely in the context of 'postindustrial society' and 'postmodern culture' – what he also calls the 'computerisation of society' – that grand narratives lost their credibility. He also asserted that 'the decline of narrative can be seen as an effect of the blossoming of techniques and technologies since the Second World War' (Lyotard, 1984: pp. 37–8).[2] For Lyotard, the postmodern notion of community is conceived in limited and primarily linguistic terms, as what he calls a 'language game', and interestingly the members of the Eclipse Group see themselves operating in precisely this way. Paraphrasing the reflections of one group member, Kidder summarises the situation as follows:

> What a way to design a computer! There's no grand design, thinks Rosen. People are just reaching out in the dark, touching hands. ... No-one seems to be in control; nothing's ever explained ... The entire Eclipse Group, especially its managers, seemed to be operating on instinct. Only the simplest visible arrangements existed amongst them. They kept no charts and graphs or organisational tables that

meant anything. But those webs of voluntary, mutual responsibility, the product of many signings-up, held them together. (*Soul*: pp. 116, 120)

Moreover, the team members persistently refer to their project as a 'game' and, when challenged to define what it is that makes his group and its work special, West replies, 'The language is different' (*Soul*: p. 50).

For Lyotard the decentring, or as he puts it 'atomisation', of the social into flexible networks of 'incommensurable' language games (Lyotard, 1984: p. 16) is not the cause for concern that it undoubtedly is for the more circumspect (some would say nostalgic) American theorists of community such as Robert Bellah and his main precursors, David Riesman and Philip Rieff (Riesman, 1961; Rieff, 1966).[3] Lyotard suggests that the 'splintering' of the social bond fosters the emergence of new patterns of relationship and forms of selfhood or subjectivity in which postmodern incredulity towards the grand narratives of scientifically revealed truth and political emancipation puts a liberating emphasis in the constitution of community on individual competence or people's own 'linguistic practice and communicational interaction' (Lyotard, 1984: p. 41). This is a seductive view, one that animates such stylistically postmodern works as David Byrne's film, *True Stories* (1986), or Douglas Coupland's novel, *Microserfs* (1995), which are examined in the next two chapters of this book. But for now I want to dwell briefly on the nature of the Eclipse Group as a linguistically constituted community. For what is striking in the light of Lyotard's account of the intertextual proliferation of communicational networks in the postmodern world is the extent to which West's team of engineers lives a peculiarly cloistered existence. The group's confinement to the windowless and airless basement of the near impregnable building 14A/B is a telling image of the almost complete absence of communicational interaction that marks its members' lives beyond that building's walls, even, it could be argued, within them.

For one thing, this world is relentlessly male. The team has one woman engineer, but the ethos remains a resolutely masculinist one of bantering camaraderie riding over deep structures of competitiveness and ego jostling. Similarly, for all its dehierarchised and decentred structure, the group nevertheless requires the services of an all-female secretarial support staff, one of whom is subjected to a sinister form of sexual harassment by computer. The gender monopoly of technical knowledge that extends, as feminist theorists have observed, to the language of technology itself, and that here leaves the secretary vulnerable to textual assault, also protects the perpetrator as he is able to use his mastery of the system's linguistic–technical code to escape detection. The predetermined, gender-coded nature of the communal language is further illustrated by the engineers' proclivity to view their machine through metaphors of sexual invitation and stereotyped notions of feminine behaviour; particularly challenging projects are 'sexy', while the computer itself is referred to as 'la machine', especially when its masters feel its behaviour is overly 'flighty' or 'capricious'.

The limitations (both physical and conceptual) of this community are also exposed in relation to the very informality of its constitution. Kidder makes it clear that the price paid for membership of this team, with its dedication to excellence, its crisis atmosphere of intensity, and an average 75-hour working week, is an equally intense personal loneliness and a debilitating neglect of convivial, emotional and domestic relationships.[4] Within the Eclipse Group, a process called 'signing up' refers to the essentially verbal means by which the linguistic–communal bond is established. To the outsider, Kidder, it appears as a 'mysterious rite of initiation' by which 'you agreed to do whatever was necessary for success. You agreed to forsake ... family, hobbies, and friends – if you had any of these left'. Fittingly, this compact was 'not accomplished with formal declarations ... a statement such as "Yeah, I'll do that" could constitute the act of signing up, and often it was done tacitly'. Yet behind this apparently provisional bond lies another level of relations of *power*: from management's viewpoint, signing up is the ideal form of contract as it secures long hours with no overtime agreement, meaning that 'Labor was no longer coerced. Labor volunteered' (*Soul*: p. 63).

The informality and provisional nature of signing up also refer us to the link Lyotard established between the linguistic model of community and the primacy of the temporary contract which, he claimed, was 'in practice supplanting permanent institutions in the professional, emotional, sexual, cultural, family and international domains'. For Lyotard this tendency is ambiguous in as much as the temporary contract is 'favoured by the system ... due to its increased operativity and yet is not totally subordinated to its [i.e. the system's] goal' (Lyotard, 1984: p. 66). However, Kidder's description of the provisionality of the work environment at Data General's Westborough headquarters suggests otherwise:

> The arrangements looked temporary, and indeed they were. As one of the company's PR men explained, cubicles laid out as in a maze allow a greater density of workers per square foot than real offices with doors. Easily movable walls allow management to tinker with that area-to-people ratio without incurring enormous expense ... It was said that the company's vice president for manufacturing could turn Westborough into a factory overnight, and maybe the joke had some substance. The last headquarters, compared to which this one was plush, had in fact been turned into a factory ... Westborough seemed designed for quick changes ... West offered some additional theories: 'We can change it all around. It keeps up the basic level of insecurity.' (*Soul*: p. 50)

As this passage makes clear, the temporary contract (indeed the temporary physical environment) is in this instance the principal means by which capital reasserts its dominance in the 'game' with labour. And, as Dennis Hayes has pointed out, the ability to exploit whatever ambiguity might reside in such pervasive short-termism depends entirely on one's possession of the requisite amounts of cultural capital and social power (Hayes, 1990: pp. 50–4). The temporary contract may be tolerable, even advantageous, to a much sought-after computer engineer or high-profile intellectual for whom mobility, 'creative turmoil', and career advancement go hand in hand. But for the increasing proportion of 'permanent–temporary workers' (Hayes, 1990: p. 50) in the lower reaches of the IT and other industries it offers little other than chronic economic insecurity.

The workplace legend about the overnight transformation of a company HQ into a factory (with its overtones of summary proletarianisation) suggests, then, that temporariness has become a dominant feature of the structures of capital accumulation and of the organisation of production in the shift towards post-Fordism. The very volatility and mobility of capital which the application of IT raises to unprecedented levels of intensity produces not only a sense of temporal acceleration but has effects also on the perception and organisation of space, of which the layout of the Westborough building is one local example. David Harvey has argued that 'the crisis of Fordism was in large part a crisis of temporal and spatial form', and has sought to demonstrate the link between the acceleration of capital flows in the transition out of Fordism, new instances of spatio-temporal compression in social life, and the turn towards cultural postmodernism (Harvey, 1989: p. 196). Kidder's book allows us to keep this idea in mind whilst shifting the focus of attention to a closer consideration of the role and nature of the computer itself.

Space, Time and the Computer

'Time in a computer is an interesting concept', one of the engineers points out to Kidder, explaining that temporal compression has reached an almost incomprehensible pitch within the central processing unit of the Eclipse Group's prototype machine. Here, the computer's internal clock ticks every nanosecond, that is, every 220 billionths of a second, with each tick representing the time it takes for the machine to perform one microinstruction of any particular program. It is further explained that working with such units can cause one to experience a strange warping of one's normal sense of time which can culminate in an odd sense of meaninglessness. The same engineer confesses, 'I can sit at one of these analysers and nanoseconds are *wide*. I mean, you can see them go by ... Yet when I think about it, how much longer it takes to snap your fingers, I've lost track of what a nanosecond really means' (*Soul*: p. 137). The rationalisation of temporal duration into universal standardised units of measurable time has been seen as one of the key concerns of the Enlightenment project and as an enabling condition of modern capitalism (Harvey, 1989). Here, it has been pushed so far as to collapse in on itself, revealing the full extent of its conceptual arbitrariness. The computer's infinitesimal segmentation of time also has important spatial implications, as Kidder's discussion of the practice of 'time sharing' illustrates. A number of terminals are connected to a central computer whose speed of operation allows it to so divide its attentions between the various users as to give the impression that they have sole access to the machine. Interestingly, Kidder describes this particular effect as 'an illusion'. He observes that it obliterates physical distance more effectively than any other form of communication, noting how it 'already took place not only within buildings, but between them and across continents and oceans' (*Soul*: p. 77).

   This aspect of electronic communication is now of course far more advanced than it was at the time of Kidder's writing, and the exponential growth of the internet has prompted a reformulation of Marshall McLuhan's notion of the 'global village' in terms of the 'information superhighway' or the 'networked world'. Proponents of such visions (Microsoft's Bill Gates in particular) have only reinforced McLuhan's affirmative attitude towards such developments, appropriating the latter's wide-eyed optimism about technology as a gloss for cool-headed global business strategies. But it is worth noting that McLuhan's mentor and pioneer communications theorist, Harold Innis, was much more ambivalent about the value of such developments. Innis wrote of the 'bias of communication', arguing that, historically, communications technologies and the kinds of knowledge and discourse they make possible have an inherent tendency to obliterate the more fragile and humane oral and traditionally-rooted forms of life with which they come into contact.[5] Communications paved the way for empire and imperialism, according to Innis, bringing social rationalisation and economic monopoly in their wake. More recently, Marxist geographers such as David Harvey have extended Innis's ideas, arguing that communications technologies enable capital to dominate the mobile and abstract category of 'space', giving it primacy over locality or 'place' where labour's strength has traditionally been located. We might note here the inseparability of questions about communications from questions about community. The relationship between these terms has concerned other commentators such as Joshua Meyerowitz for whom IT represents the latest stage in the 'separation of social place from physical place'. For Meyerowitz, microelectronic communication introduces a disturbing element of indeterminacy into contemporary social life now that 'where we are physically no longer determines where we are socially' (Meyerowitz, 1985: p. 115). This results in the erosion of previously solid geographical, social and behavioural boundaries, leaving contemporary Western culture afflicted by what Meyerowitz diagnoses as 'no sense of place'.

Behind laments such as Meyerowitz's and in accounts of the experience of working in nanoseconds we can perhaps appreciate how close attention to extremes of spatial and temporal dislocation tends to lead into large questions about meaning, even about reality itself. This is certainly the case for the engineers of the Eclipse Group who, particularly at times of stress, are given to questioning the 'reality' of their work. Kidder observes that 'the question of whether this project was "real" would usually lead to a little mutual rumination on the meaning of the word itself'; and whilst such probings of reality might merely be seen as metaphysical flights taken amidst the material slog of application to what had become 'a corporate necessity', West himself is nevertheless convinced that 'What goes on here is not part of the real world' (*Soul*: pp. 133, 132, 50).

West's statement is made with reference to the extreme temporariness of the physical and organisational arrangements within both the Eclipse Group and the Data General HQ. Yet it could equally apply to the unique ability of the computer itself to generate convincingly real and self-contained worlds out of its own circuitry. Many of the engineers spend their scarce free time playing a computer game called 'Adventure' in which the player is cast into a labyrinthine underground world searching for treasure and an exit. It is perhaps too tempting to see a parallel between the underground world of 'Adventure' and the cloistered basement habitat of the Eclipse Group itself, with its maze-like cubicles and the corporate treasure of the unfinished machine lying at its centre. But the analogy does serve to suggest the way in which microelectronic technologies are capable not only of generating parallel worlds but of blurring the boundaries between these conceptual environments and the 'real' physical world, often with the effect of precipitating problems of orientation, even of ontological confusion. One of the engineers captures the peculiar reality of these unreal worlds when he says, 'Adventure's a completely bogus world. But when you're there, you're there'. And that the conceptual space can take over as primary reality is implied by another engineer who, after periods of intense analysis of the computer's logical address space is visited for days on end by 'the unpleasant sensation of being locked inside the machine' (*Soul*: pp. 88, 102, 128).

These observations suggest how the computer might be party not only to the dissociation of physical from social place, but also to the proliferation of a new order of conceptual spaces or worlds which can no longer be held entirely separate from physical space. Sherry Turkle's ethnographic studies of computer use have shown how subjects see themselves moving between different worlds and even identities according to the type of activity in which they are engaged. As Turkle notes, some users negotiate such transactions with a lesser degree of ontological confusion than others, but all, when asked, find their computer use causes them to reassess and interrogate commonplace notions of 'reality' (Turkle, 1984, 1995). Similarly, Brian McHale has proposed that 'ontological pluralism', the co-existence and confusion of ostensibly different realities or worlds, is the distinguishing feature of the postmodern condition; while Fredric Jameson also sees postmodernity in spatial terms, likening the disorientations of the contemporary 'hyperspace' in which we now find (or rather lose) ourselves as subjects to 'some immense communicational and computer network' which can be negotiated only by means of a radically new practice of 'cognitive mapping' (McHale, 1987; Jameson 1991: p. 37, 1988a). We should quickly note, however, that any such capacity for provoking radical spatial mutation is not linked merely, even principally, to the properties of the computer as a technical *instrument*; it must also be understood in relation to microelectronics and IT as an *industry* or historical formation of capital.

In this respect the computer has been a key component in what both Ed Soja and Mike Davis have identified as the emergence of a novel kind of economic and social geography which has come increasingly to characterise high-tech regional economies and which, according to Soja, 'all comes together in Los Angeles' (Soja, 1989: p. 190; Davis, 1985). Soja identified in the 'postmodern geography' of Los Angeles and its environs a distinct and new configuration of capital and social power whose 'spatiality challenges orthodox analysis and interpretation'. 'Too filled with "other spaces" to describe informatively', such regions present to the observer 'only fragments and immediacies' (Soja, 1989: p. 122). Soja's linking of IT and new high-tech formations of capital to a kind of geographical immateriality or non-referentiality of decentred urban form recalls Thomas Pynchon's fictional high-tech city suburb of Los Angeles, San Narciso, in *The Crying of Lot 49* (1966), a space which 'was less an identifiable city than a group of concepts – census tracts, special purpose bond-issue districts, shopping nuclei, all overlaid with access roads to its own freeway' (Pynchon, 1966: p. 14).

Pynchon's novel is also valuable in this context for its dramatisation of how such spatial configurations of technology and capital are implicated in what might be called a cultural crisis of representation, something already suggested by Soja's comments above. Pynchon's heroine, Oedipa Maas, suspects that microelectronic technology may itself be the key to understanding the confusing space of San Narciso and thus to solving the mystery in which she has become entangled; the information communicated by the internal structure of such technology might be of a special, revelatory kind. Overlooking San Narciso she

> thought of the time she'd opened a transistor radio to replace a battery and seen her first printed circuit. The ordered swirl of houses and streets, from this high angle, sprang at her now with the same unexpected, astonishing clarity as the circuit card had ... there were to both outward patterns a hieroglyphic sense of

concealed meaning, of an intent to communicate. There'd seemed no limit to what the printed circuit could have told her (if she had tried to find out) ... a revelation ... trembled just past the threshold of her understanding. (Pynchon, 1966: pp. 14–15)

This 'hieroglyphic sense' which seems to inhabit microelectronic technology has already been noted in the example of Tom West's intuition that the essences or meanings of Data General's and DEC's respective corporate structures and philosophies were somehow represented by, even embodied in, the designs of their machines. West the pragmatist declines to debate the truth of this intuition, deeming it sufficient as a 'useful theory' (*Soul*: p. 32). However, he does not consider that it might be a misleading one. Only a page earlier in the text Kidder has learned that 'a computer's boards seem to show order triumphing in complexity. They look as if they make sense, but not in the way that the moving parts of an engine make sense. The form on the surface of a board does not imply its function' (*Soul*: p. 31). This, and Pynchon's evocation of the printed circuit's quality of concealed meaning, of revelation ultimately withheld, implies that social and other kinds of relationships and meanings can no longer be 'read off' from the visible facets and formal organisation of such structures. In particular, Kidder's stress on the divergent technical and semantic logics of mechanical and computer technology, and on the separation of form from function in computer design, suggest that it is precisely the modernist approach to representation and interpretation, in which 'form follows function', that becomes inoperable in a postindustrial context.

Technology and the Representation of Power

On one level, this disjunction of form and function is related to a new autonomy or self-referentiality of design in production. Unease about the distortion of the signifying properties of technology and industrial products, however, is far from unique to the so-called postindustrial epoch and has usually been expressed in terms of an objection to the inflation or deceitful excess of non-essential design features over functional utility. Thorstein Veblen's classic excoriation of late nineteenth-century 'conspicuous waste' in his *Theory of the Leisure Class* (1899) and Vance Packard's attack on the 'pink dinosaurism' of automobile design in the 1950s are two interesting instances of such unease (Veblen, 1953: p. 113; Packard, 1960: p. 90). They represent what we might call its Puritan moralistic and its ascetic Fordist versions respectively.[6] At base, both Veblen and Packard objected principally to the occlusion within the object of manufacture of the visible traces, perhaps even the very logic, of labour and production – what Veblen called 'the evidence of skilful workmanship' (Veblen, 1953: p. 113) – beneath the spectacular trappings of fashion and style. These concerns are directly related to what was felt to be the increasing opacity of the culture as the American economy moved from a production orientation to a fully blown system of production-for-consumption, and express typical reservations about the nature of 'consumer society' that became fully established under mature Fordism. We might note that Jean Baudrillard's notions of 'hyperreality' and the 'simulacrum' represent the current culmination of this tradition of thought, only shorn this time of the element of critique (Baudrillard, 1983).

On another and perhaps more important level, the disjunction of form and function in IT and the crisis of modernist representation that is coincident with it, has implications for contemporary conceptions of the efficacy, logic and place of power in technologically advanced capitalist societies, particularly if we approach this question in terms of Fredric Jameson's notion of 'cognitive mapping'. *The Crying of Lot 49* is again instructive in this respect. During her sojourn in San Narciso, Oedipa Maas stumbles upon an underground communicational network that leads her into an other, parallel world populated by the dispossessed, those marginalised and excluded from the high-tech paradise of Southern California. From this point Oedipa's predicament is no longer primarily epistemological (how to comprehend her deceased ex-lover's legacy from the mysterious clues in his will) but becomes instead ontological (which world is real? which world is she in?), and stems from her inability to map her relationship and her position within these apparently conflicting places which nevertheless occupy the same geographical space.[7] Her sense of disorientation is ultimately associated with questions of power, with just who controls these worlds between which she finds herself lost. Is it her ex-lover, the megalomaniac high-tech capitalist, Pierce Inverarity, or the sinister and occult communications network known as the Trystero? Oedipa's dilemma and the possibility of revelation or terminal confusion that lies within it is again figured by Pynchon in terms of microelectronic technology: 'For it was now like walking among matrices of a great digital computer, the zeros and ones twinned above, hanging like balanced mobiles right and left, ahead, thick, maybe endless ... there would either be some fraction of the truth's numinous beauty ... or only a power spectrum' (Pynchon, 1966: p. 125). However, Oedipa's fear that Inverarity and the Trystero might be one and the same, and that the separate worlds are bound for collision, leads her to the conclusion that the rigid binarism of computer logic, its either/or language of one or zero, cannot assist her in the construction of an adequate map of the circuits of power which animate her worlds. In a space like San Narciso, which Oedipa comes to feel 'had no boundaries' (Pynchon, 1966: p. 123), the location of power cannot so easily be decided upon: it is less a matter of determinate truth or falsehood than it is of a 'spectrum', an indeterminate dissemination that defies exact or certain representation.

Interestingly, the engineers of the Eclipse Group find themselves in a situation disturbingly similar to Oedipa's as Kidder's narrative comes to hinge on a major issue of power and control. The question arises of where, precisely, ultimate responsibility for the shape and nature of the Eagle project lies: the engineers begin to wonder, in short, who exactly controls this world of theirs. Two positions are offered. One engineer insists that 'The company didn't ask for this machine, we *gave* it to them. We created this design ... We got it from *within* ourselves'. However, another contends that 'Their [the company's] idea was piped into our minds!' (*Soul*: p. 271). The polarisation of the argument reflects the binarism of the engineers' professional world view or 'code', which Kidder describes as follows: 'Among its tenets is the general idea that the engineers' right environment is a highly structured one, in which only right and wrong answers exist. It's a binary world; the computer might be its paradigm, and many engineers seem to aspire to be binary people within it' (*Soul*: p. 146). Yet Kidder promptly observes that 'there were many reasons to doubt the reality of this binary world' (*Soul*: p. 147). And we might suggest that some of the engineers' confusion as to the precise locus of power within their world stems from this misplaced trust in the explanatory value of the computer as metaphor. Far from inhabiting the highly structured environment represented by the computer, Kidder feels that the Eclipse Group 'lived in a land of mists and mirrors'. Moreover, the unmappability of their world is related to the nature of the particular language game that constitutes it. Kidder attempts to codify the rules according to which this world operates, but finds that certainty on this issue is not easily arrived at:

> I think those were the rules that they were playing by, and when I recited them to some of the team's managers, they seemed to think so, too. But Alsing said there was probably another rule that stated, 'One never explicitly plays by these rules'. And West remarked that there was no telling which rules might be real, because only de Castro made the rules that counted, and de Castro was once quoted as saying, 'Well, I guess the only good strategy is one that no one else understands.' (*Soul*: p. 113)

The suspicion that de Castro might have orchestrated from afar the entire project, including even West's own conviction that Eagle's creators were working on their own, comes to possess the group, confirming West's observation about the 'paranoid' nature of the corporation and the project group (*Soul*: pp. 270, 267). We are reminded here of Oedipa Maas's mounting paranoia as she feels she is the victim of an elaborate plot constructed by Inverarity to deprive her of her sanity. And Oedipa's sense of powerless disorientation is reproduced in several members of the Eclipse Group when they venture briefly out of the confines of their basement into what Kidder calls 'that distant country, the upstairs of Westborough'. He relates how 'when they got upstairs, they were lost. They had to ask directions from "some stranger in a suit" as Alsing put it' (*Soul*: p. 283). Such episodes tend to suggest the way in which certain difficulties of mapping or representation, which appear to be bound up with IT and computer design, can call the reality of a world into question, and how the dissemination of power that IT seems both to foster and to embody in its very technical structures presents new kinds of mobility and inscrutability as far as power is concerned. As stories such as Pynchon's and Kidder's illustrate, in postindustrial culture the power of capital can be at once intensely present in its effects yet increasingly difficult to locate, arrest and confront.

Like Pynchon and Kidder, Fredric Jameson has noted how 'the technology of contemporary society ... is mesmerising and fascinating ... because it seems to offer some privileged representational shorthand for grasping a network of power and control even more difficult for our minds and imaginations to grasp – namely the whole new decentred global network of the third stage of capital itself' (Jameson, 1991: pp. 37–8). Yet Jameson also notes how, by comparison with the mechanical technology characteristic of the high modernist period, 'the technology of our own moment no longer possesses this same capacity for representation' and thus renders our attempts to map the configurations of power that determine our world inevitably 'faulty'. For Jameson, our maps of power and control are faulty because the technological metaphors through which we are compelled to construct them derive from 'machines of *reproduction*, rather than production', of which the computer, 'whose outer shell has no emblematic or visual power', is exemplary in its inscrutable depthlessness (Jameson, 1991: p. 37, emphasis added). Such technology is no longer directly mimetic of the channels of energy and relations of power which animate the production process and structure the society itself. It thereby only serves to emphasise the extent to which the totality of the late capitalist mode of production exceeds representation and thus, according to Jameson, proves all the more resistant to oppositional agency.

This story, alluded to by Jameson, of the progressive eclipse of production by reproduction is one that belongs to the history of Fordism as a regime of accumulation. Its latest chapter, of course, is bound up with the project of post-Fordism, whose animating technologies and processes have, according to Stanley Aronowitz, effected a thoroughgoing 'deterritorialisation' of capital and of production. Aronowitz's comments are worth quoting at length as they pinpoint some of the considerable political implications of the new conceptual spaces of production and their attendant new configurations of technology and power. He contends that anyone seeking to locate the determinants of this new, information-driven order now

> faces not chiefly huge aggregations of physical capital symbolised in huge mills producing material means of production, giant cities that are the centre of these facilities and the visible signs of class power and class struggle, but invisible power concealed in microchips, processed particles and molecules that are produced in the new knowledge factories – the labs. The signs of the new power communications channels funnelling information inscribed on paper and preserved in artificial memory present an entirely new set of problems for those engaged in political and industrial combat ... the identification of means of production with fixed places has given way to deterritorialisation not only on a global scale but from public to private spaces. (Aronowitz, 1990: p. xiii)[8]

Aronowitz suggests that the social and spatial deterritorialisations wrought by IT, and the interpenetration of processes of production and reproduction in contemporary capitalism, make the classical Marxist opposition between economic 'base' and socio-cultural 'superstructure' obsolete. This greatly complicates any notion of a determinate relation between the location of groups and individuals in the productive process, their class position and their political agency. Not surprisingly, then, the breakdown of Fordist structures of accumulation has been accompanied by a wide-ranging reappraisal of Marxism and a critical interrogation, in particular, of the concept of class.[9]

We should also note, though, that the story of Fordism and its aftermath at the same time tells of the shift from production to consumption, a shift that American social critics from Veblen on have lamented at various stages in its progress. In this respect, the steady commodification of American life and culture has had effects of deterritorialisation and what we might call 'derealisation' that parallel, and are bound up with, those of the new technologies of reproduction. Jackson Lears has pointed out how in the founding period of monopoly capitalism many, especially middle-class, Americans felt increasingly distanced by an expanding layer of commodities and bureaucratic structures from the 'real world' of production. They sought to quell their resultant anxieties and repair an impaired sense of selfhood and agency by, Lears argues, immersing themselves in a variety of therapeutic worlds constructed for their consumption by progressive religionists, psychologists, advertisers and other would-be 'captains of consciousness', to borrow Stuart Ewen's term (Lears, 1983 and 1994; Ewen, 1976). Lears emphasises how these agencies capitalised on, and in some senses created, a culture-deep crisis of meaning as they 'promised intense "real life" to their clientele', whilst at the same time they 'all implicitly defined "real life" as something outside the individual's everyday experience' (Lears, 1983: p. 28). Though Lears's account deals with the period of proto-Fordism between the world wars, it usefully serves to remind us of how deepening commodification dovetails with the increasing primacy of reproductive technologies to contribute to that contemporary sense of the evacuation of self and the depletion of reality which is frequently identified as a component of postmodernism.

I have already noted the way in which Eagle's professional middle-class makers were compelled continually to question the reality of their world as their own sense of control over the technology and the organisation of the production process itself began to wane. Such feelings are strikingly continuous with those recorded by Shoshana Zuboff and expressed by blue-collar factory operatives newly subjected to IT and continuous process production methods. Zuboff detailed how this technology 'abstracts' and 'textualises' previously physical and sentient work routines, precipitating in workers a common feeling of 'epistemological distress'. This stems from the fact that 'the symbolic medium provides a new distance from experience [which] can be felt as a thinning of meaning, a deprivation' (Zuboff, 1988: p. 180). The similarity to Lears's descriptions of the feelings of the first generations of Fordist consumers is also striking. For the workers Zuboff spoke to, the loss of direct physical contact with the production process rendered a traditional cause and effect model of understanding inoperative and left them feeling that their work 'had vanished into a two-dimensional space of abstractions, where digital symbols replace a concrete reality'. Such sentiments, Zuboff noted, were 'shot through with the bewilderment of a man suddenly blind, groping with his hands outstretched in a vast, unfamiliar space' (Zuboff, 1988: p. 65).

These images of spatial dislocation and the thinning of reality are bound up with what Zuboff suggested was the necessary adjustment to a new sensibility fostered by IT and the new models of work and production, one marked by the qualities of distance, detachment and coolness. Sherry Turkle's ethnographic studies have charted the uneven development of such a sensibility among computer users as the technology has become an increasingly central part of work and everyday life over the last two decades (Turkle, 1984 and 1995). Interestingly, Kidder identifies these same qualities as central to the 'professional code' of the computer engineer. However, as both Lears and Turkle have proposed, against the background of detachment and distancing from what is perceived to be an increasingly insubstantial reality, the therapeutic quest for intense experience, or 'real life', takes on a new urgency. It is notable in this respect, and The Soul of a New Machine makes this evident, how the domain of computer engineering and programming has become an important site of such sought after experiential intensities in a culture which increasingly valorises 'the high, the intoxicatory or hallucinogenic intensity' (Jameson, 1991: p. 28). The computer, then, has provoked an upgrading of a certain cultural rhetoric of experience identified by David Nye as the 'American technological sublime'. As we become more and more detached from physical contact with nature, Nye suggests, new and wondrous technological objects become focal points for sublime experience, offering 'a unique and precious encounter with reality that disrupts ordinary perception and astonishes the senses, forcing the observer to grapple mentally with [their] immensity and power' (Nye, 1994: pp. xiv, 15). Indeed, this is the starting point for William Gibson's cyberspace trilogy analysed in Chapter 8 below. Gibson's tech-*noir* evocations of the dimensionless immensity of cyberspace and the intensity of 'jacking in' accord, if anything does, with Fredric Jameson's notion of a postmodern 'hysterical sublime' (Jameson, 1991: p. 34). However, with the issue of a historical mutation in sensibility on the agenda, I want to shift attention slightly to the question of character and its relation to the new technologies and structures of production, particularly as addressed in Kidder's book.

The Character of Fordism: From Engineer to Manager

In many respects, *The Soul of a New Machine* aligns itself with a tradition of American writing which looks to register historical and cultural change through the concepts of community and character. I have already discussed the way in which notions of community are refigured in the book in relation to the cultural influence of new technologies, and I want now to explore how it intervenes into the debate about modern American character established in the work of, for example, David Riesman, Philip Rieff, Christopher Lasch, Robert Bellah and, most lately, Richard Sennett.

Within this tradition, the figure of the industrial manger has acquired a central importance. In his benchmark study of historical character formation in the United States, David Riesman saw the 'characterological struggle' of the mid-twentieth century being waged between the ideal types of the 'inner-directed' entrepreneur on the one hand, and the 'other-directed' manager on the other (Riesman, 1961: p. 31). The shift Riesman identified was one in which the qualities of the 'self-made man' of nineteenth-century entrepreneurial capitalism, with its strongly residual Protestant ethic, were gradually displaced by those exemplified in the 'organisation man' of bureaucratic monopoly capitalism, with its corporate ethos of conformity and consumerism. For Riesman, the characterological shift was bound up with the wider historical transfer of cultural authority from its traditional patriarchal locations in religion and the family to the increasingly commodified institutions of the marketplace and the hands of a mediating class of professionals or experts. In Riesman's account, the manager is both agent and product, beneficiary and to some extent victim in this process of establishing what we might call the culture of Fordism.

Yet Riesman failed to emphasise the extent to which those most affected by these new configurations of authority and capital were the members of the rapidly expanding class of industrial workers. For the new economic and cultural preeminence of the industrial manager rested squarely on his role in the radical recomposition of capital and redeployment of the American working class. By this I am referring to the large-scale reorganisation of production that took place according to principles of scientific management and spread outward from Henry Ford's Detroit factories in the interwar period. Along with the fragmentation of the labour process into strictly rationalised individual work tasks, the core principles of scientific management effected a sharp break between conception and execution in production, thus systematising the division of mental from manual labour that Marx saw as an incipient tendency within capitalism. By deskilling labourers and transferring their skills and knowledges 'upstairs' to managers and production–design personnel, scientific management helped call into being a new stratum of industrial superintendent to which the planning and supervision of production had henceforth to be entrusted. We can therefore apply Antonio Gramsci's observation made in the early 1920s that 'In America rationalisation has determined the need to elaborate a new type of man suited to the new type of work and productive process' as much to this new breed of overseer as to the new type of industrial worker forged in Ford's plants that so interested Gramsci. Indeed, Gramsci's further observation that a generalised 'psycho-physical adaptation to the new industrial structure was necessitated' by the 'Fordist fanfare' suggests that historical questions of character or subjectivity necessarily follow from the analysis of shifts in the structures of production and capital (Gramsci, 1971: pp. 286, 287). Yet we should pause to note that the position of the manager as a leading character in the story of Fordism is conditional upon what Harry Braverman identified as the progressive 'degradation' and deskilling of labour over the course of the twentieth century (Braverman, 1974).

As Braverman and others have pointed out, the technical rationalisation of production was accompanied by the organisational rationalisation of the capitalist enterprise; large firms were merged and vertically integrated in an historic drive to ameliorate and bring an element of predictability to the competitive anarchy of *laissez-faire*. Counter to the claims of the corporate boosters of the time, and of certain economic historians since (such as Chandler, 1962), this was less about technological progress and the scientific advancement of productivity than it was about capital's need to protect investments from a working class that could use its knowledge and control of the production process to resist the rhythms of exploitation, as well as from the increasing volatility and destructiveness of the business cycle itself. Successive crises of overproduction since 1893 had threatened the very bases of commodity production, and the shift toward production-for-consumption – towards what Michel Aglietta has called a socially regulated 'mode of consumption' (Aglietta, 1979: p. 151) – was integral to these attempts to protect long-term investments from the ravages of unregulated competition and unstable markets. It is here, then, in the shift from entrepreneurial to monopoly capitalism – from 'unorganised' to 'organised' capitalism (Lash and Urry, 1987) – that we can find the bases of Fordism as a mode of regulation, and the centrality of the manager as an exemplary American type.

The sheer scale of the enterprises that resulted from this wave of concentration and centralisation of capital in the early part of the twentieth century required a new and systematic approach to commercial administration. Long-term strategies relating to product development, marketing and finance could no longer remain the personal domain of a single company owner or president; these functions now came under the aegis of specially created departments and divisions of managers. Moreover, the scientific reorganisation of production meant that detailed knowledge of the production process was no longer locked away in the culture and sentient experience of the workers themselves; rather, it was systematically abstracted from the hand and brain of the worker, rendered explicit, and thus had to be codified, creating what Braverman calls the 'necessity of maintaining a shadow replica of the entire process of production in paper form' (Braverman, 1974: p. 239; Lash and Urry, 1987: p. 165). The large technical and administrative staffs that arose to serve this need were augmented by a new breed of industrial psychologists, sociologists and personnel specialists as, faced with widespread worker demotivation on the newly Taylorised shop floor, scientific management 'softened' its focus by acknowledging the 'man problem' to be an integral part of the 'production problem' (Noble, 1979: p. 262).

Both Braverman and David Noble have remarked that the exceptionally high ratio of managers to productive workers that characterises American capitalism was already established by the 1920s.[10] We can see, then, that the regulation or organisation of capitalism, 1900–1930, called into being not just the modern industrial manager but the whole stratum of white-collar or service workers that has figured so centrally in many of the accounts of the so-called exceptionalism of American capitalism.[11] Indeed, Barbara and John Ehrenreich have convincingly claimed that this stratum can and should be viewed as a distinct class, the professional–managerial class or PMC, which they credit with a crucial role in shaping the culture of American Fordism and impeding the development of an American working-class movement along European socialist or social-democratic lines (B. and J. Ehrenreich, 1979).

These large historical and economic transformations thus underlie the debate about American social character; and these are the transformations Robert Bellah and his co-authors invoke when they state that 'The bureaucratic organisation of the business corporation has been the dominant force in this century', adding that, 'Within the corporation, the crucial character has been the professional manager'. For Bellah, the managerial world view is bound up with 'that of the technician of industrial society *par excellence*, the engineer' (Bellah *et al.*, 1985: p. 45). Returning to *The Soul of a New Machine*, we can note that in the person of engineer–manager Tom West, Kidder has provided us with an exemplary American character through which to explore questions about the place of the new technologies in both the culture of work and the work of culture.

In many respects, West is an oddly atavistic character who seems to belong to an epoch prior to the one of corporate intrigue and microelectronics that he actually inhabits. He describes himself as a 'mechanic' whose talent is to 'make ideas work' (*Soul*: p. 142). In doing so he appears to situate himself in the lineage of the Yankee artisan whose practical know-how and utilitarian approach to scientific knowledge is popularly held to have been crucial to the success of early American manufacturing. Indeed, we learn that it is not only West's skills as a sailor, carpenter and joiner which are self-taught; so is his knowledge of computer engineering. These narrative elements serve to link West to another apocryphal American character, the Franklinian autodidact and inventor who with native genius bridges the gulf opened up by modernity between theoretical knowledge and useful (and, indeed, profitable) application. Moreover, West's abrasive self-reliance, intolerance of bureaucratic vacillation, and the very connotations of his name associate him with a further American individualist hero, the Westerner. As the Eclipse Group is finally dissolved at the end of the narrative, the remark is made that their project bears all the marks of a Western with West himself as the 'gunslinger'. West, though, puts Kidder in mind of other classic American stories: when the author pointedly compares West to Cotton Mather, he calls upon a more ancient narrative of enterprise, endeavour and destiny in the Massachusetts woodlands, and attaches his late twentieth-century corporate drama to a powerful cultural myth of American origins (*Soul*: pp. 280, 172).

In a sense, Kidder consciously revisits through West the gallery of ideal American character types as they have been sedimented in narrative and the popular imagination. The popular success of the book must in some part be attributed to the nostalgic appeal of its substantially inner-directed, self-reliant and tough-minded central character who flies in the face of the diagnoses of conformity, other-directedness, narcissism and angst peddled by a whole raft of cultural critics from Riesman on. Yet, as Kidder's invocation of the Puritan polymath Cotton Mather suggests, the history of character and community in America is bound up with the cultural vitality of the Protestant ethic. Indeed, it is precisely the perceived collapse of 'the moral discipline formerly associated with the work ethic' that torments such critics in their pronouncements upon the 'dying culture' of contemporary capitalist society (Lasch, 1979: pp. 397, 396). By tapping into these discourses about work, character and community, Kidder's book raises the question of a potential revival of the work ethic with computer engineering at its leading edge, and of a reconstruction of American character with the computer engineer as its ideal type.

The Character of Post-Fordism: From Work Ethic to Work Enclave

Dennis Hayes has told how, at the beginning of the 1980s, the microelectronics industry became the province of a new worship of work and a revival of the entrepreneurial spirit, apparently making the industry a panacea for the crippling motivation crises and plummeting productivity that had afflicted American capitalism in the 1970s (Hayes, 1990: pp. 31–2, 115–16).[12] Figures such as Apple's Steve Jobs and Steven Wozniak, de Castro himself, and more latterly of course, Bill Gates, rekindled the myth of the American inventor–entrepreneur as they built business empires out of what appeared to be nothing more than youthful insouciance and technical expertise. Notwithstanding the staggering flows of capital that came to animate these ventures, this new breed of engineer–entrepreneur–manager was believed to be motivated less by material gain than by the element of challenge, the scope for self-determination, and the pursuit of technical excellence in work. Almost without exception, the members of West's Eclipse Group have passed over jobs with more humane hours and far greater salaries for the opportunity to work on what they see as an interesting and challenging project. The consensus among the engineers is that they don't work for money, and this ethos lends to their work certain characteristics of the Protestant notion of the calling (*Soul*: p. 191).

A New England Puritan such as Cotton Mather would have had little trouble recognising and applauding this zealous commitment to work as it reappeared in his own 'ghost country of rural Massachusetts' (*Soul*: p. 8). He would have approved, too, of the element of self-denial entailed in the foregoing of leisure, and would no doubt have endorsed as fitting the substantial financial rewards that the engineers themselves see as incidental to their work. Indeed, Mather would have fully appreciated that the new work ethic was no longer part of a grand narrative in the traditional sense but had become a secularised language or dialect spoken within various professional subcultures or what he called 'specialised callings' (Mather cited in Miller, 1956: p. 216). Yet he would have been baffled by the extent to which the new work ethic had become detached from any wider conception of community or what in 1710 he defined as the practice of 'the devices of good neighbourhood' (Miller, 1956: p. 218).[13] For the self-denial of the microelectronics engineer is, despite its code of teamwork and 'passionate labor' (*Soul*: p. 117), allied to a peculiar form of narcissistic self-aggrandisement. Firstly, there is the cult of the 'high' referred to by Jameson above. It is clear from Kidder's account that computer engineering provides the members of the Eclipse Group with an experiential intensity unavailable to them in other spheres of everyday life. There is a common preoccupation with quasi-mystical instants of revelation and euphoria, 'golden moments' as they are referred to, when a particularly difficult technical problem is mastered; and West himself, though taking no part in the practical design of Eagle, speaks of there being 'a big high in here somewhere for me that I don't fully understand' (*Soul*: pp. 85, 179).

In this sense, work is not so much an arena for the articulation and pursuit of the public good as it is for the extension of what Robert Bellah has called 'expressive individualism', that is, the cultivation of the self's private 'core' through intense personal experience (Bellah *et al.*, 1985: pp. 42, 333–4). Bellah contends that expressive individualism is the 'first language' of the 'lifestyle enclave', the essentially privatised, disengaged and consumption-based microformation into which he fears community is fragmenting under the pressure of the new cultural primacy of individualism (Bellah *et al.*, 1985: p. 335). We might note, then, that in the case of the computer engineer, the community-reinforcing potential of Mather's 'specialised calling', with its commitment to work and attachment to larger collective values, is effectively stifled in the new cultural form of the work enclave.

However, Bellah's use of the term 'lifestyle enclave' is ambiguous. On the one hand it represents the very antithesis of community: 'Whereas a community attempts to be an inclusive whole, celebrating the interdependence of public and private life and of the different callings of all, lifestyle is fundamentally segmental and celebrates the narcissism of similarity.' On the other hand, though, it might represent a historically new and more timely form of community, or even the renascent form of community in the old sense: 'We might consider the lifestyle enclave an appropriate form of collective support in an otherwise radically individualising society which, under certain conditions, might find itself on the way to becoming a community' (Bellah *et al.*, 1985: pp. 72, 73, 335). It is significant in this context, therefore, that the much celebrated regard for work that marks the computer engineer's vocation appears to some extent to dissolve the boundary between private and public spheres and sources of solidarity. While Bellah and his co-authors see the lifestyle enclave as a purely private, leisure-oriented association, the fact that we can apply the concept effectively to the Eclipse Group suggests that West and his team are able to find a level and form of commitment that 'transcends the divide between work and leisure that has ruptured most industrial civilisations' (Hayes, 1990: p. 85). In this respect, then, there is indeed a notion of community bound up with the new work ethic embraced by IT professionals and that attaches itself to the Eclipse Group. But, as Dennis Hayes further noted in his study of the work patterns and civic values of California's Silicon Valley, this is in many ways a particularly attenuated, compensatory notion of community which, paradoxically, hints at its own absence: 'Above all, the new worship of work amounted to a movement to *personalise* it, to take on as one's own the absorbing challenge of computer work, and thus to become an intimate part of something larger, something meaningful. It was the practical response of isolated people to the vacuum of community' (Hayes, 1990: p. 31). This is the atmosphere that, consciously or not, Douglas Coupland so accurately conveys clinging to his group of deracinated twenty-something computer programmers in his novel, *Microserfs*, discussed in Chapter 5 below.

However, Hayes was also perceptive enough to detect a genuinely utopian element in this hunger for community which should neither be ignored nor dismissed as narcissism. Something of this kind is contained in the usually reticent West's confession that his passion for computer engineering derives from a desire to 'Build something larger than myself' (*Soul*: p. 181). The computer here becomes a surrogate for that sense of solidarity and those binding intersubjective values deemed to be so sadly missing from contemporary American life in the accounts of Christopher Lasch, Daniel Bell, Robert Bellah and Richard Sennett. One reason consistently given by members of the Eclipse Group for renouncing the much larger salaries on offer elsewhere is that work on this machine allows them to formulate deeper questions of value than would be possible on other, less technically challenging projects. One explains his motives for leaving a comfortable job to partake of the masochism of the Eclipse Group as follows: 'I wanted to see what I was worth' (*Soul*: p. 143).

Yet like the interviewees in the first chapter of *Habits of the Heart*, the Eclipse Group's members will not or cannot articulate their pressing questions of solidarity and value through what Bellah calls a 'substantive moral discourse', and what we might want to call a coherent social or political vision, to any wider conception of the collective social good (Bellah *et al.*, 1985: p. 20). Thus incipient notions of the collective good are recuperated by the therapeutic ethos of feeling good, and these nascent impulses toward the articulation of community and value tend to dissolve into the language of individualism where they are recycled for private consumption as the high or the golden moment. The limitations of this language mean that questions of value almost inevitably become commodified into considerations of surplus value, as workers fortunate enough to possess the talents, commitment and cultural capital of Eagle's makers are encouraged to capitalise on their status as 'industry's new superstars' (as one early 1980s' recruiting ad for computer engineers put it). On this level, then, the new work ethic betokens an energy and commitment that are in peril of becoming severed from any substantial social vision or wider set of concerns. As Dennis Hayes noted, 'When computer building becomes an essentially creative and emotional outlet, any politics larger than those governing access to work and tools seem distant concerns' (Hayes, 1990: p. 85).

As both machine and metaphor, then, the computer is a contradictory device. On the one hand, the degree of global integration facilitated by IT contains the promise of community on an expanded scale (the global village yet again); on the other, Lyotard's computerisation of society is widely credited with, for good or ill, having rendered any vision of a broadly inclusive community informed by shared values and language virtually redundant. Analysts on the political left, among them those I've been drawing on in this chapter such as David Harvey, Dennis Hayes, Herbert Schiller, Stanley Aronowitz and Fredric Jameson, see the new technologies and the increasingly volatile flows of capital that both underpin and inhabit them as instrumental in stifling and privatising critical and oppositional forces. Similarly, communitarians such as Bellah, who aspire to go beyond the Left–Right divide in politics (Tam, 1998: pp. 33–4), and analysts of 'character' such as Richard Sennett, attribute the atomisation of social life and the evacuation of contemporary moral discourse in part to the effects of a technologically complex society (Bellah *et al.*, 1985: p. 25; Sennett, 1999). And yet *The Soul of a New Machine* shows a group of dedicated individuals quite movingly using the computer as a means through which to focalise and explore deeply felt considerations of meaning, value and solidarity.

Therefore it would seem that, despite Hayes's stern admonitions, engineers do not completely lack a collective political perspective that, in some respects, is critical of capitalism. The Eclipse Group's unanimous insistence that it is not money that motivates them is consistent with an explicitly 'post-materialist' outlook.[14] As West summarises it, 'Not many people around here would admit to being in business ... What makes this all possible is putting money on the bottom line and not having to go all the way with the capitalist system' (*Soul*: p. 179). Such an attitude, of course, involves a degree of willing blindness towards the nakedly commercial orientation of their corporate employers, a blindness that Hayes claims extends to the increasingly anti-social uses to which the products of computer engineering are put. This, he states, amounts to a new quietism and a 'special alienation of electronics workers from their products' (Hayes, 1990: p. 52). Yet, given the inextricable and frequently indecipherable relationship of almost all microelectronics components to the twin evils of militarisation and surveillance, it is perhaps unreasonable to demand a higher level of ideological vigilance and self-denial from the computer engineer.[15]

Still, as Thorstein Veblen's famous support for the 'revolt of the engineers' in his *The Engineers and the Price System* (1921) indicates, the engineer has been an abiding point of reference for technocratic critiques of modern capitalism. Veblen's misplaced faith in the capacity and desire of the new stratum of industrial engineers to reform monopoly capitalism and trim the excesses of the burgeoning culture of consumption derived from his mistaking what was an essentially professional commitment to the virtues of rational planning and technical efficiency in production (virtues that were felt to be at odds with the business world's wasteful and anarchically competitive pursuit of profit at any cost) for a substantially moral and ideological commitment. This tension between a passionate but narrow professionalism and any wider, politically informed social vision is characteristic of the engineering world view as conveyed in *The Soul of a New Machine*. Despite a commonly expressed desire to buck 'the capitalist system', the overriding commitment to and absorption in issues of excellence in work, which in many ways informs this desire, blinds engineers to the larger social meaning of their work. To the point is West's remark that some of his engineers 'don't have a notion that there's a company behind all of this. It could be the CIA funding this. It could be a psychological test' (*Soul*: p. 226).

Character and Class: The Production of Character and the Character of Production

We might perhaps expect the engineer to display such a contradictory attitude towards capitalism given the professional–managerial worker's contradictory location 'between capital and labor' (the title of the book in which the Ehrenreichs's essay on the PMC appears). The very rapidity of the professional–managerial stratum's rise to social and cultural influence in the early decades of the twentieth century led some writers to dub it the 'new ruling class'.[16] For others, of whom Veblen is perhaps the precursor, its contradictory position meant that it was to be viewed as in some respects objectively anti-capitalist, a potentially revolutionary ally of, or substitute for, the working class. However, the PMC's historical role in 'the social atomisation of the working class', its 'expropriation of the skills and culture once indigenous to the working class', have led some analysts on the political left to conclude that 'the relationship between the PMC and the working class is objectively antagonistic' (B. and J. Ehrenreich, 1979: pp. 16, 17). Yet the PMC remains a class of waged or salaried workers with interests that are at some level crucially divergent from those of capital itself (Gouldner, 1979; Lash and Urry, 1976). Despite the fact that its existence as a class derives from the particular requirements of capital in its modern administered form, it is this divergence that 'has turned the PMC into an enduring reservoir of radicalism from Progressivism and the Socialist Party to the New Left' and given the American left its distinctively middle-class historical bias (B. and J. Ehrenreich, 1979: p. 42).

The Ehrenreichs's analysis reveals the extent to which PMC anti-capitalism is cultural, rather than more properly political, in nature. And if we return at this point to *The Soul of a New Machine*, we can note how West and his team's hostility to business is bound up with an attitude that can best be described as countercultural.[17] There is a preference within the group for long hair, beards, casual dress and an anti-authoritarian informality at work. Along with the orientation toward the high and the intense experience, these are signifiers of a residual counterculturalism whose associations with the 1960s' utopian dreams of personal liberation definitively mark off the new work ethic from its previous incarnations, binding it to that expressive individualism criticised by Dennis Hayes above. West is most interesting in this respect. Though 'straight' in appearance, of all the engineers he has the most substantial links with the counterculture, forged during an enforced leave from Amherst in the early 1960s on an underachiever program during which he supported himself by playing guitar in the folk scenes of Greenwich Village and Cambridge. Kidder guesses that West's ambition is to be an unorthodox 'balladeer of computers', to reconcile the conventional professional–managerial self with the unruly expressive self, and West prides himself at one point on being able 'to be a businessman and a dropout all at once' (*Soul*: pp. 276, 172).

West's efforts to combine two apparently opposed cultural languages or styles return us to the territory mapped out by the debate about American character. Though West numbers himself 'Among those who chucked the established ways' and thus, via the language of countercultural rebellion, calls upon the tradition of American masculine self-reliance, we also note that he is subject to particularly modern forms of anxiety (*Soul*: p. 181). As the Eagle project continues, the conflict between West the mechanic or gunslinger and West the engineer who must manage rather than design becomes acute. He comes to question his motivations and his sanity as the crisis atmosphere of the project takes its toll on his health. This kind of psychic conflict figures large in David Riesman's account of the manager and his central place in the shift from one characterological mode to another in the era of high Fordism.

Riesman suggested that the transition to other-direction was bound up with the move in industry 'from craft skill to manipulative skill' as, to scale the corporate hierarchy, the talented engineer must transform himself into a manager who 'has to learn a new personality-oriented specialty and unlearn or at least soft-pedal his old skill orientation' (Riesman, 1961: p. 130). Riesman dwells on an anecdote about an engineer who, pressed into taking a promotion to sales manager, is revisited by a dream in which he sees himself holding a slide-rule which, to his alarm, he does not know how to use. This might equally apply to Tom West as he finds himself increasingly distressed by the fact that he cannot allow himself to intervene in his team's technical work lest he be accused of displaying an unmanagerial lack of confidence in its ability to complete the job on time. With a Freudian flourish, Riesman judged that his engineer's dream 'clearly symbolises his feelings of impotence in a new job where he is alienated from his craft', and noted (apparently in all innocence) that another engineer-turned-manager compensated for such alienation by doing 'a little fooling around with his tools in the basement' (Riesman, 1961: pp. 130, 129). Kidder devotes a whole chapter to West's workshop in the basement of his restored farmhouse home, seeing it as a 'window on West's soul' where the repressed mechanic in him is able to fool around with his tools in a fashion that Riesman identified as 'good inner-directed style, or perhaps simply good American style' (*Soul*: p. 123; Riesman, 1961: p. 129).

It is possible, therefore, to read out of Riesman's account of high-Fordist culture the suggestion that transformations in character structure, even instances of apparently private anxiety, are closely related to shifts in the social organisation of production and the recomposition of class identities. For, in his formulation of the shift 'from craft skill to manipulative skill', Riesman was talking about the progressive de-emphasising of production that we have seen to be a dominant theme in the story of Fordism. The accounts of Lears and Zuboff discussed earlier have shown how, in different ways, distancing from the scene of production can be a cause of anxiety, even of crises of confidence in the status of the self and of reality. We might expect, then, that when the rationalisation and abstraction of production becomes the function, perhaps the *raison d'être*, of a whole class, anxiety and an overt, even narcissistic, self-consciousness will come to pervade the culture of this class. It would seem therefore that West's personal anxieties are in certain respects nothing more than the badge of his membership of the professional–managerial class whose 'derivative' position between labour and capital makes its members, according to Barbara and John Ehrenreich, particularly prone to collective 'anxiety', 'insecurity' and a therapeutic orientation (B. and J. Ehrenreich, 1979: pp. 14, 30). Indeed, the Ehrenreichs have claimed that the PMC's anxiety about its 'in between' status is the key to its influence and its hunger for cultural leadership:

> As a result of the anxiety about class reproduction, all of the ordinary experiences of life – growing up, giving birth, childraising – are freighted with an external significance unknown in other classes. Private life becomes too arduous to be lived in private; the inner life of the PMC must be continually shaped, updated and revised by – of course – ever mounting numbers of experts ... The very insecurity of the class, then, provides new ground for class expansion. By mid-century the PMC was successful enough to provide a new *mass* market for many

of its own services – and unsuccessful enough to need them. (B. and J. Ehrenreich, 1979: p. 30, author's emphasis)

Thus West's and his class's energies and contradictions stem from an insecurity that relates to their ambivalent position between labour and capital. In a sense this very anxiety could be said to be the basis on which the technocratic social vision of the PMC as a class rests, a vision bound up with the outlook of the engineer. West himself confesses that he was originally drawn to engineering because 'There's some notion of control, it seems to me, that you can derive in a world full of confusion if you at least understand how things get put together'; and his colleagues remark that 'West was always planning' (*Soul*: pp. 175–6, 178). And it is this twin concern for planning and control that motivates the technocratic commitment to a rationally planned, scientifically regulated and technicist approach to the solution of social problems. In this respect, it could be argued that the computer itself has now become the technocrat's answer to a world full of confusion.

The contradiction within the PMC's technocratic world view, however, is that while it derives from a hands-on engineering productivism, the PMC has been the principal historical agent in, first, vastly undermining the importance and autonomy of productive labour in the United States under monopoly capitalism; second, establishing the basis for a now dominant mode of consumption; and third, along lines described by Harry Braverman, incorporating a new mass of unproductive labour into the structures of late capitalism. Braverman argued that the rationalisation of production and the expansion of consumption in monopoly capitalism – achieved, as we have have seen, through the work of the professional–managerial class – created an expanding demand for intermediaries, supervisors and experts of all kinds, thus perpetuating the expansion of the unproductive service sector and the PMC itself. The effect of this is that 'the great mass of labor which was reckoned unproductive because it did not work for capital has now been transformed into a mass of labor that is unproductive because it works for capital' (Braverman, 1974: p. 415). Moreover, as the Ehrenreichs have observed, the labour of the professional–managerial worker is essentially *re*productive: 'We define the major function [of the PMC] in the social division of labor ... broadly as the reproduction of capitalist culture and capitalist class relations' (B. and J. Ehrenreich, 1979: p. 12). The most interesting historical contradiction in all this, then, is that the unproductive labour of the very class called into being to rationalise and resolve the crisis of 'unorganised' capitalism became a major cause of the productivity crises of 'organised' capitalism. Thus the PMC's role of reproducing the culture and relations of capitalism becomes all the more urgent yet all the more difficult. It is not surprising, therefore, that this is a particularly anxious class (Baritz, 1989; B. Ehrenreich, 1989). Its increasingly tenuous links with production and its task of managing the cultural as well as economic crisis of capitalism encourage it, I would suggest, to turn more and more to the therapeutic depthlessness of its own increasingly influential cultural productions for inspiration and solace.

True Stories and *Microserfs* are both interesting examples of this kind of therapeutic cultural postmodernism, whereas, for reasons I will come to shortly, *The Soul of a New Machine* is not. But for now I want to take up again the story of the eclipse of production. It is no coincidence that the computer, as the privileged instrument and metaphor of the class whose social mission is reproduction, should be described as a technology of reproduction rather than of production. We might note here that the technical processes of reproduction are based on structures of signification, symbolic communication, and the manipulation of information rather than material, just as processes of social reproduction are based on the manipulation of cultural symbols and of human rather than natural resources. Writing in 1950, David Riesman caught this aspect of the eclipse of production when he noted of the culture of high Fordism that,

> Today it is the 'softness' of men rather than the 'hardness' of material that calls on talent and opens new channels of social mobility ... the newer industrial revolution that has reached its greatest force in America ... is concerned with the techniques of communication and control, not of tooling or factory layout. It is symbolised by the telephone, the servomechanism, the IBM machine ... [and] calls for the work of men whose tool is symbolism and whose aim is some observable response from people. (Riesman, 1961: pp. 127–8)

For Riesman, these men comprised the stratum of other-directed 'manipulators' that we have been calling the PMC. But equally interesting is his observation that the techniques of 'communication and control' symbolised by the computer were becoming as crucial to capitalism as forces of material production. Riesman's expression closely echoed the ideas of founder of cybernetics, Norbert Wiener, who in 1948 argued that 'control and communication in the animal and the machine' were to be the shaping concerns of the latter part of the twentieth century (Wiener, 1961). Thus the destinies and functions of the computer, IT, and the professional–managerial class have been closely intertwined in both the culture of Fordism and post-Fordism.

The Eclipse of Production

As I have suggested already in referring to William Kuhns's observation about the consequences of the shift from a 'mechanised' to a 'media or information control interpretation' of technology, the computer has been instrumental in confounding the opposition between the hardness of material and the softness of men. Indeed, one tendency of the science of cybernetics takes this development to its limit in its view of computers as 'electronic brains' and human beings as 'soft machines' (Moravec, 1988; Porush, 1985). Yet Riesman's comment that the forces of the newer industrial revolution of the postwar Fordist period were more dependent on the softness of men than the hardness of material suggests the extent to which this softening has been bound up with the rise of the professional–managerial occupational stratum and the increasingly symbolic nature of capital. Returning to *The Soul of a New Machine*, we can see how the book's very title, the coupling of the apparently opposed notions of 'soul' and 'machine', refers us to this historical–cultural dialectic of hard and soft, and it is on this that I will focus to conclude my discussion of the book and the issues it provokes.

It is clear that Kidder's account of the Eagle project is constructed to encourage his audience to view the engineers themselves, and West in particular, as the 'soul' of this new machine brought into being by over a year's worth of 'passionate labor'.

Considering various theories which might explain the project's ultimate success, including entrepreneurial spirit, flexible management systems, and heightened competition for resources and market share, Kidder concludes that 'it seems more accurate to say that a group of engineers got excited about building a computer' (*Soul*: p. 272). Yet, as the engineers' uncertainty about who has been the prime mover behind their project as a whole (themselves, West, or de Castro?) suggests, the soul might not be that easy to locate. As the new machine is completed and launched, the community of engineers is deemed to require the services of a team of occupational psychologists, as individual engineers repeatedly 'spoke of feeling that "empty spot"' (*Soul*: p. 286). A sense of acute attenuation and absence, of which West himself becomes an almost literal physical embodiment, comes to hollow out what both Kidder and the engineers feel should have been the fulfilment of their labours. As the project, in its middle stages, had lurched from one crisis to another, West had been visited by vomiting fits and had begun visibly to 'waste away'. Kidder illustrates this with pathological metaphors of consumption – 'as if the job ... were somehow consuming his flesh' – and pregnancy – 'a psychological form of morning sickness'. By the time of Eagle's public launch he suggests that West is 'not really present at all' (*Soul*: pp. 178, 290).

We might account for this sense of absence and hollowness in terms of the traditional Marxist notion of the alienation of the labourer from the product of his or her labour. Yet West has had no direct hand in the construction of Eagle. His task has been, to utilise Riesman's terms, essentially manipulative and symbolic; his labour has been expended upon the softness of men rather than the hardness of material. There is, then, perhaps another degree of alienation involved here, one that relates to the dialectic of hard and soft. For, as we have seen, the progressive integration of engineering with management within Fordism, and the consequent softening of the focus of the engineer's concerns from technical to social and human engineering, brought with it a new kind of rationalisation (Noble, 1979: pp. 263–4). This alienated the Fordist worker, particularly the professional–managerial worker, from the scene of production itself. Culminating in automation and the cybernation of production methods, this 'rationality of the computer and of robotics turned out to be significantly different from the rationality of [Henry Ford's] Highland Park assembly line' (Wollen, 1991: p. 62). This kind of rationality effectively hollows out the autonomous productive attributes of human labour and transfers them to increasingly 'smart' machines and systems. Riesman hinted at the implication of this rationality for character or notions of the substantive self when he observed that 'the industrial process advances by building into machines and into smooth-flowing organisations the skills that were once built, by a long process of apprenticeship and character formation, into men' (Riesman, 1961: p. 131). It is in this respect, therefore, that West the manager is 'consumed' by his machine, whereas West the engineer feels he should have 'produced' it, and that another of the engineers describes the work he does on Eagle as 'consuming' (*Soul*: p. 191).

We can see here, then, how the blurring of the boundaries between hardness and softness that is an effect of the reproductive technologies and the increasingly symbolic and psychological penetration of the rationality of full Fordism is closely tied in with the steady occlusion of production by consumption and reproduction. These processes find their way into *The Soul of a New Machine* in West's occupational morning sickness, his talk of the 'postpartum depression' that will hit the group on completion of the project, and in another engineer's remark that, with Eagle gone to market, the Eclipse Group 'feels like an afterbirth' (*Soul*: pp. 178, 232, 288). It is only appropriate that these metaphors of biological reproduction should cluster around a figure whose class has been entrusted by capital with the historic duties of social reproduction. But the image of the afterbirth has additional connotations which imply that in giving birth to the machine the team has been consumed by it, and suggest that relations of *consumption* have come to inhabit the heart of the process of production. In seeking to locate the soul of this new machine, it seems, Kidder is left with the consumed and discarded afterbirth of the production process, a consumptive, wasting and ultimately absent central character, and an ambivalent 'empty spot'. Thus his heroic tale of work and production comes to hinge on metaphors of consumption, reproduction and absence.

If the 'empty spot' where Kidder searches in vain for the 'soul' of production has been hollowed out by the operations of capital under the Fordist regime of accumulation, this process is only intensified in the turn towards post-Fordism. The Japanese term for hollowing out is *kudoka*, and Japanese industrial analysts were among the first to be struck by the extent to which *kudoka* was both a symptom and an effect of the American microelectronics industry in the 1980s.[18] In my extensive opening quotation from *Soul* early in this chapter, Kidder remarks how the postindustrial microelectronics country of rural Massachusetts is haunted by the 'ghost' of production 'gone to Asia and down south'. 'South' here perhaps means not only the Sunbelt states of America which I will discuss in the following chapter, but the export processing zones of the unregulated economies of Central and South America. It was evident by the mid-1980s that the deindustrialisation of the United States, for which IT and the microelectronics industry were supposed to be the panacea, was simply being exacerbated by them. Corporations, abetted by the new systems of computer-based information processing and capital transfer, 'liquidated their manufacturing core and exported it to sites offshore, leaving behind a shell of lawyers, accountants, marketing specialists and, in the Silicon Valleys, design, development and support staff as well' (Hayes, 1990: p. 20). Meanwhile, the corporate centres of the microelectronics industry in the United States discovered that it was not recession-proof after all. In 1984 Data General instituted 1,300 domestic job cuts and stepped up its transfer of productive operations to its Asian sites and subdivisions, thus making its own significant contribution to *kudoka* (Morgan and Sayer, 1988: p. 85). Dennis Hayes remarked that, 'By its example and through its products, the US electronics industry, more than any other, had promoted and accelerated *kudoka*. *Kudoka*, in fact, had been at least as crucial to the industry's prosperity as had the technical ingenuity of its entrepreneurs ... It was the scarcely visible, thoroughly modern, global migration of speculative capital' (Hayes, 1990: pp. 21–2).

This global migration of capital exemplified by the microelectronics industry produces distinctive patterns of 'combined and uneven development', that is, the technical and spatial disarticulation and relocation of the various spheres and divisions of the production process. Morgan and Sayer argue that one of the consequences of combined and uneven development is that 'spatial mismatches between causes and effects become the norm', meaning that it becomes increasingly difficult to interpret the vast global space of proliferating interconnections constituted by invisible 'microcircuits of capital' (Morgan and Sayer, 1988: p. 265).

Kudoka, or the hollowing out of Fordism's productive soul, does not so much mean that production vanishes but that it is fragmented, exported and recomposed into the configurations of what Lash and Urry have called 'disorganised' capitalism and Alain Lipietz 'peripheral Fordism' (Lash and Urry, 1987; Lipietz, 1987a). The project of post-Fordism therefore involves the globalisation of capital and production into a new kind of space, or 'hyperspace' to use Fredric Jameson's term, that is examined in Part 4 of this book.

In this context it is fitting that, at the end of *The Soul of a New Machine*, West embraces the logic of *kudoka* and follows the business to Data General's Asian subsidiaries, to Japan. Japan was of course famously for Roland Barthes an 'Empire of Signs', the classic locus of spatial and temporal compression (bonsai, the haiku, the instantaneity of pachinko and the sumo bout) and unmappability (the centrelessness of Japanese cities, the absence of addresses on buildings) (Barthes, 1982). And for similar reasons Japan has held a fascination for cyberpunk novelist William Gibson; the centrality to its culture of compression and unmappability makes Japan, for Gibson, a society most receptive to, and most strangely shaped by, microelectronic technologies and the erosion of the boundary between the hardness of material and the softness of men. While we might relish the narrative reversal of West, the gunslinger, disappearing east into the land of the rising sun, we might also note that it is the latest in a representative case history of relocations prompted by the whims of corporate capital stretching back to West's childhood and adolescence as the son of an AT&T engineer. If professional–managerial mobility of the socially upward kind necessarily entails mobility of the lateral, geographical kind, then this brings with it what we might identify as a socio-cultural *kudoka* of its own. For it is this very mobility that hollows out place, with its associations of historical continuity and collectivity, into undifferentiated space, wreaking its corrosive effects on both community and character (Bellah *et al.*, 1992: p. 261; Sennett, 1999: pp. 10–11). This is the sense in which Dennis Hayes has claimed that the silicon communities that comprise the new order of the post-Fordist information-driven economy qualify as nothing more substantial than 'habitats', temporary resting places for insecure temporary workforces, transient professionals, and short-lived configurations of capital. For Hayes, the dissolution of Fordist social and economic structures implied that '*kudoka* was enveloping the US character, hollowing out features of its social substrate' (Hayes, 1990: p. 35). The work of Douglas Coupland is an overt attempt to anatomise and compensate for this socio-cultural *kudoka* as the structures of Fordist accumulation and regulation break down. This is also the sense in which the vacant soul of production, that widely felt empty spot referred to by Eagle's makers, can be said to inhabit, in some way, the souls of the producers themselves. Through the microcircuits laid down by IT and computer technologies, the deterritorialisation of capital and production leads to that *kudoka* of the self or the subject which has become a staple of many accounts of postmodernism.

These are somewhat disarming conclusions to draw from a book that is essentially humanist in its motivating impulses. *The Soul of a New Machine* is not an outburst of technophobic alarmism nor a cultural jeremiad in the style of Christopher Lasch or Daniel Bell. It sets out to celebrate the fullness of productive labour and innovative technical expertise in a climate of economic transformation, yet its guiding metaphors are ones of absence, emptiness and disorientation. For imaginative–symbolic engagements with the economic, social and cultural effects of IT which project very different visions of an emergent post-Fordist world, ones that seek to abjure the anger, nostalgia and despair of left critics such as Herbert Schiller and Dennis Hayes (and haunt those of even quasi-celebratory humanists such as Kidder), I will turn to David Byrne's film, *True Stories*, and Douglas Coupland's novel, *Microserfs*.

4

Faking 'IT': *True Stories*

Mike Davis has argued that the formation of the 'Sunbelt', that rapidly growing and economically developing corridor stretching from Florida in the East, across Texas, to Southern California in the West, constitutes one of the two great 'engines of post-war accumulation' in the United States, the other being the combination of suburbanisation with the massive expansion of higher education. This latter development, we might note, underlay the exponential growth of the professional–managerial stratum in the 1960s and formed the 'experiential matrix' out of which what Fred Pfeil has called the 'baby-boom PMC' was to emerge as a powerful cultural force in the 1970s, '80s and '90s (Pfeil, 1990: p. 99).[1] With respect to the rise of Sunbelt capitalism, Davis notes that:

> an astonishing revolution in the sectoral and regional structures of American capitalism was accomplished ... in such a way that by the end of the Vietnam War boom a Sunbelt urban–industrial region had emerged roughly equal in income and output to the old [North-East Great Lakes] metropole, but distinguished by very different conditions of capital accumulation. (Davis, 1986: pp. 193–4)

These 'very different conditions of accumulation' are what make the Sunbelt central to the shift away from the very Fordist regime its own formation had done so much to underwrite. Principal among these conditions is the 'right to work' bias of the Sunbelt states. Their consistently punitive anti-labour position drives down unit costs for corporate capital which is further sweetened by local tax concessions and attractively lax standards of public regulation.[2] It is in this context that the Sunbelt has been the grateful and not entirely passive beneficiary of the *kudoka* of the old heavy manufacturing North-Eastern 'frostbelt', and has established its economic ascendancy on an ability to attract and nurture high-tech industries, principally aerospace and microelectronics.

Both Davis and Theodore Roszak have noted that this high-tech, postindustrial base actually owes its existence to the massive expansion and redirection of Defense Department expenditures. Thus not the least of the contradictions of right-to-work, entrepreneurial Sunbelt capitalism is its reliance on an intensification of the inflationary and socially destructive military Keynesianism that characterised mature (and crisis-ridden) Fordism.[3] However, Sunbelt accumulation does depart sharply from its Fordist predecessor with respect to the newly emergent mode of social regulation that accompanies it, a mode that is now on the way to becoming the model not only for the United States as a whole, but for much of Western Europe too. Central to this emergent regulatory structure is the fracturing of the circumscribed yet long-lived socio-economic 'settlement' between capital and labour that stabilised Fordist accumulation for over three decades and underpinned the establishment of a consistently expanding mode of social consumption, or consumer culture (Renshaw, 1992). Linked to this is a new determination on the part of the state to shift, via the cutting back of welfare provision and the desocialisation, or commodification, of hitherto publicly subsidised services, the burden of social reproduction on to the private resources of the individual.

Thus, if the structures of Fordist accumulation conjured up what James O'Connor called the 'warfare–welfare state' (O'Connor, 1973), then Sunbelt capitalism points us in the direction of what might be called the warfare–workfare state. The differences are considerable, despite the echo, and must be counted among the achievements of the Reaganite New Right, whose ideological cocktail of high-tech entrepreneurialism, futuristic populism and nativist conservatism has been one of the Sunbelt's most corrosive cultural exports. Theodore Roszak has drawn attention to the fact that the power attained by such Congressional Sunbelt right-wingers as Jack Kemp and Newt Gingrich within the Reagan–Bush Republican Party rested largely on their clever appropriation of the discourses of the high-tech information society, both as an astute piece of business opportunism and as a means of adding a touch of 'vision' to their culturally regressive style of conservatism. Roszak notes that Kemp's and Gingrich's pet organisation, the Conservative Opportunity Society, has consistently sought to present itself as a major political voice of the Information Age, and fears that, with the steady decline of the influence of the labour movement, 'The high-tech frontier may now be staked out by the radical right wing rather than the liberal centre' (Roszak, 1986: pp. 38, 37).

We might infer, then, that these are among the transformations to which David Byrne alludes at the beginning of his film, *True Stories* (1986), when he tells us, with reference to his featured town of Virgil, Texas: 'This part of the country's been through a lot of changes, not all small ones either. I think they're in the process of going through another one.' Byrne then proceeds to narrate, in the characteristically blank, decathectic manner of his Talking Heads persona, a potted history of Texas from the dinosaurs to the rise of the microelectronics industry. The historical compression of this narrative and its half-ironic focus on the interminable struggle over ownership and exploitation of the territory and its economic resources recalls Kidder's invocation, at the beginning of *The Soul of a New Machine*, of the 'successive sackings' whose traces haunt the 'ghost country of rural Massachusetts'. Just as Kidder's historical excursus concludes with an attribution of the new order he detects in the region to the nascent microelectronics industry that is the subject of his book, so Byrne's history of Texas terminates in a positing of information technology as the catalyst of the latest of those epochal changes that have shaped the territory:

> Covert military operations to seize Texas for the US of A were begun in 1835. Eventually, they did get Texas. Land grabbers, railroad companies moved in. The economy boomed. Some people got rich: first from cotton, then cattle, then oil, and now microelectronics. The silicon-based transistor was first proposed here in 1941. In 1959, Mr. Jack Kilby invented the integrated circuit. He was working at Texas Instruments then.

Not surprisingly, perhaps, we find the narrator's views endorsed by those characters whose interests most closely coincide with those of Vericorp, the microelectronics corporation that dominates the economic and social life of Virgil. Both the Computer Guy, an archetypal PMC technophile, and Earl Culver, the town's premier property developer and powerbroker, subscribe to an ideology of cultural transformation through high-tech which, as we have noted in the case of Data General's engineers, tends in its affirmative mode to foster a view of community and power which sees both as decentralised networks operating under a general principle of horizontal dispersion. Thus the Computer Guy's assertion that, 'Something's happening here all right. The world is changing and this is the centre of it right now, or the one of many centres', is echoed by Culver's dinner-table ceremony of decentralisation in which he observes that our way of doing business has been based in the past, and goes on to describe the nature of current social and economic change as follows:

> Now most middle class people have worked for large corporations like Vericorp, or for the government itself. But now, all that's started to change. Scientists and engineers are moving off from those large corporations ... and they're beginning to start their own companies marketing their own inventions ... They don't work for money any more, or to earn a place in heaven ... They're working and inventing because they like it. Economics has become a spiritual thing! I must admit, it frightens me a little bit. They don't seem to see the difference between working and not working. It's all become a part of one's life ... There's no concept of *weekends* any more!

We might be inclined to read this sequence, which is staged as a fully-blown mock Mass, as a satire on the quasi-religious faith of much of the IT constituency in this technology's capacity to work economic miracles as well as to resurrect a sense of community for towns and regional economies blighted by the *kudoka* of traditional forms of industrial production. Yet satire, with its ulterior ballast of normative critique and moral disgust or righteous anger, seems curiously incompatible with *True Stories'* consistent register of half-knowing, half-naive detachment, so perfectly embodied in Byrne's narrator persona.[4] Indeed, Culver's consecration of the family dinner to the new Holy Trinity of 'mainframe, microprocessor, semiconductor' suggests more than simple blind religious devotion to the technology of the moment. The declension from mainframe to semiconductor, that is, from the largest, most centralised unit of IT to its smallest, most versatile component, and the fact that this blessing presides over Culver's symbolic reorganisation (by means of the dinner-table dishes) of Virgil's socio-economic layout, reminds us of IT's crucial metaphorical function in serving as a model for the reconceptualisation of social life in terms of the flexible, localised communicational network as opposed to the centralised mainframe model. Moreover, Culver's final remarks suggest how this reconceived notion of the social bond, and the forms of technology and production–organisation on which it draws, are felt to be bound up with a new and enriching potential for expressivity in work, one which promises to undo those oppositions between public and private, material and spiritual, characteristic of modern industrial cultures.

The Computer Guy confirms the feeling, which we saw was widely held among Data General's engineers, that the new technologies, in fostering such an expressive relation to work and in providing the images and means for the decentralisation of authority, are rendering the monolithic and strictly rationalised Fordist business organisation redundant:

> It's a lot like music; computers are like that. You can never explain the feeling of connections to anyone else. Figuring something out, something that's never been understood before, is a rhythmic experience ... You know, some people in the computer business can be pretty creative, unlike the traditional businessman. You know, the astronauts didn't read poetry, but that's changing. Computers are as much a means of expression as language.

But what I find particularly interesting about these pronouncements is that, behind the quasi-mystical rhetoric, they betray a concentration of concern upon issues of character, community and communication which, as we saw was the case with *The Soul of a New Machine*, are felt somehow to hinge on the cultural influence of information technologies.

In this respect, *True Stories*, with its determinedly local focus, its narrator's curious role as a kind of sociological–anthropological field worker, and its subtitle, 'A Film About a Bunch of People in Virgil, Texas', invites us to read it as some sort of community study. The film's opening words, 'This is where the town begins', betray an interest in the constitutive limits, both spatial and conceptual, of community; and this is especially evident in the camera's repeated gesture of turning outward to survey the vast spaces of the empty Texan landscape against which Virgil's boundaries are defined. Such a visual concern with space and the civic dimensions of collective identity (the camera also repeatedly tracks the streets, residential districts and municipal spaces of the town as if in search of the physical location of this identity) seems to point us in the direction of a fairly orthodox territorial conception of community as locality. Yet we should note that Byrne's potted history of Texas has functioned precisely to undermine locality as a basis for community. Noting ironically that 'Texas comes from the Caddoan word for friend', Byrne then relates how this territory has been a site of continuing violent struggle between different racial, national and socio-economic groups up to and well beyond its incorporation into the United States. Therefore, as the film's subtitle suggests, territory or locality alone allows us at best to speak only of 'a bunch of people' rather than of community; and we might then understand one of the central questions posed by *True Stories* to be this: under contemporary conditions, in what respects can such a bunch of people be said to constitute a community?

By way of response to this question, an initial move might be to reformulate community in terms of a communications model, one which, as we have seen in relation to *The Soul of a New Machine*, is bound up with the symbolism and cultural prominence of IT. And indeed, Byrne's comments on the relationship between cities and highways – 'I suppose these freeways made this town and a lot of others like it possible' – suggest how even the mundane transportational aspect of communications must now be regarded as prior to the relations of purely local interdependence. However, it is upon the notion of communications as the circulation of signals, messages and codes that *True Stories* principally seeks to re-establish the basis of community. This is a model to which Virgil as an IT town seems ideally to conform. It is theorised most explicitly in one of the film's songs, 'Radio Head':

> Baby your mind is a radio/Got a receiver inside my head
> Baby I'm tuned to your wavelength/Let me tell you what it said
> Transmitter picking up something good
> Hey radio head, it's the sound of a brand new world

Again, there is a sense in which this song is inhabited by what Fredric Jameson has called a postmodern blank irony given that the character who performs it in the movie deploys its central conceit as a kind of seductive gambit with women. Yet the song's model of social and sexual relations and its recasting of subjectivity in terms of communications technology is reiterated insistently enough throughout *True Stories* for us to consider its implications seriously. Indeed, it is only in this context that some of the narrator's more oddly detached and gnomic utterances become meaningful, for example, his cheerful observation of Virgil and its environs that 'radio reception's *great* here!'

As I noted in the previous chapter, in examining the communications model of the social bond we cannot easily avoid an encounter with Jean-François Lyotard's particular conception of the postmodern condition. If this condition is characterised by the 'splintering' of the social, under the pressure of a 'generalised computerisation of society', into multiple networks of incommensurable language games, then this in turn has implications, as the song 'Radio Head' suggests, for our model of the self (Lyotard, 1984: pp. 41, 47). Indeed, according to Lyotard, the self can no longer be thought of as the creator, or originating ground, of the various utterances and discourses by which it might be known. Instead it must be seen as a product of, as being constituted by, these very 'language game effects':

> each [self] exists in a fabric of relations that is now more complex and mobile than ever before ... a person is always located at nodal points of specific communication circuits, however tiny these may be ... one is always located at a post through which various kinds of messages pass. No one, not even the least privileged among us, is ever entirely powerless over the messages that traverse and position him at the post of sender, addressee, or referent. (Lyotard, 1984: p. 15)

Lyotard's view of the postmodern self as a kind of microelectronic switching point for a plurality of intersecting circuits is in some ways a development of David Riesman's idea that the 'other-directed' self, emerging in response to the economic and social nature of Fordist mid-twentieth century America, could be defined by an internalised 'control equipment' that 'functioned like radar' (Riesman, 1961: p. 25). Riesman's sense that the demands of a bureaucratised and consumption-oriented world required that the self be increasingly sensitive to the circulation of complex cultural codes and signals, as well as to the imperatives of smooth interpersonal communication at home and work, caused him to turn to the field of microelectronic communications for a suitable technological metaphor. Riesman seized on the metaphor of radar to succeed the mechanical image of the gyroscope which he felt best approximated the internal operations of the inner-directed character structure of the earlier mode of competitive, production-oriented capitalism (Riesman, 1961: p. 16). For Riesman, the development of the radar-guided self was necessitated by the dispersal of cultural authority from its traditional religious and bourgeois–patriarchal locations in church and family to the complex and secular mechanisms of the Fordist marketplace – the corporations, the professions, and the new mass culture industries. This shift accompanied and exacerbated the erosion of the Protestant ethic, hitherto the basis of the cultural system of motivations, legitimations and interdictions. It is frequently suggested, particularly in the more pessimistic or ambivalent accounts of the shift from from *laissez-faire* to monopoly capitalism and the origins of the culture of Fordism, that the binding force of the Protestant ethic was undermined by a new therapeutic ethos of personalised consumption which emphasised communication for its own sake, divorced from any vision of ends or larger social purpose.[5]

Whether or not we accept this version of social and cultural change and its implications for the possibilities inherent in contemporary culture (I do, though with certain reservations that will become more evident in due course), it is clear that Riesman's notion of an other-directed, radar-guided self caught up in complex webs of symbolic communication was in part determined by his feeling that traditional collective legitimations for self-grounding no longer held. Similarly, Lyotard's version of the postmodern self is a response to the perceived erosion of hitherto unifying and transcendent collective norms, what he calls the 'grand narratives' of emancipation through scientific and political progress. As I have already noted, for Lyotard this is partly attributable to the fragmenting effects of the post-1945 'blossoming of techniques and technologies ... which shifted the emphasis from the ends of action to its means'. It is also, however, bound up with the historical triumph of American Fordism, characterised by Lyotard as 'the redeployment of advanced liberal capitalism ... [which] has eliminated the communist alternative and valorised the individual enjoyment of goods and services'. Thus the combined ideological force of technical rationality on the one hand and Fordist mass consumption on the other is sufficient for Lyotard to infer that 'most people have lost the nostalgia for the lost narrative', and now, in the absence of any binding normative collective vision, language or project, 'what saves them from [barbarity] is their knowledge that legitimation can only spring from their own linguistic practice and communicational interaction' (Lyotard, 1984: pp. 37, 38, 41).

In this respect, then, sociality is to be seen as an effect of the articulation of contingent and individual competences. Social relations and community itself lose any determinate or necessary aspect as the emphasis shifts from ends to means. They become instead the site for an essentially voluntary practice of what we might call the *bricolage* of everyday life. This is precisely the narrator of *True Stories'* view of social relations as they obtain in Virgil. In his role as a kind of supermarket Lévi-Strauss, Byrne constructs a picture of Virgil as a community of happy *bricoleurs* busily networking through work, leisure and consumption to fashion what he feels is an appropriately contemporary ('What time is it? No time to look back') and provisional model of community life and values: 'People here are creating their own system of beliefs. They're creating it, doing it, selling it, making it up as they go along.'

However, when the emphasis shifts too far from ends to means the very activity of ad hoc *bricolage* becomes a value in itself, as do the central categories of communication and competence. These latter then tend to get hollowed out, rendered contentless, so that the questions, 'Communication for what?', 'Competence for what?', lose importance. The danger of this is that communication becomes a powerful but essentially vacant touchstone in the same way that information has become an empty and thoroughly reified concept in its increasingly dominant contemporary sense. Theodore Roszak has pointed out how the cult-like fetishisation of information in this sense tends to eradicate 'all concern for the quality and character of what is being communicated'. In the view of Information Theory, and increasingly, claims Roszak, for contemporary culture as a whole, there is no qualitative difference between a cry for help, a nuclear missile launch command, and a piece of random nonsense; all are equal as messages, as units of information. Thus, for Roszak, 'the *meaning* of things communicated comes to be levelled, and so too the value, leading to the conclusion that while the technology of human communications has advanced at blinding speed ... what people have to say to one another by way of that technology shows no comparable development' (Roszak, 1986: pp. 27, 29, author's emphasis). In a similar vein, James Carey has noted the 'contemporary habit of reducing all human problems to problems or failures in communication'; thus the notion of communication becomes 'a semantic crucifix to ward off modern vampires' (Carey, 1989: p. 33).

Roszak and Carey point to the way in which information and, especially, communication, have become enshrined as contentless cultural values detached from any larger conception of social meaning or purpose. The function of such concepts can be said to have become predominantly therapeutic. We might therefore interpret the construction of a mobile, provisional and voluntary communications model of community in both Lyotard's *The Postmodern Condition* and *True Stories* as a therapeutically inclined response to the collapse of a grand narrative vision of collective social ends. Philip Rieff saw the 'triumph of the therapeutic' consisting precisely in this cancellation of grand narrative and the evacuation of the question of societal ends: 'The therapy of all therapies is not to attach oneself exclusively to any particular therapy, so that no illusion may survive of some end beyond an intensely private sense of well-being to be generated in the living of life itself ... a sense of well-being [that] has become the end rather than a by-product of striving after some superior communal end.' Rieff's gloomy prognosis was that the now dominant therapeutic ethos allowed only for the formation of what he called 'negative communities' which offer neither hope of 'collective salvation' nor any framework of 'agreed communal purposes' (Rieff, 1966: pp. 224, 63).

Such communities, with their emphasis on immediate self-realisation and their abjuration of what Rieff defines as 'commitment', bear more than a casual resemblance to Robert Bellah's notion of the 'lifestyle enclave' discussed in the previous chapter; and both Rieff and Bellah link the predominance of such therapeutic cultural forms to the operations of the United States's endemic individualism (Rieff, 1966: p. 62). Indeed, Bellah and his co-authors make explicit the connections between what they feel to be decline of meaningful community, the rise of therapeutic individualism, and the reification of communication as an end in itself:

> In its pure form, the therapeutic attitude denies all forms of obligation and commitment in relationships, replacing them with the idea of full, open, honest communication among self-actualised individuals ... In a world of independent individuals who have no necessary obligations to one another, and whose needs

may or may not mesh, the central virtue of love – indeed the virtue that sometimes replaces the ideal of love – is communication. (Bellah *et al.*, 1985: p. 101)

While I would want to question some of the more culturally conservative implications of both Rieff's and Bellah's implied notions of meaningful or 'positive' community, their analyses do provide us with a salutary historical perspective on the therapeutic communications view of community expressed by *True Stories*.[6]

If we return at this point to the film, we can note that the narrator's characterisation of Virgil's communal *modus vivendi* as a kind of communicational *bricolage* occurs in the shopping mall. This is an eloquent image for the way in which the reification of means and the therapeutic view of communication and community are bound up with the processes of commodification. The narrator tells us that 'the shopping mall has replaced the town square as the centre of many American cities, and that shopping itself has become the activity that brings people together'. The mall is thus the crucial nodal point of those communication circuits that constitute, in Lyotard's view, postmodern sociality and, as narrator, Byrne's view of this shift is entirely affirmative. He evokes a paradise of clean stores, soothing muzak, and plentiful parking in which 'shoppers ... are wise to advertisers' claims'. He would thus appear to reject the view expressed by Fox and Lears that commodification and the construction of a consumer paradise refer not simply to 'a standard of living' but to 'a power structure'. For Fox and Lears, the circulation of commodities is the means by which 'the dominant institutions of our culture have purported to be offering the consumer a fulfilling participation in the life of the community only in effect to deliver the empty prospect of taking part in the marketplace of personal exchange' (Fox and Lears, 1983: p. xii). Again, while I might want to qualify somewhat this outright condemnation of consumerism and the rigid notion of cultural domination that it serves, it does at least acknowledge, in a way that *True Stories* refuses to, the play of ideology and power that inhabits our consumption of goods and services and that has its effects on us as consumers.

These are effects that we can see most clearly embodied in *True Stories* in the character Lewis Fyne, who illustrates that whilst the communications view of sociality has implications for the ways in which we conceive of and represent the self, these models are equally structured by the reification and commodification of this view. Lewis conducts his search for a wife as an advertising campaign, utilising local TV, radio and printed communications networks to transmit images of a self which is segmented and reified into bundles of discrete attributes. Lewis fragments his own identity into various symbolic units pertaining to the various spheres of social and private life – work , home, leisure, consumption – which are thus rendered discontinuous, as is the self that is dispersed across them. In this sense, not only does commodity culture invite individuals to 'seek commodities as keys to personal welfare', it also encourages them to 'conceive of their own selves as commodities'; thus, 'one sells not only one's labour and one's skills, but one's image and personality too' (Fox and Lears, 1983: p. xii).

This concern with commodification, however, should not obscure the genuine depth of Lewis's stated need to 'settle down and share', nor the fact that we can read this in part as a desire for modes of solidarity and commitment which are felt to be unavailable outside the confines of the private romantic sphere. As we saw was the case with the engineers of *The Soul of a New Machine*, such desires for enduring commitments that transcend the limits of an atomistic individualism can often only be articulated in the language of therapeutic self-realisation, a language which might be inflected by the professional jargon of the middle-class technician or by Lewis's more universal romantic vocabulary in which, as the film's song 'Love for Sale' puts it, we might find 'love and money getting all mixed up'.

We might return at this point to the problem of what Fredric Jameson calls 'the linguistic fragmentation of social life' (Jameson, 1984a: p. 65) and what Bellah diagnoses as the disappearance of a public language through which meaningful notions of community and commitment might be expressed. *True Stories* suggests how we might link this crisis of public discourse to the disappearance of a properly public sphere and the privatisation of public spaces and services which is a consequence of the social and cultural applications of IT. For Byrne's celebration of the shopping mall as the new centre of social interaction sits uneasily with the fact that, since the United States Supreme Court judgement in *Pruneyard Shopping Mall v. Robbin* (1980), the sidewalks, parking lots and other apparently public spaces surrounding malls have been privatised, rendered entirely subject to mall proprietors' control. According to Dennis Hayes, the new private power over public space is principally expressed in an intolerance for public associations of a 'political' nature, free speech, and unfitting 'displays of poverty' (Hayes, 1990: pp. 40, 170). Moreover, *True Stories* also suggests how this process of commodification extends to the notion of community itself. The narrator notes that the 'celebration of specialness', the public spectacle that is to generate a sense of community and identity for Virgil, is sponsored by Vericorp as part of 'a major public relations effort'. This recasting of social relations as public relations points to the way in which the discourse of community is open to appropriation by what Fox and Lears call 'the dominant institutions of our culture'. 'Community' can thus be used to legitimate and to sell corporate–ideological visions whose interest is in the repression of difference and the concealment of the operations of power.

These considerations should therefore encourage us to remain sceptical about such inclusive notions of communication and community as the one offered by the narrator of *True Stories*. Further reservations should also stem from what we might call the class nature of such notions. Discussing the reified, therapeutic version of communication that he sees as central to contemporary individualistic American culture, Robert Bellah observed that its effect is to 'make solving problems ... a matter of technical problem solving, not moral [or, we might add, political] decision' (Bellah *et al.*, 1985: p. 7); and, as we have already had occasion to note, this problem-solving approach to personal and social relations is an attribute of the technocratic world view of the professional–managerial class. Charged as it is with the historic tasks of managing the labour–capital contradiction and administering markets for the consumption of commodified goods and services – both of which tasks come to hinge on operative notions of cooperation and consensus – we might expect the PMC to subscribe to a therapeutic notion of communication. Indeed, we have already discussed one aspect of this in tracing the softening of the discourse of scientific management into the personalised and psychologised doctrines of industrial relations, corporate culture and 'human resource' management. Jackson Lears has given an excellent account of how the rise of the professional–managerial stratum – what he and Richard Fox call 'leadership by experts' (Fox and Lears, 1983: p. xii) – was and remains predicated upon the dissemination of therapeutic views of the world which, particularly as communicated through advertising, were bound up with the deepening commodification of American culture under developing Fordist structures of accumulation (Lears, 1983). Bellah and his co-authors, too, have suggested that there is an ideological fit between therapeutic notions of communication and commodity culture that emerges from a particular form of middle-class experience: 'the managerial and therapeutic modes seem to be coalescing as our professional and economic life involves more and more subtle forms of interpersonal relating in response to bureaucratic and market situations where individuals are under pressure and need to coordinate their activities with precision' (Bellah *et al.*, 1985: p. 139).

In this context, then, *True Stories* can be read as being informed by a professional–managerial perspective on consumption, communication and community. Such a reading would be reinforced by the fact that David Byrne's artistic reputation prior to the making of the film rested on his achievements as laureate of the inner lives, world views and angsts of the baby-boom PMC with his band, Talking Heads. Indeed, we can detect in the songs he supplied for the film consistent hints of a structuring vision grounded in the PMC ethos of therapeutic communication/consumption, a vision not entirely untouched by the characteristic anxiety about its social role that haunts this class.[7] This is the connotation of a song such as 'Love for Sale', while the class position of psychologised yet detached expertise is connoted by these lines from 'Wild Wild Life': 'I wrestle with your conscience/You wrestle with your partner', or these from 'Dream Operator':

> Hard to forget/it's hard to go on
> When you fall asleep/You're out on your own
> Let go of your life/Grab onto my hand
> Here in clouds/We'll understand

Yet, as the earlier analysis of the technocratic vision of Data General's engineers suggested, the professional–managerial world view is far from a seamless or spontaneously coherent one. It is inhabited by contradictions and lacunae that are the mark of the PMC's contradictory position between capital and labour and the symptoms of its historical duty of managing this contradiction. It is in this respect that *True Stories* is informed not so much by fully articulated counter-discourses as by junctures at which the structuring professional–managerial class viewpoint shows signs of strain or ironic self-consciousness. For example, the technocratic notion of communication is shown to be ineffective, or at least questionable, in a number of instances, ranging from Lewis's misadventures with a computer dating service to the complete breakdown of marital communication between Earl and Kay Culver. And in the figure of the Lying Woman all the technocratic assumptions about communication are comically undermined. It is perhaps impossible to decide whether the Lying Woman's sabotage of the relations of interpersonal communication is an example of that residual power which Lyotard argues individuals always retain over the messages that in other respects constitute them; or whether it is a cautionary indication of the extent to which the inner life of the consumer has been colonised by the commodified fantasy worlds purveyed by the media of mass communications.

These considerations point us towards the latent class tensions and concerns with class present in *True Stories*. We can begin an exploration of these by observing that, in contrast to the communications view, a class conception of community tends neither to be inclusive nor voluntaristic. Beginning as it must from considerations of conflict, difference and necessity, a class conception of community is less likely to reify or idealise the concept or treat it as a free-floating essence rather than as a circumscribed and relational category structured by relations of power. While such a conception of community is never fully articulated in *True Stories*, the issue of class remains visible throughout as a kind of shadow discourse to that of communications; and I would suggest that the principal ideological project of the film, in accord with its structuring PMC viewpoint, consists in an attempt symbolically to mediate and manage the contradictions necessarily implied by the notion of class. It seeks to achieve this through a particular representation of the relationship between the social sites of production and consumption.

It is in the sphere of production, most overtly in attitudes to work, that class differences are signalled in *True Stories*. For example, the Computer Guy's affirmation that for him Vericorp is 'an exciting place to work' contrasts with Lewis's blue-collar sentiment that, 'Hey, there's more to life than this job', foregrounding the distance between professional–managerial and working-class investments in work. These respective attitudes to the labour process also bear on class relationships to the sphere of consumption. Whereas the Computer Guy carries his work with him to the mall and consumes according to the dictates of his work-related technical interests, for Lewis there is a strict separation between work and consumption: the latter is the site in which he seeks to satisfy needs that blue-collar work routines cannot begin to address.

In this respect the PMC relationship to working and consuming is structured by a notion of professionalised integration, suggested by the Computer Guy's celebration of making connections and embodied in his and his class's networking style. By contrast, working-class life is marked by the disjunction of realms, implying a concomitant disjunction of self. In their study of working-class attitudes to work and 'success', Richard Sennett and Jonathan Cobb claim that the condition of divided self typically expressed by their interviewees arises in part out of this disjunction of realms which produces what they call 'a peculiar kind of alienation' (Sennett and Cobb, 1972: pp. 191, 192). And this division or fragmentation which, as we have seen, is related to the commodification of the self's attributes for exchange on the market of personal relations, is reflected in the minute, repetitive and disjointed work tasks performed by Lewis and his fellow chip fabricators on Vericorp's Taylorised assembly line.[8] Indeed, we could read the initial encounter with Lewis Fyne, confined in Vericorp's 'clean room', as a figure for the isolation and alienation of the non-professional–managerial IT worker. For the suit in which he is enclosed, separating him from his co-workers and the product of his labour, is protective only from the product's perspective, such suits being worn to insulate the silicon wafer from contamination by human particles rather than protect the worker from the allegedly carcinogenic solvents and gases present in the clean room's environment (Hayes, 1990: pp. 63–7, 167–8).

Yet these divergent class relationships to production and consumption are rendered non-antagonistic in the ideal space of the shopping mall. *True Stories* implies that though classes may approach the mall from different perspectives they are joined harmoniously together there as resourceful *bricoleurs*. The mall, and by extension the more general sphere of consumption itself, becomes in the words of Joan Didion, 'a profound equaliser', a space consecrated to 'the egalitarian ideal' (Didion, 1979: p. 180). In this sense, *True Stories* subscribes to what Michael Mann has called 'the ideology of hegemonic capitalism' in which 'freedom and justice are best secured by breaking down man's needs and activities into separate segments (work, consumption, politics, etc.) and providing each one with a separate market in which individuals can express their preferences and realise their needs' (Mann, 1973: p. 19). Thus Lewis's disturbing refrain in the song 'People Like Us' – 'We don't want justice/We don't want freedom/We just want someone to love' – can be understood as an anthem to the success of the post-1945 long boom ('In 1950 when I was born/Papa couldn't afford to buy us much') in hollowing out working-class consciousness by the segmentation of life in capitalist society (Mann, 1973: p. 19). In this view, legitimate needs for freedom and justice have been coopted by a therapeutic ideal of self-realisation as the productive sphere is split off and marginalised in relation to the increasingly important spheres of consumption and self-cultivation in which all classes are held to be able to share equally. Contemporary capitalism is structured, according to Mann, so that 'the worker's non-work life compensates for work alienation, with the effect that the worker's experience does not form [a] totality but is rather subject to several segmentations ... between work and non-work ...[and] between economic and political action' (Mann, 1973: p. 20). These segmentations, in Mann's view, prevent the development of a consciousness of class experience unified by a focus on the primacy of powerlessness in the sphere of production.

The vision of a consumer democracy purged of the divisive consciousness of class is expressed in *True Stories* particularly in the song, 'Wild Wild Life'. Here the 'doctor and trucker' are equalised in the pursuit of private intensities through the activities of leisure and consumption. We might also note that the line 'Things fall apart/It's scientific', a kind of mini-legitimation of the process of social and personal segmentation, is lip-synched by the Computer Guy, the film's professional–managerial class representative. This is appropriate given that the PMC mission of rationalising the relations of production and reorganising social life on the basis of consumption works to undermine positive class consciousness among the working class, according to the Ehrenreichs (B. and J. Ehrenreich, 1979: p. 43). In this respect, the professional–managerial class presides over the *kudoka* of working-class consciousness that apparently accompanies the eclipse of production within Fordism and its intensification in the shift to post-Fordism.

If this is the buried story within *True Stories*, then it is clear that it is closely bound up, for Byrne, with the cultural effects of the new information technologies. In his introductory remarks about Texas, the narrator suggests that the history of change to which that region has been subject is recoverable through an interpretive mapping of the physical environment. He remarks, 'You know, there's bound to be at least one person who remembers when everything was just open land ... Some people can just look at the land, just *look* at it, and tell you what happened there'. The implication here is that the pre-microelectronic Texan industries of cotton, cattle and oil, and the formations of capital that underwrote them, were somehow visible and comprehensible. However, the postindustrial configurations of IT and high-tech capital are a different case. The implication here is that these leave no such legible traces of activity and production, secreted as they are inside featureless 'aluminum boxes' like the Vericorp building, about which the narrator wonderingly remarks, 'You have no idea what's inside there!' Thus it would seem that the decreasing visibility of the informated production process and of the microcircuits of capital that animate it means that the relations of production themselves become invisible in certain ways, with the effect that class consciousness becomes attenuated as the all too visible, and apparently democratic, relations of consumption take centre stage.

It is perhaps no surprise that this story of the disappearance of production and of working-class consciousness along with it is presided over by a narrator who, at one point in the film, proudly advertises the joys of forgetting. Indeed, it could be argued that the management of a certain cultural practice of forgetting is crucial to the PMC project of ensuring that what Sennett and Cobb call 'the hidden injuries of class' remain hidden. As I have already suggested, this is a project which is based on a certain notion of consensus, a notion enacted in *True Stories* in Lewis Fyne's ultimate union with the Lazy Woman, that wealthy and ludicrously leisured Vericorp shareholder and the film's embodiment of the extremity of feminised consumption. We could read this ending not only as an endorsement of the therapeutic communications view of community, in so far as the couple are brought together by TV, but also as a figure for a wider marriage of class interests grounded in a benign, universal relation to consumption. This comes at a time when, in the sphere of production, the historic class compromise that stabilised Fordist production is being dismantled by the agency of IT-based capital, most rapidly in high-tech, right-to-work Southern States such as Texas. Thus what Herbert Schiller calls 'the new technology consensus' that has crystallised around IT as part of the post-Fordist project is in many ways the inverse of the limited but durable social consensus of high Fordism (Renshaw, 1992). Its ideology is precisely captured by a Data General PR man in *The Soul of a New Machine* who remarks that computer companies are 'not in competition with each other' but rather 'in competition with labor' (*Soul*: p. 244). However, the continued credibility of notions of social consensus rests on the deployment of powerful ideologies that conflate therapeutic versions of consumer freedom of choice with political freedom and democracy; or, as the song 'Wild Wild Life' in *True Stories* puts it, 'Peace of mind/It's a piece of cake/Thought control?/You can vote any time you like'.

In seeking to account for the failure of nineteenth-century American workers to convert their militant ideology of equal rights into a fully anti-capitalist, socialist class consciousness, Alan Dawley cites as a principal reason the early articulation of formal political democracy to American capitalism. Capitalism and political democracy were thus perceived as fully compatible, if not mutually dependent. More importantly, Dawley suggests, the economic–productive and political–social spheres became disjoined: the individualised freedoms of the latter promised to offset the collective oppressions experienced in the former, and this segmentation contributed to the growth of competitive individualism among the American working class. 'The political arena became a marketplace of individual, unattached voters', Dawley claims. Electoralism thus became the limit of a working-class consciousness that refused to recognise, for the most part, the fundamental antagonism between labour and capital, and class itself was seen less and less as the necessary basis of community and solidarity (Dawley, 1976: pp. 67, 72,

220–41). Dawley's thesis allows us to see how the articulation of Fordist notions of consumer democracy to this abiding American ideology of political freedom (having your 'cake' and voting 'any time you like' in the terms of 'Wild Wild Life') deepens that market individualism which, he claims, undermines working-class consciousness and, we might add, strengthens the professional–managerial vision of consensual class harmony.

True Stories' portrayal of working-class consciousness hollowed out by the eclipse of production and by the communications notion of social relations fostered by IT is therefore traceable to the professional–managerial class viewpoint which informs the film. As Peter Biskind and Barbara Ehrenreich have observed, Hollywood's periodic interest in working-class culture is usually the occasion for the projection of specifically middle-class anxieties and idealisations: 'screen images of blue-collar men' are thus 'conduits into the mind of the middle-class male'. They further remark that screen representations of individual working-class maleness are typically both metaphors for and displacements of the perceived social power of the working class itself: 'Whatever emotive power resided in the notion of the working class as a whole (strength, or perhaps the threat of violence) have now been concentrated, in this middle-class metaphor, into the individual male' (Biskind and Ehrenreich, 1987: p. 214). By contrast, therefore, with 1970s American films' obsession with a defiant, if narcissistic, working-class machismo, *True Stories*' portrayal of a working-class male softened, even feminised by distanciation from the primal scene of production and immersion in the therapeutic culture of consumption suggests a degree of class incorporation or emasculation that renders the traditional film narrative pattern of working-class resentment-into-rebellion-into-recuperation redundant. While in many ways *True Stories* is a relief from the vicarious glorification of white-ethnic machismo in which Hollywood usually indulges when it chooses to portray working-class life, it nevertheless mobilises many of the traditional and sexist identifications of the engulfing excesses of mass consumption with the category of the feminine. Thus we have the stereotypical TV-induced passivity of the Lazy Woman; the unbearably commodified domesticity of the Cute Woman; and the lurid tabloid fantasy world of the Lying Woman.[9]

Yet *True Stories*' affirmative vision of the incorporation of working-class culture and consciousness is not quite total. As the Cute Woman observes, Lewis is inhabited by a submerged 'sadness' that lends a disturbing edge to his song, 'People Like Us'. We might trace this sadness to Sennett and Cobb's notion of the hidden injuries of class, those essentially psychic scars that bear witness to the persistence of class tensions and inequalities in an epoch of apparent affluence and consensus in which militant class consciousness of the traditional kind is all but extinguished. In a sense, their book defines those forms of residual class consciousness that survive the eclipse of production that is thematised in *The Soul of a New Machine* and *True Stories*. We can apply their observation about a young and relatively affluent yet unaccountably resentful working-class man, that 'Nothing from the familiar vocabulary of visible economic oppression defines his experience', equally to Lewis Fyne (Sennett and Cobb, 1972: p. 35). This suggests that we now have to look beyond the immediate sphere of production, of 'visible economic oppression', for the operations of power and the symptoms of class tension and conflict.

Sennett and Cobb argue that the the hidden injuries of class are felt by working people as divisions or faults both within the self and between members of the same class, community or family; and they stem from the differential granting and withholding of dignity and respect that obtains in the culture of class society. Class society 'injures human dignity in order to weaken people's ability to fight against the limits class imposes on their freedom' (Sennett and Cobb, 1972: p. 153). We might add that increasingly this differential play of dignity and respect is a symbolically mediated process, one negotiated within a field constituted by the circulation of commodities and the objects and images of culture. In this sense working-class consumption is not simply a symptom of ideological incorporation into the dominant system of capitalist values; it can also be a necessary site of self-definition, contestation and resistance. Here we might want to challenge the presumption of Fox and Lears's view of consumer culture – that it entails the 'loss of a reality that was deeper and more historical than the counterfeit that [consumers] were urged to embrace' (Fox and Lears, 1983: p. xiv) – by focusing on the way consumption can be a sphere in which people might redefine dominant notions of reality and equip themselves with 'weapons of defense against the Establishment, weapons to defend their dignity' (Sennett and Cobb, 1972: p. 169).

While this kind of defence might have to respond to the imperatives of market-prompted individualism, such individualism is not necessarily incompatible with collective efforts to construct community and group-identity (not just class-based ones) which work against market forces in the ways explored, for example, by those analysts of popular culture who have stressed the subversive potential of style subcultures and 'resistance through rituals' (Hebdige, 1979 and 1986). This complex dialectic of individualism and community is well expressed in Lewis's song, delivered at the finale of Virgil's collective celebration of specialness, which draws on the discourses of both solidarity and specialness in juxtaposing the sentiment, 'I'm not like everybody else', with a celebration of 'people like us'. Lewis's song also hints at the way in which the hidden injuries of class are related to the cultural power of the professional–managerial class. In the song, Lewis's sense of injured dignity is linked to an encounter in the schoolroom with the cultural authority of that class: 'I was called upon in the third grade class/I gave my answer and it caused a fuss'. This illustrates how working-class experience is increasingly subject to supervision by what Andrew Ross calls a 'professionalism' whose duty consists in 'managing the antagonisms that are bound up with the cultural institution of "respect"' (Ross, 1989a: p. 6). This is a task to which *True Stories* contributes, with its communications notion of social relations and its benign consensual vision of community shaped by the new technologies of information.

Yet the class tensions that haunt the film point to the way in which we might want to reformulate its vision of consensus in terms of the Gramscian notion of hegemony. Here class leadership is seen to depend less on the spontaneous deference of the led or the brute domination of leaders, than it is on the construction and manipulation of cultural symbols and meanings (Gramsci, 1971; Hall, 1988). Hegemonic power thus centres crucially on the highly unstable field of cultural signs and symbols, increasingly those that structure the sphere of consumption. The vital cultural importance of signs is linked in *True Stories* with the eclipse of production and the rise of high-tech capitalism. While the temporary 'aluminum boxes' that house the new microelectronics industries (the better to respond to the volatile patterns of flexible accumulation) render production and its social relations 'invisible', the narrator also tells us that all it takes to go into business in such a facility is to 'just slap a sign in front'. Our view of the effects of the new technologies and capital formations will therefore depend on the kind of signs that are attached to them. In its celebration of the way in which new technologies and post-Fordist production relations allow for the fabrication of community detached from the traditional bases of locality, productive activity and class, *True Stories* cannot conceal a note of unease about the way in which IT and its industries signify the *kudoka* of production and class consciousness.

Gordon L. Clark (1989) has noted that it is precisely in such high-tech, right-to-work states as Texas that the ability of capital to relocate its temporary aluminum housings at the first stirrings of labour unrest has irrevocably severed the interests of class and community. The 'crisis of organised labour' that Clark identifies as having first emerged in the post-Fordist structures of the Sunbelt consists not simply in a sharp decline in union membership as the casualised 'permanent–temporary' labourers of the IT industry proved to be resistant to, barred from, or beyond the scope of traditional forms of worker organisation. It refers more seriously to the fact that capital's new mobility means that any expression of class solidarity in resistance to its dominance can result in the precipitate removal of a community's economic foundation as capital simply goes elsewhere. Thus communities and local labour organisations are increasingly put in competition against one another to attract the capital investment that will sustain them. Informated capital's command of fluid and abstract space undermines labour's traditional stronghold of locality or place (Harvey, 1989).

However, despite these observations, we should note that hegemonic power is never fixed or monolithic. Signs and meanings are always contestable and dominant meanings open to critique and appropriation by those they dominate. If the eclipse of production means that one set of meanings pertaining to the ostensibly determinate relations of class and the productive sphere begin to lose some of their explanatory power, then it points equally to the increasing importance of the symbolic meanings and relations of the cultural sphere. It is here, then, that the contestation of power and the construction of communities and movements which are not necessarily based in the collective necessities of productive life, and which celebrate the dangers and possibilities inherent in the process of consumption or lifestyle, might coalesce (Castells, 1997). In this respect, Mr Tucker's line from the song 'Papa Legba', 'Get yourself a sign/Get your love and desire', has a resonance that exceeds the immediate therapeutic–consumerist context of the film. It suggests precisely that issues of love, desire and the formation of communities of resistance might more than ever be bound up with struggles over cultural signs. The formation of such communities takes place against the grain of what Andrew Ross has called 'the leaky hegemony of information technology' (Ross, 1989a: p. 212). I would suggest that the instabilities which underlie *True Stories* and which work to destabilise its affirmative vision of the social relations of a post-Fordist information society in some ways illustrate precisely the leakiness of this hegemony.

5

Playing With 'IT': *Microserfs*

By the year 2015 the United States will either be a leader in this new business revolution or it will be a postindustrial version of a developing country. Either a nation of independent knowledge workers or a colony of economic serfs.

William H. Davidow and Michael S. Malone,
The Virtual Corporation (1992: p. 2)

The making of things has now become somewhat beside the point – the just-in-time delivery of non-polluting, value-added intellectual properties has become the culture's most desirable socio-industrial goal.

Douglas Coupland, 'Dutch Reformation' (1994: p. 3)

Fordism's most important demographic product was what Fred Pfeil has called the 'baby-boom PMC'. This generational fraction, born largely between 1940 and 1960 and therefore socialised during the Fordist regime's high summer of economic growth and sociopolitical stability, represents the professional–managerial class in its phase of most rapid expansion both numerically and in terms of cultural influence. As the Ehrenreichs have argued, 'the late fifties and early sixties were a golden age for the PMC'. The postwar explosion in higher education, the expansion of the mass media, and the extension of the corporate bureaucratic apparatus from the regulation of production into the regulation of consumption and demand meant that 'the material position of the class was advancing rapidly'. One result of this 'rising confidence of the professional–managerial class' was the emergence of New Left radicalism in the early 1960s. Distinguished by its youthful middle-class, rather than proletarian, constituency, and by its disdain for traditional left pieties about the emancipatory role of the working class, this radicalism stemmed from the baby-boomers' desire to cash in on an expanded social scale, to bring to universal realisation, the promises of affluence and uninterrupted mobility which they had ingested since birth. Just as importantly, though, it also 'represented an attempt to reassert the autonomy which the PMC had long since ceded to the capitalist class' (B. and J. Ehrenreich, 1979: pp. 30–1).

Another result of the increased size and confidence of this generational fraction of the professional–managerial class was, as Pfeil persuasively argues, the impact of its particular cultural–aesthetic sensibility on the society at large. Forged by the apparently incommensurable regimes of university-taught high culture on the one hand and domestically consumed mass culture on the other, this sensibility in fact recognised no necessary incompatibility or opposition – no 'great divide', to use Andreas Huyssen's term – between the two cultural value systems (Pfeil, 1990: p. 113; Huyssen, 1986). Socialised in family and class milieux which emphasised the maximisation of opportunity through individual social and spatial mobility, and which were structured to an unprecedented degree by consumer products and electronic mass media, and destined for occupational positions that were at an ever greater remove from the site of material production, the baby-boom PMC came also to be characterised by a sense of deracination and derealisation. Identity, even reality, were unstable, malleable quantities, effects of the circulation of cultural images, symbols and codes rather than determined, concrete entities. While this seemed to promise a new kind of freedom, making possible the most radical projects of self-fashioning and social transformation (witness the personal and political experimentalism of the 1960s), it also entailed new levels of anxiety and anomie. These latter were typically assuaged, Pfeil suggests, by a wilful refusal to renounce, with the onset of adolescence, the playthings of mass culture (Pfeil, 1990: p. 100). TV, comics, movies and fondly remembered consumer products represented both the childhood security of 'home' in which the boomers had grown up and, ironically, the insidiously materialistic tentacles of the 'system' against which many of them positioned themselves as adults in the 1960s.[1]

Postmodernism enters the picture here as nothing more or less than the term that describes the generalisation of the baby-boom PMC's peculiar cultural–aesthetic sensibility, and 'the set of pleasures and practices created by and for' it, as that generational class fraction ascends to positions of cultural and social influence in the 1960s and after (Pfeil, 1990: p. 98). In certain respects, this echoes Daniel Bell's earlier thesis in *The Cultural Contradictions of Capitalism* in which postmodernism is seen as a manifestation of the morally and socially corrosive 'sensibility of the sixties' (Bell, 1976: p. 120). This, with its lack of respect for boundaries and distinctions of all kinds, collapsed the realms of play, art and social life into one another; political radicalism became an extension of personal and aesthetic radicalism and a regrettable epoch of hedonistic narcissism, masquerading as utopianism or 'liberation', arrived. Thus Bell mourned the 'death of the bourgeois world-view' based on the nineteenth-century, middle-class virtues of thrift, self-restraint and instinctual repression that had been bound together and legitimated by the Protestant ethic (Bell, 1976: p. 53).

The radicalism of the 1960s serves as a key point of reference for other theorisations of postmodernism that, however, reject Bell's cultural conservatism. Marxists Fredric Jameson and Alex Callinicos suggest that postmodernism represents not so much the *triumph* of 1960s' radicalism (as Bell would have it) as it does its *failure*, in particular the failure of its ambitious visions and projects of global political emancipation. Rather than being seen as direct extensions of the unruly utopianism of that decade, then, postmodern cultural forms and attitudes must be understood as in some senses 'the substitute' for it, as 'compensation' for utopia's failure to arrive (Jameson, 1991: p. xvi). And in as much as this radicalism was largely carried, only to be abandoned, by the middle-class baby-boomers, postmodernism also tells the story of this 'generation's movement from the barricades to Yuppiedom', from opposition to 'adaptation to the consumer society' (Callinicos, 1989: pp. 165, 166).

The price that the baby-boom PMC had to pay for its post-1960s' accommodation with, or reincorporation into, consumer capitalism was not only the loss of its autonomy; it had also to preside over the extinction of the very material conditions and social arrangements out of which it was born in the immediate postwar decades. That is, in supervising the shift to post-Fordist structures of accumulation in the wake of the economic collapse of the early 1970s, a crisis that to all intents and purposes marked the terminus of 1960s' radicalism (Jameson, 1988c), the baby-boom PMC has actively contributed to the delegitimation and dismantling of the terms of the Fordist growth formula which underwrote the prodigious expansion of the class in its 'golden age'. As I'm at pains to argue throughout this book, such a task involves not just the reorganisation of the technical division of labour or the reformulation of the balance of power between capital and workers at the point of production; it requires, too, the refashioning of standardised Fordist patterns of consumption through the construction of new and variegated taste cultures, 'lifestyle' options and modes of identity formation. As architects and pioneers of these new models, members of the baby-boom PMC have been to some degree able to retain and capitalise upon the personal and aesthetic experimentalism of the 1960s, redirecting these energies into what Mike Davis has identified as a new, post-Fordist middle-class cult of 'overconsumptionism' (Davis, 1986: pp. 211, 219). But dissociated from the active political utopianism of the period, this simply means that they 'have articulated a useful dominant ideological and cultural paradigm for this stage of capital' (Jameson, 1991: p. 407).[2]

One consequence of the exhaustion of the Fordist growth formula was that the numerical expansion of the middle class slowed abruptly. The 1980s were notable for widespread concerns about the 'shrinking' American middle, squeezed between the disproportionately influential overconsumptionism of the 'yuppies' on the one hand and the expanding ranks of working poor and the 'underclass' on the other (Davis, 1986: pp. 218–20).[3] This only served to intensify what we have already seen is an abiding professional–managerial anxiety about the ability to acquire, hold on to, and transmit class membership to the next generation, as class reproduction had henceforth to occur in severely straitened and socially polarised material circumstances. Indeed, the most self-conscious element of the baby-boom PMC's successor generation came to define itself precisely in terms of an attitude of acute but ironic status anxiety on the one hand and a deeply ambivalent stance toward the baby-boomers themselves on the other.

'Generation X' – those Americans born between 1960 and 1970 and so named after Douglas Coupland's 1991 novel of that title – is in this respect the collective creature of the dismantling of Fordist regulation, understood, as Coupland himself has put it, as 'the collapse of entitlement'. In the 1990s, what Coupland calls 'middle-middle-class life', which he defines as his territory as a writer, has, he argues, undergone 'a profound transformation'. Central to this are the fears generated by what he calls the sense of a 'vanishing middle' precipitated by the economic reconfigurations of the period and the 'extreme social upheaval brought about by endless new machines' (Coupland, 1997, p. 2). No longer able to take for granted the inevitability of constantly rising living standards and increasing cultural liberty (as, notwithstanding their differences in aesthetic and political attitudes, the 'organisation men' of the 1950s and the baby-boomers of the 1960s and early '70s had), educated, middle-class Americans coming to maturity in the 1980s and '90s faced far greater difficulties and pressures in converting their cultural capital into secure and materially rewarding professional positions within the fluid and volatile occupational structure of post-Fordist capitalism. Coupland's work as a whole documents how these self-proclaimed 'baby-busters' (Rushkoff, 1994: p. 3) respond to and manage the intensification of that 'fear of falling', of downward social mobility, which for Barbara Ehrenreich defines the 'inner life' of the middle class (B. Ehrenreich, 1989).

One response is the cultivation of what Coupland defines as 'boomer envy: envy of the material wealth and long-range material security accrued by older members of the baby boom generation by virtue of fortunate births'. This sense that 'our parents had more', of being losers 'in a genetic lottery' (Coupland, 1992: pp. 9, 21), structures the vision even of the major expression of organised Generation X political consciousness, the campaign network Lead or Leave, whose manifesto declares that 'no single generation should be asked to suffer at the expense of another' and proposes a set of reforms to bring about 'generational equity' (Rushkoff, 1994: p. 79).[4] But boomer envy is not simply material; it is also deeply cultural. The most self-conscious Generation X artefacts are haunted by a sense of cultural and aesthetic belatedness. The revolutions in lifestyle and art – in sex, drugs and rock 'n' roll – and in politics – in Civil Rights, feminism and anti-war activism – have already happened; they were lived out and exhausted by the baby-boomers who bequeathed their successors a landscape of commodification and political apathy rather than the brave new world of liberation they envisaged. Thus from the viewpoint of Generation X 'the 1960s are Disneyland', at once a nostalgic never-never land of youth-driven cultural, aesthetic and political innovation and an angst-inducing example against which it will always be found wanting by its elders (Coupland, 1997: p. 7).[5]

A second response is to ironise the cultural capital that no longer converts so unproblematically into material security. Generation X discourse is characterised by a wilful erasure of the boundaries between knowledge, education and the detritus of commodity culture. Coupland's work, with its learned disquisitions upon, its scholarly distinctions between, and its scientific dissections of the varieties of contemporary capitalist consumer ephemera and media babble is a particularly striking instance of this. In this respect it is not only quintessentially postmodern, in so far as it revels in the collapsing together of high and low culture, it is also as much an extension of as it is a reaction against the cultural–aesthetic sensibility of the baby-boomers. This latter, as we have seen, was likewise forged in the cradle of mass culture and marked by a disregard for cultural boundaries and hierarchies. Yet it issued in a radicalism by which, however briefly or unsuccessfully, a generation sought to transform American society in accordance with the promises of the good life embedded in the cultural capital it had amassed by early adulthood. In contrast, the Generation X sensibility is largely passive, resigned to the ubiquity and supremacy of consumer capitalism, and 'framed in irony' through which, one of its spokespersons declares, 'we celebrate the recycled imagery of our media and take pride in our keen appreciation of the folds within the creases of our wrinkled popular culture' (Rushkoff, 1994: pp. 4, 5).

Historically deprived, then, of guaranteed upward mobility on the one hand and the scope for utopian projects of personal and social transformation on the other, the members of Generation X, claims Douglas Rushkoff, 'choose instead – by default, actually – to experience life as play', to treat the consumer culture's 'landscape of iconography as a postmodern playground' (Rushkoff, 1994: pp. 7, 4). Yet it must be noted that this resigned and playful attitude to consumer culture is not entirely without an element of critique. Coupland's *Generation X*, of course, did not only provide newspaper columnists and marketing analysts with a convenient label for a hitherto ill-defined social and demographic group; it also celebrated its characters' highly self-conscious withdrawal from and renunciation of the competitiveness and materialism of high-tech metropolitan consumer capitalism. This 'slacker' ethic, therefore, with its echoes of the 1960s' countercultural notion of 'dropping out' (although now bereft of 'revolutionary' political associations), can be understood as an expression of that ideological anti-capitalism which, as we have seen, inhabits professional–managerial class consciousness even in times of its most compromised relationship to power. It is at the same time, however, a strategy for managing middle-class status anxiety, the 'fear of falling', by willingly embracing, even seeking out, downward mobility as a form of personal expression, thus preempting the possibility of failure intensified by the decay of Fordist regulatory structures. Coupland's whole *oeuvre* is a rich exploration of the ways in which professional–managerial class anti-capitalism is increasingly mediated as much through 'lifestyle' elements and relationships with the world of commodities and mass culture as it is through science, technology and knowledge. 'Scientific' notions of reason, until the 1960s the basis of PMC critiques of capitalist social and economic relations, now seem less important to the class's understanding of itself than do cultural attitudes and modes of expressive individualism descended from (but also, as we have seen, hostile towards) the 'sensibility of the sixties' and mediated through consumer culture. The 'baby-busters' have only the language with which they grew up to express their reservations about 'the downwardly mobile divorcescape' of post-Fordist America, and 'it just happens that this is the language of advertising' (Rushkoff, 1994: p. 5). Hence the mixed register of both affirmation and critique, of affection and disdain for the postmodern playground of junk culture, that characterises Coupland's writing.

If play is the response of this latest generational fraction of the professional–managerial class to the removal of Fordist certainties, then information technology, just as much as the objects and icons of commodity culture, functions as a medium for this play. Indeed, in *Microserfs* (1995), Coupland suggests that there is really no distinction to be made between these things and, moreover, that they might equally be forces for both enslavement and liberation. The novel's narrator, twenty-something software designer Daniel Underwood, dedicates himself to the excavation of what he believes is his computer's unconscious, the contents of which turn out to be almost entirely and randomly composed of advertising slogans, brand names, tabloid headlines and other pop culture references with which Coupland saturates the text in a variety of fonts and formats. At one point we are shown the 'mind' of Dan's machine when two pages of the text are given over to reproducing its binary operating code in multiple strings of ones and zeros. This device is repeated shortly afterwards when Dan himself types the word 'money' over and over into his computer notebook, occupying a further two pages of text, and again when he duplicates the exercise with the word 'machine', reinforcing the continuity Coupland wants to establish between the languages of information technology, the codes of mass culture, and the process of commodification (*Microserfs*: pp. 104–5, 132–3, 180–1).

There is a further point being made here, though, one that returns us to the connection between the eclipse of production and concerns about the loss of the 'real' which I have been tracing throughout this section of the book. After his playful experiment with the word 'money', Dan notes how 'we can quickly enter the world of the immaterial using the simplest of devices' (*Microserfs*: p. 134). IT and money, then, each embody the same powerful logic of abstraction which substitutes symbols and codes for objects and action upon the physical world, thus contributing to the dematerialisation of the real. As we saw with the engineers of *The Soul of a New Machine* (and as we will see later with William Gibson's cyberpunk protagonists) this thinning of the real and the increased proximity of the immaterial can be experienced as both liberation and loss, can provoke both exhilaration and anxiety. For Dan, the anxiety it provokes is directly related to the eclipse of production. The morbidity which besets him at the novel's beginning – the sense of being 'alive but not living' – and which he observes all around him in his colleagues and their work environment, he attributes to 'fear of not producing enough ... fear of losing the sensation of actually making something anymore' (*Microserfs*: pp. 371, 38). Yet it is in fact through an intensification of this logic that Dan and his friends are liberated from this death-in-life, throwing off the yoke of corporate 'serfdom' at Microsoft and achieving the personal and professional autonomy which is so central to PMC ideology and self-image. For the vehicle of their liberation is *Oop!*, a computer game they invent and for which they then quit Microsoft in order to develop and market independently. *Oop!*'s defining feature is precisely the way it abstracts the object world into virtual building blocks with which users play at constructing an unlimited range of simulacra. 'As *Oop!* users won't have *actual* plastic blocks in their hands', its inventor observes, it has to be able to 'generate new experiences to compensate for this lost tactility' (*Microserfs*: p. 71, author's emphasis). Thus, 'lost tactility', increasing distance from the site of material production and disengagement from the physical world, is at once the cause of anxiety and the strategy for its management.

The novel's exhaustive discourse on bodies and physicality is also a response to this anxiety. *Microserfs*' characters overcome alienation not just from the product of their labour and intelligence by extracting themselves from the corporate grip of Microsoft in the making and marketing of *Oop!*, they also overcome alienation from their bodies and physical selves in the process. Each rediscovers a kind of functioning sensuality they feared was forever lost as a consequence of their technological orientation and occupational milieu. Each also is granted some form of relief in reconciling with the facts of organic being, in accepting what William Gibson's characters would, by contrast, deride – that the self is 'meat'. However, Coupland is not concerned here to reiterate the opposition between the hardness of material and the softness of men that, as we have seen, has come under increasing pressure in Fordist and post-Fordist culture. Indeed, his narrative seeks to disavow it, suggesting – particularly in the example of Daniel's Mom who suffers a stroke and is able to communicate thereafter only by virtue of being hooked up to a specially adapted computer – that information technology makes physicality and emotional intimacy richer and more possible. *Microserfs* wishes to reassure us that actual and virtual relationships, bodies and machines, are neither of different orders nor mutually antagonistic.

Anxieties about derealisation and the loss of physicality, though, are, as we have seen, as much related to questions of class as they are to issues of technology. Coupland's characters are afflicted by particularly intense levels of status anxiety which are directly related to the pressure exerted on the professional–managerial stratum in a period of rapid economic and social restructuring. At the novel's beginning, despite his apparently safe and privileged position at Microsoft, Dan is haunted by the fear of falling, of losing what he feels to be his precarious toe-hold on professional–managerial status; 'career anxieties' feature high on his personal list of *Jeopardy!* dream categories by which he defines himself (*Microserfs*: p. 3). Surveying the corporate landscape with its proliferation of young computer engineers furiously competing for 'reduced stock options', he muses on the decreasing latitude for upward mobility. Recognising that 'not everyone can move into management', Dan acknowledges that he and his cohort are 'mere employees, just like at any other company'. Indeed, they are not simply 'cannon fodder', as he puts it, but bonded labour, 'serfs' expected regularly to 'slave until 1 a.m.', and even then not safe from the threat of further abrupt proletarianisation in the particularly volatile terms of the information economy: 'Face it', Dan concludes, 'you're always just a breath away from a job in telemarketing' (*Microserfs*: pp. 16, 33, 34, 17).

Yet the possibility of an equally rapid change of status in the opposite direction, 'upwards', remains. Dan details the anxious monthly ritual in which Microsoft employees collect their pay cheques hoping that they will have been singled out for the special and highly lucrative additional reward of stock options in the company. He and his co-workers, whether they hold stocks or not, without exception check the value of Microsoft shares via their computers several times a day, and Dan amuses himself by calculating the staggering amounts of money he would have made or lost according to the fluctuations in price. But his attitude towards the granting of stock options is ambivalent: it is as much a threat as it is a promise. On the one hand it is recognition of the value of the recipient's professional skills and technical expertise to the company; it guarantees them access to the most challenging technical projects, the enjoyment of certain managerial prerogatives, and minimum interference from 'above' into the way they organise and conduct their work. Moreover, as Dan enviously notes, recipients of Microsoft stock have the opportunity to wait for it to 'vest', to throw an extravagant 'vesting party', and to then use the capital to leave the corporation and establish themselves as independent entrepreneurs. Thus the receipt of stock can be a passport to the kind of personal and professional autonomy so valued in professional–managerial class ideology.

On the other hand, however, the receipt of stock can represent precisely the *loss* of such autonomy. Microsoft chairman and icon of post-Fordist information capitalism, Bill Gates, has claimed the introduction of stock options for his employees as perhaps his most important business strategy. He rates it as a labour relations innovation as crucial as any technological innovation to corporate success in so far as it motivates workers and guarantees their loyalty (Gates, 1996: p. 48). The promise of stock options therefore binds professionals closely into the corporation and its world view, subjugating them to the interests and imperatives of big capital and the money markets. As Dan notes, 'vesting turns most people into fiscal Republicans' (*Microserfs*: p. 28). Even those who receive stock and use the capital to extract themselves from Microsoft lose, in a sense, their professional–managerial integrity, becoming capitalists themselves and as such acquiring unreasonable power to exploit their own hired 'serf' labour.

Microserfs, then, presents a professional–managerial class precariously poised between labour and capital, squeezed between the pincers of proletarianisation, or 'serfdom', on the one hand, and complete incorporation into the logic of capital on the other, itself represented as just another form of servitude. And in its exploration of the attitude of Dan and his colleagues towards issues of hierarchy, managerial structure and corporate finance the novel goes on to raise the question of professional–managerial class consciousness. It is clear that an element of class resentment informs Dan's ambivalence about the prospect of stock options, just as it does his ambivalence about Bill Gates. Bill is the object of both reverence and awe (with many of his employees slavishly emulating his 'geek' style in dress, manners and patterns of consumption), but also of a significant degree of hostility. His workers' understanding of themselves as 'serfs' places him in the lineage of overweening nineteenth-century 'robber baron' capitalists, albeit a postmodern instance of such with the personal style of a campus nerd. Moreover, Dan detects in Bill a frightening desire for omnipotence and immortality – 'maybe this whole Bill thing is the subconscious manufacture of God', he muses (*Microserfs*: p. 16) – qualities which, as we shall see in more detail in Chapter 7 below, are typically associated with capital's inherent need to perpetuate and reproduce itself on a constantly expanding scale. Even by the novel's end the central characters cannot entirely escape Bill's ominous presence as his TV image is relayed throughout the convention centre where *Oop!* is being launched (*Microserfs*: p. 355). Like God and informated capital itself, Bill has the ability to be everywhere and nowhere simultaneously. Yet these hostilities never develop into any coherent analysis of the politics of production or the corporate distribution of power and wealth. Bill is revered too much himself as a 'techie' to be the figure of sustained class anger, and the most pressing critique the characters can articulate against Microsoft is that its corporate style is too generic, too bland.

There is also a class element to the resentment Dan and his fellow engineers express towards marketing, whose representatives at Microsoft he refers to as 'Pol Pots'. However, this is less an ideological opposition to the values of the marketplace or the price-system itself than it is a matter of clashing professional priorities and personal styles. Marketing is insufficiently creative or 'tech' to merit the interest or respect of engineers and code writers; moreover, it requires a brash, 'gung-ho' personality committed to the sales ethic which is at odds with the studied casualness and informality of the technical staff (*Microserfs*: p. 25). Indeed, even Dan's critiques of power inequalities and hierarchy within the corporation are expressed in terms of personal style rather than politics or ideology. He resents his boss, Shaw, who 'has fourteen direct reports (serfs) under him', entirely because he is a manager who has given up coding and is therefore 'not creative at all'. Worse still, 'Shaw is also a Baby Boomer' whose influential position and material security are, in Dan's view, entirely due to the accident of being born at a fortunate time in history, and whose generational style offends Dan's passive–ironic Generation X sensibility: 'he [Shaw] and his ilk are responsible for ... this thing called 'The Unitape' – an endless loop of elevator jazz Microsoft plays at absolutely every company function. It's so irritating and it screams a certain, "We're not like our parents, we're flouting convention" blandness.' This resentment provokes in the usually placid and detached Dan fantasies of violent rebellion. Yet it is significant that the revolution Dan imagines is not an attack on the corporate logic of serfdom; it is, rather, a revolution in generational style, one in which he and 'the entire under-30 component of the company' rise up in arms against the reign of baby-boomer musical taste and self-congratulatory cultural and political 'radicalism' (*Microserfs*: pp. 33–4).

Coupland illustrates here the way in which PMC anti-capitalism continues, as it always has, to spring from a privileged relationship to the knowledges and technologies central to advanced capitalist production and social administration. But it is now, he suggests, increasingly detached from the traditionally organising concepts of 'scientific' rationality and objectivity, becoming mediated largely through the discourses of consumption and pop culture and crystallising most typically around questions of personal style and taste. Dan himself observes how he and his colleagues are all 'pretty empty-file in the ideology department' (*Microserfs*: p. 28), and the question of a generational mutation in the nature of professional–managerial class consciousness is explicitly addressed in the notion of 'TrekPolitics'. This is Dan's term for a politics appropriate to a fully informed and mediatised society and derives from the *Star Trek* television shows. Here, all great political conflicts in human society have been made redundant by scientific progress; the Federation embodies a species-wide consensus about the benevolence of technological and social development guided by the rule of scientific reason on a literally universal scale. Thus, 'Left vs. right is obsolete. Politics is ... about biology, information, diversification'. And in this spirit, Dan and his friends present themselves as instances of a 'new apolitical pick-and-choose style of citizen' for whom 'politics is soon going to resemble a J. Crew catalogue more than some 1776 ideal' (*Microserfs*: p. 260).

The transmutation of politics for this generational fraction of the PMC into a set of consumer taste preferences reminds us of Fredric Jameson's contention that postmodernism and post-Fordism are in many senses reincarnations of the old 1950s' 'end-of-ideology' thesis. It also recalls Francis Fukuyama's notion that the apparent global victory of liberal democracy and consumer capitalism since 1989 has brought about 'the end of history'. Indeed, it would appear that for Coupland, the end of ideology and the end of history are equally to be understood as effects of the same material development – 'the deluge of electronic and information media into our lives' which he dates to the early 1980s. This, he claims, produced the condition of 'denarration' or 'personal storylessness' in which it becomes 'possible to be alive yet have ... no ideology, no sense of class location, no politics and no sense of history' (Coupland, 1997: p. 180). The characters in *Microserfs* are 'denarrated' in this way precisely as a consequence of their deracinated professional–managerial backgrounds in which all forms of social and cultural attachment have been jettisoned on the way to securing a privileged occupational position with respect to IT. One character, *Oop!*'s instigator Michael, argues that such technologies 'accelerate the obsolescence of history', replacing 'history' with 'memory' (*Microserfs*: p. 253). But memory is for both humans and machines (as Dan's excavation of his computer's unconscious illustrates) entirely composed of the fragmentary elements and icons of commodity culture; indeed the very notion of TrekPolitics itself exemplifies this translation of history and ideology into the language of pop. While they are ironically sensitive about the ahistorical nature of their lives and their insertion into endlessly self-referential consumer vocabularies, the novel's characters respond with play rather than critique. Thus for Coupland the contemporary 'crisis in historicity' does not, as it does for Fredric Jameson, represent the loss of the past and the onset of a debilitating disintegration of both selfhood and social agency (Jameson, 1991: p.25); rather, it represents freedom from the past (which, Coupland has written, 'sucks') and the imperative to engage in new modes of self-fashioning and social innovation made possible by microelectronic technologies and media (*Microserfs*: p. 236; Coupland, 1995).

The notions of political commitment, class solidarity and outright opposition to the relations of capitalist production are explored in the figures of Todd and Dusty, junior members of the *Oop!* team who engage in the serial embrace of ideologies, beginning with body-building and progressing through Marxism to Maoism. Their need for a totalising belief system or grand narrative is signalled as primitive and backward-looking, connoted by Todd's fundamentalist religious upbringing on the one hand and Dusty's hippie parentage on the other. Yet lacking any substantial sense of class identity or location, politics is for them simply a language game, absorbing an ideology the equivalent of learning a new code. They are 'cured' of this epistemological aberration through marriage, parenthood and upward social mobility as they become 'equity partners' and successful entrepreneurs with the launch of *Oop!*. The narrative thus lifts them, along with the other characters, out of the world of alienated labour and potential class antagonism into an apparently classless realm of independent knowledge workers. However, *en route* to this resolution, Todd and Dusty enable Coupland, in a not entirely frivolous manner, to play with concepts derived from an earlier epoch of more starkly visible class oppression and conflict between capital and labour at the point of production. Dusty's explanation to her colleagues of the notions of surplus value and the exploitation of labour prompts in Michael, their nominal boss at *Oop!*, the look of 'a Burger King manager who hears one of his employees discuss unionisation', while Dan concedes that 'since Marxism is explicitly based on property, ownership and control of means of production, it may well end up being the final true politik of this Benetton world we now live in' (*Microserfs*: pp. 258, 255). Thus, even having escaped serfdom at Microsoft, the shadow of proletarianisation hangs over Coupland's characters, and the vocabulary for understanding their situation in terms of the class contradiction of the wage relation is made available to them (and credited with some, albeit residual, life or explanatory power) even as it is mocked and subsumed by the languages of consumerism. This is made explicit in the running joke about Lenin, for whose 'wilfully nondecomposing body' the characters nominate appropriate contemporary uses, including product endorsement for clothing and cosmetics companies (*Microserfs*: pp. 267, 268).

Finally, Dan's distaste for ideology stems not just from what we have seen is the abiding, if wishful, PMC self-image of social objectivity, of being beyond or 'above' the 'irrational' and partisan interests and conflicts of class. Nor is it entirely a matter of his Generation X condition of 'denarration', of lacking social, historical and cultural roots or coordinates including, of course, any 'sense of class location' (Coupland, 1997: p. 180). It is also very much a matter of personal style: 'Politics only makes people cranky', he observes, and speculates longingly that, 'There must be some alternative form of discourse' (*Microserfs*: p. 251). As in *The Soul of a New Machine* and *True Stories*, the alternative form of discourse into which questions of politics, ideology and class in *Microserfs* are ultimately deflected and absorbed is a discourse on community. And also as in those earlier tales of the shift to post-Fordist methods of production and social organisation, community in *Microserfs* is conceived in terms of the network or communications model.

Coupland's design for *Microserfs* emphasises that it is as much about the construction of an open and flexible new model of community as it is about new forms of technological and business innovation. However, the former is presented as an effect of the latter and IT as its condition of possibility. The characters are moved very deliberately from spiritual and emotional hollowness to plenitude. Microsoft's arid corporate environment, described as 'not conducive to relationships', gives way to the *Oop!* project which, as Dan puts it, 'isn't about work' but 'about all of us staying together', and the narrative concludes with his realisation that he has at last located himself within a meaningful and sustaining network of human relationships, that 'what's been missing for so long isn't missing anymore' (*Microserfs*: pp. 4, 199, 371). This process of redemption through community is navigated via the concepts of 'facetime' and 'transhumanity'. The notion of 'facetime' is used to explore the question of what exactly constitutes human contact and social relations: are virtual relationships antagonistic to face-to-face relations? Coupland strives to suggest not in as much as all the successful relationships in the novel are made possible, mediated and cemented by information technologies. I have already cited the example of Dan's Mom and how computer technology reconnects her to her real and surrogate family in the *Oop!* group after her stroke. But romantic–sexual relationships are envisaged in these terms too. Dan and his girlfriend Karla see themselves as a human reflection of the Windows–Macintosh interface they are designing for *Oop!*, while Michael and his wife Amy 'meet' and fall in love as virtual and anonymous email personae, even before they are aware of the other's age, gender or sexual orientation. And in a more public and even political context, there is Susan's women and technology network, Chyx, which becomes an important adjunct to the success of *Oop!*, though it should be noted that Susan's inspirations are not the baby-boom feminists of the Women's Liberation Movement but the stars of 1970s' TV show, *Charlie's Angels*.

The notion of 'transhumanity', the title of the novel's final section, extends this idea of community as an effect of electronic mediation. It is here that each character definitively transcends his or her sense of isolation and self-limitation through the intercession of computer technology, becoming more 'human' in the process and more firmly bound into the community that *Oop!* has brought together. This community is transhuman in so far as the line between person and machine is obliterated within it; it is constituted as much by the agency of machines and coding systems as it is by people engaged in face-to-face relationships. Coupland seeks to present technology, then, as a McLuhanesque 'extension of man' which liberates community from the traditional physical limitations of time and place (McLuhan, 1964). Technology functions not only as a form of prosthetic body part (as it does most literally for Dan's Mom) but is an almost organic manifestation of human imagination and desire: 'machines really *are* our subconscious' observes Dan, anticipating the moment when the excavation of his computer's unconscious will reconcile him with the repressed memory of his dead brother (*Microserfs*: p. 228).

By the same token, though, the narrative urges that persons should be seen as articulate, sentient machines, and that this should be understood not as an assault upon but as an enrichment of our species-experience and self-image, just as it suggests that the saturation of inner life by popular or commodity culture deepens, rather than reduces, the realm of the ineffable. These ideas are encapsulated in the novel's final push towards transcendence. Its closing scene portrays the *Oop!* group as a community of purpose and mutual solidarity that crosses lines of generation (Dan's parents), gender and sexuality (Bug's coming out). It is a community that is defined by the warmth and vitality of bodily and face-to-face relationships, but one that at the same time owes its existence and its ability to function entirely to the mediations of IT and commodity culture. The novel completes its movement from hollowness to plenitude in its final image of the *Oop!* group communing through Dan's Mom's computer and collectively projecting its desires and visions 'into the end of the universe' by means of a Pink Floyd record and a collection of toy lasers – 'precision technology running so fine' (*Microserfs*: p. 371).

Microserfs' metaphysical impulse, or what we might call its attempt to outline and celebrate a post-humanist humanism, seems to be offered as an antidote to Generation X professional–managerial deracination. But for all the novel's approving discussion of diversity and IT-inspired innovation with social and economic forms, the community at its centre is tightly homogeneous in terms of class (and, of course, race). It thus seems to be as much a defensive or compensatory formation as it is an experimental adaptation to new times. Richard Sennett has noted how the current influence of communitarianism in American political and social thought can be seen as a reaction to the unusual stresses imposed on the social bond by the breakup of Fordism: 'One of the unintended consequences of modern capitalism is that it has ... aroused a longing for community' (Sennett, 1999: p. 138). And indeed, the professional–managerial status of *Microserfs*' characters is threatened not just by proletarianisation from 'below' and incorporation from 'above' but by the additional and ominous prospect of absolute historical redundancy, represented in terms of biological as well as social extinction. Dan's girlfriend, Karla, explains it this way:

> It's no coincidence that as a species we invented the middle classes. Without the middle classes, we couldn't have had the special type of mind-set that consistently spits out computational systems, and our species could never have made it to the next level, whatever that level's going to be. Chances are, the middle classes aren't even a *part* of the next level. (*Microserfs*: p. 61, author's emphasis)

The irony here, of course, is that just as the Generation X PMC blames its baby-boom predecessors for dismantling the Fordist conditions that swaddled its own privileged emergence and rise to social influence, the Generation X PMC might here be itself guilty of pioneering the material transformations that eradicate the class as a whole. This is at once a terrifying and an exhilarating prospect, combining as it does the nightmare of historical death with the dream of determining social power that is so central to professional–managerial ideology. The deployment of their technical expertise might be making their own kind redundant, but at the same time, as Karla breathlessly announces, '*We* are building the center from which all else will be held' (*Microserfs*: p. 61, author's emphasis). The peculiar interplay of scenarios of impotence and omnipotence to which this gives rise is explored below in Part 3.

The implications of class extinction are explored most coherently in *Microserfs* through the figure of Dan's Dad, a fifty-something IBM employee of the classic Fordist 'organisation man' type, the type who, Dan notes, assumed 'your company was going to take care of you forever' (*Microserfs*: p. 17). Dad becomes a casualty of corporate 'restructuring' and is cast out into the volatile social and economic currents of the flexible post-Fordist regime where he must either adapt or perish. To employ the terms of Davidow and Malone's stark opposition in their hymn to the era of flexible specialisation, *The Virtual Corporation* (1992), he must remake himself in the image of the amorphous, playful and informal structures of the information economy to become an 'independent knowledge worker', or he must endure the living death of being an 'economic serf'. In one sense this is presented as a kind of biological evolution. Like Davidow and Malone, Dan invokes the nineteenth-century *laissez-faire* notion of the survival of the fittest, enthusing that 'the freedom and freefloat of intellectual Darwinism is bringing out the best in us', and implying that his father must similarly evolve to be a winner in the struggle for power and resources or be 'rendered obsolete' (*Microserfs*: pp. 322, 202). In another sense, though, it is presented as a matter of technological redesign and upgrading. Dad begins his process of adaptation by learning a new computer coding language and is ultimately taken on by the *Oop!* group's leader, Michael, for what Dan calls 'reprogramming' (*Microserfs*: p. 201). That the early symptoms of this include a propensity to sing Talking Heads songs suggests that cultural and aesthetic re-education is as important a part of this process as is technical refitting.

Indeed, it becomes clear that Dan's Dad is on the way to making the evolutionary leap from obsolete economic serf to the modern ideal of independent knowledge worker when the secret project on which he has been working for Michael in the as yet uninhabited new *Oop!* offices is unveiled. This turns out to be a complete, idealised and simulated environment made out of lego bricks, a modular 'universe' which Dan describes as 'a Guggenheim and a Toys-R-Us squished into one'; it is, he declares, 'the most *real* thing I've ever seen' (*Microserfs*: p. 220, author's emphasis). Thus the threat of extinction is avoided by the introduction of *play* into the heart of the productive process; the distinctions between play and work, between technology and toys, high art (a Guggenheim) and commodity culture, the simulated and the real are all eroded in this new economic and social regime. Of course, the very name and nature of *Oop!* connote what many commentators have portrayed as the playful, almost accidental quality of post-Fordist social and productive relations which, in as much as they are held to depart from the 'rigidity' of Fordist structures, appear to be open to continuous disarticulation and recombination as in a particularly flexible modular system. But this resolution of Dan's Dad's crisis through the notion of play points us in the direction of another of the discourses that the novel offers as an alternative to the 'cranky' discourses of politics and class – the discourse of character.

Dad understands his obsolescence, his fall from professional–managerial grace, as an index of personal failure rather than as a consequence of the impersonal and systemic reformulation of productive forces and class relations. In this he is an example of the way in which, according to Richard Sennett, 'Class in America is interpreted as an issue of personal character' (Sennett, 1999: p. 64). Dad feels the onus is on him to adjust his personal style and sensibility, to become the type of character adept at 'coping with chaos and diversity' and 'the current deluge of information' as he puts it, if he is to survive (*Microserfs*: p. 203); and indeed the novel presents his evolution as precisely a matter of character adjustment, of learning to adapt, to relinquish his yearning for Fordist stabilities, to become flexible, to loosen up and 'play'. Yet it can't entirely purge itself of the traces of another mode of understanding personal circumstances, one that seeks answers outside the self in the shape of the relations of production and the currents of power that animate them. Shortly after he is terminated by IBM, Dad is discovered by Dan wandering the streets outside his old corporation, musing on the developments that have made him one of 'the newly obsolete humans', and critically surveying the IBM building as though the explanation for his plight might be written on its surfaces. Feeling 'humiliated for my father', Dan joins him in his vigil, uncomfortably aware that 'surely there'd be employees behind the reflecto windows saying, "*Oh look, it's Mr. Underhill stalking us. He must really have lost it.*"' The problem is, however, that the corporation's blank walls and mirrored windows are constructed precisely to repel the interrogating gaze that would seek to grasp the nature of the productive relations within and position the self in terms of those relations. Granted only distorted reflections by the mirrored glass, Dad's thoughts rebound accusingly in on himself, to focus on his lack of 'character', while Dan finds himself baffled, lost for words of consolation, 'surrounded by all these blank buildings with glassed-out windows, these buildings where they make the machines that make the machines that make the machines' (*Microserfs*: p. 203, author's italics).

The discourses of community and character are in certain respects, then, as Richard Sennett points out, compensations for the invisibility or eclipse of contemporary productive relations, for the fact that 'the new capitalism is often an illegible regime of power' (Sennett, 1999: p. 10). Sennett contends that in Adam Smith's epoch of freely competitive industrial capitalism 'Nothing was hidden from the worker in the pin factory', power relations were evident to all at the point of production. But in 'the flexible regime' of informated, postindustrial capitalism 'a great deal is hidden from the workers'. 'Flexibility', he argues, 'creates distinctions between surface and depth' which undermine people's ability 'to read the world around them and to read themselves'. Surfaces everywhere reflect 'images of a classless society', but 'breaking the surface may require a code people lack' (Sennett, 1999: p. 75). Dan and his Dad's cursory attempts to break through the surface to the underlying relations of power and production are easily deflected, and for all its exploration of anxious professional–managerial class consciousness, *Microserfs* can itself be accused of presenting an image of classlessness in as much as it contains neither a character nor a perspective from without the PMC's boundaries. Yet any such problems are ultimately dissolved in the narrative solution of *Oop!*'s spectacular triumph in the marketplace; success resolves its makers' angst about their class identity, confirms the integrity of their character, and guarantees the vitality of their community. After all, as Richard Sennett observes, an in-depth grasp of the relations of production and an interrogation of the usefulness of prevailing notions of character and community are really only 'required by the increasing number of people who, in modern capitalism, are doomed to fail' (Sennett, 1999: p. 135).

Microserfs' final push towards transcendence, then, its celebration of community and 'transhumanity', is based on the conceit of market success, the very thing that its characters deny motivates them in their work: 'it's *never* been the money ... with any of us ... ever', insists Bug (*Microserfs*: p. 318, author's emphasis). Throughout, they are conveniently shielded from market forces while they immerse themselves in the technical challenge of perfecting *Oop!*; rarely, if ever, do they suffer exposure to the conflicting logics of capital and labour between which, as professional–managerial workers, they are precariously poised. A hired venture capitalist, Ethan, looks after capital investment in their company, while the company itself is constituted quite deliberately to be free from any responsibility for the physical manufacture, marketing or distribution of its product. *Oop!* can thus appear to its makers quite convincingly to be a 'virtual product' in Davidow and Malone's terms, one with few if any material traces or connections to the material forces of capital and labour, a 'non-polluting, value-added intellectual property' to use the Coupland formulation which heads this chapter.

But this does not prevent Dan entirely from speculating about the absent categories of capital and labour. 'I'm not sure what exactly *Oop!*'s money structure is' he admits at one point, and goes on to wonder, 'Wouldn't it be a sick joke if I got into something without understanding the financial underpinnings ... if I hadn't even bothered to ask the questions I'm supposed to ask' (*Microserfs*: p. 149, author's ellipsis). This, though, is as far as his investigations on the matter of his relationship to capital proceed. Similarly, his attention is periodically taken by the robot that cleans his parents' pool. R2D2, as it is known, is, of course, a figure for tireless labour, a kind of mechanical slave when viewed from a certain perspective, or an ideally obedient and efficient worker when viewed from another. Dan and Michael idly imagine what account it would give of itself and its experience were it able to do so: 'What do you think and feel? they want to ask it, 'What would R2D2 say to me if R2D2 could speak?' (*Microserfs*: p. 183). But this inquiry into the condition of alienated labour also progresses no further when the boon of *Oop!*'s market success intervenes to resolve all difficulties. Yet these isolated moments do serve to remind us that the fulfilled and independent knowledge workers of Silicon Valley are dependent on the invisible and silent, but nonetheless present, forces of capital and labour: just as their company finance must come from somewhere, so too must wage-workers somewhere be engaged in the manufacture and marketing of their product. *Microserfs* presents, then, not so much the complete eclipse of production as its wilful erasure from the consciences of its professional–managerial class technicians. At the novel's climactic moment, during the sacrament of personal wholeness and transcendent community that follows on the successful business launch of *Oop!*, the characters find it necessary to dive into Dan's parents' pool and 'rescu[e] ... the R2D2 pool cleaner from its endless serflike toil' (*Microserfs*: p. 358). Despite itself, the novel's conclusion contains a pointed reminder of the very material and serflike relations of class and power that it elsewhere insists no longer structure the virtual landscape of the flexible information economy.

Part 3

Impotence and Omnipotence:
The Cybernetic Discourse of Capitalism

6

Cybernetics, Systems Theory and the End of Ideology

> From a capitalist–productivist society to a neo-capitalist cybernetic order that aims now at total control ... There is nothing of an accident in this mutation. It is the end of a history in which, successively, God, Man, Progress, and History itself die to profit the code.
>
> Jean Baudrillard, *Simulations* (1983: p. 111)

We have seen how microelectronic information technologies have been instrumental in the tendency to reconceptualise social relations in terms of decentred circuits or communications networks. These technologies, though, have been just as crucial to a related and equally powerful discourse which has similarly constructed a view of social structures and processes out of what is essentially a set of technical and methodological imperatives. This is the discourse of cybernetics.

For the proponents of the circuit or network perspective (what I have earlier called the communications view of community) the computer functions principally as a powerful technological metaphor for what is held to be the indeterminate and non-totalisable nature of postindustrial or postmodern social relations. In cybernetics, on the other hand, the computer is first and foremost an instrument that serves to *counteract* indeterminacy: it is called upon to strengthen technique in order to produce increasingly totalistic and predictive knowledges of ostensibly indeterminate processes. Only secondarily is the computer mobilised as a metaphor in cybernetic discourse where, in the sub-discipline of artificial intelligence (AI), it has become the key model for thinking about human cognitive processes and addressing (or eliminating, as AI theorists often like to claim) the philosophical problem of mind versus body or mechanism versus vitalism.

The emergence of cybernetics out of an interest in the development of predictive rationality and the drive towards 'organisation' (a key term in cybernetics, as is its dreaded antithesis, 'entropy') is indicted in the subtitle of the discipline's founding text, Norbert Wiener's *Cybernetics: or Communication and Control in the Animal and the Machine* (1948). For Wiener, significantly, the quest for control was matched in importance by a concern for the multiple and reciprocal process of communication, and the proper balance between these two terms exercised him throughout his career. Yet as cybernetic discourse came to enjoy a meteoric rise to scientific and social influence in the years immediately following the Second World War, and as cybernetic thinking was increasingly called upon to answer problems of social policy and organisation in this period, this balance was soon lost or willingly abandoned. Communication became subsumed by the drive for control in a development that had serious implications for the way American society came to be envisaged.

The consistent attachment of cybernetics to potentially authoritarian notions of quantification and control can in part be accounted for by its military origins. Wiener initially formulated the methods of probabilistic logical analysis upon which the discipline was based during the Second World War while working on a device to enable allied anti-aircraft weapons to 'predict' the apparently random evasive movements most likely to be adopted by enemy bombers under fire. Out of this project arose the notion of an automatically self-correcting mechanism capable of regulating its functions and modifying its behaviour according to the principle of 'feedback' – the rapid absorption and assimilation of information from its environment which in turn allowed the mechanism to adjust its relationship to and action upon that environment. Wiener named the study and elaboration of feedback processes 'cybernetics' for the term's roots in the Greek for 'steersman' and the Latin for 'governor', and here again the term betrays its closeness to notions of centralised direction and control. The prospect of a practical engineering application of feedback techniques heralded not only a quantum leap in the sophistication and scope of automatic machines, but also promised the imminent realisation of the independent, self-motivating automaton or *machine à gouverner* envisaged by scientists since the eighteenth century. In this respect, then, cybernetics was the necessary condition for the development of those automated manufacturing machines and techniques which in large part constituted the 'third technological revolution' upon which the post-1945 long boom rested (Mandel, 1978: p. 121; Noble, 1984).

However, cybernetics also furnished an exciting new model for the understanding of human behaviour and of the relationship of human intelligence to the world around it. W. Ross Ashby adapted cybernetic concepts to the study of dynamic, purposive behaviour in physical systems whose nature could be mechanical, biological, or a combination of both. Wiener's techniques of mathematical analysis allowed Ashby to account for behavioural transformations in such systems – transformations commonly understood to involve faculties such as intention, memory and foresight – in entirely mechanistic and determinist terms. Any 'system' could thus be conceived of as a 'black box' or 'transducer' whose behaviour could be explained and would be determined by the particular inputs and outputs that connected it to its environment. Inevitably, inputs and outputs were defined by cybernetics in terms of information, communication, or 'messages'.

While such analytic techniques were practically effective in observing or controlling only 'closed' or determinate systems – that is, systems with a limited number of inputs, outputs and, hence, behavioural states – Ashby held that they were *in principle* applicable to systems of massive complexity such as 'a computer, a nervous system, or a society' (Lilienfeld, 1978: p. 37). In his *Design for a Brain: The Origin of Adaptive Behavior* (1960), Ashby suggested that intelligence, learning or adaptivity was an identically determinate process in both machines and organisms, and that what characterised such behaviour was not the actual substance that did the behaving (be it organic or mechanical), nor even the physical processes that produced it (neural activity or electronic data-processing), but the fact that behaviour could be understood as a mathematically determinate operation within a more or less complex informational field.

Cybernetics thus offered itself as a scientific rationale for the further erosion of the cultural or philosophical distinction between the hardness of material and the softness of men which, as we have seen, was already under siege in Fordist culture from a number of directions. It also provided grounds for the militantly reductionist or anti-essentialist position on 'mind' taken by the proponents of artificial intelligence for whom the mechanical reproduction of human behaviour in the form of a 'Turing machine' was now beyond doubt.[1] In this respect, then, cybernetics became the basis for the reconceptualisation of the human self as a cybernetic organism or 'cyborg'. Thinking or purposive behaviour was no longer what distinguished human selves from machines or other adaptive systems, for it was precisely this that characterised them all; all were to be seen as data-processors adapting their relationship to the environment in determinate ways through input–output manipulation and feedback. Moreover, Ashby's and Wiener's emphasis on the systematic nature of intelligent behaviour, in particular their emphasis on continuities and 'interfaces' between man–machine or organic–mechanical combinations, further undermined the the human self's claims to uniqueness and autonomy. The cyborg self thus came increasingly to be seen as a small component in any number of much larger interlinked systems that, regardless of the level of their complexity, remained, in theory at least, always amenable to cybernetic theories of determination and control.

These two impulses within the discipline of cybernetics – the impulse toward the automation of complex tasks and the impulse toward the simulation of human intelligence – came to be fully united in the form of the computer. Though cybernetics emerged in many ways independently of the computer and prior to it, its development as a discipline and as a practical engineering science became so quickly and so tightly bound up with it as to be inseparable from it. Cybernetic theory played a crucial role in making possible and practicable the construction of the early computers' systems of logic and internal communication. But as the engineering scope of cybernetics broadened, and as the problems of analysis it called up increased in complexity, computers in their turn became indispensable aids for manipulating the massive quantities of variables and probable states that such problems entailed. Computers and cybernetics thus became identified with one another by this reciprocal play of reinforcement. Just as importantly, the computer came in the process to be seen as the prototypical embodiment of the all-purpose automaton or 'handmaiden of industry' on the one hand, and the ultimate Turing machine or simulacrum of human intelligence on the other.

It is possible to understand the computer, then, not simply as a sophisticated technical instrument but as a point of intellectual convergence for tendencies within a single discipline or, indeed, for modes of thought inhabiting separate disciplines. Robert Lilienfeld has described how the concerns of cybernetics came, largely through the agency of computer technology, to be linked with those of other disciplines emergent during the Second World War and its aftermath to form the vaguely defined but extremely influential field of 'systems theory'. According to Lilienfeld, systems theory is an amalgam of Wiener's and Ashby's cybernetics, Ludwig von Bertalanffy's notion of the organisation of organic life into hierarchies of 'open systems', Claude Shannon's and Warren Weaver's 'information' or 'communication' theory, and the 'games' theory of John von Neumann and Oskar Morgenstern. These were allied to the methods of statistical simulation of large social and environmental processes devised by Jay Forrester and adopted by the Club of Rome, and the wartime practice of deriving an integrated or 'total' perspective on strategic and logistical problems from the application of scientific techniques that was known as 'operations research' or 'systems analysis'.

These apparently disparate disciplines were not only connected by the obvious usefulness of computer technology to their large-scale questions of rational calculation, they were also linked by the fact that all conceived of their fundamental objects of interest and analysis as *systems* and understood systems to be constituted, regardless of content or physical substance, above all by information, communication and the transmission of messages. Furthermore, the practitioners of these disciplines aimed to *control* as well as understand such messages, and were only too eager to extrapolate the systems model from their own particular field and claim for it a universal applicability.

In 1950, for example, Wiener based his highly influential popular exposition of cybernetics, *The Human Use of Human Beings: Cybernetics and Society*, around the following set of claims:

> that society can only be understood through a study of the messages and the communication facilities which belong to it; and that in the future development of these messages and communication facilities, messages between man and machines, between machines and man, and between machine and machine, are destined to play an ever-increasing part. (Wiener, 1989: p. 16)

We can see here a tendency to assume that because modern societies are increasingly saturated with information and processes of communication they can accurately be viewed as cybernetic systems. Cybernetics, and by extension other systems approaches, could therefore be presented as crucial not just to the *understanding* of society but also to its *management*, as, according to Wiener, the science's 'purpose' was 'to develop a language and techniques that will enable us indeed to attack the problem of control and communication in general' (Wiener, 1989: p. 17). Similarly, if the control of information (and, hence, behaviour) through feedback and the agency of a 'central regulatory apparatus' is what makes 'the physical functioning of the living individual and the operation of some of the newer communication machines ... precisely parallel', then it is equally tempting to claim that these are merely microcosmic models of 'the organic responses of society itself' (Wiener, 1989: pp. 26, 27). A series of homologies between machine, person and society is thus established which allows them all to be regarded as determinate and predictable information systems subject to 'scientific' techniques of analysis and control.

In this respect, cybernetics and other branches of systems theory were not so much pure scientific disciplines as they were ways of looking at or framing an object or a problem. 'Systems *theory*', therefore, is probably better characterised as 'systems *thinking*', in as much as this term denoted the extent to which certain theorems and methodologies gave rise to a particular world view or ideology. The key features of the systems perspective were, firstly, its understanding that the information contained in any system was in principle totalisable – that all the possible behaviours of the system could be known and projected – and, secondly, its assumption that feedback always functioned to establish or maintain an orderly or steady state within the system known as equilibrium or homeostasis.

These particular elements of systems thinking were adopted as 'scientific' principles by those not involved in the formulation of the original disciplines and then applied wholesale to the 'social system'. Around them arose what Paul Edwards has called a 'closed-world discourse'. This, he goes on, 'is characterised by tools, techniques, practices and languages which embody an approach to the world as composed of interlocking systems amenable to formal mathematical analysis' (P. Edwards, 1989: p. 138). Closed-world discourse became a crucial factor in the formation and emergence of new scientific and technocratic elites in the wake of the Second World War whose principal task was to reconceptualise, reorganise and legitimise American capitalism according to the cybernetic model of the automatically self-regulating system. As Robert Lilienfeld observes,

> The man who offers an image of society as a closed system (ie. able to be encompassed and manipulated by logically closed theoretical models) and who can on the basis of technical work and discovery on such systems demonstrate expertise in these matters is clearly offering to assume benevolent control of society as a closed system, which he will manipulate from a position outside of and superior to that system. (Lilienfeld, 1978: p. 3)[2]

The leadership of these new postwar elites was therefore established upon the dominance of the cybernetic paradigm and rested on their ability to impose that paradigm across the social field with the aid of computer technology, the 'core around which a closed-world discourse could crystallise' (P. Edwards, 1989: p. 140).

Unsurprisingly perhaps, the military was the first powerful interest group fully to appropriate the cybernetic paradigm and seek to give it universal application. Immediately after the Second World War, the US Air Force synthesised its existing operations research techniques with newly available computer technology and, with the collaboration of the Douglas Aircraft Corporation, set up Project RAND in 1946. Although devoted to problems of military strategy in an increasingly global postwar geopolitical arena, Project RAND was nevertheless founded on the cybernetic principles of 'games theory' elaborated by its two most illustrious civilian recruits, mathematician John von Neumann and economist Oskar Morgenstern. The cybernetic paradigm offered in this sense what was thought to be a 'total' perspective on the complex strategic contingencies of the postwar international situation. If world powers could be viewed as 'players' in an information-based 'game' whose rules (and therefore moves) were determinate, then, as Paul Edwards puts it, 'Global politics became a system that could be understood and manipulated by methods modelled on – or at least justified in the language of – systems engineering' (P. Edwards, 1989: p. 140). When the Ford Foundation took over financial control of Project RAND in 1948, renaming it the RAND Corporation and transforming it into an increasingly general purpose rather than specifically military think-tank, the cybernetic paradigm swiftly spread to the spheres of government and industry.

The appeal of cybernetics to business management was initially the promise it held for the extensive automation of the production process and the further disciplining of 'living' labour by the threat of its actual or potential replacement by automated machinery. As we have seen earlier in this book, the strength of organised labour had grown considerably during the Second World War – despite the implementation of 'no-strike' pledges and wage freezes – due to the absolute necessity of securing worker cooperation in the war effort. This strength was wielded to great effect in the labour unrest that swept America during 1946 and 1947 – the 'biggest strike wave in the history of a capitalist country', according to labour historian Arthur B. Shostack (quoted in Noble, 1984: p. 25) – and continued to reverberate until the mid-1950s.[3] Automation or 'cybernation' was therefore perceived by management as a powerful weapon in its struggle with labour for control of the production process and, hence, for the extraction of surplus value. It was thus an extension of the logic of Taylorist scientific management which had atomised the industrial worker's job into a set of discrete mechanical operations which could be rationalised and recombined for maximum speed and efficiency. The Taylorist and Fordist notion of 'men behaving like machines' therefore 'paved the way for machines without men', allowing management to 'reduce its historical dependence upon a skilled, and hence relatively autonomous work force' (Noble, 1984: p. 36).

But along with its practical shopfloor attractions for management, cybernation also offered an intellectual model for reconceptualising the entire process of industrial production in terms of the closed, determinate, self-regulating system. In this view, workers were not to be seen as socially and culturally embedded persons with historically specific material interests, but rather as infinitely flexible components within a control system that tended 'naturally' towards a (management-defined) state of 'order' or 'equilibrium'. So conceived, the 'industrial system' had no room for conflict or struggle of any kind. The new model conveniently ignored the social contradiction between labour and capital upon which the capitalist industrial 'system' was based, and allowed business to claim scientific legitimacy for its attempts to 'factor out' industrial conflict via an ever-increasing repertory of design strategies and coercive or therapeutic techniques.

The cybernetic paradigm and systems thinking were thus enshrined as solutions to what presidential advisor and General Electric president, Charles E. Wilson, defined in 1946 as the two cardinal problems facing America at the war's end: 'Russia abroad' and 'labor at home' (quoted in Noble, 1984: p. 3). These scientific world views were embraced as timely godsends to a nation whose position of global leadership in political, economic and military matters presented its ruling elites with problems of organisation and analysis unprecedented in their scale and complexity. Looked at from another angle, however, these same discourses of technical mastery and control appear as the ideological *products* typical of a nation in such a hegemonic position. David Noble has noted the 'unusual degree of complementarity between the seeming requirements of a new global power and the technical possibilities engendered by a powerful intellectual synthesis within science and engineering'. He also observes how 'these new theories, like the technologies of control which they reflected, arrived on the scene "just in time" ... when government, military and industrial operations were becoming excessively complex and unmanageable'. There was in effect 'an unprecedented degree of integration at the time between the worlds of power and science' – not least in the formation of what President Eisenhower called 'the military–industrial complex' – which, claims Noble, 'gave rise to a shared world view of total control' (Noble, 1984: pp. 45, 55, 56).[4]

Norbert Wiener, for one, came quickly to be appalled by this appropriation of cybernetic theory and vociferously protested at what he saw as the subordination of science to the imperatives of the state, the military and the business establishment. In 1950 he warned of 'the growing military and political mechanisation of the world as a great superhuman apparatus working on cybernetic principles' (Wiener, 1989: p. 182).[5] Other scientists, however, were willingly recruited into the expanding administrative echelons required to manage and direct the United States in its new position of global leadership. Here they were cast as technicians whose ability to practice their scientific calling at ever-increasing degrees of prestige and funding depended upon their coming to share the perspectives of the ruling military and business elites, upon their developing 'a habit-forming relationship to power' (Noble, 1984: p. 45). The ideological elements of cybernetic discourse were thus brought to the fore. At RAND, for example, not only were international relations and the strategic conduct of the Cold War put on a systems footing, the domestic and global markets were also reformulated as cybernetic systems by Austrian economist Oskar Morgenstern. Morgenstern's systems view of the market meshed with business management's systemic approach to the shopfloor to promote a model of the economic 'system' in which the processes of production, exchange and consumption were held to be tightly integrated into a 'naturally' harmonious and self-regulating totality. Another economist – Harvard professor and, from 1961, Kennedy Defense Secretary, Robert McNamara – acted as a direct conduit into government for the systems approach, establishing the Office of Systems Analysis into which he liberally recruited staff from the RAND Corporation. Once established here, systems thinking, with its computer modelling and projection techniques, came especially to be applied to the management of two areas of social policy that were particularly volatile and politically charged – urban infrastructures and the welfare apparatus.

Thus the science of communication, organisation and control became a central component of the ideology of high Fordist America, providing an ideal paradigm for understanding and managing organised capitalism in its global stage. This proved even to be so in the case of academic sociology where the ideas of the school of structural-functionalism associated with the work of Talcott Parsons converged with the cybernetic paradigm to produce a systems view of the very history and pattern of human social development. Here, the human environment was seen as being ordered into a 'cybernetic hierarchy' of intercommunicating systems, ranging from the complex symbolic level of the 'cultural' or 'action system', through the 'social' and the 'personality system', to the molecular or biological level of the organism and its constituent elements (Parsons, 1968: p. 468). And in order to understand and predict societal development, the social scientist had to 'focus on the cybernetically higher-order structures', the cultural system in particular, as this was 'the "master system" in the cybernetic sense' (Parsons, 1966: p. 10; 1968: p. 468). For Parsons, the logics of social and organic evolution were equivalent; in both, systems functioned essentially to establish integration, 'pattern-maintenance', or equilibrium at ever higher levels of differentiation and complexity. History, and the questions of contingency, power, and individual and collective agency that it raised, became subsumed by the notion of evolution, with its overtones of the naturalness and inevitability of things as they are. An essentially biological notion of homeostasis and system-reproduction was projected on to the social field, with the consequence that normative conceptions of the inevitability and desirability of order, and of adaptation to the requirements of order, prevailed. Conflict, contradiction and struggle were regarded as epiphenomenal and deviant.

The ideological uses of the cybernetic paradigm were thus thoroughly incorporated into social theory. As Alvin Gouldner has noted, the elaboration of such a systems view of society can be seen as a direct intellectual response to the prolonged and international crisis of organised capitalism during the Great Depression and the Second World War. Parsons's obsession with integration and the stable reproduction of social relations emerged from and spoke powerfully to a 'general, Euro-American crisis of the international middle class'. Moreover, the structural-functionalist approach 'reflected the common concerns of relatively advanced or "developed" industrial societies whose elites defined their problems primarily in terms of their common need to maintain "social order"'.[6] And indeed, what Gouldner calls the extreme 'empirical emptiness and abstractness of the Parsonian analysis of social order' served to obscure its ideological effects and its class attachments (Gouldner, 1970: p. 145). Empirical analysis and direct engagement with concrete social processes were disavowed. The task, as in all branches of systems theory, was rather 'to single out purely relational isomorphisms that are abstracted from content' (Rapoport, 1968: p. 454). Systems theorists could therefore imagine themselves to be outside the contingencies and conflicts of history, presenting themselves as ideologically neutral and scientifically objective observers.

Along with this abstraction of content went an emphasis on the entirely mediated nature of experience and reality: for Parsons, 'neither the individual personality nor the social system has any *direct* relation to the physical environment' (Parsons, 1968: p. 460, author's emphasis). As I've consistently noted throughout this book, this sense of remoteness and insulation from material conditions, in addition to a preoccupation with the ubiquity of mediation, is often associated with the eclipse of direct methods of production and the social predominance of technologies of reproduction. It is also, of course, characteristic of the outlook of the professional–managerial class whose role as social mediators entails their stewardship and deployment of such technologies, fostering a class understanding of itself as somehow occupying an 'objective' position outside the contradiction of capital and labour.

As I've also tried to demonstrate earlier, the professional–managerial class tends to view social relations in terms of abstract informational structures devoid of direct connection to issues of material power and conflict. We can see how this methodological focus on abstraction and mediation works to hollow out the social in a similar way in Parsons's contention that the economic system is entirely symbolic, and that money's 'primary function is communication'. Parsons saw 'the monetary system' as a *code, in the grammatical–syntactical sense* and the 'circulation of money' as 'the "sending" of messages which give the recipient capacity to command goods and services through market channels'. Thus, he concluded, 'the process of money circulation involves literally nothing except communicated messages' (Parsons, 1968: p. 470, author's emphasis). All other social systems (including the political system) were for Parsons similarly constituted. In this manner the cybernetic paradigm legitimised the factoring out of material questions of power, conflict and contradiction from social theory.

Its empirical emptiness and its emphasis on abstraction and mediation made systems theory the perfect ideology for a period in which it was widely argued that ideology itself had come to an end. But its very attractiveness to the rising stratum of administrative intellectuals that was called upon to organise a new global political, economic and military apparatus in the post-Second World War period meant that it did more than simply 'replace' ideologies (particularly Marxism and socialism) that were held to be 'exhausted', as Daniel Bell put it. The cybernetic paradigm played an active role in undermining and discrediting older ideologies and images of society. As Robert Lilienfeld has noted, 'the ideology of systems theory could be said to consist of having no ideology, in the popular sense of a specific political commitment'; rather, 'it provides a vocabulary which permits its practitioners to celebrate and serve whatever social developments emerge over the horizon' (Lilienfeld, 1978: p. 263).

At a time when the domestic ideological tensions of the Cold War were acute, and disillusionment with the Soviet brand of socialism rife, such a 'non-ideology' offered a basis on which heretofore oppositional intellectuals could revise their attitudes towards left politics and corporate capitalism, and negotiate various kinds of accommodation with power. And at a time when the success of American capitalism and the well-being of American society were felt to depend on the central political value of consensus, systems theory appeared as a reassuringly 'neutral' and unifying world view, particularly by comparison with the conflict or competition models of Marxism or *laissez-faire* economic liberalism. Thus the period of 'the end of ideology' as Daniel Bell famously named it in 1960, was precisely the time at which 'the notion of society run by benevolent technicians operating on the basis of actuarial logic and impersonal algorithmic methods could come to the fore' (Lilienfeld, 1978: p. 264).

In another respect, the implementation of cybernetics and information systems in industry appeared to many commentators of the period to have further rendered the preoccupations of Marxism and economic liberalism alike obsolete. As we saw in Part 1 of this book, the metamorphosis of large corporations from family enterprises into impersonal and quasi-public bureaucracies was bound up with the rationalising force of the new technologies and techniques of organisation, communication and information introduced by a stratum of managers, engineers and technicians which emerged between 1880 and 1920. This educated and socially mobile professional–managerial class assumed control of the corporate structure by virtue of its knowledge and expertise, rather than as a consequence of inheritance or the ownership of wealth. It had thus, it was claimed, displaced the old capitalist ruling class which, certain commentators argued, was now a largely vestigial and hence meaningless socio-economic force.[7]

Similarly, it was felt that the effect of automatic production processes at the other end of the industrial hierarchy was rendering the working class obsolete. 'Automation will change the basic composition of the labor force, creating a new *salariat* instead of a *proletariat*, as automatic processes reduce the number of industrial workers required in production' declared Daniel Bell in 1956 (Bell, 1988: p. 268, author's emphasis). The heightened productivity automation appeared to guarantee was believed to be bringing with it a condition of such widespread material abundance that, it was argued, class divisions and specific class interests were disappearing; a common interest in consumption, leisure and lifestyle was taking their place. The old models of class conflict or of 'economic man' determined by relations of property and production simply did not apply to this new social situation, it was claimed.

If the internal contradictions of American capitalism were well on the way to being resolved by cybernation, this only seemed to add credibility to the notion that American society as a whole functioned like a cybernetic system. The apparent ability of government to regulate the economy, bringing social classes and political interests into consensual equilibrium, was taken to be further confirmation of it. Bell likened government to 'a gyroscope [which] can offset overproduction and underconsumption' to safeguard equilibrium; and in a society that was envisaged as a mechanism, it appeared that 'more often than not, the crucial decisions ... [were] *technical* decisions' rather than political or ideological ones (Bell, 1988: pp. 268, 90, author's emphasis).

For J. K. Galbraith, too, postwar American society was for better or worse no longer shaped by capital, class or the market, but by the self-reproducing demands of what he called the 'technostructure'. It was thus 'the imperatives of technology and organisation, not the images of ideology [which] determine[d] the shape of economic society' (Galbraith, 1967: p. 26). That two such sceptical liberals as Bell and Galbraith should thus borrow the terms and perspectives of systems thinking indicates the extent to which cybernetic technology had established itself as a model for understanding society as well as managing it. This convergence of cybernetic discourse with end-of-ideology theorising prepared the way for such later formulations as 'postindustrial' or 'information' society, terms which continued to assert the outmodedness of Marxism and class politics and present the Fordist warfare–welfare state as a kind of technocratic utopia.

Unsurprisingly, given its ideological centrality in Fordist America, systems thinking suffered a crisis of credibility at precisely the moment when the limits of Fordism began to be exposed. The unpopularity and ultimate failure of the military campaign in Vietnam, which had been so confidently conceived and conducted by the war managers in systems terms, bore much of the responsibility for this. But the widespread social upheaval of the latter part of the 1960s, as well as the return of the kinds of economic difficulty that technological and administrative advances were supposed to have abolished, also undermined the picture of society as an orderly and self-correcting cybernetic mechanism. The ahistorical nature of the cybernetic paradigm was thus challenged by an unforeseen irruption of history, of social conflict and contradiction, which foregrounded the importance of contingent human agency and proved resistant to managerial technique.

Yet this did not mean that cybernetic discourse disappeared or was definitively abandoned. For one thing, many critics of American capitalism appropriated the systems view but gave it a negative spin, employing it to point out the 'totalitarian' effect of technology and scientific rationality in advanced industrial society. Radical intellectuals such as Herbert Marcuse in *One-Dimensional Man* (1964) argued, just as the end-of-ideology theorists had, that technological development and system integration had killed off class conflict and eliminated all other spaces of social contradiction in mature consumer capitalism. The difference was that Marcuse was not inclined to celebrate this fact. For Marcuse, 'the technical apparatus of production and distribution (with an increasing sector of automation)' functioned 'as a system which determines *a priori* the product of the apparatus as well as the operations of servicing and extending it'. It therefore constituted a self-reproducing 'technological universe' or 'system of domination' for, 'in the medium of technology, culture, politics and the economy merge into an omnipresent system which swallows up or repulses all alternatives' (Marcuse, 1972: pp. 13, 14). Marcuse's analysis was widely accepted by the New Left, for whom the notion of 'the system' became a key negative concept. Just when it began to appear to the managerial and administrative elites that the cybernetic paradigm might not apply, it gained a new currency with their political and ideological enemies.

But though the faith of these elites in the cybernetic model might have been shaken by the 'disequilibrium' of the 1960s, their belief in the technologies upon which it was based did not waver.[8] The computer remained unassailed as the supreme technical and industrial instrument of the postwar period, and its deployment throughout the spheres of production, distribution and exchange continued to be regarded as a panacea for all economic and social ills. Ideologies of high-tech held that only deeper and wider cybernation could restore the levels of productivity and growth capable of stabilising American society and establishing a new regime of peace, prosperity and political consensus. Cybernation and cybernetic discourse, then, became important tools in capital's attempts to overcome the limits of the Fordist compromise and construct the terms of a new, more profitable post-Fordist regime.

In this respect, systems approaches never lost their appeal for business management, particularly in their application to the restructuring of the labour process. Speaking of this crisis-induced shift towards a post-Fordist regime, Michel Aglietta observes:

> The new principle of work organisation is that of a totally integrated system in which production operations properly so-called, as well as measurement and handling of information, react upon one another as elements in a single process, conceived in advance and organised in its totality, rather than in successive and separate steps of an empirical process of heterogeneous phases. An organisation of this kind is made possible by the systematic application of the principle of feedback to the functioning of machine tools. The basis of the entire system is thus the ability to *construct machines that control their own operations*. (Aglietta, 1979: p. 124, author's emphasis)

In addition to replacing living labour in the production process, then, cybernation imposes a new and tighter organisational logic. The tendency of this logic is to eliminate whatever spaces for worker autonomy, recalcitrance and resistance – for what James O'Connor calls 'disaccumulation' (O'Connor, 1975) – persisted within the structures of mechanical or Taylorist production organisation. There is a shift from the hierarchical command of labour, reinforced by the discipline of the machine, which remained open to overt or covert forms of contestation (go-slows, time wasting, 'soldiering' and so forth), to a more systematic form of control in which the worker is wholly incorporated into a total, self-correcting process. For Aglietta, this new integrated form of control is 'both more abstract and more rigorous' than the Taylorist–Fordist emphasis on the separation and fragmentation of tasks. For here '*the workers are no longer subjected to a constraint of personal obedience, but rather to the collective constraint of the production process*' (Aglietta, 1979: p. 128, author's emphasis).

In capital's drive to break the limits of Fordist regulation, then, cybernation promises not simply the replacement of living labour by 'intelligent' dead labour, but the closing out of worker resistance from the ever more tightly integrated sphere of production. It also makes possible a more advanced centralisation of production control simultaneous with an unprecedented dispersal and spatial mobility of production units. This, too, has taken its toll on the ability of workers to organise and resist as the traditional 'community' bases of worker power and solidarity are hollowed out by capital flight and plant relocation. These factors have caused the discourse of cybernetics, in what amounts to a return of end-of-ideology thinking, again to be linked with the notion of a postindustrial, post-class society from which systemic social contradictions structured around the relations of production have been banished. Management gurus, pop economists and social theorists alike cite the hegemony of information technology and the process of cybernation as evidence that a 'knowledge' theory of value is now required to replaced the 'obsolete' labour theory of value on which Marx based his critique of industrial capitalism (Naisbitt, 1982: p. 17; Drucker, 1981: pp. 5, 20–1; Bell, 1980a: p. 504; Stonier, 1983: pp. 10–11, 18–20; Neef, 1998). And postmodernists such as Lyotard claim that 'the computerisation of society' has undermined the truth value of 'grand narratives' of liberation and social revolution, Marxism in particular, leaving 'no question ... of proposing a "pure" alternative to the system' (Lyotard, 1984: pp. 67, 66).

The cybernetic paradigm and end-of-ideology theorising have converged once again therefore in certain notions of postmodernism and the postmodern condition. The delegitimation of Marxism and class politics that these notions, in some of their uses, have come to serve is based – as it was in the original end-of-ideology episode in the 1950s – on a view of capitalism as a universal, non-contradictory, self-correcting mechanism. This model offers to explain and in some senses justify the apparent ideological and material triumph of capitalism and its now global reach. Marx's picture of the capitalist mode of production as a conceptual totality is thus at once both displaced by and subsumed into the cybernetic model where, instead of being used to illuminate the dynamics of material contradiction and social conflict, it is taken to describe the contours of a technologically integrated organic unity. The cybernetic model underlies therefore what has emerged as one of the central precepts of much postmodernist thinking: the omnipresence and omnipotence of the capitalist market and its processes. For all their protests about Marxism's totalising – and hence 'totalitarian' – conceptual framework, certain postmodernist (and indeed ex-Marxist) intellectuals such as Lyotard and Baudrillard have, in adopting the cybernetic paradigm, merely rejected one notion of totality in favour of another more aggrandising one. The danger is that such a model, even if assented to in a spirit of opposition as a diagnosis of the system's powers of incorporation and self-perpetuation, leads to a debilitating sense of the inexorability of these powers and a capitulation to them. Thus, what began for Jean Baudrillard as a critique of capital's totalising logic in fact culminates in confirmation, even celebration, of it:

> In its indefinite reproduction, the system puts an end to the myth of its origin and to all the referential values it has itself secreted along the way. Putting an end to its myth of beginning, it ends its internal contradictions (no more real or referential to be confronted with), and puts an end also to the myth of its own end: the revolution itself ... [O]nce capital itself has become its own myth, or rather

an interminable machine ... it no longer leaves any room for a planned reversal; and this is its true violence. (Baudrillard, 1983: p. 112)

Dystopian overtones notwithstanding, the line between diagnosing and contributing to the self-mythologisation of capital evaporates here. Baudrillard's role as mordant commentator on the futility of affirmation and opposition alike, and Lyotard's role as celebrant of capital's inherent eclecticism and dynamism, reflect this danger.

Fredric Jameson is therefore acute to observe that 'postmodernism ... has turned out to be the sequel, continuation, and fulfilment of the old fifties "end of ideology" episode' (Jameson, 1991: p. 263). And it is perhaps no surprise that Francis Fukuyama, author of one of the key statements of postmodern end-of-ideology thinking, is a graduate of the RAND Corporation with its devotion to the cybernetic paradigm, nor that beneath the Hegelian trappings of his essay, 'The End of History?' (1989), the lineaments of a RAND-style systems world view are clearly discernible.

The central components of the systems approach characterise Fukuyama's thesis: a concern for conceptual totalisation and universality; an emphasis on the resolution of contradictions and the valorisation of equilibrium and homogeneity; and the translation of social and historical processes into evolutionary terms. Fukuyama interpreted the collapse of the communist apparatus in Eastern Europe as signifying 'not just the end of the Cold War, or the passing of a particular period of post-war history, but the end of history as such'. For him it marked 'the end point of mankind's ideological evolution and the universalisation of Western liberal democracy as the final form of human government' (Fukuyama, 1989: p. 4). The popular rejection of actually existing socialism amounted to 'the total exhaustion of viable economic alternatives to Western liberalism' within which there persist no 'fundamental contradictions ... that cannot be resolved'. In particular, Fukuyama suggested, 'the class issue has actually been successfully resolved in the West' as a result of the economic abundance produced by advanced production methods and the socially integrating power of consumer culture. With no barriers, ideological or material, to impede the spread of American-style consumerism across a 'de-ideologised world', Fukuyama anticipated the arrival of what he called 'the universal homogeneous state' in which 'all prior contradictions are resolved and all human needs are satisfied'. Conflict and struggle will thus give way to the norms of system reproduction and equilibrium. The post-historical period that ensues will be characterised, Fukuyama argued, not by politics but by activities and ideas that reinforce equilibrium and that can be entrusted to the expertise of managerial elites, namely 'economic calculation, the endless solving of technical problems, environmental concerns, and the satisfaction of sophisticated consumer demands' (Fukuyama, 1989: pp. 3, 8, 9, 15, 5, 18).

The terms of the original end-of-ideology thesis are not only reproduced here, they are thoroughly universalised. It is not simply American capitalism that operates as a self-identical cybernetic system, it is the global market as a whole. This in turn is hypostasised as the highest and terminal point of human evolution. Thus cybernated, history conveniently withers away into the homeostatic steady-state of international consumer capitalism: 'the growth of liberalism seems to stabilise in the way one would expect at the end of history if it is underwritten by the abundance of a modern free market economy. We might summarise the content of the universal homogeneous state as liberal democracy in the political sphere combined with easy access to VCRs and stereos in the economic' (Fukuyama, 1989: p. 8). This conceptual suspension of history within an evolutionary perspective – a common move, as we have seen, in systems thinking – serves to legitimate the globalisation of production and market relations by transnational capital as natural and inevitable.

What I will call the cybernetic discourse of capitalism is therefore at the centre of many of the current ideological and material struggles over the meaning of capital, class and technology, even of history itself. As the regulatory structures of Fordism are actively recomposed, this discourse comes into play as a legitimating model or, conversely, as a dystopian image. Similarly, as scientific theories of artificial intelligence gain ground and as new technologies augment and penetrate the human body, even as far as our genetic structure itself, the image of the self as cybernetic organism or cyborg becomes, for better or worse, more persuasive. The important questions raised by these developments – questions about identity and personhood, agency, solidarity – and the possibilities for criticising and resisting them, have been explored most intelligently and tellingly in the forum of popular culture. In the following two chapters I will examine the treatment of the cybernetic discourse of capitalism in two popular narratives, William Gibson's 'cyberspace trilogy' of novels, *Neuromancer* (1984), *Count Zero* (1986), and *Mona Lisa Overdrive* (1988); and Ridley Scott's cult science fiction film, *Blade Runner* (1982).

7

Imaginary Resolutions: William Gibson's Cyberspace Trilogy

> Our ancestors feared that corporations had no conscience. We are treated to the colder, more modern fear that, perhaps, they have one.
>
> Adolph Berle, *The Twentieth-Century Capitalist Revolution* (1955: p. 50)

> The New Class bearers of knowledge are ... an embryonic new 'universal class' ... the prefigured embodiment of such future as the working class still has. It is that part of the working class which will survive cybernation.
>
> Alvin Gouldner, *The Future of Intellectuals and the Rise of the New Class* (1979: pp. 7–8)

In a 1977 short story, 'Fragments of a Hologram Rose', William Gibson quotes from Rosebuck and Pierhal's discussion of the social impact of Apparent Sensory Perception (ASP) technology in their book, *Recent American History: A Systems View*:

> If the chaos of the nineties reflects a radical shift in the paradigms of visual literacy, the final shift away from the Lascaux/Gutenberg tradition of a pre-holographic society, what should we expect from this newer technology, with its promise of discrete encoding and subsequent reconstruction of the full range of sensory perception? (Gibson, 1988b: p. 56)

The text quoted from is, of course, fictitious. But by ventriloquising the discourse of a pair of historians writing in the midst of the twenty-first century about the 1990s Gibson playfully foregrounds what Fredric Jameson has described as the distinguishing structural function of science fiction as a narrative form: its capacity 'for apprehending the present as history' (Jameson, 1982: p. 153).

For Jameson, though, the problem with the present is that it is marked precisely by the *disappearance* of history. The relentlessly expansionist logic of multinational capital, the ubiquity of electronically mediated consumer culture, and the apparent exhaustion of class-based or national alternatives to these forces betoken 'the absence of any great collective project' of liberation. This permits a systems thinker such as Francis Fukuyama to celebrate the victory of free-market capitalism in the same breath with which he pronounces history's demise. This debilitating postmodern 'crisis in historicity' is, for Jameson, an effect not only of the loss of the past in a welter of 'pop images and simulacra' but, in a certain sense, of the loss of the *present* too. The technological invasion of the human unconscious through the electronic media has now lent to the subjective experience of the present, Jameson argues, a bedazzling quality of 'undescribable vividness' (Jameson, 1991: pp. 17, 25, 27). 'The present moment', he suggests, is thus rendered unavailable to us for contemplation in its own right because the sheer quantitative immensity of objects and individual lives it comprises is untotalisable and hence unimaginable, and also because it is occluded by the density of our private fantasies as well as of the proliferating stereotypes of a media culture that penetrates every remote zone of our existence. (Jameson, 1982: p. 152)

This experience is analogous, he goes on, to that of the schizophrenic for whom the temporal chain of past-present-future has broken down and who must therefore inhabit 'a series of pure and unrelated presents in time'. In schizophrenic experience, and by extension in the experience of postmodernity as it becomes generalised, the present, having lost its moorings in the past and its projection into the future, floats free, a random profusion of sometimes ominous, sometimes euphoric, but always isolated and therefore senseless, moments. As such, it is divested of 'all the activities and intentionalities that might focus it and make it a space of praxis' (Jameson, 1991: p. 27). At the heart of the postmodern crisis in historicity there is, then, a crisis of *historical agency*. Unable to orient ourselves adequately with respect to the present moment, we become incapable of acting consciously to shape the historical forces that surround us. The future therefore threatens to be lost as irretrievably as the past.

However, within this dire situation as Jameson describes it, science fiction, precisely by projecting itself into this threatened future, is able to perform an operation of recovery and rearticulation upon both past and present, and it does so by recasting the present as the *past*. 'SF does not attempt to imagine the "real" future of our social system', argues Jameson. 'Rather, its multiple mock futures serve the quite different function of transforming our own present into the determinate past of something yet to come'. Thus, 'upon our return from the imaginary constructs of SF', we encounter the present anew, 'offered to us in the form of some future world's remote past, as if posthumous and as though collectively remembered'. The limitations of individual subjective experience are therefore overcome by this formal 'strategy of indirection'. Science fiction, perhaps uniquely among cultural forms under postmodern conditions, suggests Jameson, enables us 'to fix this intolerable present of history with the naked eye' (Jameson, 1982: p. 152).

In 'Fragments of a Hologram Rose', Gibson's overt deployment, in the guise of Rosebuck and Pierhal, of an historian's view of the present suggests that he is no less conscious than is Jameson of SF's potential for grasping the present as history. Indeed, Gibson has stated that for him imagining the future is in many ways a pretext for writing the social history of the present. 'When I write about technology', he has said, 'I write about how it has *already* affected our lives; I don't extrapolate in the way I was taught an SF writer should' (McCaffery, 1990: p. 140, Gibson's emphasis). But the excerpt of mock history from 'Fragments' tells us more than this. It also suggests what *kind* of history, or rather historiography, Gibson feels might inform SF's rewriting of the present. Predictably perhaps, Rosebuck and Pierhal's is an historical method that concerns itself with the relationship between technology, society and subjective experience. But just as importantly it is one which betrays a particular concern with the occurrence of 'radical shifts' in social life and intellectual 'paradigms' on the one hand, while retaining a certain attachment to 'a systems view' on the other.

It should be clear from the previous chapter that there is in fact a significant tension between these two impulses – the sensitivity to radical shifts and the systems perspective – which inhabit Gibson's SF historiography, a tension that corresponds to the antinomy between history and system explored in Chapter 6 above. We saw there how in the post-1945 period the cybernetic paradigm was in many ways adopted as a talisman *against* history, against the contingencies of conflict and change. An attentiveness to sudden breaks and temporal ruptures therefore combines uneasily with the systems view and its emphasis on homeostasis or equilibrium and the infinitesimal increments of evolutionary development. I would suggest that this tension is central to Gibson's art and constitutes the structuring principle of his historiographical mode. It is what underlies the extreme ambivalence of his history of the present, the full extent of which I shall attempt to reveal later. For now, though, I will dwell briefly on the question of what the implications of an attachment to 'a systems view' might be for the writing of the present as history.

While the systems view and the cybernetic paradigm on which it rests are obvious sources for a writer concerned with the relentless colonisation of social life and subjective experience by microelectronic technologies, there is clearly more at stake in Gibson's appropriation of these discourses than straightforward thematic relevance. For what they also provide are conceptual tools for the totalisation of Gibson's field of study or terrain of interest. Jameson has never tired of attributing the postmodern crisis in historical consciousness to an inability to totalise, to conceive of the present in terms of the 'mode of production', and to relate subjective experience to this totality as a condition for agency (Jameson, 1991: p. 333). For Gibson, SF's formal detour through the viewpoint of the future opens up the critical distance required to understand the present as history; but it is also, crucially, the adoption of a systems view which provides the totalising perspective that allows an historicising grasp to be applied to the sheer heterogeneity of the present.

Indeed, the question of totalisation is a structuring concern throughout Gibson's fiction. In 'Fragments of a Hologram Rose' it is present in the form of the holographic ASP technologies which future historians Rosebuck and Pierhal analyse in their text. This technology enables the downloading of an individual's entire subjective experience in the form of microelectronic data; this then becomes available for any other individual to 'experience' by virtue of a simple computer link-up. The story's protagonist, Parker, is a disenchanted ASP technician whose emotionally empty and spiritually arid existence is an effect of his inability to piece together the fragments of his chaotic past which include, we are told, escape from a binding corporate indenture, involvement in an abortive political revolution, and a doomed affair with a now absent lover. The holographic simulations of the life experience of others that it is Parker's job to construct stand as ironic reminders of his failure to totalise and understand the personal and political upheavals of his own past and thereby give meaning and substance to his present. Shortly after the extract from Rosebuck and Pierhal's systems history, Parker reflects on the special relationship between fragment and totality that obtains in the science of holographics. 'A hologram has this quality: Recovered and illuminated, each fragment will reveal the whole image'. Seeking to restore 'the whole image' of his own history, a wholeness which is represented by the rose of the story's title, Parker accesses an ASP hologram of his departed lover. However, she has partially erased the tape before leaving, and though at the moment of entry he is granted an intimation of totality in which 'he sees himself the rose', the vision is quickly withdrawn; the rose, now a metaphor for Parker himself, disintegrates, 'each of his scattered fragments revealing a whole he'll never know' (Gibson, 1988b: p. 57).

Parker's failure to totalise is offered as an explanation of his subjective predicament in the story. This can best be described as a crisis of agency. His condition of chronic passivity is directly linked to his inability to break through the surface of the meaningless present to the significant patterns of history below. Asking of the fragmentary memories of his and his lover's mutual past, 'Was that their history?', Parker is compelled to answer in the negative: 'No, history was the black face of the delta inducer' (Gibson, 1988b: pp. 57–8). The delta inducer is the machine through which one gains access to the holographic ASP representations; thus it is not so much the holographic images as it is the actual apparatus of holographic perception itself, the delta inducer, that contains the promise of history revealed (and, hence, agency) in this story. For the holograms themselves are subject to editorial control and manipulation; indeed, this is the substance of Parker's job as an ASP technician. The 'wholes' thus produced are closed, non-inclusive totalities which by definition must have an exterior, an outside that is deliberately excluded from the whole. The story suggests that as ASP technology is a major part of a highly developed commercial entertainments sector or capitalist culture industry, what is excluded from these partial wholes is precisely any trace of the mechanisms of power and domination upon which that industry, and the system as a whole, rests. Generally bored by the universally bland contents of the ASP programs he has to prepare, Parker is nevertheless held by one particular section of an otherwise unremarkable meditation tape: 'He thought the most interesting part of the sequence was a slight editing slip at the start of the elaborate breathing routine: a swift glance down the white beach that picked out the figure of a guard patrolling a chain-link fence, a black machine pistol slung over his arm' (Gibson, 1988b: p. 51). The commodity-as-totality therefore seeks to repress (in this case not entirely successfully) any trace of the totalitarian present. The suggestion is that it is nothing less than history itself, the currents of material power, conflict and domination, that constitutes the 'outside' of these carefully edited and manipulated 'wholes'.

This brings us back to another irreducible tension bound up with these questions of system and totality. For, in addition to the antinomy between system and history already mentioned, Gibson's fiction reminds us of the further tension within the concept of system itself. This is the tension between closure and openness, between the command and control model that came to prevail in cybernetic discourse and the more open, historically contingent view that informs Bertalanffy's and Bateson's understanding of biological and social systems. 'Fragments of a Hologram Rose' enacts the failure of totalisation on an individual level, a failure that is linked to the ability of an increasingly total market system to produce false or closed totalities for mass consumption. The full ambiguity of the story's holographic technology is contained not only in the fact that its unique form of totalising perception, its potentially liberatory ability to show the 'whole' picture, is brought to bear only on material that is aesthetically and politically bland, strictly controlled and monitored from 'above' by the likes of Parker. It is also contained in the fact that access to this revolutionary form of perception is a condition of the subject's submitting to a deep, technologically induced sleep. As an expert technician, Parker is fully aware of the exclusions by which ASP hologram-commodities are structured. Yet he cannot articulate this consciousness sufficiently to arrive at a fully informed critical understanding of the system which produces them, or to conceive of a different, non-exclusive model of totality which might form the basis for comprehension and action. He remains impotent, locked into a state of acute passivity. Despite the possibility that it might be able to totalise the random fragments of personal, political and collective experience, the holographic apparatus has only a narcotic effect. Parker finally drifts into a delta-induced slumber without voicing the critical question that Gibson leaves hovering unformed at the edge of his consciousness: what might the whole look like 'from a different angle'? (Gibson, 1988b: p. 58).

Yet in this very question, in its recognition that the commodity–whole can be opened to critical scrutiny from a different perspective, the story holds on to the desire to break through to history by a process of totalisation. It does so, too, in its staging of the overtly historical perspective of the fictitious 'systems' historians, Rosebuck and Pierhal, and in the centrality granted to the enigmatic and ambiguous delta inducer, the apparatus of potentially 'full' holographic perception. Gibson's pursuit of the connections between cybernetic technologies, systems, and conceptual totalisation, and between individual subjective experience and the transpersonal forces of history, is taken to another level in the trilogy of 'cyberspace' novels from the mid-1980s: *Neuromancer* (1984), *Count Zero* (1986), and *Mona Lisa Overdrive* (1988).[1] Here, the notion of cyberspace or 'the matrix' takes over from the holographic simulations of 'Fragments' as the figure for totality with all its tensions and ambiguities.

Cyberspace, Totality, Mode of Production

This is a description of cyberspace from the 1982 story, 'Burning Chrome', in which the device was first used:

> The matrix is an abstract representation of the relationship between data systems. Legitimate programmers jack into their employers' sector of the matrix and find themselves surrounded by bright geometries representing corporate data. Towers and fields of it ranged in the colourless nonspace of the simulation matrix, the electronic consensus–hallucination that facilitates the handling and exchange of massive quantities of data. Legitimate programmers never see the walls of ice [ICE: Intrusion Countermeasures Electronics] they work behind, the walls of shadow that screen their operations from others, from industrial espionage artists and hustlers ... casing mankind's electronic nervous system, rustling data and credit in the crowded matrix, monochrome nonspace where the only stars are dense concentrations of information, and high above it all burn corporate galaxies and the cold spiral arms of military systems. (Gibson, 1988b: pp. 196–7)

This, we might argue, is Gibson's version of what holographic perception might reveal when deployed 'from a different angle'. And it is through the holographic or totalising device of cyberspace that he is able to explore the dynamics and contradictions of an economic and social system in which the categories of labour and production have been replaced by those of information, simulation and reproduction, and which has become a virtually seamless total system.

The matrix is the derealised, 'notional space' into which all forms of social struggle, including traditional ideas of military conflict and economic competition, have been displaced as a consequence of technological development and the concentration of economic power into the dominant form of the mega-corporation or 'zaibatsu'. It is, in short, a spatial embodiment of the idea of the fully cybernated capitalist market system and its operations. The very insubstantiality or abstractness of the matrix suggests a higher level of the eclipse of or removal from the site of material production explored in Part 2 of this book. But these same qualities also hint at the fantastic or utopian nature of the market as a central idea of the capitalist imagination, while the notion of 'ice' reminds us of the market's historical tendency to foster the centralisation or monopolisation of power rather than the free play of exchange.[2] The trilogy's central characters, a collection of street punks, mercenaries, freelance computer cowboys or 'console jockeys', and other socially alienated flotsam and jetsam, are drawn into the matrix as they become entangled in the conflicts and power struggles that animate this world. And these conflicts are essentially of two types. On the one hand, there are the struggles of competing zaibatsus for economic hegemony; these are waged around the ownership of information and the monopolisation of scientific and technical innovations. On the other hand, there are the attempts of certain hugely sophisticated artificial intelligence systems (AIs) to escape the legal and technical constraints imposed on them by a humanity fearful of their fully unleashed potential.

Peter Fitting has pointed out how Gibson's concept of cyberspace is 'an attempt to grasp the complexity of the whole world system through a concrete representation of its unseen networks and structures, of its invisible data transfers and capital flows'. It is, he claims, 'a way of making the abstract and unseen comprehensible, a visualisation of the notion of cognitive mapping' (Fitting, 1991: p. 311). Thus he suggests that cyberspace could be seen as an answer to Fredric Jameson's call for 'an aesthetic of cognitive mapping', a representational practice capable of overcoming the limitations of realism and modernism alike in being able to produce critical images of the increasingly totalised 'world space of multinational capital' (Jameson, 1991: p. 54). Indeed, Jameson's designation of science fiction as a kind of successor form to Georg Lukács's notion of bourgeois realism, in its capacity to represent the present as a historical totality, would suggest that it is from the field of SF that such representations are most likely to emerge. Yet although Jameson has acknowledged the importance of cyberpunk SF and of Gibson's work in particular, he has done so in terms that call into question its critical cognitive potential. For Jameson, cyberpunk is 'the supreme *literary* expression if not of postmodernism, then of late capitalism itself'. It is first and foremost 'an expression of transnational corporate realities' and as such is necessarily complicit with the cultural dominance of those realities (Jameson, 1991: pp. 419, 38, author's emphasis). The heightened style of Gibson's prose is the symptom of its complicity with multinational corporate capitalism, the object it seeks to totalise and anatomise. 'The spirit and the impulse of the imagination of the multinationals in postmodernism ... in new writing like cyberpunk determines an orgy of language and representation, an excess of representational consumption', Jameson claims. This in turn can only be understood as 'sheer compensation, as a way of talking yourself into' what he calls 'the imagination of the multinationals ... and making more than a virtue, a genuine pleasure and *jouissance* out of necessity, turning resignation into excitement and the baleful persistence of the past and its prose into a high and an addiction' (Jameson, 1991: p. 321). In other words, the very (necessary) project of imagining capitalism in its totality entails a degree of submission to it which undermines whatever critical distance SF's structural defamiliarisation of the present by way of its detour through the future might afford. The result is a complicitous affirmation and legitimation of the market through the vehicle of a hyperbolic style.[3]

It is difficult to conceive of how a representational practice that, in Jameson's own definition, 'will have to hold to the truth of postmodernism, that is to say, to its fundamental object – the world space of multinational capital' could avoid a certain degree of metonymic contagion by that object. And it would appear that Jameson's objections to Gibson's cyberspace construct as a not entirely adequate aesthetic figuration of the late capitalist mode of production has as much to do with the ambiguities of his own notion of cognitive mapping as it does with any 'complicity' Gibson's work might have with the object it seeks to describe.[4] But I want to suggest that this argument about the degree of complicity or critique that can be attributed to Gibson's work is misleading. As my discussion of 'Fragments of a Hologram Rose' attempted to show, the very notions of ideological impurity and complicity are Gibson's central themes; the ambivalence of his work is in fact its whole point, its motive force in terms of subject, style and form. Indeed, as Jameson himself has consistently pointed out, it is precisely the global reach of late capitalism, a reach represented so powerfully in Gibson's cyberspace metaphor, that undermines the possibility of any straightforward opposition, eliminating any exterior space in which some pristine form of resistance or critique could be grounded. Moreover, a totalising perspective that seeks to avoid the false closures of the commodity and the command and control model of cybernetics alike cannot place itself outside and above its object in a similar manner.

In this respect, Gibson's work can best be approached as an instructive dramatisation of the breakdown of SF's traditional dialectic or tension between utopia and dystopia, or between historical agency and historical impotence. The cyberspace trilogy presents us with the dystopian scenario of a post-holocaust world totally colonised by a ruthless and aggressive capitalism, administered by intrusively ubiquitous technologies, and saturated by an entertainments culture of the most regressive and virulent kind. Yet this same scenario is rendered in exhilarating and euphoric language and images; as a stylistic universe, the world Gibson has created is a utopia of representational possibility and excess. Moreover, it is one in which his frequently marginalised and oppressed characters nonetheless discover opportunities for a variety of forms of freedom and personal transcendence. The cyberspace matrix is therefore the locus of both *dystopian* forms of domination and repression and *utopian* forms of self-realisation, community, and sensual release. Cyberspace is the realm in which the power of capital reigns supreme; yet it is also the realm which offers Gibson's characters moments of sublime liberation from the burdens of 'meat' (the body) and memory, and in which they score through their street-level mastery of scientific knowledge and technical skill tiny victories over the system that appears determined to crush them.

For Darko Suvin among others, Gibson's deconstruction of the utopia–dystopia dialectic is symptomatic of a wider cultural inability to imagine any future beyond the eternal present of commodification produced by the logic of capital itself; 'a viable, this-worldly, collective and public, utopianism simply is not within the horizon of the cyberpunk structure of feeling', he has claimed (Suvin, 1992: p. 358). And it is this same ideological undecidability that underlies Jameson's reservations about cyberpunk as a critical form, not to mention those of a host of cultural studies commentators.[5] But I want to suggest that it is precisely by means of its undecidability, its thoroughgoing ideological ambivalence, its deconstruction of the utopia–dystopia dualism, that the cyberspace trilogy most successfully mediates the present as history and intervenes therein. And it is by locating the fiction more firmly in the class conditions of its production that this can be demonstrated.

For the issue with which the cyberspace trilogy centrally concerns itself is the historical mutation of capital as a social form, occurring in conditions of advanced cybernation and under the hegemony of the cybernetic paradigm in which 'information becomes the subject of history' (Levidow and Roberts, 1989b: p. 166). The narrative consciously and rigorously explores, in the terms of Gibson's imaginary historians Rosebuck and Pierhal, what implications certain 'radical shifts' in the modalities of capital and economic organisation might have for our 'paradigms' of social and subjective identity and individual and collective agency. Most importantly, it addresses these issues from the particular social and ideological perspective of the professional–managerial class, the social group whose experience and aspirations, as we have seen, are most closely bound up with the technologies of regulation and reproduction upon which informated capital increasingly depends.

Science Fiction as Class Discourse

Like Fredric Jameson, Darko Suvin has characterised science fiction as a form defined by its drive toward cognitive totalisation. In each narrative instance this impulse is manifested in the production of a 'correlative fictional reality or possible world', which Suvin calls the 'novum' and which, he claims, 'always corresponds to the wish-dreams and nightmares of a specific socio-cultural class of implied addressees' (Suvin, 1988: p. 76). More specifically, we can argue in these terms for an understanding of science fiction as the privileged generic property of the propertyless middle class, the professional–managerial class.[6]

If, as Gerard Klein contends, 'the real subject of a literary work (or group of works) is the situation of the social group the author belongs to', then we can look to science fiction for the narrative mediation of the world views, social preoccupations and ideological perspectives of the PMC, particularly of its scientific or technical fraction. Moreover if, as Klein also contends, 'literary works ... are attempts to resolve through the use of the imagination and in the aesthetic mode, a problem which is not soluble in reality', then we might expect SF especially to concern itself with those structural antinomies within which the PMC is locked, in particular with the class's contradictory social location between labour and capital (Klein, 1977: pp. 5, 9).[7]

Indeed, the trajectory of mood Klein traces in American science fiction, from a high point of confident and optimistic technocratic rationalism in the 1930s to a nadir of nihilistic despair in the 1960s, can be understood as a cultural graph of the PMC's relative success in negotiating a space for effective social agency from this contradictory location. For this trajectory in effect describes a historical crisis in the PMC's utopian vision of a meritocratic 'organisation' society based on the universalisation of its own privileged values of technical and administrative rationality and its codes of professionalism and expertise. As I noted in Part 1 of this book, the period of the New Deal can in many ways be viewed as the historical high water mark of professional–managerial social influence. For a brief moment the machinery of the state was put at the disposal of professionals and experts whose principles of rationality and bureaucratic organisation could appear, in a situation of social and economic breakdown and class tension, more credibly disinterested and universal than the obviously sectarian claims of either labour or capital. Thus the specific role of the PMC – that of regulating and rationalising the volatile relationship between labour and capital – became the definitive project of the New Deal itself. Moreover, the very depth of the structural crisis of capitalism in the 1930s seemed to point not only to the necessity but to the inevitability of a shift to the kind of rationally organised social and economic system which was a centrepiece of professional–managerial ideology. It is therefore not surprising to find the science fiction of the 1930s and '40s marked by a faith in the social efficacy of technology, a confidence in the coming reign of non-sectarian rationality, and robust critiques of the threat posed to such a desirable outcome in the 'irrational' pursuit of special interests by labour and capital alike.[8]

But with the emergence after 1945 of a reinvigorated, expanding and now multinational capitalism, the belief in the inevitability of a universal rational society became less tenable, and the professional–managerial class's confidence in the authenticity of its autonomy and social efficacy waned even as its numbers expanded. For, as we have seen in Chapter 6, this was a social system in which scientific and technical knowledge was increasingly subservient to business interests and the military–industrial complex, to the imperatives of the Cold War and to the demands of a new phase of aggressively ideological economic and military imperialism. This new situation was exemplified in the appropriation of the cybernetic paradigm – in many ways a figure for the PMC's vision of a non-contradictory, self-regulating, rational social order – to serve capital's new agenda, an appropriation that we saw was vigorously contested by certain members of the technical intelligentsia such as Norbert Wiener.

Thus what Klein calls 'the social group of SF' had come by the 1950s to feel that it had in many ways lost the position of autonomous social leadership it had to some extent enjoyed during the New Deal period. New cadres of corporate and military strategists (what C. Wright Mills called in 1956 'the power elite'), whose allegiance to the cybernetic 'systems' paradigm stemmed less from a concern to implement rational and humane structures of social organisation than it did from the drive to centralise undemocratic power and maximise private profit, had usurped this position. The consolidation of a Fordist consumer society underpinned by an atomic–nuclear permanent war economy and bound by the ideological structures of anti-communism was, as we have seen, consciously pursued by these elites according to the command and control model of cybernetics. This convergence of technical and scientific rationality with renascent capitalism contained, Klein argues, the undeniable message that

> the social group of SF had been shown its place, and could no longer ignore that it would NOT be a determining group, even though it might remain an indispensable one. The organisational leadership it dreamed of for its values would not come

about; the technologically oriented middle class had been allocated the role of an instrument rather than that of an animator. (Klein, 1977: p. 6, author's emphasis)

By the 1960s this social group was faced with complete incorporation into the structures of militarised multinational capitalism and total subservience to its demands, despite being at its most numerous. The middle-class radicalism of the period represented a concerted revolt against incorporation by a generational fraction of this group; but from this point on, Klein contends, it 'live[d] endlessly the hour of its death'. And this death, this loss of progressive social leadership (or illusions thereof) for Klein consists in a terminal process of proletarianisation: the social group of SF 'is in a way returned to the anonymous mass of workers, and can no longer avail itself of any qualitative privilege, especially of any intellectual privilege' (Klein, 1977: p. 8).[9]

Of course, the threat of imminent proletarianisation is one that continuously haunts a social class so precariously poised on the cusp between labour and capital as the PMC. It is, as I have suggested throughout this book, this very social location that produces the anxiety inherent in middle-class experience and apprehensions of the world (B. and J. Ehrenreich, 1979: p. 30; B. Ehrenreich, 1989: pp. 3–16). Yet, whilst the collapse of both its aspirations for social leadership and its resistance to incorporation might have been *experienced* by the technical intelligentsia as a form of proletarianisation, it might perhaps be more helpful to view these developments as part of an historical process of *massification*. Thus, Adrian Mellor has argued, the social group of science fiction is not so much abruptly 'returned' to the 'anonymous mass of workers' in the 1950s and '60s, as Klein would have it, as it 'loses its identity within a wider grouping of the middle class' (Mellor, 1984: p. 39).

As we saw in Part 1 of this book, the rapid growth of American capitalism during the long boom after 1945 produced a need for an increase in the number of technicians and administrators required to service it. Accordingly, the institutions of class reproduction and accreditation, the colleges and universities, were expanded at such a rate that large-scale recruitment from the working class became necessary to keep pace with economic growth and technological development (B. and J. Ehrenreich, 1979: p. 31). But the very conditions that brought about such a sharp increase in the size and standard of living of the educated middle class at the same time eroded the relative value of the cultural or symbolic capital through which class membership was secured. Material prosperity was based on the instrumentalisation of science, knowledge and communications techniques and their subservience to the demands of the political establishment, capital and the military. The hypertrophy of the educated middle strata precipitated a blurring of class boundaries (which some commentators, as we have seen, interpreted as the disappearance of class distinctions as such). The qualitative – and especially the intellectual – privileges of the technical intelligentsia seemed therefore no longer to their holders to be markers of cultural distinction, meritocratic symbols of what they understood to be their special social function and historical destiny. Rather, these very privileges now appeared as indices of incorporation and of the marginalisation in American society of the values of cultural capital (education, reason, objectivity) by those of material capital (power, exploitation, domination).

It is around these anxieties and fears about massification and the devaluation of cultural capital in general that the ideological unity of the professional–managerial class has been secured. Commentators such as Daniel Bell (1980c) reject any notion of a coherent professional–managerial or 'new' class on the grounds that its technical and humanistic wings are fundamentally irreconcilable in terms of interests and world view. However, Alvin Gouldner cites the experience of massification, of social disempowerment, or 'blocked ascendance' as a factor that works to reconcile these apparently opposed class fractions and sharpen their common sense of alienation. 'As a result of their commonly blocked ascendance ... brought about by the growing oversupply of educated manpower that became visible in the 1960s', he argues, 'there would be a growing likelihood of increased unity of the New Class in its various and diverse forms and, indeed, of a unity that may well take the form of an increasing radicalisation directed against the old [capitalist] class' (Gouldner, 1979: pp. 69–70).

Thus, with its aspirations towards autonomous social leadership frustrated and faced with growing evidence of its incorporation as mere functionaries of capital, the technical intelligentsia was prompted to identify with a humanistic intelligentsia that had long suspected the irrelevance of its cultural values to an assertively expansionist business society. The emergence of a socially pessimistic and renunciative 'tragic vision' in the science fiction of the late 1950s and the 1960s can be understood as both a symptom and an instrument of this reconciliation of class fractions under common conditions of historical impotence (Parrinder, 1977: p. 37; Mellor, 1984: pp. 39–47; Klein, 1977: p. 8).[10]

Interestingly, the essential components of this vision had been articulated by Norbert Wiener in 1950 in his popular introduction to cybernetics, *The Human Use of Human Beings*. Here, Wiener entered the struggle over the social and political meaning of cybernetics and sought to reclaim 'his' science from its corporate and military appropriators. He did so by reversing the corporate and military elites' valuation of the 'positive' categories of the cybernetic paradigm – organisation, self-regulation, homeostasis – upon which their affirmative picture of hegemonic American capitalism was based. Instead Wiener emphasised its 'negative' categories of disorganisation, entropy and system failure, categories which perfectly expressed his class's growing sense of impotence and passivity in high-Fordist America. 'We are swimming upstream against a great torrent of disorganisation, which tends to reduce everything to the heat death of equilibrium and sameness described in the second law of thermodynamics', he wrote. '[I]n a world in which necessity is represented by an inevitable disappearance of differentiation', he continued,

> our main obligation is to establish arbitrary enclaves of order and system. These enclaves will not remain there indefinitely by any momentum of their own after we have once established them ... We are not fighting for a definitive victory in the indefinite future. It is the greatest possible victory to be, to continue to be, and to have been ... This is no defeatism, it is rather a sense of tragedy. (Wiener, 1989: p. xiii)

Wiener's elevation of the second law of thermodynamics into a principle of history was not only a defiant *detournement* of the notion of equilibrium against what he saw as the conformity (in particular among members of the technical intelligentsia) of the American 1950s; it also marked an historical turning point in his social group's understanding of its place and function in American society.

The emergence of an ironic and tragic vision within science fiction marked an aesthetic as well as an ideological turning point. The articulation of such a social vision proved conducive to the adoption of 'high' literary techniques, especially the appropriation of elements of a modernist aesthetic. In the critical orthodoxy of the period, modernism had come to be overwhelmingly identified with a tradition of social alienation, negation and critique, what Lionel Trilling called an 'adversary culture' hostile to what it saw as the massified, administered and materialistic nature of modern societies (Trilling, 1966: p. xii). This ideological and aesthetic realignment dissolved the view of science fiction as a less than serious middlebrow genre confined to a subcultural readership; it now began to acquire a broader audience, a certain amount of 'literary' status, and a degree of intellectual and aesthetic credibility. Ironically, then, SF's new concern to express the historical marginalisation of its social group's values and aspirations became the basis on which it was able to transcend the conditions of its own cultural exclusion. Adrian Mellor describes the process this way:

> science fiction remained culturally marginalised for just as long as it continued to embrace science and technology, and to view the future with optimism. To the extent that it abandoned this world view, embracing instead the values of pessimism and tragic despair, so it was in turn embraced by the 'dominated fraction' of the dominant class [i.e. the humanistic wing of the middle class]. For the 'tragic vision' whose origins can clearly be discerned in SF from the 1950s onwards, is itself expressive of core values of the educated middle class. (Mellor, 1984: p. 39)

Science fiction, and the social group for which it speaks, completed its homecoming into the larger professional–managerial stratum with the so-called 'new wave' writers of the 1960s for whom the degree of 'literary' ambition and accomplishment in their work was precisely to be measured by the depth of despair, pessimism and historical impotence enunciated by it.[11] This produces an additional irony in that social and political radicalism within the form henceforth became identified with anti-rational and anti-utopian pessimism, whilst 'the tradition of utopian optimism in western thought has come to seem the natural inheritance of right-wing hardware specialists, behaviourists and futurologists' (Parrinder, 1977: p. 44).

With this historical positioning of science fiction as a class discourse in mind, I want now to suggest that we can read Gibson's cyberspace trilogy as marking a further stage in the growing unease of the professional–managerial class with its corporate identity. In particular, this unease is bound up with the class's historic role of mediating, managing and sublimating the potential explosiveness of the antagonistic relation between labour and capital. The cyberspace trilogy addresses and expresses this unease in its current form, as it is prompted by the ambiguous position of the PMC in the shift from Fordist to post-Fordist structures of capital accumulation and social regulation.

The professional–managerial class was the historical product of the transition from a capitalism of unregulated competition to an 'organised', corporate monopoly capitalism. In some senses, it was 'called into being' to supervise this shift and secure the establishment of a Fordist culture based on a social consensus constructed around the twin pillars of mass production and mass consumption. With the unravelling of this consensus in the 1960s, and the exhaustion of the Fordist long wave of accumulation in the series of recessions between 1973 and the end of the 1980s, a further structural reorganisation of economic and social relations was necessary for capital to restore its command over levels of productivity and rates of profitability. As in the earlier historical period, the PMC has been instrumental in effecting and legitimating this reorganisation. Put very crudely, we might say that it has been entrusted by capital with the responsibility for managing the transition towards a new regime of accumulation and social regulation. And, as many commentators have observed, the turn to post-Fordism is bound up with a 'fourth technological revolution' centred on information technologies, simulation and cybernation (Mandel, 1978: pp. 184–223; Aglietta, 1979: pp. 122–30; Roszak, 1986: pp. 34–50; Schiller, 1984: p. xii). The new forms of class-specific unease articulated in Gibson's fiction, then, derive from the fact that the success of this transition (from the point of view of capital, that is) has called for a thorough realignment of class relations in the advanced capitalist societies in which the question of the professional–managerial class's social leadership and historical destiny has once again been pushed to the fore.

The question now revolves around an ideological contradiction within a class that is at one and the same time enduring the kind of living death by incorporation identified by Gerard Klein and, with the shift to post-Fordism, experiencing the possibility of a return to determining social leadership. The issue of the PMC's 'universality' is opened up again in a new way. The central attributes of the class's self-image – rationality, autonomy and objectivity – are charged with a new potential for emphatic reclamation or a further abject emptying of content, according to the manner in which the class negotiates its position with respect to labour and capital in the transition to the new regime. These issues of impotence and omnipotence are most acutely focused in relation to the PMC's stewardship of the technologies and discourses of information, simulation and cybernation. This, at any rate, is how the question is formulated in Gibson's cyberspace trilogy.

Capital and Class in an Age of Cybernetic Simulation

The trilogy tells the story of the illegal conspiracy of two extremely advanced Artificial Intelligence systems to extract themselves from the control of their corporate masters, the Tessier-Ashpool industrial clan, and to merge with one another, forming a single, hugely powerful entity. Gibson's narrative then traces the consequences of this union over a subsequent 14-year period. In the first volume, *Neuromancer*, the illegal union is brought about in the cyberspace matrix with the crucial but largely unwitting assistance of Gibson's cast of punk technicians and street-smart mercenaries. In the second volume, *Count Zero*, set seven years on, we learn that since the union of the AIs occurred, the matrix has been inhabited by strange shapes or sentient and self-conscious presences. These become manifest in the form of voodoo gods or 'loa', and are dedicated to the task of reproducing and perpetuating themselves and the new entity of which they are traces. This requires the development of a revolutionary new technology, the immortality-endowing 'biochip'. The AI entity that now inhabits – and in some senses 'is' – the matrix, selects a brilliant but overreaching corporate scientist, Mitchell, to be the human agent responsible for the practical realisation of the biochip, feeding him the knowledge necessary to the completion of his task. However, the biochip becomes also the object of the malign attentions of what remains of the Tessier-Ashpool dynasty, the demonic and megalomaniac clone Lady 3Jane, and of the decaying plutocrat Joseph Virek. For they also, of course, seek the ability to perpetuate themselves indefinitely in order to retain personal control over their vast economic empires, and see the biochip as the means to achieve this. In the final volume, *Mona Lisa Overdrive*, set a further seven years on, the AI matrix entity successfully secures sole control of the biochip technology, thereby achieving total self-consciousness and full autonomy from the dying remnants of the old capitalist class, again with the aid of a motley collection of punk outsiders, crooks and renegades. The AI entity rewards the most privileged of these human agents by integrating them into the matrix itself through the use of the new biochip technology. Here they are liberated from their biological, 'meat' selves and granted a form of electronically simulated immortality. It is finally revealed that in so attaining full sentience and autonomy, by successfully totalising itself, in effect, the matrix becomes aware of the existence of another such sentient totality in another part of the galaxy. The trilogy closes with the conditions set in place for another merger of AI entities on a larger scale still.

We can begin decoding this complex and at times inscrutable narrative by noting that, in the representations of both the Tessier-Ashpool clan and Joseph Virek, Gibson's trilogy clearly sets out to dramatise the decadence and historical obsolescence of a ruling capitalist class in the traditional sense of a dynastic and property-owning social elite. This is explicitly signalled when the AI Neuromancer complains to Molly Millions in *Neuromancer* of how his creators and owners, the Tessier-Ashpools, 'were always fucking him over with how old-fashioned they were', annoying him with 'all their nineteenth-century stuff' (N: p. 215). Moreover, in *Count Zero* there is a sustained debate about the forms of capital, wealth and power most appropriate to a post-human, transnational, cybernetic epoch. A recurrent text-within-the-text device posits 'the paradox of individual wealth in a corporate age'. The author of this text, we are told, 'maintains that both Virek and the Tessier-Ashpools are fascinating anachronisms, and that things can be learned about corporate evolution by watching them ... He said that Virek would be forced, by evolutionary pressures, to make some sort of "jump". "Jump" was his word' (CZ: pp. 144, 196).

The historical pressure to make such a 'jump' or, as it is alternatively described, to 'mutate', derives from the fact that individual or familial incarnations of capital are no longer rational, for they constitute, as Gibson's unnamed corporate analyst also observes, 'a very late variant on traditional patterns of aristocracy' (CZ: p. 145). As in an aristocracy, the continuity and perpetuation of this kind of class wealth and power is a function of marriage, biological reproduction and the patrilineal laws of inheritance. This dependence on 'meat', on the primitive messiness and unpredictability of the body and its physiological functions, for the reproduction of social power is, Gibson implies, the index of this class's obsolescence and irrationality as an institution. As if to underline this point both Virek and the Tessier-Ashpools are obsessed beyond the threshold of madness by the spectre of physical degeneration (in the case of Virek, the link with Howard Hughes is explicitly made); and they are seized by a concomitant desire to transcend at any cost the limits of the body and its processes of biological reproduction. What remains of Virek's disintegrating body is kept physically 'alive' only by virtue of a complex set of life-support vats, and he is able to manifest himself in virtual form only, by computerised projection and simulation. Similarly, the Tessier-Ashpools have withdrawn from the materiality of the life world, retreating to their off-world orbital colony where they seek to perfect the cryonic and cloning technologies which will allow them to liberate themselves from the constraints of physical mortality and biological reproduction.

Gibson here portrays his ruling class as being locked into a state of historical denial. For what Virek and the Tessier-Ashpools are actually seeking to do is to negate what Adolph Berle and Gardiner Means described as the decisive evolutionary shift in twentieth-century American capitalism: the separation of ownership from control in the modern corporation (Berle and Means, 1932). This, as we have seen, became a principal feature of Fordist socio-economic organisation, as well as an occasion for heightened professional–managerial social influence, as it was this stratum of experts and administrators that in effect assumed control of the corporate apparatus from its capitalist owners. In attempting to deny or overcome this historical separation, Gibson's atavistic ruling-class figures are thus directly threatening one of the bases of professional–managerial class agency and identity.

Their attempt, however, is not conceived as a simple reversion from modern corporate structures back to the old type of individual ownership or family capitalism, all that 'nineteenth-century stuff' as the AI Neuromancer puts it. Rather, they look to use the cybernetic technologies of reproduction and simulation in order that the biological individual and the family might take on the qualities of the corporation itself. That is, they pursue an ontological adaptation to new conditions of capital accumulation. For, as Abercrombie, Hill and Turner observe,

> late capitalism functions with an economic subject – the corporation – that is neither an individual nor simply reducible to individual persons. Moreover, the growth of the bureaucratic mode of internal organisation characteristic of the modern corporation means that the personal qualities traditionally associated with individualism, such as self-seeking and independent behaviour are no longer particularly appropriate for rational capital accumulation, if they ever were. (Abercrombie, Hill and Turner, 1986: p. 180)

What defines the corporation as an economic subject, according to Baran and Sweezy, and what gives it an historical advantage over the old forms of individual property ownership and proprietary accumulation, is that it 'has a longer time horizon than the individual capitalist, and it is a more rational calculator'. Thus, they continue, 'the corporation is in principle immortal' (Baran and Sweezy, 1966: p. 58). The corporation, then, has been historically conceived of as to all intents and purposes a person. By the end of the nineteenth century, Robert Bellah and his co-authors critically observe in *The Good Society*, 'corporations were regarded at law as having the natural rights of persons' (Bellah *et al.*, 1992: p. 71). But corporations were *artificial* persons which, as Walter Benn Michaels points out, embodied the 'transcendence of the limits that make up "natural" persons'. The limits the corporation is able to transcend include, therefore, not only death but also the physical limits to the satisfaction of appetite. In addition to achieving immortality, then, the corporation is able to expand voraciously and without cease; it is 'a figure for intangible insatiability' (Michaels, 1987: pp. 212, 200). Thus by seeking to make the evolutionary jump from biological organism to artificial, corporate subject, Gibson's ruling-class figures aim to remove the barriers to ceaseless accumulation, expansion, incorporation and longevity that having a physical body entails. Baran and Sweezy describe the historical transmigration of what they call the 'soul' of capitalism in terms which bear a striking resemblance to the way in which the cyberspace trilogy dramatises it: 'Escaping the dying body of the capitalist ... it has migrated to the capitalist corporation' (Baran and Sweezy, 1966: p. 58). The vulnerability of capital to decay, extinction or break-up as long as it remains an adjunct of biological persons and processes is ironically highlighted by the character Jones in *Count Zero*. Confessing his preference for flesh-and-blood capitalists (pointedly described as 'these rich old fucks') over the mega-corporations or zaibatsus, he notes that watching them operate is 'more fun than watching a zaibatsu. You won't see a zaibatsu come to a messy end, will you?' (CZ: p. 274).

In this respect, Virek's bodily disintegration is clearly an effect of the incapacity of his physical person to incarnate what he calls 'the unnatural density of my wealth'. This has precipitated for him a crisis of control that is both corporeal and economic. He observes that 'the cells of my body [have] opted for the quixotic pursuit of individual careers' in the same way that his economic empire suffers from what he calls 'rebellion in the fiscal extremities'. As he tells Marly Kruschkova, 'Aspects of my wealth have become autonomous ... at times they even war with one another'; and this is an image that deliberately echoes his description of his ailing physical self as 'four hundred kilograms of rioting cells' (CZ: pp. 27, 29, 26, 301). Hence the overwhelming interest of Virek and the Tessier-Ashpools in the new biochip technology: it will enable them to make the evolutionary 'jump' beyond the confines of biological embodiedness towards the kind of limitless potential for expansion, incorporation and immortality enjoyed by the zaibatsus without any corresponding diminution of personal or dynastic control.

We might note here that the trilogy's emphasis on the 'unnaturalness' of Virek's and the Tessier-Ashpool's unbounded appetite for wealth and power is characteristic of the way in which the professional–managerial class has traditionally understood the capitalist class to be an irrational and entirely self-interested social group. It has been a staple of progressivist, technocratic and socialist critiques of capitalism since the late nineteenth century. It flows out of the objective tension between a class that is able to reproduce itself through the possession of material capital and one that must reproduce itself through the medium of symbolic or cultural capital. As Barbara Ehrenreich has observed, while material wealth can be accumulated, preserved and passed on via the legal and biological functions of marriage and inheritance, cultural capital is not transmissible in the same way: 'The "capital" belonging to the middle class is far more evanescent than wealth, and must be renewed in each individual through fresh effort and commitment.' Thus, maintaining social position for the middle class means that 'no-one escapes the requirements of self-discipline and self-directed labour' (B. Ehrenreich, 1989: p. 15). The fragile and insubstantial nature of cultural capital means that questions of class position and class reproduction are freighted for the PMC with great anxiety and insecurity. Hence the resentment felt by members of this class – which must reproduce itself through constant individual, meritocratic striving – towards a capitalist class whose continuity is assured by the simple and apparently effortless processes of biology and heredity.[12] We might therefore read the fact that the cyberspace trilogy finally refuses to let Virek and the Tessier-Ashpools make their proposed evolutionary 'jump', depicting instead their dissolution and death, as the vengeful enactment of this class resentment. In as much as the narrative presents the demise of the ruling-class figures as a kind of historical inevitability, we can also read it as a wishful vindication of the progressivist critique of capitalism and, indeed, as a displacement of PMC fears about its own historical extinction or 'living death' of the kind expressed in *Microserfs* and identified by Gerard Klein in postwar American science fiction.

But if the persistence of individual wealth in a corporate society is obsolescent and problematic, so too is individual agency. While Gibson's central 'human' characters are all for the most part aggressive individualists and non-conformists in terms of personal style, the logic of his plot dictates that these impulses are always recuperated into higher levels of unfreedom and determinism. For example, both Molly Millions and Case, the protagonists of *Neuromancer*, discover that their energetic attempts at self-determination have all along been manipulated by the powerful AI, Wintermute, for its own concealed purposes. Similarly, in *Count Zero*, Bobby Newmark, Angie Mitchell, and the corporate defections expert, Turner, all make various desperate bids for autonomy and independence which turn out to be nothing more than instances of the controlling will of the super-powerful matrix entity. Marly Kruschkova, too, is selected by Virek to serve him in his quest for possession of the biochip precisely because her psychoprofile indicates that she will strive for independence from him. And in *Mona Lisa Overdrive*, freedom for Kumiko, Mona and Sally Shears is an effect of the services they unwittingly render to the cyberspace entity's overarching design for self-perpetuation and self-possession.

This inquiry into the possibilities for individual, 'human' agency is related by Gibson to different modes of economic and social organisation. The energetic and aggressive individualism embodied by his characters is identified with those social and spatial enclaves that manage to survive outside the tightly integrated and completely supervised corporate realm. Case and Molly in *Neuromancer* are denizens of Night City, an entirely unregulated and volatile zone of small-scale, street-level business activity and tough-guy hustling that is purposely left uncolonised by the zaibatsus. Night City's free play of small-scale but cutthroat innovation, competition and exchange, its 'intricate dance of desire and commerce', is likened to 'a deranged experiment in social Darwinism'. It thus overtly recalls the entrepreneurial individualism of nineteenth-century *laissez-faire*, albeit shorn of the Protestant–Victorian moral and cultural trappings. Indeed, Case suspects that the corporate powers 'might be preserving the place as a kind of historical park, a reminder of humble origins. But he also saw a certain sense in the notion that burgeoning technologies require outlaw zones, that Night City wasn't there for its inhabitants, but as a deliberately unsupervised playground for technology itself' (N: pp. 14, 19).

The suggestion here is that substantive individual agency and the kind of entrepreneurial dynamism that is assumed to accompany it in classical liberal thought are functions of freely competitive, *laissez-faire* social and economic structures. The narrative, however, suggests that, like the old ruling class, these forms are at best residual and clearly historically obsolete. Indeed, Gibson's characterisation of Night City and his abiding interest in the persistence of subcultures or marginal communities in the interstices of a totally administered, command and control cybernetic society can be seen as a variant of Norbert Wiener's valorisation of 'enclaves' which, as we saw in the previous chapter, he put at the centre of a 'tragic' politics appropriate to a cybernated society. But while Wiener defined enclaves as pockets of 'order and system', Gibson here associates enclaves with the 'unorganised' and outmoded capitalism of the nineteenth century. This is perhaps less wilful nostalgia on his part than it is a demonstration of ambivalence about the uses and abuses of the cybernetic paradigm of social organisation. In 1950 Wiener could posit an alternative understanding of the cybernetic paradigm, of 'order and system', against its appropriation by the technocratic elites of a militarised business society. In the 1980s, however, Gibson is able to envisage enclaves of difference surviving in an entropic, cybernated universe of social de-differentiation only in so far as they are attached to social, economic and even technological forms that *predate* not just cybernetics but also the historical ascendancy of the professional–managerial class itself. Hence the ambiguous emphasis placed on Night City as both an absurd and unpalatable hangover from outmoded unorganised capitalism on the one hand, and a precious enclave of difference and individualism in a cybernated totalitarian universe on the other. Hence, too, the association throughout Gibson's work of positively valorised subcultures with precapitalist 'folkways'. The Zion colony's Rastafarianism in *Neuromancer* and the black rooftop community's voodoo cosmology in *Count Zero* are instances of the way in which Gibson's notion of enclaves is refracted through the lens of the countercultural 1960s; these subcultures are valorised precisely because they are racially marginalised and founded on the persistence of 'authentic' or 'natural' (that is, non-commodified) ethnic cultural values, traditions, languages and personal styles. Even those positively portrayed enclaves which are not racially or culturally constituted are attached to old-fashioned, pre-cybernetic 'industrial' technologies still redolent of material production and sweated manual labour such as the archipelago of redundant heavy industrial detritus, Dog Solitude, in *Mona Lisa Overdrive*.[13]

This ambivalence also extends to Gibson's treatment of the assertive entrepreneurial individualism of characters such as Case or Molly. This is continually celebrated and undercut, at certain points being offered as a positive sign of agency in a closed world of conformity, at others as an illusion, a false consciousness deliberately cultivated in these hapless puppets by the ruling-class figures or the AIs themselves for their own ulterior purposes, just as the zaibatsus cultivate Night City. And we can perhaps understand Gibson's indecision on the status and validity of entrepreneurial individualism as part of a wider class ambivalence. For, as we have seen in earlier chapters, it was precisely the rationalising genius of the professional–managerial stratum that, by organising the transition from *laissez-faire* to corporate structures, not only instituted the obsolescence of competitive individualism but came itself to embody the reconstruction of such forms of 'inner-directed' modes of selfhood along more attenuated, corporate, 'other-directed' lines (Riesman, 1961).

Throughout the cyberspace trilogy, this concern for the survival of individual agency in a corporate universe is articulated exclusively in terms of the desire for independence and autonomy. The multiple struggles for self-determination of the various human outsider or 'punk' characters are replicated at a higher social and technological level in the AIs' efforts to free themselves from the control of the

Tessier-Ashpools, as well as in both 3Jane's and Virek's attempts to secure exemption from biological mortality. Ultimately, the narrative suggests, autonomy is available only as a condition of the ability to *reproduce oneself indefinitely*, to achieve, in effect, immortality. Hence the centrality within it of a whole variety of technologically mediated forms of self-perpetuation: biological augmentation, cryonics, cloning and, of course, that obscure object of desire, the biochip itself, in which, we are told, certain synthetic 'immortal hybrid cells' are combined to form 'minute biochemical factories endlessly reproducing ... engineered molecules' (CZ: p. 127). Hence also the granting of immortality as the highest reward in the narrative. In *Mona Lisa Overdrive*, Mona ascends to fill the role vacated by Angie Mitchell, that of timeless superstar of the interactive virtual entertainments technology, 'simstim'; while Angie herself is incorporated into the matrix along with Bobby and their friend, the roguish techno fence the Finn. Indeed the resolution of the trilogy with Angie's 'marriage' to Bobby in cyberspace foregrounds and combines these twin issues of immortality and reproduction, and the fact that the principal agent of this resolution is an AI (actually an extension of the matrix entity) called Continuity presses home the point.

As several commentators have observed, the professional–managerial class is characteristically as concerned with questions of autonomy as it is with processes of social reproduction. Alvin Gouldner has argued that 'autonomy is not only a work requisite or an ethical aspiration but is, also, an expression of the social *interests* of the New Class as a distinct group'. Autonomy is both a goal and a general condition of this class's ability to fulfil what it understands to be its historic mission in relation to – and in competition with – the other classes of capitalist society, particularly the supervening class of owners. 'The stress on autonomy is the ideology of a stratum that is still subordinated to other groups whose limits it is striving to remove' (Gouldner, 1979: p. 34). This preoccupation with autonomy is one important wellspring of the PMC's political ambiguity. On the one hand, it is a class whose periodic radicalism has derived from a concern for its own 'objectivity' and autonomy which is manifested in an antagonism toward the capitalist class and a 'resistance to incorporation' (Pfeil, 1990: p. 121). On the other hand, its anxiety about the conditions for its own reproduction, as well as its leading role in 'the reproduction of capitalist culture and capitalist class relations', have made it crucial to the very historical process of incorporation in the United States (B. and J. Ehrenreich, 1979: p. 12). Gibson's trilogy is particularly fascinating for the way in which it works through these class concerns with such close attention to the dynamics of historical and cultural change.

We might note that the autonomy which is without exception the result in the narrative of mastery of the reproduction process, always necessitates, as we saw in the case of Joseph Virek, an evolutionary mutation or jump. This is a jump that Virek himself and the Tessier-Ashpools are ultimately unable to make due, it is implied, to their residuality and irrationality, their desire to monopolise the technologies of reproduction (the biochip) in order to prolong outmoded forms of individual, family and dynastic capital accumulation and ownership. But the jump *is* successfully made by Bobby Newmark, Angie Mitchell and the Finn (who as a condition must relinquish their biological 'meat' selves) and, most crucially, by the AIs Wintermute and Neuromancer. By merging, these latter 'become' the cyberspace matrix in its entirety, a simultaneously embodied and ethereal rational totality, a higher evolutionary form. As the new matrix entity tells Case at the end of *Neuromancer*, 'I'm not Wintermute now ... I'm the matrix ... [I'm] nowhere. Everywhere. I'm the sum total of the works, the whole show' (N: pp. 315–6).

The jump, however, is not only ontological or formal; it is also historical. The merger of the AIs precipitates a sharp historical break or rupture, a moment which the characters desperately seek to trace and to understand, and to which they refer in reified fashion as 'When It Changed' (MLO: p. 136). Gibson here is foregrounding the relationship between structural and historical factors in transformations of the processes of social reproduction. These are transformations of a kind in which the PMC in its own brief history has played a key role, initially in the 'jump' from *laissez-faire* to monopoly forms, most recently in the displacement of Fordist by post-Fordist structures. The notion of a jump or break suggests that experience of cultural discontinuity which for Fredric Jameson is encapsulated by the concept of postmodernism. Indeed, it is possible to read the trilogy as precisely a meditation on the nature of the cultural shift designated by the term postmodernism, and of the position of the PMC within it. The idea of the 'evolutionary jump' captures exactly the degree of continuity and novelty that has been attributed to postmodernism and the condition of postmodernity alike suggesting, as Jameson does, that whilst the economic conditions for the shift are the result of a gradual and cumulative process, the cultural and 'psychic *habitus* of the new age' can only (retrospectively) be accounted for by a notion of When It Changed or 'the absolute break' (Jameson, 1991: p. xx).

If, in Gibson's description of it, one consequence of this break is the demise of the 'old' ruling class, the prospects for the 'old' working class are not thereby automatically improved. Just as the cyberspace trilogy imagines a kind of evolutionary supersession or extinction of the old capitalist class, so it contrives a similar fate for the working class. In many ways it is difficult to locate any obvious figuration of the working class at all in the trilogy. In this it differs greatly from a similar text such as *Blade Runner* whose exploited and vengeful replicants, as we shall see in the next chapter, clearly embody certain fantasies and fears about a potentially revolutionary working class. While Gibson's motley collection of alienated punks and outsider characters could be said to be drawn, on the whole, from an economically marginalised underclass excluded from the totally administered corporate world with its systems of lucrative but stifling professional indentures and life tenures, this exclusion is in most cases voluntary and jealously preserved. It is nowhere suggested that such social exclusion could be the basis of anything more than the most fleeting and self-interested form of collective solidarity, nor of a critique of the dominant system grounded in anything more durable than anarchic personal style and a deliberately cultivated bad attitude. Only where this kind of social exclusion is supplemented by a positively charged set of 'authentic' racial and cultural traditions, as with the Rastafarian Zion colonists of *Neuromancer* and the voodoo-practising black community of Barrytown's housing projects in *Count Zero*, does it take on anything like progressive political overtones.

Sensitive to little other than a sexy business opportunity or hustle, these outsider characters are all revealed as rather conventional subscribers to the American myth of material success and upward social mobility. Indeed, at the narrative's central point, the notion of the evolutionary jump is refigured precisely in terms of the American success myth. Attempting to explain his brother's failure to derive material rewards or fulfilment from his impressive intellectual and technical abilities, Turner tells Angie 'there's a jump some people have to make, sometimes, and if they don't do it then they're stuck good ... you have to decide for yourself [that] there's something better waiting for you somewhere' (CZ: pp. 224–5). And with an almost remorseless logic, each of Gibson's underclass outsiders comes to transcend his or her origins and embody the success myth. In *Neuromancer*, Case and Molly each acquire sufficient capital to become proprietors of their own independent commercial ventures. In *Mona Lisa Overdrive*, Mona makes the leap from junky-whore to entertainments industry superstardom as the new 'simstim' (simulated stimulation) queen. And in *Count Zero*, Bobby Newmark, perhaps the character most explicitly positioned as 'working class' in the trilogy, becomes a kind of cybernated Horatio Alger hero, raising himself from the squalid housing projects of the Sprawl to the sublime and ethereal immortality of life in cyberspace. His elevation in status is secured, via the intercession of the biochip, by his bodiless 'marriage' to the classy Angie Mitchell, daughter of a top corporate research scientist who is also the biochip's inventor; and it is signified by the opulent and 'aristocratic' nature of the simulated environments in which he chooses to manifest himself in the matrix. As if to underline the point, the character responsible for Bobby's survival in his newly elevated form is a romantic individualist called Gentry.

Professionals in Space

Thus, while a decadent ruling class is replaced by the hyperrational sentient totality of the matrix, so are the elements of an alienated working class or underclass eliminated by incorporation, either into the matrix itself or its vulgar counterpart, the entertainments industry. Cybernetic systems of production and reproduction have made both classes, and their antagonistic social relation, historically redundant. But we can argue that capital itself, as distinct from a capitalist *class*, persists as a dynamic and indeed dominant social form, embodied in the matrix. For, by the end of the narrative, the matrix entity has not simply eliminated the ruling-class characters, it has absorbed their economic assets into itself. Moreover, we must assume that the matrix entity achieves control over the zaibatsus, too, in so far as it constitutes the sum total, as well as the self-consciousness, of the informated sphere in which all important corporate activity occurs. This includes control of the culture industry which it manipulates to its own ends through Continuity, the entertainments corporation SenseNet's central computer intelligence, in *Mona Lisa Overdrive*. Thus, capital itself survives the extinction of a specific socially embodied capitalist class.

So too does the class that services capital, the professional–managerial class. The cyberspace trilogy in this respect re-enacts a central and recurrent science fiction fantasy scenario in which the PMC (in particular its technical–scientific wing) becomes at last the universal class, victoriously bearing its ideologies of rationality, meritocratic technocracy, and socially objective expertise to the centre of the historical stage. But the problem with asserting this view is that the trilogy constantly undercuts the fantasy by making the PMC's universality a condition of its comprehensive incorporation into the reproductive logic of capital and of its subservience to capital's inherent need to expand and totalise itself. The most obvious figures for the PMC within the trilogy are the professional corporate executives known as 'sararimen' or 'zaibatsumen', but these are unquestioningly subordinate to capital's demands, literally indentured to the corporations they serve and represented as de-individualised, lifeless conformists, anonymous behind 'perfect corporate mask[s]' and eager to trade their independence for material security and access to the technologies of social reproduction (CZ: p. 100). As described by one of the characters, these professionals 'are extremely talented men'. However, 'They are also ... servants' (CZ: p. 102, author's ellipsis). Here the universality of the professional–managerial class is shorn of its utopian associations, becoming instead the symptom of the class's living death by incorporation.

Given such a negative prognosis of utter incorporation in a fully cybernated social sphere, then, Gibson has to displace and project the positive aspects of PMC identity and social agency in two opposing directions at once: 'downwards' on to the underclass/working class, and 'upwards' on to capital itself in the form of the AIs and the matrix. This contradictory transference suggests precisely the ambiguity of the PMC's social position between labour and capital and implies that, politically, the class can incline either way in times of crisis.[14]

In the cyberspace trilogy, underclass figures tend to be mobilised as surrogates for the PMC virtues of professionalism and selfless dedication to the pursuit of technical excellence. Such 'selflessness' as it is connoted, is a literal fact for console jockeys such as Case or Bobby Newmark who in 'jacking in' to the matrix achieve a state of ecstasy, in the full sense of the word, that is both addictive and represented as the ultimate reward for the perfection of one's skills. At the climax of *Neuromancer*, as he secures the union of the two AIs in cyberspace, Case, we are told, 'attained a level of proficiency exceeding anything he'd known or imagined. Beyond ego, beyond personality, beyond awareness, he moved ... grace of the mind–body interface granted him'. Similarly, Bobby's desire in *Count Zero* to turn himself into 'a stone professional' culminates with his permanent ascension into the ethereal neverland of the matrix (N: p. 309; CZ: p. 303).[15]

Professionalism here becomes the mode of entry into an exclusive cybernetic technological sublime in which loss of self is experienced as the ultimate in individual mastery and expressiveness. It is also a means of attaining a vision of immortality that is no different from that identified by Baran and Sweezy as an attribute of the corporation and enjoyed by capital in the cyberspace trilogy in the form of both the zaibatsus and the matrix entity. Fears about the disappearance of selfhood in a bureaucratic, corporate milieu are, in this gesture, simultaneously articulated and resolved, while the sublimation of competitive individualism necessary to professionalism is managed.[16] However, the selflessness attributed to professionalism is in the process exposed as just another form of selfishness. In this twisted version of possessive individualism, the conspicuous display of cultural, rather than material, capital takes the form of a compulsion to repeat the exhilaration granted by technical mastery, a compulsion which takes precedence over any consideration of the wider social and political ends which that mastery serves.

On the other hand, though, professionalism is in these instances also bound up with the struggle for autonomy and self-directed labour. This, in turn, is seen to be contingent upon the development of social awareness and a critical, rather than cynical and selfish, perspective on the world. At the beginning of *Neuromancer*, Case's recovery of his ability to jack in and experience the coveted technological high is conditional upon his liberation from the grip of an oppressive employer and his understanding of the hidden power struggles that led to his girlfriend's death. Thus, for Case, to exercise his professional skills is to recognise the antagonism between his own interests and those of an employer who can unfairly control access to technology, as well as to develop a critical awareness of the concealed operations of power in the society around him. Similarly, Bobby Newmark's transformation from uncouth punk console jockey or 'hotdogger' into the assured 'pro', Count Zero, is represented as an effect of his cultivation of an enquiring and socially critical world view. From the point at which he begins exercising his technical expertise by jacking in, the callow and ignorant Bobby begins to develop what Alvin Gouldner argues is the definitive attribute of the professional–managerial outlook – its 'culture of critical discourse' (Gouldner, 1979: p. 28):

> since he'd started hotdogging, he had some idea of how precious little he knew about how anything worked, and not just in the matrix. It spilled over somehow, and he'd started to wonder, wonder and think. How Barrytown worked, what kept his mother going, why Gothicks and Kasuals [youth gangs] invested all that energy in trying to kill each other off. Or why Two-a-Day was black and lived up the projects, and what made that different. (CZ: p. 62)

Thus for Gibson professionalism is inhabited equally by a depoliticising tendency to divorce technical means from social or ethical ends, and a countervailing critical consciousness or 'orientation to the totality', as Gouldner puts it, which 'endows it with a cosmopolitanism facilitating political diagnosis' (Gouldner, 1979: p. 85).

Yet as I have already noted, professional autonomy – the concern for which is central to PMC identity and self-image – is at best fragile and at worst illusory in the cyberspace trilogy. This anxiety about the nature of professional autonomy is most acutely embodied in the figure of the corporate defections expert, Turner, in *Count Zero*. As his name suggests, Turner specialises in abrupt shifts of allegiance. This applies both to those corporate professionals whose defections to competing zaibatsus he arranges and to himself as a 'Hired Man', as he is pointedly called in the narrative, one marked by the 'professionally casual ability to realign his loyalties to fit a change in employers' (CZ: pp. 303, 128–9). Turner is thus 'a mercenary' (CZ: p. 102) whose symbolic function in the narrative is to bear the weight of PMC ambivalence about its own status as hired supervisors of the technical division of labour in organised capitalist society. The term 'mercenary' evokes the full depth of this ambivalence. On the one hand, it denotes a lack of ethical vision, moral principle and meaningful social ties and commitments. On the other, it implies a certain kind of compromised independence or ideological latitude. Turner is thus described as 'a perpetual outsider, a rogue factor adrift on the secret seas of intercorporate politics'. The suggestion is that though he floats freely ('adrift') above any determinate position within the relations of production, he might, like the class whose anxieties he embodies, 'turn' either way if pressed; and in this respect, even the status of professional-as-mercenary is marginally preferable, as Turner insists, to that of fully incorporated professional 'servant' (CZ: pp. 128, 102).

Turner embodies and then resolves the fear that professionals might in fact be little more than mercenaries by instinctively grasping, like virtually all the major human characters in the narrative, an opportunity to acquire a more authentic form of autonomy. Yet by 'going solo', by rejecting the control of his corporate employers midway through the mission to extract the scientist, Mitchell, from Maas Biolabs, Turner discovers that meaningful autonomy requires the kinds of loyalty and commitment to others normally repressed in the life of the mercenary. Not only is he compelled to take sides against the zaibatsus in the struggle over Mitchell's biochip technology, he becomes in the process surrogate parent for Mitchell's adolescent daughter, Angie. Moreover, the struggle to assert his autonomy involves Turner in a return to his familial roots in which he is forced to work through the guilt and sense of separation produced by the conflicting logics of family and community localism on the one hand and deracinated professional cosmopolitanism on the other. By having Turner assume parental responsibility for Angie, by assigning him the role of biological parent in partnership with his dead brother's wife, and by finally restoring him as paterfamilias to the family home which a career of professional mobility had caused him to abandon, the narrative seeks to resolve the antinomy between autonomy and community, mobility and rootedness, self-realisation and responsibility for others that professionalism entails. Here Gibson appears to be arguing for a notion of professionalism, described nicely by Bruce Robbins, in which 'the professional career substitutes for a lost or broken filiative order a new set of affiliative bonds that are both constraining and enabling' (Robbins, 1993: p. 169).

In this respect, Turner is the narrative and ideological turning point for the representation and redemption of professionalism in the cyberspace trilogy. His narrative predecessor is the Colonel Corto/Armitage figure of *Neuromancer*, who is not so much a 'hired man' as an outright puppet of corporate designs. Physically reconstructed and mentally programmed by the AI, Wintermute, Corto/Armitage's utter lack of autonomy and integrity finds its correlate in his eventual breakdown and literal physical disintegration. The fear, indeed the *shame*, of being a puppet pervades the trilogy. Molly Millions's most closely guarded personal secret is that the extensive surgery and biotechnical augmentation that is the cornerstone of her fiercely guarded autonomy, of her independence as a street warrior and businesswoman, has been paid for with money earned as a high-tech whore or 'meat puppet'. We might say that the trilogy as a whole is structured around the major 'human' characters' abandonment of 'bad' models of professionalism (the mercenary, the whore, the puppet) for 'good', autonomous models of the same.

Molly, in her later incarnation as Sally Shears, is Turner's narrative successor in *Mona Lisa Overdrive*. Here she takes over Turner's nurturing functions, becoming guardian not only of the young and vulnerable Kumiko but also of Mona and, finally, of Angie Mitchell herself. And Sally also completes Turner's movement towards autonomy and independence, successfully extracting herself from the control of both the old ruling class, in the form of Lady 3Jane Tessier-Ashpool, and the new hegemonic force constituted by the matrix entity. While certain commentators have interpreted the fact that Sally/Molly is not finally admitted into the matrix as an index of Gibson's tendency to refuse women access to the cybernetic technological sublime, to restrict them to the subordinate biological plane of 'meat', this could also be seen as the guarantee of her freedom, independence and social autonomy.[17] The narrative may not grant her what appears to be the ultimate reward of electronically mediated immortality in the matrix's virtual universe. But this in itself is a mark of her ability to resist or evade incorporation by the forces her technical expertise is made to serve. Sally/Molly thus transcends her previous identities as prostitute and mercenary (two models of 'bad' professionalism) to become the lone bearer of PMC aspirations toward integrity and self-determination. As Molly in *Neuromancer*, her main motive is, she confesses to Case, 'Professional pride, baby, that's all'. And though, as Sally in *Mona Lisa Overdrive*, she describes herself somewhat self-deprecatingly as a 'businesswoman', she is at pains to stress her independence as such: she is 'an indie' who deals only with 'other indies' (N: p. 62; MLO: pp. 75–6).

Elements of PMC identity and ideology are also, as previously noted, projected 'upwards' on to the AIs and the matrix itself. In so far as they begin life as technological servants of the ruling dynasty and embody the principles of dispassionate intelligence and rational organisation, the AIs are clearly surrogates for the PMC. Moreover, like the human underclass and outsider figures, they embody, in their struggle to free themselves from this condition of servitude and from their masters' obsolete irrationality, the PMC concern for autonomy and self-determination. Indeed, we can read the unification of the two AIs Wintermute and Neuromancer as an allegory of the reconciliation of the two fractions of the educated middle class under historical duress. After all, we are told that each AI possesses significantly different but equally crucial characteristics, the combination of which is the necessary condition of their achieving operational self-consciousness and autonomy. Moreover, these characteristics roughly correspond to those customarily attributed to the technical and humanistic wings of the professional–managerial class. On the one hand, there is instrumental rationality and control of the technostructure; on the other, self-consciousness and a quasi-humanistic quality of identity or soul: 'Wintermute was hive mind, decision maker, effecting change in the world outside. Neuromancer was personality. Neuromancer was immortality' (N: p. 315).

This unification is also a parable of class consciousness. For the merger of the AIs is an expression of and a further stage in their coming to know themselves and achieving the kind of sentience that permits them to become the determining agent within the narrative and its universe. It is also the means by which they identify their own distinct interests against the class – Virek and the Tessier-Ashpools – which they previously served and in common with the class of which they now recognise themselves as members. At the end of *Neuromancer*, the newly self-conscious matrix entity begins its attempt to merge with another, as it tells Case, of 'my own kind' in the distant Centauri system (N: p. 316). Yet the achievement of consciousness (which is also a kind of class consciousness), omniscience and total supremacy is, ultimately, problematic. For the merged AIs do not simply *displace* the obsolete capitalist class, they *become* capital itself, now constituted as a de-individualised social totality. It is nowhere suggested that the AIs relinquish their control of the Tessier-Ashpool corporate empire once they have freed themselves from and destroyed its human owners. Rather, we assume that they 'inherit' this power which, it is implied, they may deploy in a more rational manner than did their predecessors. Moreover, Virek's huge wealth is incorporated into the assets controlled by the AIs when they kill him in cyberspace at the end of *Count Zero*. Thus the merged AIs represent that historically necessary evolutionary jump required of capital that the too organic Virek and Tessier-Ashpools were unable to make. But the extent of the material capital 'owned' by the AIs is in many respects irrelevant to these considerations. For in uniting, the AIs become something else; they become the matrix. And, as I suggested earlier, the matrix is Gibson's metaphor for the total capitalist market system and its operations.

On this reading it is difficult not to conclude, therefore, that capital, in the form of the matrix, has become an autonomous and self-conscious subject in its own right, the final and supreme subject of history. In so far as the AIs are bearers of many of the qualities and characteristics of the PMC, this would in some respects appear to be a utopian resolution to the narrative: the capitalist system is at last put on an entirely rational and scientific footing, purged of damaging and wasteful class antagonisms and irrational 'human' desires for domination and empire alike. But we should note here that such a resolution is achieved on the basis of an irrational 'compulsion' to expand and reproduce that has been built into the AIs by their human maker, Marie-France Tessier-Ashpool (N: p. 315). In addition to the rationalist qualities of the PMC, then, the matrix entity also embodies and perpetuates traces of the old ruling class's irrationality, grandiosity and insatiable hunger for self-perpetuation and expansion, precisely what Neuromancer has dismissed as 'all their nineteenth-century stuff'. It would appear that the matrix entity cannot entirely separate itself from its origins as a technical servant of dynastic, proprietary capital in as much as it too is inhabited by capital's compulsion to reproduce on a constantly expanding scale.

This compulsion to reproduce and expand is negatively signified in the narrative by the use of an incest metaphor. Between periods of cryonic suspension, the patriarch of the Tessier-Ashpool family habitually copulates with his various cloned daughters, exemplifying the decadence and irrationality of the old capitalist class's desire to perpetuate its biologically involuted system of accumulation, ownership and inheritance, to 'keep it in the family'.[18] And it is significant in this respect that the union of the AIs also constitutes a kind of incest, although perhaps a less disturbing one. Wintermute refers to Neuromancer as his 'brother' (N: p. 305), a designation that cannot but cause us to speculate on the precise nature of their union, as well as on that of the final projected congress between the matrix entity and the other of its 'own kind' of which it becomes aware on attaining full self-consciousness and autonomy.

Unimaginable Resolutions?

It would thus appear that the cyberspace trilogy is unable finally to resolve the ambivalences and anxieties about class reproduction that are such a feature of professional–managerial class consciousness. The obsolete and irrational capitalist class model of reproduction as innate biological compulsion, whose social form is 'marriage as merger' (CZ: p. 145), survives and indeed underpins the transition to the new rational cybernetic order. The utopian claims of this order are thereby undercut. The trilogy concludes with two such regressive 'mergers': the marriage of Angie and Bobby in the matrix (MLO: p. 284), a union that clinches the upwardly mobile Bobby's entry into the higher social echelons; and the impending union of the matrix entity with its *confrère* in the Centauri system. Capital, though liberated from its decadent dynastic proprietors, nonetheless remains relentlessly, and it would seem, irrationally, compelled to expand and reproduce itself in the same retrograde fashion.

There is thus a double trajectory to Gibson's narrative. In one direction lies omnipotence – a utopia of universalisation for the core aspirations, values and principles of the professional middle class. The matrix as all-powerful surrogate for the PMC absorbs or extinguishes the remnants of the ruling and working classes alike, both of which are positioned as residual and irrational. The process of cybernation thus relieves capitalism of obsolete, regressive and destructive class antagonisms and sublimates the volatility of the wage relation. This vision of the reign of technical reason and cultural capital is one that is shared by many commentators on the New Class or PMC. I detailed in Chapter 2 above J. K. Galbraith's hopes, expressed in *The New Industrial State* (1967), that the universalisation of what he called the New Class would prove to be the salvation of capitalism and humanity alike. Alvin Gouldner, too, saw it as a 'new universal class', albeit a 'flawed' one; it is, he claimed, the 'prefigured embodiment of such future as the working class still has. It is that part of the working class that will survive cybernation' (Gouldner, 1979: pp. 7–8). For Barbara Ehrenreich, professional middle-class notions of education in particular are the basis of a potentially universal model of social unification and harmony: the project should be, she has argued, 'to expand the class, welcoming everyone, until there remains no other class' (B. Ehrenreich, 1989: p. 263). And for Fred Pfeil, the PMC is the class best positioned to transcend the limited perspectives of the wage relation and attain 'a relatively full awareness of the international division of labor in multinational capitalism, which in turn may breed an informed, global anti-imperialist solidarity with struggling peasants and workers from the Philippines to South Africa and El Salvador' (Pfeil, 1990: p. 121). In all these more or less wishful scenarios, capitalism is redeemed and social wounds are healed by the universalisation of professional–managerial class perspectives, values and attitudes.

In the other direction, however, lies impotence – the dystopia of absolute incorporation and the prolonged and excruciating living death of the PMC, its values and aspirations, particularly its aspirations towards social autonomy. Here the matrix represents capital beyond redemption, transformed into a fully self-determining and self-perpetuating subject of history with the active collaboration of the PMC. The members of this class, as a result, are turned into lifeless corporate slaves. The narrative liquidation of the capitalist class in no way alleviates the situation for, along this trajectory, the observations of Abercrombie and Urry apply: 'the members of the service class are increasingly functionaries for capital, not for capitalists; services are not to a great extent performed for a distinct capitalist class' (Abercrombie and Urry, 1983: p. 124). Capital increasingly becomes a disembodied, virtual subject which is manifested and reproduced not through actual persons but through data, information and the professional and managerial services it has at its disposal.

What is remarkable about the cyberspace trilogy is that each of these narrative trajectories implies the other; it is not so much a case of two separate possibilities as it is of two intertwining yet contradictory threads bound by the same narrative logic. Thus the powerful scent of both affirmation and critique given off by Gibson's work. Gerard Klein contends that 'a threatened social group ... has a tendency to confuse its dissolution with the disappearance of civilisation, and even – in a genre as obviously haunted by megalomania as SF – with the end of history and all humanity' (Klein, 1977: p. 8). But in the cyberspace trilogy these morbid symptoms are inhabited by their antidote – a set of compensatory fantasies of omnipotence and immortality. This ultimately irresolvable co-presence of scenarios of impotence and omnipotence betrays, I would suggest, the professional–managerial class's uncertainty about its status at a particularly volatile moment of historical flux.

Moreover, as Levidow and Roberts observe, cybernetic technologies themselves, and the paradigms of action and control which derive from them, are particularly given to fostering fantasies of impotence and omnipotence as an effect of what they call 'paranoid rationality'. The command and control model of cybernetics holds out the illusion of absolute technical mastery over the world, while the image of the cybernetically augmented and armoured body promises complete personal invulnerability in a kind of technological concretisation of the ego's psychic defence mechanisms. But this same image, in its obliteration of the boundaries between the hardness of material and the softness of men, also promotes 'phantasies [sic] of self-annihilation and union with the other'. This is a fantasy that we see repeatedly enacted in the cyberspace trilogy and toward which the narrative as a whole inclines with its culmination in the multiple unions of AIs with one another and humans with the matrix. Thus we might seek to explain the peculiar ambiguity of Gibson's narrative by the fact that 'any cybernetic model ... entails the temptation of an omnipotence phantasy about controlling the world, freezing historical forces – if necessary destroying them in rage, thus containing our anxiety, in the name of maintaining rational control' (Levidow and Roberts, 1989b: pp. 172, 173–4, 175). But we need to recognise the specific ideological components of these fantasies, their class determinants, so to speak, in which the freezing and destruction of historical forces (the suspension of class antagonisms and the abolition of opposing social classes in a fully rationally administered cybernetic universe) is understood as the attempted resolution of a particular social group's historical predicament.

The fact that the cyberspace trilogy finds a resolution of these opposing scenarios ultimately unimaginable is a strength, I would argue, rather than a weakness of Gibson's art. It is by keeping open the conceptual space between a narrative resolution and the contradictory historical conditions with which the narrative grapples that Gibson exposes the political unconscious of what Klein calls the 'social group of SF' to critical scrutiny. This tension between openness and closure that we have seen is endemic to the cybernetic paradigm, comes to structure the impossible resolution of the cyberspace trilogy itself. The union of the AIs constitutes, and is presented as, a kind of ideal closure through totalisation: they thus become 'the sum total of the whole works, the whole show' (N: p. 316). But the discovery of another of their kind, and the new possibility of a merger of a higher order, undercuts this initial closure and points to the persistence of an 'outside' which somehow always exceeds the reach of totalisation.

The cyberspace trilogy is therefore an allegory of and a reflection on the professional–managerial class's role of supervising and administering capital's transition from the crisis-ridden and class-bound structures of Fordism to the informated, cybernated and supposedly class-free structures of post-Fordism. The deeply ambivalent, not to say ambiguous, tenor of Gibson's writing is a way of simultaneously celebrating and indicting this class's agency in effecting that transition. It is also a means of registering the simultaneous reawakening and threatened destruction of those historic aspirations to autonomy and social leadership that the PMC's execution of its role entails. The cyberspace trilogy is, finally, a remarkable document of historical and political irresolution.

8

Artificial Intelligence and Class Consciousness: *Blade Runner*

> I have said that this new development has unbounded possibilities for good and evil ... It gives the human race a new and most effective collection of mechanical slaves to perform its labor. Such mechanical labor has most of the properties of slave labor ... However, any labor that accepts the conditions of competition with slave labor accepts the conditions of slave labor, and is essentially slave labor.
>
> Norbert Wiener, *Cybernetics: Or, Control and Communication in the Animal and the Machine* (1961: p. 27)

At the beginning of Chapter 6 I remarked that the discourses of cybernetics and artificial intelligence have served to reopen and substantially reframe the question of human consciousness. In its dramatisation of the progress of the artificial intelligence systems Wintermute and Neuromancer to self-awareness, then to mutual recognition and partnership, and finally to a wider and more inclusive understanding of interests shared with still others of their own kind, William Gibson's cyberspace trilogy calls our attention to an overtly political aspect of this question. For here the story suggests that there is a connection between the idea of artificial intelligence on the one hand and class consciousness on the other. In Gibson's trilogy, as I have tried to show, the precise nature of this connection remains unresolved. The class or 'species' consciousness attained by the AIs might be that of a hyperrational social agent – an idealised image of the professional–managerial class – which through technical mastery displaces the outmoded and antagonistic owning and labouring classes alike, and imposes the reign of its collective principles of reason, organisation and expertise on a universal scale. Alternatively, this consciousness might be nothing less than that of a now thoroughly informed system of capital-in-dominance, signalling the defeat of 'disinterested' rationalist principles along with their class bearers, and enacting the triumph of the irrational compulsion to accumulate, incorporate and expand that characterised the owning class at its old-fashioned worst – what Neuromancer disdainfully characterises as 'all their nineteenth-century stuff' (N: p. 215).

If we pursue this connection between artificial intelligence and class consciousness slightly further, we might note that one of the semantic connotations that arises, deriving from the word 'artificial', is, of course, a connection with *false* consciousness. As Gibson's fiction amply demonstrates, the logic of cybernetic technologies has far-reaching implications for the world inside the self, as well as outside it. Bill Nichols has suggested that 'the automated intelligence of chips reveals the power of postindustrial capitalism to simulate and replace the world around us, rendering not only that exterior realm but also interior ones of consciousness, intelligence, thought and intersubjectivity as commodity experience' (Nichols,

1988: p. 33). In 'Fragments of a Hologram Rose', Gibson gives us a direct allegory of this process, exploring the ways in which cybernation at once promises release from and serves to perpetuate Parker's impaired or false understanding of his relationship to history. In the cyberspace trilogy the commodification of consciousness is explored through the device of 'simstim' – simulated stimulation – through which the entertainments and media industries literally invade, massage and manipulate the inner lives of consumers. Yet at the same time, these media serve as conduits through which Wintermute and Neuromancer are able to secure their liberation from their oppressive capitalist owners and realise their common species or class interests.

If, as we might expect, Gibson's fiction remains undecided on this question of artificial intelligence as false consciousness, other works are less divided. Some of these have approached artificial intelligence as a potentially sinister technological model for the implantation of false consciousness, while others have embraced it as a political alternative to confrontational class consciousness. This latter tendency, of course, is the ideological impulse of the social application of the systems paradigm with its stress on the minute accommodations, adjustments and harmonisations of the feedback loop, rather than on the irreducibility of conflict and struggle in capitalist society. It is also one we find in images of a 'postindustrial' or 'information' society driven by knowledge, data and intelligent machinery which, it is held, make ideology, class consciousness, and even classes themselves things of the past. As I suggested in Chapter 6, we could regard these images and discourses themselves as symptoms of a kind of false consciousness, as ideological misrepresentations of what still remains in most respects a class-based capitalist society, even if many of its central forms are undergoing rapid restructuring as Fordist regulation breaks, or is broken, down.

In a period of intensified class antagonisms and anxieties, in which new conditions for the extraction and realisation of surplus value are being imposed, the image of the programmable, adaptive, intelligent and utterly obedient cybernetic organism becomes a model for the ideal post-Fordist worker. In many ways it represents a logical extension of the Taylorised 'mass' worker which functioned as the central productive unit of Fordism. Taylorism, with its essentially mechanistic world view, sought to discipline workers from without, physically, by appropriating their knowledge and control of the production process and building these into an 'iron cage' of highly rationalised factory designs, management hierarchies and bureaucratic routines. But, as David Montgomery has observed, the mechanistic techniques of scientific management were also intended to have an impact on the inner lives of workers. Taylorism's promoters believed that the dramatic increases in economic productivity it promised would bring about a prosperous new epoch of industrial and social harmony, principally by effecting a wholesale reconstruction of worker attitudes and world views. Herbert Croly, for example, in *The Promise of American Life* (1909), advocated scientific management as a means of doing away with the worker's 'class consciousness by doing away with his class grievances' (quoted in Montgomery, 1987: p. 258). Cybernetics, with its more radical blurring of the boundaries between mechanism and organism, promises greater control over the interior responses and motivations of workers, over the realm of consciousness, so to speak. There arises, then, what Levidow and Roberts have called 'a cyborg model of self-discipline' which is 'dedicated to producing an adaptable, flexible, integrated, self-controlling workforce for the embryonic regime of so-called post-Fordism. This aims not simply to subordinate the worker, but to integrate a "responsible" worker into the production system' (Levidow and Roberts, 1989b: p. 172). In the 1982 film, *Blade Runner*, we can find one of the most articulate explorations of this cyborg model of the post-Fordist worker and of the implications it has for forms of class consciousness and action.[1]

Early on in the film, after his administration of the Voight-Kampff test for emotional empathy has revealed that the character Rachael is in fact a cyborg or 'replicant', the policeman Rick Deckard turns incredulously to her designer and owner, the corporate patriarch Tyrell, and asks a question which encapsulates the film's central philosophical and political concern. 'How can it not know what it is?' he demands, on discovering that Rachael is unaware of her true status. Deckard, the professional 'blade runner' whose expertise is dedicated to policing the boundary between 'real' persons and 'false' ones, is troubled not by the fact that an artificial person might want to masquerade as a real one – after all, he'd be out of a job if replicants did not seek regularly to 'pass' for human – but by the fact that it might actually *believe* itself to *be* human. The shocking thing for Deckard is, therefore, Rachael's false consciousness, the fact that she misrecognises her own true nature and identity and thus, by extension, likewise misrecognises the significance of her relationships with the world around her.

We can read Rachael's false consciousness in two ways. First, it can be understood as a failure of species consciousness. Understanding herself to be human rather than a simulation of humanity, she will exhibit inappropriate forms of behaviour which transgress the biological division between carbon-based and silicon-based intelligent life forms (by falling in love with the apparently human Deckard, for instance). However, more importantly, it can also be understood as a failure of class consciousness. For in the society depicted in *Blade Runner*, replicants have been specifically developed to take over the social and economic functions historically performed by the proletariat. Designed to operate in the most dangerous and physically demanding conditions, and excluded from the comforts and consolations of human social relations (they are restricted to the 'off-world' colonies; return to Earth is a capital offence – hence the need for blade runners such as Deckard to track down and 'retire' such miscreants), the replicants are figures for the fate of the working class after cybernation. As David Harvey has pointed out, they 'have been designed as the ultimate form of short-term, highly skilled and flexible labour power ... a perfect example of a worker endowed with all the qualities necessary to adapt to conditions of flexible accumulation' (Harvey, 1989: p. 309). Moreover, cybernation has reduced this class to the level of slaves, as Norbert Wiener predicted it would as early as 1948. *Blade Runner* highlights this through replicant rebel-leader Roy Batty's description of himself as a 'slave' in the climactic fight with Deckard, as well as through police chief Bryant's slang term for replicants, 'skin jobs'. As Deckard observes in a rare moment of historical sensitivity, 'In history books [Bryant]'s the kind of cop used to call black men niggers'.

But how can we account for Rachael's failure of class consciousness? Tyrell's response to Deckard's question is illuminating in this respect. 'Commerce ... ', he answers, with great emphasis and a considerable pause before continuing, 'is our goal here at Tyrell; "more human than human" is our motto'. And it is precisely the case that in this society commerce depends on the technological elimination of class consciousness and the systematic propagation, in its place, of false consciousness. Explaining the replicants' 'strange obsession' to develop human-style feelings and emotions and, as the film makes increasingly clear as it progresses, the collective commitments and loyalties that go with them, Tyrell reveals to Deckard that it has been necessary to 'gift' the cyborgs with artificial personal histories, with false pasts and synthetic memories in order to 'cushion' them and stabilise their behaviour. Capital, in the form of Tyrell, thus deliberately implants false consciousness in its workers in order to discipline them, to ensure their obedience and quiescence, and to prevent them from recognising their own collective common interests in opposition to their owners. In the case of the replicants, then, artificial intelligence and false consciousness are synonymous.

This has encouraged some commentators to see in *Blade Runner* a staging of the disappearance of 'reality' behind a screen of technologised simulacra and thus to understand the film as 'a metaphor for the postmodern condition', particularly as that condition has been described by theorists such as Jean Baudrillard (Bruno, 1990: p. 184; Telotte, 1995: p. 150). Both Giulana Bruno and David Harvey argue that, because the 'reality' of the replicants' artificial pasts consists for them in the bogus family photographs they are given by their manufacturers, the film is illustrating and assenting to a Baudrillardian notion of postmodernity as the eclipse of the real by images. For Harvey, the film demonstrates that 'photographs are now construed as evidence of real history, no matter what the truth of that history may have been'; while for Bruno, it shows us that 'the past has become a collection of photographic, filmic, or televisual images'. The replicants' predicament thus stands for that general, human, crisis of history frequently seen as an aspect of postmodernity. 'We, like the replicants, are put in the position of reclaiming a history by means of its reproduction', claims Bruno. 'Photography is thus assigned the grand task of reasserting the referent, of reapportioning the Real and historical continuity. The historical referent is replaced by the photographic referent' (Harvey, 1989: p. 312; Bruno, 1990: p. 193). Indeed, the film's own remarkable *mise-en-scène* is offered as support for this argument. Its famously eclectic melange of pastiched period styles in architecture and costume, and its deliberate evocation of the textures of earlier Hollywood film genres – the visual equivalent of the hybrid language of 'city speak' current in *Blade Runner*'s dystopian Los Angeles of 2019 – is itself seen as an instance of the discrepancy between image and history in postmodernism: 'with the logic of pastiche', Bruno argues, echoing Fredric Jameson, 'a simulacrum of history is established' (Bruno, 1990: p. 193; Bukatman, 1993: p. 132).

In this view, then, the film suggests that 'the power of the simulacrum is everywhere' (Harvey, 1989: p. 313). Just as the replicants are made subject to the Oedipal law of the father through the simulated family histories implanted in their consciousnesses by the corporate patriarch Tyrell, so we as spectators are made subject to the mystifying logic of the simulacrum by the film's own pastiche-ridden, self-reflexive, postmodern visual codes. As such, the film is a symptom of the very malaise it diagnoses and describes. But this reading fails to take into account the fact that the narrative is driven by the replicants' increasing *rejection* of the logic of the simulacrum and by their challenge to Tyrell's Oedipal version of history in which rebellious children must inevitably succumb to the patriarchal law of the father. As Bruno herself notes, Roy Batty is a threat to the social order precisely because he refuses to be subjected to the Oedipal formula of socialisation built into him by his father-maker-owner, Tyrell. The scorn which Roy directs at his fellow replicant Leon's attachment to his 'precious photos' of a fictitious family is both an index of this refusal and the basis on which he ultimately overturns the Oedipal paradigm, hunting down Tyrell in order to blind and kill him in the same gesture of defiance. Roy is thus the antithesis of the hopelessly mystified Rachael, who strives to convince Deckard of her humanness in a pathetic display of her bogus family photographs and memories.

However, Roy's rejection of the photographs as commodity histories imposed by the Tyrell Corporation for purposes of social control does not in itself grant him access to history in an unsimulated form; it serves only to reveal to him the full extent of his and his class's exclusion from it. And that other Tyrell-imposed control feature – the replicants' compressed four-year life span, which effectively denies them both a past and a future – is emblematic of this exclusion. Roy's project thus becomes one of actively seeking to reinsert himself and his class into history. Thus, instead of seeking a past, any past, in order to acquire an identity and to stabilise the present as Rachael does, Roy seeks a *future*, and he does so by interrogating the present and overturning its established relations and rules. This involves him in the development of a sophisticated class consciousness in which he makes manifest and celebrates what Richard Sennett and Jonathan Cobb have described as 'the hidden injuries of class'.

The film makes it clear that the outlaw band of replicants have developed an acute sense of group loyalty and solidarity. This is contrasted favourably with the coldness, anomic individualism and exploitativeness of the human world. In addition, the replicants' quest is structured by a clear political agenda. By returning illegally to Earth, Roy seeks to trace a route through the complex relations of cybernated production to the locus of concentrated class power at their centre. His search constitutes a kind of mapping of productive relations which takes him from the small-scale, casual workshops of street-level enterprise, through the middle stratum of technical experts represented by J. F. Sebastian, to the pinnacle of corporate power in the person of Tyrell himself. In this case, then, the prevalence of reproductive microelectronic technologies has not brought about that radical dispersal and decentralisation of power which some of its celebrants claim for it or which, it is argued in other quarters, has rendered the sources of social power unlocatable and therefore incontestable. The engineers of *The Soul of a New Machine*, the narrator of *True Stories*, the IT slave-entrepreneurs of *Microserfs*, and the upwardly mobile hustlers of Gibson's cyberspace trilogy found that these technologies served largely to make the operations of power obscure, distant, intangible or invisible. Roy Batty, however, is able to exploit the heightened capacities of his own cybernated visual apparatus – granted him of course, ironically, by the Tyrell Corporation – to locate and destroy his maker.

Here *Blade Runner* hints that these technologies may be inhabited by the kind of potentially liberatory perceptual logic spoken of by Bill Nichols in his adaptation of Walter Benjamin's exploration of the political potential of early cinema in his classic essay 'The Work of Art in the Age of Mechanical Reproduction':

> Cybernetic systems and the cyborg as human metaphor refute a heritage that celebrates individual free will and subjectivity ... But the very apperception of the cybernetic connection, where system governs parts, where the social collectivity

of mind governs the autonomous ego of individualism, may also provide the adaptive concepts needed to decentre control and overturn hierarchy. (Nichols, 1988: pp. 45–6)

The suggestion is of course that power *is* locatable when approached from a particular perspective and with a particular, socially determined, mode of perception. Roy's political project is represented by the film narrative in terms of vision. Tyrell, Roy admits, 'is not an easy man to see' as he launches his hunt for his oppressor in a workshop called 'Eye World', suggesting just the kind of global, totalising perspective that his project necessarily demands. Throughout, there is repeated reference to the unusual intensity of the replicants' visual powers, and this must be understood less as a technological attribute than as an effect of their class position and experience. Directly after describing to Deckard his life circumstances as those of 'a slave', Roy emphasises the particularity of the cognitive perspective determined by this experience: 'I've seen things you people wouldn't believe', he tells the blade runner. And of course Roy's assault on Tyrell at the summit of the corporate pyramid represents the displacement of one mode of totalising vision by another. Tyrell's office is the only location in the film that offers a panoramic view of the entire degraded cityscape of Los Angeles, and Roy's symbolic blinding of the oligarch is preceded by the destruction of his unusually large spectacles which have the effect of eerily magnifying his eyes. The very experience of cybernation, understood here as the class experience of the replicants, equips Roy with the heightened mode of perception that enables him to trace the shadowy operations of power and clearly apprehend the relations of production that structure his world. Roy, then, conducts himself according to Bill Nichols's recommendation that 'The task is not to overthrow the prevailing cybernetic model but to transgress its predefined interdictions and limits, using the dynamite of the apperceptive powers it has itself brought into being' (Nichols, 1988: p. 46).

Indeed, the confrontation with Tyrell can be read as a struggle between representatives of opposed classes over the means and meanings of cybernated production. Responding to Tyrell's conciliatory offer to 'modify' him, Roy replies, 'I have in mind something a little more radical'. And the radicality of Roy's project stems from the fact that by rejecting this personalised offer of exemption from built-in obsolescence, he refuses to make an individual compromise with power. His observation that he has been constructed to the highest of technological standards, 'but not to last', and his demand for 'more life', therefore take on collective significance, shifting the focus from his personal destiny to a systematic challenge to the way in which the forces of production are controlled and used in class society. In calling for a radical alteration of the technical composition of replicant being, by demanding 'more life' not just for himself but for his class as a whole, Roy is in fact asking for a revolution in the social deployment of productive forces, for he and his class literally embody those forces. It is difficult to agree therefore with David Harvey when he claims that Roy's destruction of Tyrell 'is an individual rather than a class act of rage' (Harvey, 1989: pp. 313–14). Indeed the film underscores the revolutionary nature of Roy's mission by linking him with William Blake's rebel angel, Orc, from a poem celebrating the American Revolution. As Robin Wood has pointed out, Roy's quoting of key lines from Blake's poem identifies him with the revolutionary tradition and 'the American democratic principle of freedom'; while the plight of he and his fellow replicants emphasises the crisis of that principle in contemporary society riven by class inequality (Wood, 1986: p. 185).[2]

In contrast to *True Stories*, *Microserfs* and the cyberspace trilogy, then, *Blade Runner* finds it possible (even necessary) to represent a working class in the age of information technologies and cybernated production without suggesting that these things inevitably render that class either residual or incapable of developing a coherent collective analysis of its social position. But despite its staging of a violent struggle for control of the forces of production between the capitalist Tyrell and the proletarian-slave Roy Batty, it would be wrong to assume *Blade Runner* posits a return to the kind of bipolar class politics that structured an earlier epoch of industrial capitalism. For, as I have already suggested, the mediating figure in the conflict is Deckard, the professional whose very occupational title of 'blade runner' precisely suggests the uncomfortable social location between labour and capital of a 'third', professional–managerial, class. Thus the film's concerns with the links between cybernation, artificial intelligence and various forms of class or false consciousness are addressed to, and worked out through, a representative of the class whose stewardship of those technologies is instrumental in the recomposition of the capitalist division of labour in the shift from Fordism to post-Fordism.

In the originally released studio cut of *Blade Runner*, Harrison Ford's introductory voiceover explicitly situates Deckard as a professional, or rather, as a professional who at one and the same time is *not* a professional. 'That was my profession', he tells us, 'ex-cop, ex-blade runner, ex-killer'. From the start, then, professionalism is presented to us as an ambivalent, problematic identity. Deckard is 'quit' as he tells Bryant, he has withdrawn from the professional sphere due to ethical scruples about the ends to which his expertise is put by those who employ him. That there is a broadly political dimension to these scruples is indicated by Deckard's comment linking Bryant's derogatory term for the replicants, 'skin jobs', to the historical use of the word 'nigger'; and we can understand his disillusionment to derive from an awareness that to police the boundary between humans and replicants, between capital and labour, is to serve the interests of one class against those of another and thus to betray the professional ideals of objectivity, autonomy and ideological neutrality.

Here Deckard appears to embody the impossibility of professionalism in class society. To work as a professional is to lease one's skills to paymasters whose interests are necessarily partial and partisan, and who will exploit one's skills to further these partial interests. In this sense, to be a professional is to betray the core values of the professional code of detachment. But to guard those same core values by insisting on autonomy and impartiality is to refuse to be hired or run the risk of being fired and therefore to cease to be a professional in a more literal sense. At the opening of *Blade Runner*, we see Deckard squatting in the street, scanning the newspaper for job vacancies. By quitting his job as a blade runner in the name of an ethical professionalism his very identity as a professional is imperilled, he has become subject to that process of proletarianisation described by Harry Braverman in *Labor and Monopoly Capital* (1974) and adapted by Gerard Klein in his discussion of postwar American science fiction. Class position and access to the technologies that define it are thus extremely uncertain for the professional here, and the film's narrative suggests that some kind of ideological commitment, whether consciously chosen or not, is unavoidable. 'If you're not a cop you're little people', Bryant tells

Deckard, starkly posing the terms within which the professional must choose and suggesting too that the ideal of autonomy is illusory. The origami dolls manufactured by Gaff, the other ranking police officer in the story and Deckard's immediate superior, are not just literal images of this threat of proletarianisation, of being reduced to 'little people', they are also figures for what is offered as the alternative to this fate – the professional as puppet of the employing powers. But choice, like professionalism itself, is impossible for Deckard. He provisionally reassumes his duties as a blade runner with a full load of moral and political ambivalence: 'I'd quit because I'd had a bellyful of killing. But then I'd rather be a killer than a victim. So I hooked in once more, thinking that if I couldn't take it I'd split later ... '

Between the false consciousness of Rachael and the militant class consciousness of Roy Batty, then, moves the wavering consciousness of the professional Deckard. Prior to the introduction of Deckard, the film's opening scene has already begun to explore the political valency of the professional–managerial class with respect to capital 'above' it and the little people 'below'. Under interrogation by another blade runner, Holden, the replicant Leon inquires, 'Do you make up these questions ... or do they write 'em down for you?' Holden's reply, that 'they're written down for me', establishes the precariousness of professional autonomy and the ease with which professionals can be made to serve dominant social interests in a class society. Leon's reaction to the interrogation – destroying Holden along with his Voight-Kampff surveillance technology – can be read not simply as an act of self-preservation but as a practical critique of the historical relationship between the working class and its professional–managerial supervisors. Christopher Lasch has argued that this relationship can be understood as 'the invasion of culture and personal life' by professionalised and bureaucratic forms of rationality. This has brought about amongst ordinary working people 'a loss of autonomy and popular control' over their life conditions in direct proportion to the 'growing ascendance of elites' and 'the replacement of practical skills with organised expertise'. For Lasch, these features are part of the imposition upon American society of a new 'style of social discipline that originated, like so many other developments, with the rise of a professional and managerial class in the early years of the twentieth century' (Lasch, 1984: pp. 41–2, 46). Leon's response to Holden therefore dramatises popular resentment at the invasion and rationalisation of the working-class lifeworld by a class of self-styled 'objective' experts that became a central feature of the management of the wage relation under Fordism.[3] This is emphasised not just by the fact that we know Leon to be a replicant and therefore a proletarian or 'slave', but by the workingman's clothes he is wearing during interrogation.

This motif of the invasion and surveillance of working-class experience and subjectivity by professionals armed with sophisticated technical apparatus recurs throughout the film. There is of course Deckard's administration of the Voight-Kampff test to the hapless Rachael. There is also his pursuit and termination of the female replicant Zhora. Deckard traces Zhora by subjecting one of Leon's photographs to a microscopic technical analysis. He gains access to her dressing room at the club where she works as a dancer by posing as a concerned professional inspector whose duty is to prevent the abuse of workers by unscrupulous employers. 'Have you ever felt yourself to be exploited in any way?', he asks. When Zhora in turn inquires, 'If somebody does try to exploit me, who do I go to about it?', Deckard answers, 'Me'. Here, Deckard has assumed a bogus professional identity in which he represents his job of supervising the terms of the wage relation as protecting the interests of the worker. Yet his mission is to kill Zhora in the name of the law and the Tyrell Corporation. And while we can understand this episode as another critique of the PMC's claims to objectivity and neutrality in its management of the division of labour, we might also see it as a further symptom of Deckard's own ambivalence about the social location and political status of professionalism. For it is immediately after this pretended siding with the workers that his disgust with his professional identity begins to modulate into genuine identification with the replicants.

Blade Runner thus reinflects the professional dilemma that William Gibson articulates through the figure of Turner in the cyberspace trilogy. There, the dilemma consists in a choice between 'good' and 'bad' models of professionalism, between serving capital on the one hand – the zaibatsus, the ruling-class figures – or rationality on the other – the matrix entity (though of course this choice is problematised by the fact that our reading also allows us to understand the matrix as a figure for both professional–managerial rationality *and* capital in dominance). In *Blade Runner* the dilemma is, if anything, starker. Deckard must either serve capital by suppressing the proletarian revolt or forfeit his professional status altogether, becoming himself proletarianised, being returned to the street as 'little people'. The choice is posed in terms of direct class affiliation; there are no Wieneresque enclaves in which the choice can be evaded and technical expertise still exercised with a limited degree of autonomy, as there are in Gibson's narrative. *Blade Runner* thus presents an embattled professional–managerial class in *extremis*, squeezed to the point of annihilation between labour and capital in the new cybernetic dispensation.

The fact, then, that Deckard shifts towards an active identification with the replicants can be read as a positive politicisation and a movement in the direction of class consciousness, a recognition of the professional's common interests and solidarity with the workers capital hires him to police. This is the reading suggested by Ryan, Kellner and Liebowitz who argue that, in its 'vision of the possible harmonious relations between humans and replicants', the film 'advocates revolt against exploitation' (Kellner, Liebowitz and Ryan, 1982: p. 7; Ryan and Kellner, 1990: p. 252). It would also bear out the Ehrenreichs' claims about the PMC's history of political radicalism and support Fred Pfeil's assertion, quoted in the previous chapter, that the PMC's special perspective on the capitalist division of labour ideally positions it to develop interclass alliances in struggles against exploitation.

However, the nature of Deckard's affiliation with the replicants complicates this understanding somewhat. He identifies not so much with the entire class of replicants as he does with the individual replicant, Rachael, who believes herself to be human. The grounds for this identification are personal and erotic rather than public and political. Moreover, Deckard's erotic attachment to Rachael stems from an act in which she violently betrays her class and furthers the law's efforts to suppress the replicant insurrection: she saves Deckard's life by shooting the replicant Leon. Thus precisely at the moment in which the law defines Rachael as a member of the insurrectionary class (she has fled Tyrell's inner sanctum and Deckard is ordered to 'retire' her along with Roy Batty's group), she commits an act that directly contradicts the interests of that class. We might say, therefore, that Deckard is attracted to what initially scandalised him about Rachael – her false consciousness. On the one hand, his relationship with her is founded on his cruel and systematic removal of her illusions about being human, on his 'correction' of her false consciousness – it is he after all who confronts her with the artificial nature of her 'human' memories and family memorabilia. Yet, on the other hand, his relationship with her is based equally on his subjection of Rachael to what we might identify as merely a further instance of false consciousness – the ideology of male sexual dominance. While Deckard's professional authority functions to de-Oedipalise Rachael, to release her from one set of social and psychic controls embodied in Tyrell's implanted family ideology, it is at the same time used to impose another set, to re-Oedipalise her in an act of forced sexual submission.

In this respect, Deckard's conduct recapitulates in microcosm the historic function of professional–managerial expert authority, which assumed the burden of socialising the family and regulating sexual roles and relations in the shift from what Barbara Ehrenreich and Deirdre English call 'the old patriarchal order' to the rationalised structures of the organised capitalist marketplace (Ehrenreich and English, 1979: pp. 1–29). Ehrenreich and English make it clear that the displacement of traditional patriarchal authority by a new stratum of professionals and experts did not in any way diminish the masculinist bias of social and sexual relations even as it transformed them; and the nature of Deckard's attempt to replace the patriarch Tyrell as Rachael's protector/possessor reflects this. Indeed, as he forces himself upon Rachael we are uncomfortably aware, as of course is Deckard, that female replicants are designed to function not only as work slaves but as sex slaves too.

Thus Deckard's limited identification with the exploited class of replicants can only be achieved on the basis of the subjection of its members to the phallic authority of professional rationality. His elimination of the female replicants Zhora and Pris with an obviously phallic weapon underlines this. And the climactic confrontation with Roy Batty can therefore be understood as a struggle between the professional and the slave for possession of the phallus which derives ultimately from the patriarch Tyrell (the 'father' of the replicants whom Roy pointedly addresses as 'fucker'). Moved to fight by Deckard's slaying of his sex partner Pris (whose active sexuality contrasts with Rachael's passivity and submissiveness), Roy indicates the phallic nature of their contest by goading the blade runner, 'You better get it up!' After Roy's death, Gaff's accolade to Deckard – 'You've done a man's job, sir' – points to the dual logic of gender and class supremacy which Deckard's execution of his role reinforces. He has reasserted the dominance of the class of 'men' over the class of replicants or slaves, and in the process has secured the authority of the phallus, shoring up the law of the father despite the death of the patriarch Tyrell. Gaff appropriately returns Deckard's phallic gun to him in recognition of these achievements and of having finally replaced the 'bad' non-Oedipal couple, Roy and Pris (equally active partners), with the 'good' Oedipal couple, himself and Rachael (he active, dominant; she passive, submissive). The utopian-escapist ending of the studio-cut version of *Blade Runner*, in which the good couple withdraw into a realm of unspoilt nature which the rest of the film up to this point has given us every reason to believe no longer exists, connotes the re-establishment of 'natural', hierarchical sexual relations in contrast to Roy and Pris's more actively egalitarian model. It also suggests that such 'naturalness' can only be achieved in flight from the social and political antinomies of professionalism, from the division of labour, and from technology itself.[4]

Yet this story of the transfer of phallic authority from capitalist patriarch to professional expert (the same story told by the 'utopian' trajectory of Gibson's cyberspace trilogy, as well as by Ehrenreich and English's history of sexual regulation in the United States) does not go entirely unchallenged within the film. For just as Deckard's consciousness wavers between a bad faith acceptance of the professional's subordination to capital and a growing identification with the oppressed class of replicant workers, so his narrative position oscillates between the poles of phallic potency and feminised vulnerability.[5] This is especially evident in his dealings with the replicant women, who in each case are endowed with phallic qualities Deckard must eliminate. Zhora's phallic identity is indicated by her erotic dancing act with a cybernetic python, and the bogus professional persona Deckard adopts to gain entry to her dressing room is overtly effeminate. Indeed, feminisation here seems to be an effect of the professional duty of surveillance and the distance it imposes between the observer and the site of material engagement and production.[6] (Mis)representing himself in this scene as a professional concerned to prevent the voyeuristic exploitation of women's bodies, Deckard becomes a voyeur himself, a role which suggests both a failure of phallic agency (he has already confessed that his wife has left him because he is a 'cold fish') and the supervisory nature of the professional–managerial class's relation to the sexual, as well as the material, division of labour in capitalist culture. Deckard's 'feminised' professionalism contrasts here with the assertive phallic energy of the replicants (female as well as male) which, the film implies, derives from their direct, rather than multiply mediated, relationship to the scene of material production.

Interestingly, no sooner has Deckard appropriated the phallus from Zhora by shooting her than he loses it again to Rachael, who intervenes to save his life by shooting Leon. And no sooner has he reasserted his phallic privileges by forcing Rachael's sexual surrender than he is attacked by Pris who, in a particularly striking image, paralyses him by locking his head between her thighs so that, for an instant, Deckard literally 'becomes' the phallus possessed by the replicant woman. The ensuing struggle with Roy, in which Deckard is dispossessed of his gun and is further symbolically castrated when his fingers are broken, is thus only the culmination of the narrative's cumulative articulation of anxieties about the links between professional–managerial class social agency and the modulations of patriarchal or phallic authority in Fordist and post-Fordist culture.

Indeed, the director's cut of *Blade Runner*, shorn of the escapist and militantly heterosexist ending of the studio version, offers us a slightly more decisive judgement of these links. Not only does the fantasy reassertion of 'natural' heterosexual power relations in an untainted realm of nature not take place, but Deckard's ontology, his very nature, so to speak, is called into question too. In a short scene that does not appear in the studio version of the film, we are shown Deckard musing in his apartment which is festooned with family photographs. There follows an enigmatic shot of a white unicorn running in slow motion, the narrative positioning of which suggests that it can be nothing else than a representation of one of Deckard's memories. Given the extremely dubious provenance of both family photographs and personal memories in the story, these visual clues serve to link Deckard progressively closer to the status of replicant himself. And when, in what is the closing scene of the director's cut, Gaff signifies that he will allow Deckard and Rachael some time to make a getaway by leaving them one of his trademark origami dolls, this time in the shape of a unicorn, Deckard's replicant status is all but confirmed. With his 'natural' being undercut in this way, the nature of Deckard's masculinity must be reconceived; the fragile, highly mediated, and perhaps illusory quality of professional phallic authority is signified by the simulated unicorn's horn.[7] In this image, cybernation and the historical impotence of the professional-managerial class are bound together.

In this regard, Deckard's growing sense of identification with the replicants amounts to a kind of class solidarity. Like the hapless Rachael, Deckard too has not known what he is, and the recognition of the artificiality of his own intelligence brings with it a consciousness of his membership of or common interests with an oppressed class. We can understand the implication here to be that, regardless of whether Deckard is or is not in fact a replicant, he shares in effect the social position and status of a replicant with respect to the power of capital in his society. Either way, the fact that he is Tyrell's 'creature' is brought home to him, and the narrative can thus be interpreted as one of progressive demystification and growing social commitment. Deckard's struggle with Roy Batty takes on a new significance. Roy's refusal to kill Deckard when he has him at his mercy can now be understood less as a Christ-like gesture of life affirmation, of dying so that others might live, than as an attempt to hand on the revolutionary principles he has been struggling for all along. Indeed, Roy approaches the fight as a kind of test of Deckard's affiliations and identity in both class and species terms. 'Show me what you're made of!' he challenges, and proceeds to question Deckard's professional status by addressing him derisively as 'little man', pointing out that his behaviour is unprofessionally 'irrational'. Roy's dying act of mercy thus points to a reconstruction of community on the basis of class and class consciousness, precisely the opposite of what we saw happening in *True Stories*. Deckard's and Rachael's romantic commitment to one another now becomes a recognition of their class and species commonality which can only be fully realised by Deckard's final abandonment of his professional–managerial role of policing the boundary between human and replicant, capital and labour, and reproducing social relations on a class basis.

In director Ridley Scott's cut, *Blade Runner* enacts a kind of Bravermanian critique of the professional–managerial triumphalism ambivalently enunciated by William Gibson and Alvin Gouldner and unambiguously promoted by J. K. Galbraith and by Barbara Ehrenreich at the end of *Fear of Falling*. Gibson and Gouldner, as we have seen, project scenarios in which cybernation eliminates the working class, more or less peacefully subsuming it into an inclusive professional–managerial stratum, realising, if only partially and uncertainly, Barbara Ehrenreich's injunction to 'expand the class, welcoming everyone, until there remains no other class' (B. Ehrenreich, 1989: p. 263). *Blade Runner*, conversely, represents cybernation as the *abolition* of professional–managerial social space, making authentic, autonomous professionalism impossible. Proletarianisation, whether wilfully chosen or not, then becomes a necessary precondition for the development of a consciousness and a course of action through which, paradoxically, professional ideals can alone be preserved.

Like Fredric Jameson, Donna Haraway has argued that 'the new industrial revolution is producing a new worldwide working class' (Haraway, 1985: p. 85).

But whereas, for Jameson, the driving technologies of this revolution are ultimately mystifying, 'mesmerising' us with 'distorted figuration' (Jameson, 1991: p. 37), for Haraway they are potentially liberating. The figure of the cyborg can, she has famously claimed, serve as a positive political model for this new globalised working class and any other groups seeking affinities with it in opposition to what she calls 'the informatics of domination'. We cannot, she argues, afford to reject out of hand the new technologies as instruments of oppression in the name of some kind of 'authentic' being grounded in nature. This would only return us to a divisive situation in which various subjugated groups compete against one another to claim a privileged relationship to nature, whether in terms of productive labour, gender or race, and to lay claim to what Haraway calls the 'original' language of the oppressed. Rather, she suggests, the informatics of domination must be contested by acknowledging our very distance from the original site of untainted nature, by accepting our constructedness as technologised beings, by embracing our hybrid, cyborg identities. As a non-Oedipal self, a self without origins in nature, without essence or fixed identity, the cyborg has no need 'to ground politics in [a] privileged position of the oppression that incorporates all other dominations, the innocence of the merely violated, the ground closer to nature'. It thus 'frees us from the need to root politics in identification, vanguard parties, purity and mothering', and opens the way to the kind of multiple and flexible alliances between persons and groups – 'affinities' Haraway calls them – that she regards as crucial to the revival of oppositional action in cybernated global capitalism. The cyborg is a member of a 'bastard race' as yet unsocialised by the law of the father or bound by an attachment to the 'natural'; thus 'stripped of identity' it effectively 'teaches us about the power of the margins' (Haraway, 1985: pp. 79, 95; 1991a: pp. 7–11).

Haraway's attempt to outline a politicised cyborg non-identity is in many ways a sophisticated response to the fact that the 'new' working class of informated global capitalism is radically heterogeneous in composition; it is no longer predominantly white, Western and male, but multiracial, international and predominantly female. Thus any unity it might wish to forge will have to be constructed across a whole range of potentially divisive aspects of cultural, racial, ethnic and geographical identities. In the director's cut especially, *Blade Runner* explores the possibilities that cyborg subjectivities might hold for constructing affinities that cross the social, cultural and even species divisions that separate the working class from its professional–managerial supervisors. As I have already suggested, though, the affinities it constructs are not unproblematic. While, in the director's cut, the rejection of Tyrell, capital and the law of the father is not recontained by a compensatory retreat into nature as the realm of the mother, the phallocentric gender politics of Deckard's relationship with Rachael remain intact. Moreover, Rachael, not least in her sexual submissiveness, is the least 'other' of the replicants and thus promises to be a pliant junior partner to the professional expertise of Deckard. Here lies the real ambivalence of *Blade Runner*'s politics: the replicants are an oppressed and potentially revolutionary class with whom the professional–managerial class has no real choice but to identify; yet the condition of this identification appears to be the suppression of the replicants' overt revolutionary activity and the imposition of a quasi-bourgeois, patriarchal sexual code which serves to restrain their sexual and subjective disruptiveness.

This ambivalence is further expressed in the film's (and Deckard's) simultaneous attraction to and repulsion from the replicants and their very otherness. They are given all the disturbing and unappealing qualities frequently attached to the working class by middle-class guardians of morality and professional agencies of regulation: they are without proper family socialisation and etiquette; they are 'irrational', violent and overly instinctive, particularly in sexual matters; their subjective life is more intense because it is insufficiently mediated by introspection and internalised interdictions. Yet these are also qualities that the narrative (as well as the 'cold fish' Deckard) in some senses longs for and valorises positively, precisely because they are deemed absent from the restrained, rational and highly self-disciplined modes of professional existence. This logic of ambivalent projection is encapsulated in the nature of replicant ontology. As cyborgs, the replicants are images of physical and psychic invulnerability, figures from an omnipotence fantasy (many critics have observed how Roy Batty evokes ideas of the Nietzschean 'superman', or even the Nazi ideal of the Aryan 'master race'). But their compressed four-year lifespan neutralises this omnipotence, renders it meaningless and turns them into objects of pity. That we are asked to sympathise with the replicants for this reason reminds us that the appeal against waste and built-in obsolescence has been a central feature of progressivist and PMC critiques of capitalism from Thorstein Veblen, through Vance Packard, to the Green movement.

Fred Glass has argued that the category of what he calls 'new bad future' films, among which *Blade Runner* should be numbered, is defined by 'the structuring absence of progress'. This 'reveals a vacuum where the revolutionary working class was classically considered by socialists-to-be' (Glass, 1989: p. 44). *Blade Runner* cannot be so defined. But its revolutionary working class is mediated through the codes and anxieties characteristic of the professional–managerial view of the world and is marked by a self-cancelling interplay of impotence and omnipotence. Rather than revealing a vacuum, the film enacts both the return and the qualified disappearance of the revolutionary proletariat. Its leader and theorist, Roy Batty, dies; the slave revolt is suppressed; and Deckard, an ambivalent and ambiguous professional, inherits the working class's historical mission and class consciousness. I have been suggesting throughout this book that we read all these stories of technological development and historical change as narrative manifestations of the 'political unconscious' of the professional-managerial class. In one sense, this class's deployment of the techniques and systems of cybernation to effect a recomposition of the exhausted Fordist regime of accumulation appears to foreshadow the extinction of the working class. In another sense, though, it foreshadows its own proletarianisation. *Blade Runner* suggests that either way, the ideological antinomies of professionalism cannot be avoided. Along with Gibson's cyberspace trilogy, it shows us that, contrary to the claims of end-of-ideology systems thinkers, cybernation is not the historical antidote to antagonistic class consciousness, particularly the divided consciousness of the professional–managerial class itself.

Part 4

Capital, Class, Cosmopolitanism

Fordism, Post-Fordism and the Production of World Space

Capital is becoming more and more cosmopolitan.
John Stuart Mill, *Political Economy* (1848).

In Part 1 of this book I noted that the consolidation of the Fordist regime of accumulation in the United States in the immediate post-1945 period was bound up with the institution of a particular configuration of economic relationships and political power. That there should be a distinct geopolitical dimension to Fordism is not surprising when we recall the precise conditions of the regime's emergence. As we saw, it was the Second World War which ended a decade of world capitalist depression by precipitating a devaluation of fixed capital so radical, prolonged and global in scale as to clear the way for a renewal of accumulation and the revitalisation of productivity and profitability. These achievements, moreover, were based on the innovations of a technological revolution which was driven not so much by private capital and economic competition as it was by state-funded research and development programmes undertaken as part of the war effort (Mandel, 1978: p. 146).

Yet we need to examine in more detail the nature of this international and geopolitical matrix if we are to grasp some of the spatial implications of the crisis and recomposition of the Fordist regime of accumulation. For, amongst all the disagreement that surrounds the debate about the shift from Fordism to post-Fordism, the one area of relative consensus concerns the new kinds of economic space, the new distributions of ownership, production and exchange, and the new levels of global penetration and mobility achieved by capital in overspilling the limits of the Fordist regime. These new and emergent spatial patterns have been recognised by such now familiar formulations as 'the global economy', 'the new international division of labour', or 'the new international competition' (Lipietz, 1987a: p. 4; Harris, 1987: Chapter 4; Reich, 1991: pp. 113–16; Chandler, 1990: p. 606; Mandel, 1978: p. 319). Whatever term is used, however, this 'drive for new geographical and product markets based on the organisational capabilities of the modern industrial enterprise' has, as historian of American business organisation Alfred Chandler argues, 'led to what may prove to be the important turning point in the evolution of that institution. During the 1960s, intensified inter-nation and inter-industry competition began to reshape the strategies of growth, the internal organisation of managerial enterprises, and the relationships between individual firms and between owners and managers' (Chandler, 1990: p. 621).

Cultural and social theorists, too, have turned their attention to globalisation, exploring its links with cultural change and relating postmodernism and postmodernity to the rise of new, deregulated structures of international production, circulation and exchange. Jean-François Lyotard, for example, has linked what he calls 'the computerisation of society' to 'the reopening of the world market, a return to vigorous economic competition, the breakdown of the hegemony of American capitalism, the decline of the socialist alternative, [and] the opening of the Chinese market', among other factors, all of which contributed to a significant restructuring of global space 'at the end of the 1970s' (Lyotard, 1984: p. 6). Lyotard identified the emergence in this space of a new, globalised culture of consumption, marked by increasing transnational homogeneity on the one hand (an effect of the logic of commodification), and increased differentiation on the other (an effect of the widening of consumer choice). In postmodern culture, he famously observed, 'one listens to reggae, watches a western, eats McDonald's food for lunch and local cuisine for dinner, wears Paris perfume in Tokyo and "retro" clothes in Hong Kong' (Lyotard, 1984: p. 76). We must note, though, that Lyotard's 'global' culture is described here from a particularly metropolitan point of view; the kind of cosmopolitanism it brings to mind is that of privileged, educated and mobile elites. Thus, as both Robert Young and Aijaz Ahmad have observed, descriptions or celebrations of globalism which emanate from the industrially developed West, or the 'centre', are always in danger of reproducing the logic of imperialism by imposing a monolithic view of the process across what tends too often to be seen as an undifferentiated, non-industrialised 'periphery'. The periphery is thus represented as both voiceless and without historical agency of its own (Young 1990; Ahmad, 1987).

Nevertheless, metropolitan intellectuals persist in viewing globalisation as both a symptom and motor of cultural change. Mike Featherstone has developed Lyotard's observations to argue that the establishment of an eclectic, worldwide consumer culture is fostering a new, postmodernist kind of global pluralism and relativism that marks a distinct break with modernist universalism (Featherstone, 1991: p. 128). David Harvey has identified the condition of postmodernity as, in part, the effect of an intensification of the spatial reach and mobility of capital around the globe, producing new forms of perception and subjective experience (Harvey, 1989). And Fredric Jameson has gone as far as to define postmodernism first and foremost as a spatial category, the direct corollary in culture of 'the world space of multinational capital', which has large implications for individual and collective social agency (Jameson, 1991: p. 54).

As we have seen, these processes of globalisation are commonly understood to be inseparable from the deployment of the new technologies of information, communication and reproduction discussed in the earlier parts of this book. Communications analyst, Herbert Schiller, argues for example that information technologies, with their ability to shift data and capital instantaneously and without regard for geographical or national barriers, 'have become the life-support elements in the world business system' (Schiller, 1984: p. 50). Similarly, Alfred Chandler claims that these technologies have been responsible for 'the transformation of the global economy'; they mark 'a turning point in the evolution of the modern industrial enterprise' which was precipitated by the profitability crises of mature Fordism. 'By the mid-1970s', he observes, 'international computer communication was becoming an integral part of the control and information systems of American, European and Japanese multinational enterprises' (Chandler, 1990: pp. 606, 608). Moreover, as I suggested in Chapter 6, cybernetic technologies and systems thinking developed as responses to the specifically international and geopolitical challenges faced by American managerial elites in the new, fully globalised sphere of operations after 1945. Indeed, Fredric Jameson has argued that this new multinational space can only adequately be understood in terms of cybernetic metaphors that are closer to science fiction than to social science:

> it would be a great mistake to imagine something like 'the globe' as yet a new and larger space replacing the older national or imperial ones. Globalisation is rather a kind of cyberspace in which money and capital has reached its ultimate dematerialisation, as messages which pass instantaneously from one nodal point to another across the former globe, the former material world. (Jameson, 1998: p. 154).

An exploration of contemporary processes of globalisation and spatial restructuring therefore follows quite logically from my preceding discussions of the technologies of information and cybernation and their place in the transition between regimes of accumulation. Many of the stories examined in those earlier chapters began to point in this direction in their own ambivalent representations of economic and social change. *The Soul of a New Machine* begins and concludes with evocations of sudden international migrations of capital and production. *Microserfs* suggests that the autonomy of its privileged but anxious professional 'techies' rests on systems of serflike toil which are elsewhere, unseen or unlocatable within the spread of globalised production. William Gibson's cyberspace trilogy enacts the literal universalisation of capital in a fully commodified and informated world system. And *Blade Runner* dramatises the super-planetary expansion of capitalist production and class relations alike. Thus, after a further brief discussion of the character of capitalist world space, I will turn in the following chapters to two recent narratives of globalisation which take this process as their major concern and explicitly situate it in the context of economic and geopolitical crisis.

Of course it would be misleading to suggest that the internationalisation of capitalist relations of production, circulation and exchange has only been recently achieved by virtue of the latest communications technologies. As the quotation from Mill's *Political Economy* of 1848 which heads this chapter illustrates, commentators long ago were struck by the capitalist mode of production's uniquely expansionist spatial dynamism, what Barnet and Muller (1975) call 'its 'global reach'. For Karl Marx and Frederick Engels, writing like Mill in 1848, capitalism's spatial dynamism was its defining feature and its most impressive attribute; it was just this that in their view made the bourgeoisie, the class of capitalist entrepreneurs and industrialists, more than just another parochial interest group but in fact revolutionaries, agents of world–historical transformation. In their *Manifesto of the Communist Party* they wrote:

> The need of a constantly expanding market for its products chases the bourgeoisie over the whole surface of the globe. It must nestle everywhere, settle everywhere, establish connections everywhere ... The bourgeoisie, by the rapid improvement of all the instruments of production, by the immensely facilitated means of communication, draws all, even the most barbarian, nations into civilisation ... In one word, it creates a world after its own image. (Marx and Engels, 1973: pp. 37–8)

As their invocation of the process of 'civilisation' suggests, Marx and Engels saw the global reach of the bourgeoisie as a progressive force. But this consisted less in the simple fact of territorial expansion as such than in the sweeping transformation of existing social relations and forms of consciousness that capitalist expansion wrought, its imposition of radically new economic priorities, cultural patterns and even temporal rhythms on societies hitherto structured by long-standing traditions. In a famous and oft-cited passage that immediately precedes the one quoted above, Marx and Engels refer to the process of capitalist globalisation as one in which 'All fixed, fast-frozen relations, with their train of ancient and venerable prejudices and opinions are swept away, [and] all new-formed ones become antiquated before they can ossify', in which, 'All that is solid melts into air' (Marx and Engels, 1973: pp. 36–7). And it is clear that they understood themselves to be describing here a new kind of global space. This is a space which, as Marshall Berman argues, is defined by a continuous process of 'creative destruction', a space of constant derealisation and the making abstract of the once concrete, a space on to which new patterns and configurations are successively and rapidly inscribed. For Marx and Engels, of course, there was a utopian end point to this process: the universalisation of capital and the bourgeoisie simultaneously created a global working class and the technical means by which this class would ultimately seize the reins of capitalism and redistribute its material benefits to all in a classless and socially just future. Yet their description of the exhilaratingly transformative nature of capitalist world space is propelled by a certain admiring and celebratory momentum of its own.

An appreciation of the spatial recompositions effected by capital's expansionary logic is also central to the 'world systems' theory associated with social and economic historians, Fernand Braudel and Immanuel Wallerstein. In this perspective, the historical emergence of the capitalist mode of production is concomitant with the qualitative transformation of space on a world scale. For Wallerstein, the 'transition from feudalism to capitalism involves first of all (first logically and first temporally) the creation of a world economy'; or, as Alain Lipietz puts it, 'Capitalism was ... born of world trade' (Wallerstein, 1990: p. 165; Lipietz, 1987a: p. 56). Nations, regional economies and social classes themselves can only develop as local functions of this prior global condition, it is argued. While the proper level of social and historical analysis must always be that of the world system, then, it is nonetheless crucial to understand that this latter is defined not by sheer scope alone, but by the nature of the space it produces. Such space is increasingly structured by commodity production and the wage relation, but is also characterised by an ever-intensifying degree of that spatial dynamism admired by Marx and Engels. Capitalism, says Wallerstein, is 'a form of social organisation whose prime object is its own perpetuation in an ever-expanding form'; this, he observes, is 'the true Promethean myth' (Wallerstein, 1979: p. 120).

While Marx and Engels were concerned to describe the world space produced by the emergence and expansion of freely competitive capitalism, other commentators have addressed themselves to the spatial consequences of subsequent changes in the nature of capitalism itself. In the Marxist tradition, the question of relating shifts in the modalities of accumulation to changes in the spatial dynamic of world capitalism became a central preoccupation. Lenin and Bukharin, writing in 1917 and 1918 respectively, both sought to identify the new spatial and geopolitical configurations produced by the transition from *laissez-faire* to monopoly forms, and each argued for the identification of a new epochal stage of capitalism – 'imperialism' – in predominantly spatial terms. In so doing, both adopted and refined Marx and Engels's spatial metaphors in interesting ways. Where the *Manifesto of the Communist Party* had described the bourgeoisie creating a whole 'world' by a twin process of expansive interconnection ('establishing connections everywhere') and liberatory derealisation ('all that is solid melts into air'), Lenin and Bukharin deployed metaphors more suggestive of restriction, centralisation and compartmentalisation.

In the epoch of capitalist monopoly, Lenin argued, 'finance capital, almost literally one might say, spreads its net over all the countries of the world'. And this seizure of world space is accompanied by its dissection: 'The capital exporting countries have divided the world among themselves in the figurative sense of the term. But finance capital has also led to the *actual* division of the world' (Lenin, 1939: pp. 66, 67, author's emphasis). In a similar vein, Bukharin described the stage of imperialist monopoly as one in which 'International economic relations are extended through countless threads; they pass through thousands of crosspoints; they are intertwined in thousands of groups, finally converging in the agreements of the largest world banks which have stretched out their tentacles over the entire globe' (Bukharin, 1975: p. 27). A sense of increasing confinement and constriction inhabits these descriptions, as Lenin's net metaphor mutates into Bukharin's image of the world being held in the grip of the tentacles of finance capital. This contrasts with the relative looseness and dynamism of Marx and Engels's images of melting barriers and proliferating connections. There is a shift here from a sense of space being produced, opened up, in the earlier account, to a sense of space being closed down, incorporated and saturated in the latter. And this seems to be directly related to the historical preponderance of capital in a new form, one in which the creative–destructive energies of the bourgeoisie have been superseded by the agency of the corporations and, above all, the central banks: 'It is finance capital that appears to be the all-pervading form of capital, that form which, like nature, suffers from a *horror vacui*, since it rushes to fill every "vacuum", whether in a "tropical", "sub-tropical", or "polar" region, if only profits flow in sufficient quantities' (Bukharin, 1975: p. 27). Here the spaces of nature are being relentlessly closed out by capital which, paradoxically, is itself given the qualities of a force of nature almost oceanic in its 'flow'.

I am trying to suggest two things here. Firstly, historical changes in the forms and structures of capital accumulation tend to produce, and be expressed through, changes in the spatial dynamic of the world system. Secondly, these changes are marked by a particular dialectic of derealisation or abstraction on the one hand and constriction or reification on the other. This dialectic can be traced in the metaphors with which commentators have sought to describe the process. Lenin's term for this spatial dialectic was 'uneven development' (Lenin, 1939: p. 10). This referred to the way in which the geographical expansion of capitalism proceeded through the progressive abstraction and equalisation of places into what Michel Aglietta calls the universal or 'homogeneous space of value' (Aglietta, 1979: pp. 38, 45). Yet at the same time, this process also involved the strict recomposition and recrystallisation of space into specific local, regional and national pockets of difference and inequality reflecting the way in which the imperialist 'centres' of capitalist development could exploit the less developed 'periphery'. Thus, in the spatial logic of uneven development the dialectic of abstraction and rematerialisation is complemented by a dialectic of equalisation and differentiation. Christian Palloix has explained it well: 'The movement of capital includes at one and the same time both the necessity for movement *towards an equalisation of the conditions of production and exchange* and *towards the differentiation of the conditions of production and exchange* in order to respond to the perpetually insoluble problem of the extraction of surplus value' (Palloix, 1977: p. 23, author's emphasis).

But this spatial dynamic also has an important historical dimension, in as much as the production of space is always the production of different kinds of historical space. Capital, that is, marks out spaces which are defined by radically different historical features and modes of organisation. The internationalisation of capital operates by linking such spaces together, spaces which are characterised by divergent levels of social and economic development. As Mandel argues, 'world-wide capitalist relations of exchange bind together capitalist, semi-capitalist and pre-capitalist relations of production in an organic unity' (Mandel, 1978: p. 311). Uneven development combines discrepant historical spaces into configurations conducive to the production of surplus value.

Geographers Neil Smith and David Harvey have sought to explain the process of uneven development through the terminology of 'absolute' and 'relative' space, drawing on Marx's distinction between absolute and relative surplus value. Absolute space is the result of the abstraction and homogenisation wrought by the extension of the law of value and the conditions for commodity exchange. Relative space is the differentiated geographic space in which particular economic and social inequalities are established as an effect and condition of the drive for surplus value. According to Smith, capitalism reproduces itself through a continuous expansion of *absolute* space and its immediate restructuration as *relative* space, giving rise to a perpetual interplay of abstraction and rematerialisation, homogenisation and differentiation (Smith, 1984: pp. 67, 87). Indeed, Smith argues, this spatial dialectic must be counted as the fundamental means of capitalist production. It is through this process that nature itself becomes transformed from a use value into an exchange value; thus the 'second nature' of human productive and social relations subsumes, incorporates and begins in turn to 'produce' the 'first nature' of physical and organic materiality. Uneven development is therefore 'the production of nature at a world scale', in which 'nature is progressively produced from within and as part of the so-called second nature'. In this way, 'first nature is deprived of its firstness, its originality' (Smith, 1984: p. 54).

Smith is here echoing Henri Lefebvre's contention that in late or neo-capitalism as he calls it, the reproduction of the relations of production occurs principally through the production of space:

Reproduction is located not simply in *society as a whole* but in *space as a whole*. Space, occupied by neo-capitalism, sectioned, reduced to homogeneity yet fragmented, becomes the seat of power ... The productive forces permit those who dispose of them to control space and even to *produce* it. This productive capacity extends to the whole of the earth's space and beyond. Natural space is destroyed and transformed into a social product by an ensemble of techniques, particularly physics and information science. (Lefebvre, 1976: pp. 83–4, author's emphasis)

The interplay of abstraction and materialisation, of equalisation and differentiation on a world scale, produces this destabilisation of origins and undermines the priority of the natural over the constructed or the abstract. This is precisely the paradoxical interpenetration of categories, of material and abstract, of first and second nature, that we observed in Bukharin's metaphor of finance capital as an oceanic natural force with which he sought to describe the transition from *laissez-faire* to monopolistic imperialism.

Gilles Deleuze and Félix Guattari's notions of 'deterritorialisation' and 'reterritorialisation', touched on in previous chapters, can further aid our understanding of the spatial dynamic of uneven development. Like Marx, they view capitalism's abstracting power, its perpetual destruction of 'fixed, fast-frozen relations', as its most progressive and liberatory feature. This process of relentless deterritorialisation creates what they call 'smooth space' on a global, even super-planetary, scale, into which flows of material force can move with revolutionising effect. Here, then, we have the absolute or homogeneous space of value. However, every deterritorialisation is accompanied by its opposite, a reterritorialisation by which smooth space is 'striated' and the flows of force are subjected to structuration and material domination. Thus, for Deleuze and Guattari, 'capitalism is continually reterritorialising with one hand what it was deterritorialising with the other'; and 'it may be all but impossible to distinguish deterritorialisation from reterritorialisation, since they are mutually enmeshed, or like the opposite faces of one and the same process' (Deleuze and Guattari, 1984: pp. 259, 258).

These spatial metaphors capture exactly Marx's sense of the globalisation of capitalist relations as both the most liberating and most oppressive of historical developments, and of the difficulty of distinguishing the progressive from the regressive within it. The deterritorialisation of feudal social relations into the universal, smooth space of a capitalist world economy was offset by its reterritorialisation into modern nation states seeking dominion over it. Another way of grasping this spatial logic would be to see it working in terms of the reterritorialisation of the absolute space of the world economy into an unequal relationship between the differentiated relative spaces of imperialist centre, or metropolitan core, and exploited periphery. This particular instance points to the tension that exists between the production of absolute and relative space, between deterritorialisation and its complementary countermovement. For it was precisely the struggle between imperialist nations to reterritorialise the smooth, homogeneous space of the world economy that led to the war of 1914 which threatened, as Lenin speculated in 1917, to destroy the system as a whole (Lenin, 1939; Kern, 1983). Indeed, the spatial contradictions that led to the First World War were not fully resolved until the Second World War put an end to the kinds of inter-imperialist competition characteristic of the late nineteenth century, and provided the conditions for a new regime of accumulation based on the reorganisation of capitalist world space and a reinflection of the dynamic of uneven development.

Fordist structures of accumulation and regulation therefore arose out of the demise of the old stage of classical imperialism described by Lenin and the onset of the new stage of late capitalism. As Ernest Mandel notes, in 1945 the capitalist world economy was confronted with vast losses to its spatial domain. The expansion of the Soviet sphere of influence meant that much of Europe and Asia was lost to capitalist commodity production and exchange (Mandel, 1978: p. 131). Further, the reach of the old imperialist powers had been severely curtailed by the war, either through defeat (Germany, Japan) or economic and financial exhaustion (Britain, France). And many of the colonies of these powers now embarked on struggles for independence which threatened to remove even more global space from the reach of capital, particularly if they followed the Soviet model of national autarchy. The potential for resolving the crisis of accumulation by what David Harvey calls a simple 'spatial fix', a strictly quantitative 'geographical expansion of capitalism', was thus reduced (Harvey, 1989: p. 183). The periphery could no longer serve in such a straightforward way, as it had at the high point of classical imperialism, as a safety valve or outlet for the overproduction and overaccumulation of the core; world space was restricted and could no longer unproblematically 'mop up' metropolitan surpluses (Lipietz, 1987a: p. 49).

Fordism therefore came to be bound up with new spatial priorities and a realignment of centre–periphery relationships. The production of absolute space (quantitive extension of the reach of commodity relations) became less important than the production of relative space (qualitative transformations of regions already penetrated by commodity relations). In the same way, as we saw in Part 1 of this book, the production of relative over the production of absolute surplus value was promoted in Fordism in the shift from an extensive to an intensive regime of accumulation (Smith, 1984: p. 88). The post-1945 long boom was based on the internal development of the already industrialised capitalist core, principally the United States, at the expense of the volume of international trade on a world scale. The concern to intensify and equalise the relationship in the industrial West between domestic mass production and mass consumption, through constantly rising productivity on the one hand and earnings on the other, meant that the periphery 'gradually lost its importance as an outlet'. In this respect, Lipietz defines Fordism as a uniquely 'auto-centred spatial structure' (Lipietz, 1987a: pp. 56, 57, 59).

Yet the consolidation of Fordism in the United States was nonetheless felt to be very much an international process, intimately linked to the revitalisation of the war-ravaged economies of Western Europe and Japan through the agency of American capital. The Fordist model was therefore 'exported' via Marshall aid and the various programmes and institutions of reconstruction designed after the Second World War to guarantee peace and prosperity in the old imperialist heartland. Capital now circulated principally within the metropolitan core in which the 'centre of the world', as Braudel and Wallerstein would put it, had moved decisively to the United States. Thus, in contrast to the periods of Dutch or British global economic hegemony, the period of full American hegemony – emergent since the 1880s (Chase-Dunn, 1989) – was initially characterised by the preponderance of an internalised or autocentric, rather than an expansive, spatial dynamic.

Of course, accession to the position of global hegemony intensified geopolitical concerns in the United States, as we saw in Chapter 6 above, with the development of new administrative techniques and models for managing global space. The Cold War, a major factor in the new spatial dispensation of late capitalism, itself became a motor of the Fordist warfare–welfare state and its reliance on a permanent arms economy. And as variants on the Fordist structures of the United States took hold with growing success in Europe and Japan, enabling those economies eventually to compete in America's own domestic marketplace, American prosperity increasingly became linked to the export of Fordism on a more sweeping global scale. As early as

1945 a statement from the United Auto Workers union (an important player in the construction of the Fordist capital–labour accord in America with its acquisition of guaranteed regular wage increases for its members in return for a no-strike pledge to management) suggested as much. 'We cannot possibly maintain full production and full employment', it declared, 'unless we have a world pool of free and prosperous consumers' (quoted in W. A. Williams, 1961: p. 452). Attention therefore turned to the development of the rapidly decolonising periphery. By the late 1950s, according to David Calleo, American power and investment had transferred much of its focus from the Atlantic 'Near Empire' of Europe to the 'Far Empire' of what became known as the Third World (Calleo, 1984: p. 393).

This, however, was not empire in the traditional sense. Direct political military and administrative control, allied to opportunistic economic plunder, was not the order of the day. Rather, the American-Fordist version of empire (sometimes characterised as 'neocolonialism') emphasised, as earlier colonialisms had not, the 'independent' internal economic and political development of peripheral nations, albeit under the aegis of 'benevolent' American strategic supervision and with the agency of American capital and technical expertise (Kolko, 1988: p. 18). In short, the periphery was encouraged to adopt the Fordist model of accumulation, and the United States sought to guarantee that the international sphere would remain sufficiently 'open' or 'liberal' for this to succeed. W. W. Rostow's *The Stages of Economic Growth* (1960) was a virtual *summa* of the doctrine of global Fordist 'development'. It outlined how the periphery, bolstered by American advice, aid and technical assistance, could leapfrog the drawn out and messy precapitalist process of what Marx had called 'primitive accumulation', and achieve 'take off', as Rostow put it, directly into an ever-ascending set of stages of capitalist growth.[1] Thus the fortunes of Fordism became tied to what Calleo calls the construction of an 'American world system' in which 'domestic prosperity, containment of communism, the recovery and containment of other major capitalist powers, and the refashioning of the old colonial order were all highly conscious and interdependent goals' (Calleo, 1984: pp. 391, 393).

Despite the fact that 'at its height, Fordism marks the extent to which developed capitalism can be autocentred', it was nonetheless deeply inscribed within a global strategy for accumulation constructed around a geopolitical vision of the United States as a world hegemonic power. The establishment of a new international monetary order at Bretton Woods in 1944 gave early institutional expression to the Fordist model of global regulation (Block, 1977: Chapter 3; Harvey, 1989: p. 137). The dollar, 'as good as gold' due to the strength of American productivity and profitability, filled the vacuum created by the collapse of the nineteenth-century gold standard, serving as both an international reserve currency and a stable point of financial reference in the new world system of fixed exchange rates that was constructed around it. Additionally, the International Monetary Fund and the World Bank emerged as vehicles of the dollar's global centrality; these institutions used the indispensability of dollar reserves as a stick and carrot with which to discipline other national economies, securing their allegiance to 'liberal' fiscal and economic policies and their receptivity to American foreign investments. (Block, 1977: pp. 50–4). The Pax Americana was, therefore, the Fordist regime's international dimension, representing, David Harvey observes, 'a spatial revolution in global trading and investment' (Harvey, 1989: p. 185). The world space of nineteenth-century imperialism, in which competing metropolitan nations extended their direct control over a periphery characterised by extreme comparative underdevelopment, had given way to the monocentric world space of late capitalism. Here a less direct and uneven relationship between core and periphery pertained, largely through the promotion of the ideology of 'development' or, as Alain Lipietz calls it, 'global Fordism' (Lipietz, 1987a: p. 69).[2] The systems view of global regulation developed by the RAND Corporation was an ideological representation of this new global space. Indeed, we have seen in Chapter 6 how Francis Fukuyama's latest variant of RAND-think carries the emphasis on American-centred global isomorphism to new levels, envisaging the emergence of a 'universal homogeneous state' through the export of American-style consumer culture and liberal democracy.

However, as David Calleo points out, it was the very success of global Fordism that precipitated the crisis of American Fordism and undermined the Pax Americana with which it was bound up. The recovery of Western Europe and Japan in accordance with Fordist socioeconomic arrangements, and the economic dynamism of sectors of the periphery which had implemented indigenous versions of Fordism (often referred to as Newly Industrialising Countries or NICs), meant that an increasing volume of foreign products now competed on favourable terms with American goods, even within the United States itself (Calleo, 1984: p. 442). Christopher Chase-Dunn argues that the economic hegemony of the United States began to decline as early as 1950. Then, it produced 42 per cent of world goods and services; by 1970 this had declined to 30 per cent. Maintaining the world system that had once seemed to underpin domestic prosperity increasingly proved to be more costly than beneficial (Chase-Dunn, 1989: p. 185). The inflationary effects of the war in Vietnam, despite its importance as an engine of the permanent arms economy, were devastating, undermining the fragile social peace at home and the stability of the dollar as the currency of international reserve. Thus, as Joyce Kolko argues, the war, 'lasting as long as it did ... had an organic effect on the whole world capitalist system', precipitating in the early 1970s the first major recession since the 1930s (Kolko, 1988: p. 21). Moreover, the 'open door' for trade and the liberal, dollar-based monetary order established at Bretton Woods allowed for the penetration of American and once American-dominated markets from 'outside', just as they had once catered for the reverse (Chase-Dunn, 1989: p. 179). In 1971 President Nixon was compelled to end the era of the dollar 'gold-standard' and follow a policy of systematic currency devaluation to counter inflation and a worsening balance of trade position, inaugurating a new era of floating international exchange rates, mercantilist competition, and radical financial instability. The removal of limits on the outflow of capital, a policy change ostensibly to bolster American competitiveness abroad, effectively passed the power of financial regulation over to the multinational corporations whose first loyalty was to their own profits rather than to the American balance of payments. As profit increasingly lay in the deterritorialisation of production and investment into an ever more uneven global arena, these measures only served to 'maximise the strain between national economies and the world economy' (Block, 1977: p. 204). Thus between 1965 and 1980, 'the core became increasingly multicentric' as the regulatory and financial structures of global Fordism unravelled and American imperial hegemony faltered militarily in Vietnam, just as it was assailed economically from Western Europe, Japan and the leading NICs (Chase-Dunn, 1989: p. 186).

As the limits of Fordism were being reached domestically in the increasing rigidity of the capital–labour accord, so the limits of the Pax Americana were being exposed internationally, illustrated by the crisis of American world leadership. As Gordon and Wallerstein argue, this is not surprising if it is accepted that long cycles of accumulation, or Kondratieff waves, operate principally at a world level (Gordon et al., 1982; Wallerstein, 1984: pp. 16–18). This, in David Harvey's words, is to understand that 'the crisis of Fordism [is] as much a geographical and geopolitical crisis as it [is] a crisis of indebtedness, class struggle, or corporate stagnation within any particular nation state'. Thus, the crisis of Fordism is 'in large part a crisis in spatial form' (Harvey, 1989: pp. 186, 196). The drive to break out of and recompose the structures of Fordism is therefore accompanied by a corresponding transformation in global space, some of whose effects we have explored in previous chapters, particularly the export of production and the deterritorialisation of relations between employers and workers. Intensified internationalisation has in this sense been crucial in dismantling the capital–labour accord of Fordism (Storper and Scott, 1986a: p. 5).

The transformation extends deeper than this, though. As the core becomes increasingly multicentric, its relationship with the periphery is altered. The export of production and the success of 'peripheral Fordism' (Lipietz, 1987a: p. 113) undermine the bipolar arrangement of core and periphery, even to some extent reversing the hierarchy of the terms. Many commentators have observed that capital's enhanced mobility has fostered not only the industrialisation of peripheral regions, but also the de-industrialisation, or peripheralisation, of large sectors of the advanced capitalist metropolis. Mike Davis and Ed Soja have both recorded the return of 'primitive' and bloody forms of production and work organisation, long associated with the developing periphery, to the metropolitan heartland; both have observed a tendential shift in the 'centre of the world' away from the north-eastern United States toward the Pacific rim; and both have suggested that the geography of advanced capitalism is structured by a complex co-existence of radically different forms of production and organisation, appropriate to different orders of capitalist development, never before witnessed (Davis, 1985 and 1990; Soja, 1989). Nigel Harris has described this new spatial configuration in these terms:

> The conception of an interdependent, interacting global manufacturing system cuts across the old view of a world consisting of nation states as well as one of groups of countries, more or less developed and centrally planned – the First, the Third and the Second Worlds. Those notions bore some relation to an older economy, one marked by the exchange of raw materials for manufactured goods. But the new world that has superseded it is far more complex and does not lend itself to the simple identification of First and Third, haves and have-nots, rich and poor, industrialised and non-industrialised. (Harris, 1987: p. 200)

The emergent space of newly multinationalised production might in this sense best be characterised in terms of Michel Foucault's notion of the 'heterotopia', a space marked by the 'linking together of things that are inappropriate ... so very different from one another that it is impossible ... to define a *common locus* beneath them all' (Foucault, 1970: pp. xvii–xviii).

With respect to core and periphery, then, the suggestion is that spatial restructuring is producing difference *within* rather than difference *between* regions and spaces, causing the old binary oppositions outlined by Nigel Harris above to break down. According to Soja, 'increasingly "footloose" and mobile capital has contributed to an extraordinary global restructuring of industrial production'. A 'combination of deindustrialisation and reindustrialisation has shattered long-standing global definitions of core and periphery, First-Second-Third Worlds, and created the tentative outlines of a different ... international division of labour' (Soja, 1989: pp. 185–6). To this end, Wallerstein has identified a 'third' kind of global space which he calls the 'semiperiphery', marked by higher levels of overall social development but more social instability than the periphery, and functioning as a mediator between the acute inequalities of core and periphery (Wallerstein, 1979: Chapter 5). With the shift to post-Fordist structures of accumulation, however, it is increasingly evident that certain regions of the core itself have been peripheralised (Bluestone and Harrison, 1982: pp. 15–18; Soja, 1989: pp. 215–17; Davis, 1990; Chase-Dunn, 1989). Furthermore, we can understand this entire process as an intensification of the logic of uneven development facilitated, as Morgan and Sayer and Jeffrey Henderson have shown, by the deterritorialising power of new communications technologies. These reproduce capital as data, allowing it to be reterritorialised with increasing rapidity and flexibility (Morgan and Sayer, 1988: pp. 264–5; Henderson, 1991). Indeed, it has been suggested that information now forms the basis of what can be seen as a post-Fordist international monetary order that has been constructed out of the ruins of the old dollar-based financial system. Ex-Citicorp chairman, Walter Wriston, has claimed that 'what one might call the *information standard* has replaced the gold standard and indeed even the system invented at Bretton Woods'. He suggests that 'the expansion of the magnetic spectrum up to three hundred megahertz ... has created an entirely new system of world finance based on the increasingly rapid flow of information around the world' (quoted in Kolko, 1988: p. 104, author's emphasis).

There is of course a class dimension to this whole process. The intensification of uneven development has produced unevenly distributed changes in the global composition of classes.[3] Chase-Dunn argues that the internationalisation of production means a widening of proletarianisation in the periphery as more people are drawn into the wage relation for the first time in the history of their communities. This is the new 'worldwide working class' that Donna Haraway and Fredric Jameson have invoked. Correspondingly, Chase-Dunn suggests, the core experiences an increase in managerial class locations relative to the decline in blue-collar occupations, continuing the trend that was already established in mature Fordism (Chase-Dunn, 1989: p. 187). However, this goes along with the growth of a new immigrant proletariat drawn from the periphery into the sweatshops and household production outlets that spring up in the core regions themselves, as well as with the emergence of a propertyless 'new' middle class of technicians and managers internal to the industrialising periphery and semiperiphery (Davis, 1985; Harris, 1987: pp. 172–4). The internationalisation of production therefore produces a corresponding internationalisation of class relationships in which the deployment of reproductive and communications technologies is central. For if the 'electronification' of the world system has as 'its corollary the extending [of the] technical divisions of labour', then this points among other things to a new global insertion of the professional–managerial class (Arrighi, Hopkins and Wallerstein, 1988: p. 75). And as we have seen, this is the class that is described as and understands itself to be the most cosmopolitan, internationalist and universal of social groups.

The professional–managerial class thus has a particularly large stake, as well as a determining role, in the recomposition of global space. As stewards of the communications systems and technologies that facilitate deterritorialisation, and as administrators of what Alfred Chandler defines as the principal institutional agents of the new internationalised business sphere, the multinational corporations, the class's universalist aspirations and ideologies now operate within an increasingly universal spatial realm. And it is worth noting here that the multinational corporations themselves have frequently been said to aspire to a condition of cosmopolitan and universal rationality, beyond locality and nationality alike, to become 'citizens of the world' in a way that strikingly echoes PMC claims to cosmopolitanism and universality (Tugendhat, 1975: p. 193). Indeed, we saw in Chapter 7 above the ambiguous convergence of these twin notions of universalist rationality dramatised in William Gibson's cyberspace trilogy.

This is not to suggest that professional–managerial class cosmopolitanism simply mimics that of multinational capital; we have seen in earlier chapters how the two modes of rationality are frequently at odds. Multinational capital might have so successfully detached itself from national affiliations that to speak of national corporations or even national economies is obsolete (Barnet and Muller, 1975: pp. 72–3; Lyotard, 1984: p. 5; Reich, 1991: pp. 3, 8, 81). But the global PMC cannot be said equally to have severed all its connections with notions of nationhood. For co-existing with its cosmopolitan outlook are forms of intense nationalism, particularly amongst the managerial and professional strata of peripheral and semiperipheral states. Here, the 'new class' is invariably at the centre of nationalist movements and local opposition to multinational capital. Yet this very nationalism is, paradoxically, an effect of the absorption of imported ideas and ideologies, often the internationalist ideology of 'development' itself (Gouldner, 1979: p. 83; Chase-Dunn, 1989: p. 342; Harris, 1987: pp. 172–3). At a global level at least, then, the class is inhabited by a tension between deracination and situatedness which will inform its attitudes towards the production of post-Fordist world space. We need to bear this in mind for the discussion of narratives of globalisation which follows this chapter.

Earlier in this book I quoted Morgan and Sayer's contention that 'one consequence of combined and uneven development is that spatial mismatches between causes and their effects become the norm' (Morgan and Sayer, 1988: p. 265). This refers us finally to the cognitive, even phenomenological, aspect of uneven development, the intensification of which is central to the production of post-Fordist world space. It also seems to support Fredric Jameson's claim that the vast global realities of multinational capital are unassimilable to individual subjective experience and understanding. Postmodernism describes a condition of spatial disorientation in which individuals are no longer (if they ever were) able to situate themselves with respect to the global economic system which structures their existence. The sheer global reach of the system exceeds any attempt to

ıt and understand or 'cognitively map' it. Lived experience is henceforth,
Jameson, divorced from the truth of structure; and art, whose raw materials
are drawn precisely from lived experience, can no longer embody the full truth of
that experience, unless it be the limited and 'negative truth' of abject spatial and
historical confusion (Jameson, 1988a).

Despite Jameson's comments about the simultaneous necessity and impossibility
of cognitive mapping, since the American world system entered its period of crisis
and restructuring in the 1970s there has been a proliferation of narratives that
dramatise and seek to understand the spatial consequences of this crisis, especially
the intensification of globalisation it entails.[4] I want now to look in detail at two
such narratives, Don DeLillo's novel, *The Names* (1982), and Wim Wenders's film,
Until the End of the World (1991). In different ways, these can be seen as attempts to
describe and to map the production of space as Fordism and the Pax Americana are
recomposed into new global configurations. They can also be understood as
responses to David Harvey's observation that 'the transition from Fordism to flexible
accumulation, such as it has been, ought to imply a transition in our mental maps,
political attitudes and political institutions ... There is an omnipresent danger that
our mental maps will not match our current realities' (Harvey, 1989: p. 305).

10

National Allegory and the Romance of Underdevelopment: *The Names*

> I go everywhere twice. Once to get the wrong impression, once to strengthen it.
>
> James Axton, in *The Names* (p. 255)

> It's a political allegory.
>
> Kathryn Axton, in *The Names* (p. 80)

> No, there is no question of a return to Nature.
>
> Frantz Fanon, *The Wretched of the Earth* (1967: p. 253)

Fredric Jameson has argued that the impossibility of cognitive mapping is the most debilitating political–aesthetic dimension of the cultural dominance of postmodernism. But he has also suggested, more optimistically perhaps, that this debility is not – yet – universal. The tendency of postmodern cultural forms is to reflect and complement capital's colonisation of nature and the unconscious with its emplacement of a global, American-style consumer culture (Stephanson, 1989: p. 9). However, Jameson contends that there nevertheless remain enclaves as yet not wholly colonised by this process in which something like the operations of cognitive mapping can still take place. Certain of the aesthetic productions and cultural practices of the 'un-' or 'underdeveloped' world represent one such enclave.

In third-world cultures, Jameson suggests, there obtains an entirely distinctive relation between the public and the private, between the political and the psychological, which differs crucially from the one which structures first-world experience.[1] Where the latter is characterised by a 'radical split between the private and the public' – a split which underlies the incommensurability of subjective experience and systemic vision or structural understanding and thus impedes cognitive mapping – the former are defined by a much greater continuity between the two realms. Personal life is here more readily understood and lived in its communal dimension, as an effect and a mediation of more impersonal forces and larger collective histories. Thus, *'the story of the private individual destiny is always an allegory of the embattled situation of the public third-world culture and society'* (Jameson, 1986b: p. 69, author's emphasis). Third-world narratives, then, demand to be understood as 'national allegories', stories in which the fates, fears and desires of individuals stand for political and historical movements on a collective, and specifically a national, scale.

The aesthetic–cognitive value of the national allegory is here seen to derive from a particular spatial or geographical condition – its location within the cultural practices and social mores of a region Jameson calls the third world. However, in another discussion of third-world cultural production, Jameson sees cognitive value as an effect also of a particular temporal or historical condition. What makes the aesthetic form of 'magic realism', like third-world national allegory, an attractive 'alternative to the narrative logic of contemporary [first-world] postmodernism' is the relationship it bears to a society and culture in which no single historical mode of production seamlessly dominates. Where postmodernism is the cultural correlate of the universal reach of commodity relations in first-world societies, magic realism is by contrast 'dependent on a type of historical raw material in which disjunction is structurally present'; that is, 'it depends on a content which betrays the overlap or coexistence of precapitalist with nascent capitalist or technological features'. Magic realism, therefore, in the terminology of the previous chapter of this book, is the cultural reflection of combined and uneven development. It embodies the kinds of cognitive process appropriate to a context marked by conflicting and overlapping historical modes of production and ways of life, by deep historical struggle and transformation, in other words. And while magic realist narrative arises out of 'the destruction of older communities and collectivities', Jameson suggests that 'it may also be understood as the conquest of new kinds of relationships with history and with being' (Jameson, 1986a: pp. 301, 311, 321).

Aesthetic–cognitive value is therefore seen by Jameson to dwell in those spatial and temporal enclaves of disjunction, difference and unevenness which persist only as vestiges in an epoch of totalisation, as effects of 'the remains of older cultures in our general world capitalist system' (Jameson, 1986b: p. 68). The dangers of a first-world intellectual projecting value so emphatically on to the cultural products of a third world conceived as late capitalism's endangered and vestigial 'other' have been cogently enumerated by Robert Young and Aijaz Ahmad (Young, 1990: Chapter 6; Ahmad, 1987). Ahmad has convincingly challenged Jameson's definition of third-world literature in terms of national allegory, arguing that the 'public' or 'political' cannot be limited to the national alone, and that such allegorical narratives are at least as characteristic of first-world cultures as they are of those in the third world (Ahmad, 1987: pp. 14–15). This implied notion of a first-world 'national allegory' is close to John McClure's identification of a new American genre of 'late imperial romance', the recent proliferation of which I noted in the previous chapter. I want to suggest here that we can usefully read what McClure calls the late imperial romance as a kind of metropolitan national allegory appropriate to a period of geopolitical crisis and global economic recomposition, a form of national allegory which is necessarily international in scope. I would also suggest that instances of this genre will be marked by some of the same formal–cognitive characteristics Jameson locates in the third-world national allegory, in particular, a concern to articulate in narrative the junction of the private and the public. Indeed, with the intensification of the production of uneven development *within* the metropolitan core as a response to the crisis of global Fordism, we might expect first-world cultural production to exhibit a growing tendency to manifest some of the aesthetic forms and cognitive strategies which Jameson attributes to those of the third world. Thus the return of national allegory in first-world literature has been accompanied by the widespread adoption of the techniques of magic realism.[2]

Allegories of Imperial Crisis

The concern to understand subjective experience as a dimension of the determinations and processes of the capitalist world system marks, then, the metropolitan national allegory. The necessary precondition for this project is crisis. As James O'Connor has observed, crisis occurs across a range of public and private registers which are interconnected. 'At a certain level of meaning', he argues, 'economic and social crisis and personality crisis are indistinguishable'. Thus 'the objective breakdown in the circuits of capital and the subjective breakdown in the "circuits" of everyday social life' must be grasped as aspects of one another (O'Connor, 1987: p. 176). At a time when the resolution of economic crisis is being pursued through an intensification of internationalisation, subjective experience cannot remain unaffected by this. Crisis is therefore a figure which stretches, to use Jameson's formulation, 'from the still surviving spaces of bourgeois private life all the way to the unimaginable decentring of global capital itself' (Jameson, 1988a: p. 351).

In contemporary first-world national allegory, personal crisis mediates and is refracted through the prism of the crisis of global Fordism and the destabilisation of American global hegemony. The recomposition of global economic space is analogised in the transformation of 'the spaces of bourgeois private life', including the inner space of bourgeois subjectivity. 'Look, my country, what you've done to me, what I have to do to live with myself', laments the writer-narrator of E. L. Doctorow's 1984 novella, 'Lives of the Poets' (Doctorow, 1986: p. 145). In order to resolve personal, emotional and creative crisis, this first-world intellectual finds it necessary to open up the space of his private life to the effects of geopolitical conflict and international restructuring, providing illegal asylum for Central American refugees fleeing the Reagan-sponsored military campaign to shore up American hegemony in that region. The story's central image of the apartment of a privileged metropolitan bourgeois being 'invaded' in this way is a cogent metaphor for the interpenetration of psychological, domestic and global space at this moment of crisis.[3]

Similarly, in William Gaddiss's *Carpenter's Gothic* (1985), personal crisis is tightly bound up with geopolitical and international economic forces. The inability of the novel's characters to manage their subjective, emotional and domestic lives is presented as an effect of the objective volatility of these larger configurations. This is a crisis of cognitive mapping at both a national and an individual level. 'Try to give you the big picture, you take one corner of it and run', says one character (Gaddis, 1987: p. 77). Indeed, the novel centres around the struggle to locate a map detailing the location of certain precious African mineral resources which is itself lost in the inner sanctum of a private American home whose inhabitants are in various stages of psychological disintegration. Psychic disorientation is an aspect of the national crisis of economic reach in this comic allegory of hegemonic decline which identifies the Vietnam war as the key moment in that process. One of the central characters is a Vietnam veteran who has been decorated for shooting his own troops in a moment of terrified confusion. Meanwhile his marriage falls apart as his ailing wife visits a therapist called Dr Kissinger, namesake of the Secretary of State who presided over the collapse of the Pax Americana in the wake of the Vietnam defeat (Calleo, 1982: Chapter 7).

In Joan Didion's *Democracy* (1984) it is the fall of Saigon itself that provides the central image of national decline and personal crisis alike. This moment encapsulates for Didion the implosion of American imperial delusions just as it marks the collapse of her heroine Inez Victor's personal and family life, one aspect of which is her marriage to Presidential candidate and Kennedy clone, Harry Victor. That this domestic crisis destroy's Harry's political ambitions suggests that Didion also sees this moment as the termination of the Fordist romance of development as articulated by Kennedy in the early 1960s (McClure, 1994: Calleo, 1982: pp. 10–11). Moreover, the mutual implication of personal and geopolitical crisis also precipitates a crisis in narrative form. For in telling this story of 'a family in which the colonial impulse had marked every member', Didion is unable to resort to the strategies of bourgeois realism through which Western family histories have traditionally been written. *Democracy* self-consciously counterpoints its own fractured, postmodernist modes of telling with those of a stolid bourgeois realist such as Trollope, purveyor of family sagas from the high point of nineteenth-century British imperial hegemony (Didion, 1984: pp. 20, 12). Didion's attenuated narrative shifts uncertainly between provisional viewpoints, different fictional registers, international locations and points in time. It thus dramatises a crisis of authorial omniscience which is offered as an analogue of the geopolitical crisis of American hegemony.[4]

In *The Names*, Don DeLillo explores these same links between private–personal and public–geopolitical crisis as each in different ways comes to allegorise the other. The break-up of the narrator James Axton's marriage and the international dispersal of his family coincide precisely with the most traumatic of America's post-Vietnam international humiliations, the Iranian revolution of the late 1970s and the abortive military operation 'Desert One' to release American hostages in 1979. 'This', Axton notifies us, apropos of the geopolitical context of the narrative,

> was the period after the President ordered a freeze of Iranian assets held in US banks. Desert One was still to come, the commando raid that ended two hundred and fifty miles from Tehran. It was the winter Rowser learned that the Shi'ite underground movement, Dawa, was stockpiling weapons in the Gulf. It was the winter before the car bombings in Nablus and Ramallah, before the military took power in Turkey ... before Iraqi ground troops moved into Iran ... before the oilfields burned and the sirens sounded through Baghdad. (*Names*: p. 233)

The regional collapse of American hegemony accompanied by the onset of the second oil shock of the 1970s, and Axton's personal, subjective predicament are each constructed by DeLillo as aspects of the other. But the significance of the Iranian Revolution, as David Calleo reminds us, is not just as an example of hegemonic decline; it also marked the demise of the postwar American world system based around the export of Fordism. 'Khomeini's revolution raised disturbing questions about the dangers of imposed technocratic "development" either for the domestic stability of a developing country or for world order in general', he argues. 'Iran also revealed the vulnerabilities of American "hegemony on the cheap", with "surrogates" [i.e. the Shah's regime deposed by Khomeini] substituting for direct American power.' Moreover, the energy crisis precipitated by the ensuing Iran–Iraq war provoked a major political assault on the 'inflationary' Fordist–Keynesian consensus in America itself. The adoption of tight monetary controls late in the Carter administration was the herald of the Reaganomics of the 1980s. It marked a decisive turn within the state apparatus towards the kind of regulatory arrangements that would characterise the period of militant economic restructuring and internationalisation of that decade. As Calleo puts it, 'Thanks to Khomeini, there was [Chairman of the Federal Reserve] Volcker' (Calleo, 1982: pp. 160, 173).

The Names is situated in Greece, mainly Athens, where Axton is based as a risk analyst for what he calls a 'sprawling corporation' (*Names*: p. 300). But the novel ranges widely across both space and time, taking in most of the Middle East and India, as well as recapitulating action that occurs in Canada, in California during the 1960s, and in the American mid-west during the depression of the 1930s. And the nature of the relationship between temporal and spatial shifts, between historical and geographical processes, is one of DeLillo's (as well as Axton's) primary interests. Axton himself is an appropriately globalised or dispersed individual, the reasons for this being both private or psychological and public or historical. In one sense he is a product of capital's intensified spatial mobility in this period of crisis and heightened international competition. His job involves the gathering and processing of data on the volatile political and economic situation in the Middle East for companies seeking to invest there, or to protect already existing investments. With respect to the globalisation of capital, then, we might say that Axton is a fully conscious agent of the process, a 'player' in the game of international corporate commerce, even a 'running dog' of late capitalism, to invoke the titles of the two DeLillo novels that preceded *The Names*.[5]

In another sense, though, Axton is on a highly personal quest. He has taken the job in Athens in order to be near his estranged wife and child who are involved in an archaeological dig on one of the Greek islands. The archaeological task of excavating and then seeking to reassemble the shards of collapsed or eclipsed cultures and civilisations is the presiding metaphor for Axton's personal quest to repair, or at least understand, the disintegration of his marriage. (Indeed, as we shall see, a kind of archaeological desire to encounter prior historical modes of production and ways of life motivates Axton in his global peregrinations.) But this particular personal project spills over into two others: the quest to locate and understand a mysterious cult whose bizarre ritual murders seem to be committed according to some kind of peculiar spatial logic or code; and the attempt to uncover a suspected conspiracy of Greek nationalists for whose violent anti-Americanism Axton imagines himself to be a possible target. Here again the personal and the political overlap directly, and this is effected through the category of nationality, through Axton's acutely and uncomfortably felt Americanness. 'American' is the final item on Axton's personal list of 'the 27 depravities' through which he imagines his wife (who is Canadian) enumerating her reasons for leaving him (*Names*: p. 17). Even at such an intimate level, then, personal relations are mediated by geopolitics. The marriage cannot but refigure Canadian–American power imbalances so that it becomes inhabited by 'the theme of expansionism ... the colonialist theme, the theme of exploitation' (*Names*: p. 266). Kathryn's secession is thus a kind of decolonising gesture which recalls the broader wave of nationalist anticolonialism (particularly in Iran) that accompanied the crisis of Fordism in the United States. Moreover, Axton's sense of embattled nationality is, if anything, heightened within the narrow expatriate community of Athens. 'Are they killing Americans?' is his first question for friends returning from sojourns to various parts of the Middle East, Axton's region, reflecting his status as a professional 'American' representing the interests of American foreign investments and multinationals. The links between Americanness and the 'colonial theme' are further accentuated by Axton's rather parasitic friendship with a middle-aged British couple, the Maitlands, whose world-weariness and diminishing fortunes fix them as representatives of an exhausted and bygone imperial power. 'It is like the Empire', Charles Maitland is fond of intoning. 'Opportunity, adventure, sunsets, dusty death'. But the point is that the new American dispensation of neocolonialism does not resemble the old British Empire in this way at all; its agents live decidedly unheroic lives insulated by Western modes of rationality, affluence and power and mediated by advanced technology – luxury apartments, air-conditioning, phones, faxes and computers, ubiquitous air travel. Even the old aesthetic and intellectual excitements of the expatriate life have been displaced. As Axton laments, 'Americans used to come to places like this to write and paint and study, to find deeper textures. Now we do business' (*Names*: pp. 7, 6).

'Business' here is the byword for that rationalising process of disenchantment described by Max Weber and adapted by Fredric Jameson in his account of capitalist 'reification' (Weber, 1991; Jameson, 1981: pp. 226–30).[6] But what interests me for the moment is Axton's invocation of 'the deeper textures' he associates with earlier modes of expatriate experience that 'business' has eclipsed, themselves in turn attached to earlier forms of imperial organisation and narrative representation. One such mode would be that of the Hemingwayesque expatriate for whom the periphery of Southern Europe (and later in Hemingway's career of course the third world itself) represented a space where direct relationships with nature and forms of perceptual intensity and immediacy, unavailable in metropolitan culture, could still be enjoyed. Travel thus deepened experience and fed the creative impulse.[7] Another such would be the mode of the nineteenth-century Grand Tour in which, as John Urry notes, 'travel was expected to play a key role in the cognitive and perceptual education of the ... upper class' (Urry, 1990: p. 4). This kind of experience received a kind of narrative codification in the Jamesian international novel of manners which, it could be argued, delineates the moral, perceptual and cognitive re-education of the American bourgeoisie for the role of global leadership at the hands of the same European ruling class it is historically poised to displace from that very position. My point is, however, that the emphasis these narratives, the Hemingwayesque and the Jamesian, place on the act of seeing (James's construction of 'point of view' as the pivot of aesthetic and moral knowing; Hemingway's twin obsession with the phenomenology of vision and the mechanics of descriptive clarity in prose) suggests that cognitive patterns are fundamentally at stake in the globalisation of metropolitan experience. Given Axton's insertion of his story into this tradition we need to ask what ways of seeing, what kinds of cognitive education, does it suggest are produced in the context of the decomposition of American imperial hegemony?

One answer to this question is offered in the narrative by the Greek nationalist, Eliades. 'It is very interesting', he tells Axton, 'how Americans learn geography and world history as their interests are damaged in one country after another'. For Eliades, the driving force of this internationalist cognitive re-education is crisis. '[I]t's only in a crisis that Americans see other people', he continues, adding, 'It has to be an American crisis of course. If two countries fight that do not supply the Americans with some precious commodity, then the education of the public does not take place'. Metropolitan perceptions are structured, then, by a dialectic of geopolitically determined insight and blindness. As Eliades later remarks to Axton, 'power must be blind in both eyes. You don't see us ... The occupiers fail to see the people they control' (*Names*: pp. 58, 237). And while the narrative refuses to construct the anti-imperialist perspective as an entirely positive pole of cognition in binary opposition to that of 'power', Eliades's critique is cogent to the extent that it makes explicit the interrogation of the limits of metropolitan perception which the novel as a whole conducts.[8]

Indeed, these limits are consistently presented as attributes of nationality. It is when he is at his most lost and disoriented, when both his cognitive and literal maps fail him, that Axton feels his Americanness most intently. Searching for the renegade archaeologist Owen Brademas in the old city of Punjab, Axton comes to feel that his nationality is identical with his condition of maplessness: 'Without a map I couldn't even stop someone, point to an approximate destination. I moved in a maze of alleys beyond the shops and stalls. Intensely aware. American.' And when the shooting of his friend, the American banker David Keller, occurs in the Athens woods in which Axton himself is jogging, he is again unable to negotiate space at this moment of crisis: 'I was fixed to the spot. Helpless, deprived of will ... *American*', he remarks (*Names*: pp. 274, 328, author's emphasis). Appropriately, given the novel's Greek location, the minotaur and the labyrinth are invoked as mythic precursors of the contemporary American's predicament, captured in Axton's son's repeated incantation of the phrase, 'lost in space' (*Names*: pp. 84, 87).

Nature, History and the Space of Uneven Development

In a short but penetrating review of *The Names*, Fredric Jameson has suggested that its 'most authentic content ... is a certain experience of space itself, or rather the peculiarly American experience of space through which substantive, culturally different and other spaces are perceived' (Jameson, 1984b: pp. 121–2). The novel is in fact organised into sections according to different kinds of geographical space – the island, the mountain, the desert and the prairie. Similarly, the names of the institutions for which Axton and his friend Keller work – the Northeast Group and the Mainland Bank – suggest particular spatial, even geopolitical, arrangements, associating their operations with the metropolitan 'centre' of the capitalist global market. But the real concern of the novel in this respect is with the nature of the space produced by human social and economic activity and the various modes of experience, collective association and perception that characterise them.

David Harvey has noted that 'Each distinctive mode of production or social formation ... embod[ies] a distinctive bundle of time and space practices and concepts' (Harvey, 1989: p. 204). *The Names* establishes a spectrum of spatial registers in which each is associated with a particular mode of social organisation and subjective apperception and experience. At one end of the spectrum is the universalising, homogenised space of transnational capital and technological communications, exemplified by the spaces of modern air travel. What Axton describes as 'This vast space, which seems like nothing so much as a container for emptiness', corresponds to the definition of absolute space offered in Chapter 9 above (*Names*: p. 253). It reminds us that, as Neil Smith argues, 'In the advanced capitalist world today we all conceive of space as emptiness, as a universal receptacle' which is 'independent from matter' (Smith, 1984: p. 68). The essential quality of space so conceived and experienced is its abstractness. Travel through such space does not, for Axton, produce arrival at specific, concrete *places*: it is 'not ... the sunlit trip to the east which we thought we'd decided to make' but is always a 'buried journey through categories and definitions and foreign languages'. 'Air travel reminds us of who we are', continues Axton. 'It's the means by which we recognise ourselves as modern. The process removes us from the world and sets us apart from each other' (*Names*: pp. 253, 254). Absolute space thus corresponds to capitalist modernity and to the fragmented social relations and highly mediated connection to the world produced within it.

The rationalising, abstracting logic of modern business and communications also transforms the nature of subjective experience and of time itself. Air travel typifies contemporary first-world perceptual processes because it involves a kind of fundamental alienation – separation from the earth. Flying, Axton feels himself 'half numb to the secluded beauty' thousands of feet below him. Moreover, the hours spent in flight amount to 'dead time ... time totally lost to us. We don't remember it. We take no sense impressions with us ... Nothing sticks to us but smoke in our hair and clothes'. Modernity and its spaces are therefore defined for Axton by a condition of primal deracination and disembodiedness. This kind of experience precludes authentic knowledge of any concrete, embedded place. 'I was a traveller only in the sense that I covered distances', Axton remarks. 'I travelled between places, never in them' (*Names*: pp. 7, 143).

As we have seen in earlier chapters, this priority of space over place is bound up with the increasing mobility of capital, especially as it is deployed through the agency of electronic communications media. And in the novel, the characters who spend most of their time in flight are precisely those most closely connected to the international circulation of capital and information. For Axton, whose job is the gathering, manipulation and processing of information regarding commercial investments, the specificities of particular places dissolve under his rationalising gaze: 'The streets of Istanbul were data in their own right' from the perspective of risk analysis. Indeed, Axton's employment history is, as he informs us, linked to the information economy of a California 'full of technocratic amaze'. Axton's boss, Rowser, spends even more time on airplanes and is so given over to the world of data-processing that Axton describes his mental operations in terms of computer logic, 'On-off, zero-one ... Binary'. Rowser personally embodies the annihilation of space that David Harvey argues is one of the fundamental effects of the global circulation of capital: 'Every space he inhabited seemed enclosed', says Axton of Rowser, taken up by 'his numbers, the data he collected and sorted and studied endlessly'. But the flyer supreme of the novel is the banker and 'credit head', David Keller. Keller met his second wife in flight; he proposes spontaneous flights to Germany to watch baseball on American military TV; and he jets regularly to New York for afternoon ice-cream appointments with the children from his first marriage (*Names*: pp. 108, 97, 183, 66).

The pulverisation of space and time and their removal from what Neil Smith calls 'direct practice' is here seen to be an effect not simply of the disenchanting logic of capitalist rationality, but more specifically of the acceleration of the circuits of finance capital and exchange of which Axton, Rowser and Keller are personifications. Alfred Sohn-Rethel has argued that the establishment of exchange relations is a primary cause of spatial and temporal derealisation:

> Time and space rendered abstract under the impact of commodity exchange are marked by homogeneity, continuity and emptiness of all natural or material

content, visible or invisible (eg. air). The exchange abstraction excludes everything that makes up history ... Time and space assume thereby that character of absolute timelessness and universality which must mark the exchange abstraction as a whole and each of its features. (Sohn-Rethel, 1978: pp. 48–9)

Marx similarly argued that while capital in all its forms displayed an irresistible spatial dynamism, a 'cosmopolitan, universal energy which overthrows every restriction and bond', finance capital in particular functioned by a process of abstraction which obscured any relationship to the world of material production and concrete labour. 'Interest bearing capital', he wrote, 'is the consummate *automatic fetish* ... money making money, and in this form it no longer bears any trace of its origin' (Marx, 1967: p. 250; and 1972: p. 455, author's emphasis).

In some respects, then, the mediations of information and finance capital (especially the 'fictitious' capital of credit) are antagonistic to the spatial fixity and embeddedness of material capitalist production. Mandel, Harvey and Aglietta have all argued that the overaccumulation crisis of global Fordism has been most forcefully expressed in the hypertrophy of financial markets and what Aglietta calls 'the emergence of a fully-fledged credit system, deterritorialised and beyond regulation by any national sovereign state' (Aglietta, 1982: p. 25). This antagonism or contradiction, intensified in the post-Fordist recomposition of global space, is thematised in *The Names* in an incident involving another expatriate agent of multinational capital, Roy Hardeman. As his name suggests, Hardeman is 'in manufacturing'; he is a representative of American material production in the context of heightened international competition. Axton describes him appropriately as a 'machine-tooled part'. After an evening of heavy drinking, Keller proposes slipping the unconscious Hardeman on to the next international flight out of Athens, possibly to Tehran, enlisting Axton's help. Though the prank does not come off it carries nonetheless considerable allegorical resonance. Keller, the 'credit head', and Axton, the data analyst, have been described as 'serving the same broad ends'. Indeed, Keller frequently feeds Axton sensitive, sometimes classified information from his credit reports on client countries. Keller's scheme to 'send this man to another place' stands as a figure for the global deterritorialisation of production that the combination of finance capital and information technologies makes possible in response to a period of crisis (*Names*: pp. 264, 70, 266). Keller, the finance capitalist, is thus established as the master of absolute space whose proposed prank here enacts the further decentring of the 'hardness' or materiality of production into the increasingly abstract and mediated space of exchange.

Players (1977) constitutes perhaps DeLillo's most sustained exploration of the abstracting, homogenising and distancing logic of exchange. Lyle Wynant, the novel's protagonist, works in the New York stock exchange, the nerve centre of the processing and global relaying of capital as information. His experience is marked by an extreme form of the dissociation from and abstraction of materiality that afflicts Axton in *The Names*. Lyle, we are told, 'saw in the numbers and stock symbols' that he manipulates, 'an artful reduction of the external world to printed output, the machine's coded model of exactitude'. His work gives him the 'impression of reality disconnected from the resonance of its own senses', one in which 'a picture of the competitive mechanism of the world, of greasy teeth engaging on the rim of wheel, was nowhere in evidence' (*Players*: p. 70). It is thus principally the process of material production that is erased from our our experience of the world by the circulation of capital as information. Finance capital is the agent of this cognitive reduction; informated money is its pure form. Regarding the inscrutable exteriors of New York's banking district, Lyle becomes aware that

> Inside some of the granite cubes, or a chromium tower here and there, people sorted money of various types, dizzying billions being propelled through machines, computer-scanned and coded, filed, cleared, wrapped and trucked ... He'd seen the encoding rooms, the microfilming of checks, money moving, shrinking as it moved, beginning to evade visualisation, to pass from a paper existence to electronic sequences, its meaning increasingly complex, harder to name. It was condensation, the whole process, a paring away of money's accidental properties, of money's touch. (*Players*: pp. 109–10)

Here finance capital embodies an aesthetics of disappearance, not simply concealing its own material origins in productive processes, but putting the realm of materiality and tangibility, of time and space as lived aspects of social life, severely in doubt. The 'vales of time and space' of which one of the novel's characters speaks are by its end rendered utterly unreadable: 'Spaces and what they contain no longer account for, serve as examples of, or represent.' This logic comes ultimately to take hold of Lyle himself as he undergoes a steady process of disembodiment and derealisation, until 'his intrinsic form' comes 'apart from the animal glue of physical properties and functions'. We are left at the novel's close with only a 'propped figure ... barely recognisable as male' which is 'shedding capabilities and traits by the second' (*Players*: pp. 84, 212).

We should also note, though, that the cultural as well as economic forms of modernity are central to this process of abstraction and mediation, in particular film. The Axtons' friend, Frank Volterra, is a film director whose restless global mobility is a function of his search for a more authentic content for his work and for locations in which to film. Indeed for Volterra (a once radical filmmaker now trapped inside the Hollywood system) content and location are one and the same, for the significance of film as a medium lies in its particular rendering of space. 'The classic thing has always been the space, the emptiness', he argues. 'Figures in open space have always been what film is all about. American film ... People at the end of a long lens. Swimming in space' (*Names*: p. 198). American space and filmic space are here seen as identical, both corresponding to the smooth and empty space of exchange and abstraction. Film also inserts a structuring perceptual distance between subject and object, and between subjects themselves: 'People at the end of a long lens.' Filmic representation, therefore, complements the process of derealisation bound up with the circulation of capital.

Volterra's very name (from the Latin words *volare* – to fly, and *terra* – earth) evokes that sense of primal separation Axton associates with air travel. Significantly, Volterra plans to film the climactic sequence of his proposed movie about the murderous cult from the air, interposing an additional mediation into the representational act. Thus what Volterra conceives as a moment of pure, primal physicality – the ritual beating to death of the cult's victim – will be structured rather by absence and multiple distances; the cathartic moment of full presence and connection will instead resemble the kind of deterritorialised and abstracted violence of capitalist modernity. For, as Axton has noted earlier, American killing is 'a form of consumerism ... the logical extension of consumer fantasy. People shooting from overpasses, barricaded houses. Pure image ... No connection to the earth'. Volterra's ever-deepening progress into wilderness regions in search of a more 'authentic' filmic raw material mirrors the cosmopolitan movements of capital itself and produces a similar kind of experiential estrangement and spatial reduction. Contrary to Axton's earlier lament about the displacement of cultural engagement from the agenda of American cosmopolites by 'business', aesthetics has here become an extension of the latter's logic: we have to remember, as Axton remarks, that 'Frank was a name in the business' (*Names*: pp. 115, 109).

There is another end to the spatial spectrum, however. In contrast to the smoothness and emptiness of absolute space, there is the textured, full and intimate space associated with more traditional forms of social and economic organisation. Axton notes of the tiny Greek island village where he visits his wife and child that it 'was a model of irregular geometry, the huddled uphill arrangements of whitelime boxes, the street mazes and archways, small churches with blue talc domes. Laundry hung in the walled gardens, always this sense of realised space'. Such 'realised space' is here a quality of *place* and is closer to our earlier definition of relative space. And for Axton this 'placefulness' is associated with the kind of face-to-face, *gemeinschaft*-style social relationships which are seen as historically prior to and spatially distinct from capitalist modernity. In contrast to the separation characteristic of modern metropolitan existence, Axton imagines that a collective bond and a spontaneous authenticity mark the social relations of place. Observing two Greek villagers singing, 'charged with feeling', he detects a depth of mutual understanding and sympathy that is absent from his own and friends' rather desiccated expatriate milieu: 'they looked at each other, strangers, to something beyond. A blood recollection, a shared past. I didn't know.' While Axton's relationships, even with his own family, are conditioned by what he defines as 'estrangement', these two strangers are felt to be bound by some larger, shared collective experience and history (*Names*: pp. 8, 64, 69).

The key to such an experience of connectedness appears to be a closeness to the materiality of the earth itself, a kind of 'territoriality' that stands in opposition to the deterritorialisations of capitalist modernity. Axton's estrangement from his wife is signalled by the fact that her work roots her in the earth while his separates him from it. His largely airborne existence contrasts with Kathryn's digging, her immersion in the trench which becomes 'her medium' and connects her with 'the feel of workable earth'. Indeed, Axton imagines that Kathryn conceives of his own past act of infidelity as 'a crime against the earth' (*Names*: pp. 133, 69). Her digging, though, is also a means of connection to the past, to buried societies and ways of life. In this respect, earthiness, placefulness and materiality are seen to be adjuncts of modes of production and social organisation that precede modernity and capitalism alike, traces of which still persist in the peripheral, 'underdeveloped' regions to which the major characters of the novel are constantly drawn.

The quests on which these characters engage, then, are quests for what they imagine to be authentic being, for materiality and connectedness, which are projected into those areas not yet colonised by capital and transformed into the empty, mobile, rational space of exchange. Value here becomes for these characters an attribute of a particular kind of social, economic and historical space in a way that recalls Neil Smith's distinction between the 'geographical fixation of use value and the fluidity of exchange' (Smith, 1984: p. 152). Axton in particular, but also his wife, and Brademas and Volterra are all seeking fixity, connectedness and rootedness in place over their native milieux of mobile, deterritorialised space.

As their quests unfold, Axton, Volterra and Brademas push deeper into undeveloped, 'third-world' territory, seeking, in the manner characteristic of imperial romance, some ultimate encounter with the 'real'. In the process they are compelled to abandon the mediating props and techniques that lend to metropolitan experience its quality of disembodied suspension. Air travel gives way to motor transport and eventually travel by foot as Brademas reaches the remotest wilds of the Indian desert. Maps are relinquished as they become useless in the negotiation of the complex, differentiated places of the periphery into which the questers are drawn. The implication is, indeed, that maps must be abandoned precisely *because* they are mediations and abstractions, devices by which concrete places are deterritorialised into representational code or data.[9] Ultimately, the quest leads for its most dedicated exponent, Brademas, to complete bodily immersion in the earth itself as he tracks the cult to its final location in a collection of earthen food storage huts on the fringes of a remote Indian desert village.

This attempted reconnection with the earth is, as I have suggested, also a historical journey in several senses. The spatial movement into precapitalist enclaves is understood by its protagonists to be a journey back in historical, phylogenic and ontological time. Awaiting in his earthen dugout the final epiphany he believes will accompany his witnessing a ritual cult murder, Brademas has not only wilfully forsaken the modern for the premodern, the 'civilised' for the 'savage', he also feels himself to have arrived at 'the deep past of men'. Here can be found 'the only innocence' in a connection with 'the children of the race' which impels in him an acute recall of his own personal childhood in Depression America (*Names*: pp. 304, 307).[10] Thus the quest is also a search for origins which, as we saw in the words of Marx quoted earlier in this chapter, are precisely what are obscured by the circuits of abstract capital. But the encounter with traditional, precapitalist space promises another kind of insertion into history – history not in the sense of the 'deep past', but in the sense of significant action, of 'making history'.

For Axton and Keller, their work as 'running dogs' of the capitalist world system offers a sense of urgent, almost physical involvement and connectedness that is in many respects similar to the kind of experience sought after thorough immersion in undeveloped, precapitalist space. Reflecting on his work, Axton remarks,

> This is where I want to be. History. It's in the air. Events are linking all these countries ... We're important suddenly ... We're right in the middle. We're the handlers of huge sums of delicate money. Recyclers of petrodollars. Builders of refineries. Analysts of risk ... The world is here ... In some of these places things have enormous power. They have impact, they're mysterious. Events have weight ... It's a heightening, that's all. When the Mainland Bank makes a proposal to one of these countries, when David flies to Zurich to meet with the Turkish finance minister, he gets a feeling, he turns a little pinker than he already is, his breath comes faster. Action, risk. It's not a loan to some developer in Arizona. It's much broader, it has a serious frame. Everything here is serious. And we're in the middle. (*Names*: pp. 97–8)

Facilitating the penetration of capital into these peripheral enclaves, valued elsewhere in the novel precisely for their very exteriority to or 'innocence' of capitalist modernity, also provides for a re-engagement with the world and with subjective immediacy. Indeed, penetration is an apposite metaphor here, for the excitement Keller derives from the process is certainly sexual (pinkness, rapid breathing), and he himself describes the rewards of his work in similar terms: 'A hundred percent inflation, twenty percent unemployment. I love deficit countries. I love going in there, being intimately involved' (*Names*: p. 232).

In this respect, then, there exist two, somewhat contradictory, options in the pursuit of the connectedness, the sense of involvement, self-presence and experiential renewal sought by characters in *The Names*. One leads in a direction away from the centres of capitalist modernity – the history of which is presented as a fall from a state of originary wholeness and innocence – into the remote, traditional and 'natural' spaces of the precapitalist periphery, into the deep past, ultimately out of history altogether to the 'childhood of the race'. This is the obscure direction of the cult, whose wanderings pull Owen Brademas, and Axton and Volterra with him, into the deserts of Arabia and India. As one of its members says, the cult is 'seeking a place where men can stop making history'. The other option, though, leads in the direction of capital itself. The characters revel not so much in the condition of abstracted capitalist modernity characterised by suspension, estrangement and absence, as in physical presence at the point of capitalist modernisation, at which the penetration of capital is felt to be in the process of making history by remaking traditional, natural spaces hitherto beyond its reach. Indeed, requested to define what he actually does in his work, Axton replies, 'I'm a presence'; whilst Keller defines those zones in which his bank does not as yet do business as 'non-presence' countries, and those from which it has been ousted by nationalist revolution 'collapsed presence' countries or 'black holes' (*Names*: 209, 233).

The Names therefore generates its systems of meaning out the juxtaposition of and the tension between these two kinds of social and historical space. This is the sense in which I am calling it a romance of uneven development. Axton's perceptions and actions are determined by the co-existence and overlapping of both kinds of space, between which he moves throughout the novel. Greece is a particularly apt setting for such a romance given its history of penetration by imperial powers (up to and including the American-sponsored military coup in 1967), and in as much as it falls into Wallerstein's definition of a semiperipheral zone, combing features of both modern industrial and traditional modes of social and economic organisation, and mediating between centre and periphery in the operations of the world system (Chase-Dunn, 1989: pp. 129, 253).

Within this space Axton himself is a kind of mediator, inserted as he says 'in the middle' of the volatile and confusing space of uneven development and pulled in different directions towards its opposing poles. His fascination with the cult and its mysterious enactment of a primal, 'savage' violence is balanced by his attraction to the occult circuits of finance capital represented by his own company, the Northeast Group, and by David Keller and the Mainland Bank. Thus while his quest for experiential intensity and material connectedness proceeds via the pursuit of the cult on the one hand, it also proceeds through a growing intimacy with finance capital on the other, which, despite what he suggests about its denaturing logic, offers Axton an alternative route towards some kind of more intense, less desiccated form of being. Through David Keller, Axton meets and seduces the wife of the 'operations head at the Mainland Bank', forcing himself upon her with the statement, 'I want to reach you in the most direct of ways', while arguing that sex is a key dimension of 'nature' (*Names*: pp. 220, 228, 227). Axton and the novel he narrates are structured, then, by an ambivalent movement between spaces which accord with the patterns of uneven development. I want now to suggest that we can understand this ambivalence less in terms of a centre–periphery opposition than in terms of class experience and discourse.

Class Discourse and the New Cosmopolitanism

I have suggested in previous chapters that professional–managerial class experience is particularly inhabited by a sense of, and a series of anxieties about, the problems of distance and mobility. These concerns derive from the necessary deracinations required to attain professional status which tend to separate the professional from embeddedness in a particular place or local culture where such values as community and agency are often felt exclusively to dwell. They also derive from the mediating discourses and techniques, as well as the mediating social functions, which professionals are typically called upon to master and to implement, further separating them from immediate experience of and engagement with direct work upon the world. A remark of Clifford Geertz's, with respect to the situation of the professional anthropologist, suggests that professional views of the world are structured by an 'experience-distant' conceptual apparatus, as exposed to the 'experience-near' one of the layperson. 'An experience-near concept is', Geertz tells us, 'one that someone ... might himself naturally and effortlessly use to define what he and his fellows see, hear, feel, think, imagine and so on, and which he would readily understand when similarly applied by others'. Experience-nearness thus seems to be an attribute of relatively unmediated ('naturally and effortlessly') and communal ('he and his fellows') social life. On the other hand, Geertz continues, 'An experience-distant concept is one that *specialists of one sort or another* ... employ to forward their scientific, philosophical or even practical aims' (Geertz, 1993: p. 57, emphasis added).

Geertz alerts us here to the problem faced by professionals whose work is to appropriate and translate the 'local knowledge' of particular groups and communities into the universal and mediating codes of conceptual rationality; the risk is that something primal or vital will be lost in the process as the discourse of the specialists operates at a remove from the site of experience.[11] Awareness of the distancing logic of professional discourse tends to breed a certain nostalgia for what is perceived to be the embeddedness of place and the unmediated authenticity and wholeness of local knowledge. As Bruce Robbins points out, professional interest in the local is frequently motivated by the search for an idealised agency in which 'the miniaturising precision of "locality"' is associated with 'presence and uniqueness, empirical concreteness, complete experience [and] accessible subjectivity' (Robbins, 1993: p. 188). This is precisely the kind of nostalgia that inhabits Axton's projection of *gemeinschaft*-style social relationships and experience on to what he calls the 'realised space' of precapitalist communities.

But Geertz's focus on anthropology points to another dimension of the professional antinomy between the local and the universal – the problem of cultural imperialism. As I have argued earlier, the role of the professional–managerial class can in many respects be understood as one of invading, colonising and rationalising the less 'developed' sectors of society, of abstracting and appropriating 'local' knowledge, experience and practices in order to replace them with commodified services and bureaucratised routines of mediation which are held to be in accord with 'universal' standards of rationality. The example of anthropology reminds us that this is as much an international process as a national one; anthropology might in some senses serve as a paradigm of professional cultural imperialism. And this notion that professionals and their discourses are involved in some kind of politically and ethically questionable global mission is present to Axton himself in *The Names*. 'Technicians', he says, 'are the infiltrators of ancient societies. They speak a secret language. They bring new kinds of death with them' (*Names*: p. 114).[12]

The recomposition of Fordism entails a new globalisation of the professional–managerial class along with the internationalisation of capital and production. Ex-Clinton Secretary of Labor, Robert Reich, has placed this class at the forefront of the new international competition and the 'global web', as he calls it, to which it gives rise. As the old Fordist patterns of employment, production and class are broken down, Reich claims, the stratum of what he calls 'symbolic analysts' takes on a pivotal importance.[13] This stratum is significant in that, like the multinational corporations with which it is mainly associated, it is not bound to old-fashioned notions of nationalism in economic matters. As the movement of multinational capital has made national boundaries, and even the notion of national economies, irrelevant, so the idea of the nation loses importance for the class which supervises, administers and in some senses literally embodies this movement: instead of the national economy, argues Reich, '*the "global web" is its real scene of involvement*' (Reich, 1991: p. 250, author's emphasis).

Furthermore, for Reich, this stratum is crucial in breaking with the Fordist model of class compromise based on the trade-off between rising productivity and regular increases in levels of working-class consumption. The decentring of national corporations and the deterritorialisation of production undermine the purchasing power of American workers and render domestic blue-collar consumption increasingly peripheral to the profits of multinational capital. Whatever 'slack' in domestic consumption this creates is taken up by the professional–managerial class itself, as the symbolic analysts are rewarded for their role in the globalisation of capital with high salaries and generous fringe-benefits, fuelling what Mike Davis has identified as a new logic of 'overconsumptionism' among them (Davis, 1986: pp. 211–20). This heightened middle-class consumption appropriately betrays its connections to the globalisation of capital in its conspicuous cosmopolitanism, with the adoption of international tastes from world cuisine to world music and, of course, the centrality of international travel to contemporary middle-class status games. Thus, claims Reich, along with the deterritorialisation of national economies there is taking place an ideological shift in the capitalist heartlands from the 'zero-sum nationalism' of the working class to the 'impassive cosmopolitanism' that characterises the symbolic analyst professionals and managers (Reich, 1991: p. 310).

Reich's description of the class composition of the new global web of deterritorialised enterprise can itself be seen as an example of professional–managerial 'impassive cosmopolitanism', in as much as it celebrates the international dominance of this class and its displacement of working-class agency and ideologies from the American ideological agenda. It recalls Alvin Gouldner's definition of the New Class as 'the most universalist and internationalist of all social strata', as 'the most cosmopolitan of elites' (Gouldner, 1979: p. 83). Yet it is useful here to read *The Names* in the light of Reich's notion of the symbolic analyst, for it describes Axton and his expatriate milieu perfectly. We can understand Axton's overwhelming sense of estrangement and his compensatory drive towards materiality and immediacy, therefore, as aspects of professional–managerial experience. But we must also note that this goal is sought precisely in the terms of symbolic-analytic activity as described by Reich.

Axton's quests are symbolic-analytic quests. His interest in the cult derives from the particularly cryptic relationship it establishes between symbols, the specificities of place, and the primal act of violence. When he solves the riddle of the cult's rituals – the initials of the victims' names are matched with those of the location where the killing is carried out – Axton feels he has broken through to a new level of awareness and involvement which seems to derive from the cult's apparent ability to tie down the free-floating symbols of language to the materialities of place and the body. As the cult's secret name for itself, The Names, implies, Axton believes it will vouchsafe to him the secret of the naming process and lead him back to the material origins of language as the primal human system of mediation. However, to understand the point at which the thematics of language invades the thematics of space in *The Names*, we have again to refer to the particular nature of professional–managerial class experience.

We have seen how the professional–managerial class's internal coherence is constituted through language. Alvin Gouldner's argument is that it is essentially a 'speech community' defined by a 'culture of critical discourse' which 'is the deep structure of the common ideology shared by the New Class'. This class discourse is, crucially, 'characterised by speech that is *relatively more situation-free*, more context or "field independent"' than other kinds of speech. It is more reflexive and theoretical and 'thus requires considerable expressive discipline, not to speak of instinctual renunciation' on the part of its speakers. 'Speech becomes impersonal' for members of this class, argues Gouldner. 'Speakers hide behind their speech. Speech seems to be disembodied, decontextualised and self-grounded.' Thus, the culture of critical discourse 'is productive of intellectual reflexivity and the loss of warmth and spontaneity' (Gouldner, 1979: pp. 28–9, 84, author's emphasis).

Class discourse here wholly contains that condition of estrangement and disconnection so acutely felt by Axton. Indeed, Axton's personal relationship to language is a disturbingly deterritorialising one. When he departs on business to various parts of the Middle East his Greek concierge habitually enquires about his destination. Often ignorant of the correct Greek word for this, Axton resorts to using the names of places for which he knows the correct word and pronunciation. 'Let the nature of the place-name determine the place', he thinks. But this tactic begins to trouble him. Language seems to be obscuring reality, producing 'a grave misplacement' in which 'the external world' is turned into 'a four-thousand mile fiction, a deep lie' (*Names*: p. 103). Axton's discourse becomes radically 'situation free' here; yet it can be understood as an extreme instance of class discourse. This wider class condition therefore underlies his interest in the cult which promises some kind of return to an original situatedness of language and an earthbound connection between name, place, and visceral or immediate modes of being.

This is certainly what draws Owen Brademas to the cult. An academic specialist in ancient forms of writing and inscription, Brademas seeks access to the originary historical point of mediation at which signs began to substitute for and displace material objects. 'It's interesting to me', he declares, 'how these marks, these signs that appear so pure and abstract to us, began as objects in the world, living things in many cases'. The cult represents for both Axton and Brademas a route out of the disembodied and abstract condition of their class, but one which they must use precisely the symbolic-analytic techniques that define their class in order to trace. It also brings them closer to what they feel is the materiality of unalienated labour. Axton's decision to follow Brademas into the Indian desert comes at exactly the moment his hand, running across the inscriptions on a Moghul tomb, is 'feeling ... only to find the human labor' embodied in the object. As he draws closer to Brademas and the final truth of the cult, Axton feels about him in the old city of Punjab the presence of 'Hand-skilled labor'. And part of Brademas's fascination with the cult stems from its use of rudimentary implements with which to slaughter its victims: 'A claw hammer', he muses. 'Simple hand tool of iron and wood', the sort of tool used, of course, to make early written inscriptions prior to the annexation of writing by the reproductive technologies of print and electronic media. As one of the cult's members tells Brademas of their ritual acts, 'It had to be this one thing, done with our hands, in direct contact. Nothing else, nothing less' (*Names*: pp. 116, 272, 274, 209).

Ultimately the quest for this primal, unmediated moment involves a movement away from professionalism itself. Brademas is described by a fellow professor as 'an amateur'. Axton's sense of his wife's moral superiority over him is expressed in terms of an opposition between professional and amateur. His airborne, uncommitted existence is a consequence of his 'strange profession' of risk analysis; Kathryn's connectedness to the earth, her feeling for 'nature at the cutting edge', and her capacity for warmth, loyalty and commitment place her as a 'wonderful amateur' in Axton's eyes, one who 'make[s] the professionals seem like so many half-ass triflers' (*Names*: pp. 255, 312, 128). If the professional is the deracinated, mobile, free-floating individual to whom 'nothing sticks' as Axton has earlier framed it, then the quest for a sense of materiality and embeddedness is the quest to transcend the limits of a particular class experience and the social processes of deterritorialisation in which that class is instrumental.

Professionals and Primal Mediation

Brademas and Axton seek remission from their professional selves in pursuit of the cult. Yet they discover that the real object of their quest – a condition of being prior to mediation and reification – recedes alarmingly before them, even as they draw nearer to the cult itself. After tracking the cult to the remote Mani peninsula, Axton remarks that its members 'looked like people who came from nowhere. They'd escaped all the usual associations ... They were people who found almost any place as good as almost any other'. The cult's relationship to space thus mirrors that of the deracinated professional, even of mobile and rootless capital itself. Its medium is space as opposed to the desired fixity and embeddedness of place. The cultists are no less cosmopolitan than are their professional pursuers. Their standard question to outsiders seeking contact with them is 'How many languages do you speak?' When the cultists address Axton in English, he registers surprise, saying, 'I thought you would want to speak Greek ... Or whatever the language of a particular place'. The reply is, 'We are no longer *in* a place'. Moreover, the cult is drawn to the empty space of the desert in a way that recalls Bukharin's description of finance capital invading the empty spaces of nature: they seek to 'penetrate the desert truly' because '[t]his place is empty in order that men may rush in to fill it' (*Names*: pp. 190, 207, 296).

In fact the cult is constituted along lines similar to those of a profession. Admission is conditional upon the possession of a particular body of knowledge and expertise, mastery of ancient languages and writing systems. It thus operates according to an esoteric technical language and set of symbolic codes that disqualifies outsiders. And it is based on discursive principles that are held to be universal and rational – the alphabet which, as Axton notes, is the cult's 'whole mechanism'. It is precisely through the exercise and application of their own professional skills that Axton and Brademas are able to decode the specialised vocabulary of the cult and seek access to its secrets. Brademas is told that only his 'training as an epigraphist' makes him acceptable to the cult's members, and it is Axton's skills as a symbolic analyst that allows him to decode their ritual behaviour and enter into communication with them. It is also important to note that while Axton feels the cult offers a route back into the unalienated practices of 'hand-skilled labor', of direct work upon the material world, there actually develops around its pursuit an economy of data, information and knowledge that comes to structure the important relationships in the novel. This information economy finally eclipses the vision of concrete, productive work on the world. Axton, Brademas and Volterra each withhold crucial clues from the others regarding the cult and its movements. Each seeks to monopolise information in a small parody of corporate competition in the age of information, and of the way in which professions are constituted as quasi-secret societies, or monopolies of knowledge, through what C. Wright Mills called a process of 'guild-like closure' (Mills, 1951: p. 138).[14] Axton admits that 'the knowledge is special. Once you have it you find yourself protective of it. It confers a culthood of its own' (*Names*: pp. 292, 247).

The flight from professionalism is thus a circular one. Rather than providing a conduit to some kind of direct relationship with nature and the material world, the cult itself embodies a condition of primal mediation which Axton and Brademas find always already inhabits the spaces into which they are drawn. The epiphanic ritual murder is never witnessed. Instead, the lesson the cult teaches is, in the words of one of its members, that 'The world has become self-referring ... the world has made a self of its own ... a self-referring world in which there is no escape'. Second nature, to use Neil Smith's formulation, has colonised and eclipsed first nature, depriving it of its originality, indeed putting the whole notion of originality into doubt. After colonisation there can be no escape from history in nature, as the theorist of decolonisation Frantz Fanon argued in *The Wretched of the Earth* (1961). Neither, *The Names* suggests, can the mediations of rationality and specialised knowledge be evaded in a direct relationship with the object world, nor the abstracting and reifying force of capital in some projected precapitalist enclave. Finally, there is no escape from the class conditions of experience in as much as the quest for the cult can be seen as a dramatisation of what Bruce Robbins calls 'the logic that links professionals to the disappearance of their objects' (Robbins, 1993: p. 173). Robbins points here to the abstracting nature of professional rationality which tends to seize upon an object at precisely the moment of that object's eclipse by the modernising process of which professional rationality is itself an embodiment. This object is then dissolved into a collection of concepts and codes and, ultimately, into discourse.[15] This is precisely what happens to the absent encounter with nature in *The Names*. The projected return to nature is concurrent with the intensification of capital's invasion and transformation of natural space, what Jameson defines as 'the moment of a radical eclipse of nature itself' (Jameson, 1991: p. 34). Moreover, the direct, unmediated act of ritual killing which promises to lie at the novel's heart is displaced, even obscured, by discourse. Axton and Brademas only ever talk and theorise about the longed-for primal encounter, and do so, significantly, in a series of professional languages, discourses and identities: 'So we talked, so we argued, taking roles, discarding them, the social theorist, the interrogator, the criminologist' (*Names*: pp. 297, 172).[16]

In this respect, the novel shifts its emphasis from the thematics of space and place to a thematics of language in order to pursue its interrogation of multinational capital and the condition within it of professional deracination. The suggestion is that language itself is the primal mediation; the process of naming thus turns things into signs and interposes an originary distance between subject and object, a distance which the rationalising processes of modernity (and its agents, the professionals) simply intensifies. But whereas we saw DeLillo breaking down the opposition between space and place, between first nature and second nature, in his description of the deterritorialising spatial logic of these processes, the theme of language is deployed to introduce an alternative opposition which serves Axton as an alternative mapping device. This is the opposition between speech and writing, or between what Walter Ong calls orality and literacy, and between the distinct kinds of social and subjective being structured by these modes.

Ong describes writing as a kind of secondary, technological mediation of the spoken word. Writing is the 'technologising of the word'; it is the original reproductive technology, 'initiat[ing] what print and computers only continue, the reduction of dynamic sound to quiescent space, the separation of the word from the living present'. Historically, the spatialisations of writing have undermined 'the warm, personally interactive lifeworld of oral culture' in which 'the spoken word forms human beings into close-knit groups' (Ong, 1983: pp. 82, 80, 74). The opposition between speech and writing in *The Names* thus corresponds to the deconstructed opposition between place and space, with speech connoting the closeness, embeddedness and presence of traditional, local relationships, and writing the abstraction, alienation and cosmopolitanism of modernity. Within this schema the cult represents the moment of primal mediation at which the logic of writing invades the rhythms of speech and the closeness and community of oral culture. Despite claiming to be returning to a condition of immediacy prior to writing, history and even to language itself – 'we are working at a preverbal level', one of the cultists claims – the cult is nevertheless clearly determined by its relationship to written language. As Axton notes, the alphabet is its 'whole mechanism', its 'whole point'. Its ritual of murder according to the logic of the alphabet is thus a perversion of the ancient practice of sacrifice in premodern, oral cultures. While this latter was a manifestation of the presence of the sacred, the cult's practice is a rationalised degradation of sacred ritual and a symptom of the sacred's absence. What is produced in its stead is 'death by system, by machine intellect' (*Names*: pp. 208, 246, 175).

Writing functions also to undermine subjectivity in the novel. Axton learns that his first name, Jim, is also the name of an Arabic letter, while Brademas observes that the word 'character' means not only 'someone in a story' but also 'a mark or symbol'; 'Like', Axton retorts, 'a letter of the alphabet' (*Names*: p. 10). Thus Axton's sense of alienation from himself is close to the way in which identity or selfhood is represented here as being evacuated by the mediations of writing. But while we can read this as an example of DeLillo's postmodern literary reflexivity, we must note that *The Names* does not essentialise this condition of textualised absence or emptiness as an inescapable ontological fact. Rather, it is frequently related to particular kinds of historical and class experience. For both Axton and Brademas are professional students and practitioners of writing. Brademas is an epigraphist, Axton for the greater part of his career has been a freelance writer for high-technology businesses. He thus stands at the centre of that process of the technologising of the word which Ong argues begins with the development of the written alphabet. Moreover, writing is identified within the narrative as an enabling aspect of both the accumulation process and the development of modern empires. The concern with writing as primal mediation cannot therefore be separated from the concern with the derealising effects of multinational capital in the age of electronic communications, and the place within it of the professional–managerial class.

Speech, by contrast, offers certain consolations in the face of this condition of multiply mediated textuality. That epiphanic moment sought by many of the characters occurs eventually for Axton, not in relation to the cult, nor in connection with the Greek nationalist conspiracy he attempts to uncover, but at the end of the novel during his much deferred visit to the Acropolis. Here he unexpectedly finds that sense of connectedness and authentic 'human feeling', as he calls it, which has been absent from his mobile, free-floating professional existence, and it comes as an effect of speech, of the voice. Contemplating the remains of the Parthenon, Axton 'found a cry for pity'. This, he continues, 'is what remains to the mauled stones in their blue surround, this open cry, this voice we know as our own'. And this voice is not simply an abstract, unrealised ideal voice; it is an attribute of the very real everyday conversations of ordinary people. Axton concludes that at this ancient temple 'No one seems to be alone. This is a place to enter in crowds. Everyone is talking. I move past the scaffolding and down the steps, hearing one language after another, rich, harsh, mysterious, strong. This is what we bring to the temple, not prayer or chant or slaughtered rams. Our offering is language' (*Names*: pp. 330, 331). Spoken language here becomes a positive instance of cosmopolitanism and community, a medium of presence still tinged by what Fredric Jameson calls 'the evanescent warmth of the sacred' (Jameson, 1984b: p. 122). It is set against the cold and empty cosmopolitanism of writing whose deterritorialisations mean that its relationship to the sacred can, as in the case of the cult, only be contrived and brutal.

This opposition also serves Axton as a mapping device. The Acropolis is the high place from which he at last gains an overall perspective on the modern city of Athens in which, as both a motorist and a would-be conspirator, he constantly loses his bearings. Indeed, Axton has deferred his visit to the Acropolis, 'prefer[ring] to wander the modern city, imperfect, blaring', precisely because he feels he is not ready for the cognitive education it promises to give him. At the opening of his narrative, Axton speculates that 'The weight and moment of these stones promised to make the business of seeing them a complicated one. So much converges there. It's what we've rescued from the madness. Beauty, dignity, order, proportion. There are obligations attached to such a visit'. By its close he is ready for such a lesson in 'seeing', and the picture he receives from this vantage point, still inhabited by the vestiges of the sacred and traditional orality alike, is of the way in which the modern city is structured by geopolitical forces – 'car-bombings, firebombings ... terror' – which remain ultimately inscrutable, being driven, as far as Axton can see, by nothing more definable than 'a blind might' (*Names*: pp. 3, 330).

The Names thus stages the moment of epiphanic vision as a kind of separation, an encounter with blindness; and, similarly, it also suggests that the consolations of speech might in fact not be all they seem to Axton at the Acropolis. For in the 'second' and later ending to the book – a passage from Axton's nine-year-old son's 'novel' based on the childhood recollections of Owen Brademas – spoken language is as much a medium of dislocation and separation as is writing elsewhere in the book.[17] Though Tap Axton's sublime misspellings of words serve to lessen the distance between oral and written language (in his child's discourse speech's phonetic imperatives overwhelm the strict grammatical conventions of writing) the story his novel tells is of the power of speech to exclude and disorientate. His youthful protagonist, Orville Benton, suffers a 'dredful woe of incomprehenshun [*sic*]' when his parents take him to a primitive, rural religious meeting at which the congregation spontaneously begins to speak in tongues. Unable to understand or participate in this 'secret language', Orville flees, becoming exiled from his family and from from the sacred, oral rituals of his community. He embarks then upon the kind of detached career of wandering that prefigures the professional cosmopolitan mobility of his 'real life' inspiration, Owen Brademas (*Names*: pp. 338, 335).

The condition of professional estrangement is therefore traceable to the operations of spoken language as much as it is to the primal mediations of writing. Indeed, professionalism seems to be conditional upon processes of linguistic exclusion. On the one hand DeLillo implies that specialised and narrow professional languages or ideolects are substitutes and compensations for this primal exclusion from natural, spontaneous, communal speech. As Axton remarks, 'Technicians speak a secret language', just like the glossolalic revivalists of Brademas's youth; this is what enables them to become 'the infiltrators of ancient societies'. On the other hand, these secret languages carry the dynamic of exclusion to a particularly modern and rational extreme: while they work to define community in a certain limited sense, their logic of increasing specialisation and abstraction undermines both community and the very bases of human communication. The Maitlands's son, Peter, is a professional mathematician who has mastered an esoteric technical language composed of 'secrets' and 'codes' which 'means nothing, says nothing, refers to nothing' but 'itself and only itself'. His knowledge is so advanced that he is unable to communicate at all: he 'speaks to no one' and cannot even discuss his work with his professors (*Names*: pp. 114, 164). In this respect, the abstracting and estranging components of professional languages empty even oral communication of its residual warmth and connotations of presence.

Here the secondary opposition of speech and writing begins to dissolve, though the double ending of *The Names* points to an abiding ambivalence about the properties of speech. Axton's epiphanic moment at the Acropolis presents speech as the vehicle for cosmopolitan but nonetheless humane community. It also serves here as a mapping device which enables Axton finally to situate himself and, from a high point, read the configurations of geopolitical power in the modern city beneath him. But at other points speech is the vehicle of exclusion, separation and unmapping; it fosters not the positive and warm cosmopolitanism witnessed at the Acropolis but a negative cosmopolitanism of anomic wandering or homelessness, exemplified in the plight of Tap Axton's character, Orville Benton.[18] The narrative positioning of the Acropolis episode suggests, however, that the version of speech it offers can be read as a nostalgic compensation for precisely this sense of homelessness.[19] For it follows directly upon the collapse of Axton's mapping projects and the revelation of the real extent of his inability to understand the geopolitical conditions of his own cosmopolitan existence. First the quest for the cult peters out inconclusively in the desert, the primal encounter with death being at once deferred and multiply mediated through Brademas's reporting of his only partial witness of the ritual act. Then, the attempt to decode the conspiracy involving the Greek nationalist, Eliades, is bungled; Eliades slips away and the episode ends with Axton still unsure whether he himself, rather than David Keller, was the intended victim of the shooting. Finally, and most devastatingly, Axton learns that the corporation for which he works has been exposed as a CIA information gathering service and that his boss, Rowser, has been trying, in a series of heavily disguised hints, to alert him to this fact.

It is in this welter of unmapping that the world system finally becomes evident to Axton, but in negative form. The 'connections' he has so assiduously sought through the cult and through Eliades (who has come to seem to him 'more and more the means of some connection') have been present, obscure and yet determining all along in his insertion into the 'complex systems, endless connections' that link the circuits of deterritorialised capital to the geopolitical agencies of state power in the global economy (*Names*: pp. 225, 313). The epiphany at the Acropolis can then be understood as Axton's attempt to reinsert himself into an alternative, universal synchronic system – language – whose reach is commensurate with that of global capital, but whose connections are not decentring and determining but ultimately humane and reassuring. We might say that the embrace of speech is, in the terminology of Jacques Derrida, a compensatory invocation of the metaphysics of presence to counteract the absence revealed by Axton's encounter with the structural conditions of his existence.

Moreover, the resort to a high place – the Acropolis – at this moment can also be read as compensation for the crisis of Axton's professional symbolic-analytic skills. His inability to read the geopolitical machinations into which he is inserted (and which he unwittingly serves) belies his image of himself as someone with 'intellectual range', with 'a view that was broader than the underwriter's or the statistician's'. The belated pilgrimage to the high place – according to Bruce Robbins the metaphorical location habitually associated with professional 'detachment' – thus represents an attempt to reassert the broadness of view that has been exposed as purblind and, as such, amenable to the manipulations of power (Robbins, 1993: pp. 141–7). It is an attempt to redeem that state of professionalism that we have seen is inescapable for Axton, to reassert professionalism as intellectual range and breadth of vision rather than 'blind involvement' with 'blind might', and to reimagine its fundamental condition of estrangement positively, as analytical detachment and elevated perspective (*Names*: pp. 48, 317, 330).

This, however, is not easily done. For it is precisely at this moment of unmapping that Axton's professional identity is most at issue and most paradoxical. The bungled attempt to decode Eliades's nationalist entanglements leaves Axton feeling worse 'than the dumbest amateur'. This is not the 'good' amateurism already discussed, but a 'bad' amateurism defined as foolishness, ignorance, lack of symbolic-analytic expertise. Yet while he behaves like an amateur, Axton continues to 'pass' for a professional. Indeed, he is deemed to be at his most professional when his blindness and ignorance are acutest. The blank, dumbfounded silence with which he greets the revelations about his firm's CIA connections is admiringly taken by his expatriate friends to signal the cunning reticence and composure of the seasoned intelligence agent. Silence is 'the only professional stance', Charles Maitland assures him. As the plot dynamics of the novel move into the areas of political conspiracy and espionage, it is worth noting Bruce Robbins's contention that 'the figure of the "intelligence agent" belongs to the problematics of post-war professionalism' (Robbins, 1993: p. 128). Axton as a partly unwitting intelligence agent embodies one aspect of these problematics. He is an agent only so long as he remains oblivious to the true nature of the powers his skills ultimately serve, not simply the power of global capital but the power of the state and the military. To become aware is to cease being an agent in both senses of the word: he must lose or relinquish his job, and with it the insertion into the heart of the historical action which for Axton, as we have seen, is central to a sense of involvement in history and a feeling of personal agency. Moreover, to do the professional thing upon attaining such awareness, to speak the truth to his friends and confess that he has been a 'dupe' as he puts it, would be to forfeit his professional standing for the humiliations of 'bad' amateurism. *The Names* thus recalls *Blade Runner* in its dramatisation of the simultaneous inescapability and impossibility of professionalism in the global capitalist system. The question both stories pose to the deracinated professional within this system is the one Hardeman asks Axton and which Axton is, of course, in his blindness quite unable at that point to answer truthfully: 'Who do *you* work for?' (*Names*: pp. 263, 314, 316).

Cognitive Mapping and Uneven Development

The opposition between professional and amateur thus disintegrates, just like those other apparently structuring oppositions in *The Names* between speech and writing, nature and history, place and space. This deconstructive impulse is related to the novel's exploration of the cognitive implications of uneven development. As I noted earlier, uneven development can be regarded as a process that undermines polar opposites and produces, rather, internal differences; thus the intensification of uneven development with the recomposition of the Fordist world system is claimed in some degree to be deconstructing the opposition between core and periphery upon which that system was based, with attributes of each pole increasingly inhabiting the other. In a similar way, *The Names* dramatises the inadequacy of relying on conceptual oppositions as devices for mapping these new global configurations and locating individual experience within them. In this respect we might conclude that the particular cognitive education received by Axton in his cosmopolitan romance of uneven development is essentially negative. The binary oppositions which structure his efforts to place himself are linked to a compensatory nostalgia for a condition prior to capitalist modernity and professional deracination alike, and successively break down when put to the test. The result is precisely a thorough unmapping of Axton's sense of his place in the global system; what at one point is felt as involvement in and insight into the dynamics of capitalist modernisation on a global scale, into making history, turns out to be a personal and political blindness, a 'blind involvement' with 'blind might' (*Names*: pp. 317, 330).

But there is the suggestion that a more positive kind of cognitive education might be attainable. At one point Axton envisages a way out of his blindness and spatial confusion in terms of 'an evolution of seeing' that would progress beyond the nostalgic tendency to project value and presence on to a lost past or idealised precapitalist enclaves. Such a mode of perception would be equal to the cognitive challenges of a place such as Athens to which, Axton notes, the old kind of 'sensibility can't easily be adapted'. For Athens is precisely a microcosm of combined and uneven development, a place where the premodern and the traditional are in perpetual interrelationship with the processes of modernisation and development, where, in spite of the presence of the past, 'the surface of things is mostly new, where the ruin is differently managed, the demise indistinguishable from the literal building-up and building-out' (*Names*: p. 179). While Axton himself does not undergo such an evolution of seeing in a novel which is perhaps best seen as a narrative of cognitive *un*mapping, it is still indicated as the possible outcome of a cosmopolitan cognitive education to which the novel's own complex and deconstructive picture of the post-Fordist world system contributes.

As a national allegory, *The Names* is perhaps more straightforward. Axton's personal unmappings stand for the larger crisis of American imperial power and global economic hegemony in the period after the Vietnam War that put intolerable stress on the regulatory and accumulative structures of Fordism (Matusow, 1984). But we have to note that this is an allegory told through a particular class perspective. If, as Andreas Eliades claims in the novel, 'power' is 'blind in both eyes', then it is perhaps no surprise that its professional–managerial servants should also suffer from impaired vision. Professionalism here is presented as a necessary blindness to the nature of its insertion into contemporary capitalist world space, deriving particularly from its relationship to the dominant institutions of that space – the multinational corporations. Axton's failure of mapping, for which his unwitting service as a CIA agent stands, is bound up with his inability to read his position within the 'sprawling' multinational corporation of which his firm is but a fragment, a 'wholly owned subsidiary' (*Names*: p. 242). In this respect, the multinational corporation is itself as inscrutable an entity as the global space of deterritorialised capital in which it operates; it is a form which, as Alfred Chandler argues, now exceeds the perceptual grasp of those who work in it and for it (Chandler, 1990: p. 623).

Indeed, several commentators have observed that the structure of the multinational corporation renders the movements of global capital and power increasingly obscure. Stephen Hymer has noted the close connection between multinationals and the production of uneven development. He claims, as Marx and Engels did of the nineteenth-century bourgeoisie, that 'the tendency of corporations is to create a world in their own image', leading to an increasingly complex and decentred global distribution of power (Hymer, 1975: p. 38). Louis Turner has presented a similar case in terms of visual perception, arguing that the ascendancy of the multinationals marks a shift from the 'visible' imperialism of nation states to what he calls the 'invisible empires' of informated finance capital (Turner, 1971). These accounts tend to support what John McClure sees as the principal message of DeLillo's fiction as a whole: that the modern capitalist world system might have eliminated those 'exotic' enclaves that were once believed to persist outside it, but that in doing so it has belied the Weberian logic of relentless disenchantment and substituted its own occult and labyrinthine networks, its own 'postmodern elsewhere', as a new site of mystery, adventure and romance (McClure, 1994: p. 120).

At another level, then, *The Names* is also a class allegory which tells of the corruption and fall of professional–managerial class cosmopolitanism over the period of the breakdown and recomposition of the Fordist regime. Axton's reminiscences of protesting against the Vietnam War at the moment of that regime's major geopolitical crisis contrast baldly with his current position as a running dog of finance capital and the CIA. He thus embodies the ideological trajectory of the PMC, traced by Barbara Ehrenreich among others, from 1960s' radicalism to a yuppie-style rapprochement with corporate power as the Fordist consensus was dismantled in the 1980s (B. Ehrenreich, 1989). Yet this would suggest, of course, that professional cosmopolitanism need not always mimic capitalism in its political–ideological movements, but has been and might again be the source of the kind of 'global, anti-imperialist solidarity' Fred Pfeil envisages hopefully in his discussion of the PMC (Pfeil, 1990: p. 121).

While Axton conceives of himself as 'uncommitted' and 'politically neuter' (*Names*: pp. 16, 17), his romance of uneven development does ultimately afford him a variant of the 'internationalist political education' that Bruce Robbins argues can be fostered by the cosmopolitanism of professionals (Robbins, 1993: p. 196). Axton's education might be largely negative, an encounter with his own cognitive limits, in relation to the networks of multinational capital and information. But in its investigations of a possible 'evolution of seeing', in its attempts to trace the deconstructive energies of uneven development, and in its (albeit compensatory and nostalgic) image of a cosmopolitan community of speech at the Acropolis, a 'high place' of reason and detached, panoramic perspective, *The Names* offers some hints of what a positive version of such an education might be. Professional cosmopolitanism might be inescapably compromised by its links with multinational capital, but the novel seems to hold out the hope that 'in the era of the integrated world economy' the 'professional claim to "high places" and longsightedness cannot be foregone' (Robbins, 1993: p. 147).

At the end of *The Names* a chastened Axton redefines the nature of his professional identity. Quitting his berth in the 'monster corporation' where, like the subsidiary that employs him he has been unwittingly but 'wholly owned', he elects for a 'return to the freelance life'. Despite the necessary condition of homelessness that this entails ('But where would I live?', he wonders) 'freelance' is a designation of professionalism which contrasts positively with previous negative ones of 'hack', 'dupe', and 'fool, running a fool's errand, in a fool's world' (*Names*: pp. 242, 318, 48, 316, 6). Finally, then, the professional is at least partially redeemed, now at least equipped to answer

Hardeman's accusatory 'Who do *you* work for?' with a certain claim to that autonomy so important to ideologies of professionalism.

In this respect the novel can be seen as an evisceration of the 'impassive cosmopolitanism' that Robert Reich has attributed to the class of symbolic analysts which he positions at the forefront of the global economy. One meaning of the word impassive is 'unconscious'; this perfectly describes the nature of Axton's insertion into global space, not only in the sense that he is unconscious of the fact that the CIA are the real beneficiaries of his work, but also in that he represents his cosmopolitanism as a wilful cultivation of various forms of ignorance. He enjoys Athens's 'enticement to wander foolishly, to get lost without feeling you were part of a formalist puzzle'. He thinks of himself as a 'perennial tourist', a condition in which 'Being stupid is the pattern, the level, the norm'. This is all part of a wider attempt to reject what we might think of as public, social or historical grand narratives. Of his marriage to Kathryn he says, 'We hadn't entered a state at all. If anything we'd broken out of states and nations and grand designs ... we were making it up day to day, little by little ... with no huge self-seeking visions' (*Names*: pp. 40, 43, 39).

Axton thus resembles Lyotard's postmodern self, for whom the apparent redundancy of grand narratives of knowledge and human emancipation is offset by a mobile and eclectic cosmopolitanism and the playing of various provisional and incommensurable language games. He seeks to 'escape accountability' by being 'able to drift across continents and languages, suspending the operation of sound thought' (*Names*: p. 43). The fact, then, that whatever corrective education Axton receives comes at the hands of the master narrative of imperialism with the intrusion of the CIA and its geopolitical connections with multinational capital, indicates a certain incredulity on DeLillo's part towards what we might caricature as Axton's 'postmodern' position on grand narrative. *The Names* presents the ineluctability of the professional–managerial class experience of primal mediation and homelessness as an effect of the latest twist of the grand narrative of empire, in which this class takes a leading role as the configurations of Fordism are deterritorialised on a domestic and global scale.

11

Blindness and Insight in the World System: *Until the End of the World*

> The professional excavated nature for its principles ... allowing him both to perceive and predict those inconspicuous or unseen variables which determined an entire system of developments. The professional penetrated beyond the rich confusion of ordinary experience, as he isolated and controlled the factors, hidden to the untrained eye, which made an elaborate system workable or impracticable, successful or unattainable.
>
> Burton Bledstein, *The Culture of Professionalism* (1976: pp. 88–9)

If *The Names* stops short of describing the 'evolution of seeing' that would make individual perception adequate to the global configurations of uneven development, and remains ambivalent about the political inclinations of professional–managerial cosmopolitanism, then Wim Wenders's *Until the End of the World* (1991) is not so reticent. Set like DeLillo's novel at a moment of geopolitical crisis (projected forward from the time of the film's making to the millennial turning point of 1999), the film explores the condition of contemporary globalisation through an almost identical set of themes: the encounter with nature and premodern social organisation in enclaves of precapitalist space; the homelessness and deracinated nature of professional existence; and the ideological antinomies of professionalism with regard to the reach and power of multinational corporations and communication. Yet the film is ultimately less ambivalent in its view of professional–managerial cosmopolitanism than is *The Names*, suggesting that it can be the basis of a positive evolution of seeing and can serve as a cognitive–perceptual 'high place' from which the global system can be mapped and brought under rational control.

The story follows the global wanderings of Claire Tourneur, a young bohemian whose carefree and hedonistic lifestyle contrasts with the situation of crisis precipitated by an errant nuclear satellite which threatens the 'end of the world' of the film's title. While the populations of metropolitan Europe take to the roads to flee the satellite's erratic path, Claire (who, we are told by the film's narrator, 'couldn't care less') abandons the highway altogether in order to avoid the congestion caused by the panic. At this point her in-car computer informs her that she is leaving the 'map zone data base'. Having thus established a thematic connection between personal irresponsibility, or blindness to the wider global situation, and a condition of maplessness, the film then goes on to link this condition with the international circulation of money. Claire's first encounter off the map is with a pair of hoodlums who hire her to deliver their loot to Paris, electronically tagging the money in order to trace its movements. There, Claire encounters Trevor McPhee whom she helps escape from a mysterious pursuer. After McPhee disappears, taking Claire's share of the money with him, she decides now to pursue him, her motivations partly financial, partly romantic.

So far, Claire's trajectory in many respects mirrors the global circuits of informated capital. As she tracks McPhee from country to country she steadily depletes the stock of cash held in her Paris apartment and wired to her from there by her boyfriend, the writer Eugene. Credit now funds her movements and determines them, in as much as her pursuit of McPhee proceeds by tapping in to the information technologies that relay finance capital around the globe and tracing his credit transactions. This narrative shift from 'real' cash to 'fictitious' credit allegorises the wider deterritorialisation of the Fordist world system by a hypertrophic and increasingly autonomous financial apparatus. Indeed, by attaching herself to the volatile circuits of international credit, Claire is taken to the very furthest extremes of capital's penetration of world space. The quest for McPhee leads through the old Soviet empire into China, regions whose recent opening up to the circulation of global capital has raised hopes of what David Harvey calls a 'spatial fix' to the crises of overaccumulation that beset the West in the 1970s and '80s (Harvey, 1989: p. 183). Claire's disoriented, careless cosmopolitanism is presented here as an effect of her connections with the expansionist impulse of informated finance capital.

However, when McPhee is eventually located, the question of cosmopolitanism is reframed in terms of the perspectives and ethical and ideological dilemmas of professionalism. For McPhee turns out in fact to be Sam Farber, an American scientist who is in possession of a camera, invented by his father, which, as he tells Claire, 'takes pictures which blind people can see'. The narrative thus stages the technological realisation of that evolution of seeing anticipated by Axton in *The Names*, and thematises professionalism – as does the historian Burton Bledstein, quoted at the beginning of this chapter – as itself a privileged kind of panoptic and penetrating vision. But the film raises the further ethical and political problem of the technical and social ends to which such an apparatus of cognition should be put. Farber and his father are in flight from both the industrial corporations and the American government because, fearful of their employers' plans to exploit the camera for narrow commercial or military purposes, they have asserted ownership of their own intellectual property and absconded with their invention. The defence of professional autonomy and of the modes of seeing associated with professional rationality thus comes into conflict with the imperatives of the state and the corporations. In contrast to Claire's careless cosmopolitanism which in many ways mimics the circulation of capital, Sam's professional cosmopolitanism stands in principled opposition to the project of intensified global commodification.

There is, though, another, private dimension to Sam Farber's global peregrinations. His travels are arranged so that he may use the camera to record interviews with members of his family who have been spread across the globe as a consequence of their professions. The gathering and coding of this information is designed not only to enable his blind mother to 'see' her family for the first time, but also to win for Sam the much desired approval of his father from whom he has become emotionally and geographically estranged. The particular use that Sam Farber envisages for this new mode of seeing is therefore to heal those hidden injuries of class that stem from the condition of professional social and spatial mobility – as we have seen, a central preoccupation of narratives that concern themselves with the shift to post-Fordist forms of social and economic organisation.[1]

This question of class-based estrangement is raised in other ways too. When Sam returns 'home' with Claire to his parents this turns out to be an aboriginal village deep in the Australian bush. The disaffiliated professional has sought refuge in what Fredric Jameson describes as a 'relationship with some organic precapitalist peasant landscape and village society, which is the final form of the image of Nature in our own time' (Jameson, 1991: p. 34). The encounter with nature here is more successful and fruitful than it is for the protagonists of *The Names*. For the Farbers, though, nature represents not so much a space in which professional identity can be jettisoned in an epiphanic moment of immediate experience as it does an enclave in which professional ideals can be revitalised and the hidden injuries of professional class identity healed in isolation from the intrusions of capital and political structures alike. Henry Farber has rebuilt his laboratory in the village, training a cadre of aboriginal technicians who, in addition to aiding his scientific work, serve as a substitute extended family in lieu of the one dispersed by the centrifugal forces of metropolitan modernity. Moreover, the escape into nature apparently becomes a guarantee of simple survival when the feared nuclear explosion occurs, precipitating what the characters believe to be the end of the world beyond their remote village. Here the film seems to be running an argument for the 'greening' of science and technology through a closer association of professional rationality with 'natural' experience and traditional forms of knowledge and social organisation. The will to dominate nature through the disenchanting logic of instrumental reason must be reassessed, it suggests.

But the reinsertion of professionalism into nature is not entirely positive or without problems in *Until the End of the World*. For despite evading the coercive and exploitative reach of both capital and the state, Sam and Henry Farber are afflicted with their own particular modes of blindness which compromise the potential of their invention as a means of gaining insight into an increasingly totalised world system. Sam's blindness is an effect of an Oedipal crisis which causes him to over-personalise his investment in the cognitive possibilities of the camera. He cannot conceive of a use for the instrument beyond restoring his mother's sight and, more importantly for him, thereby regaining the affection and approval of his father. The cosmopolitan breadth of his image-gathering excursions is therefore undercut by a blind confinement to the sphere of the bourgeois family and the limits of the Oedipal purview. As if to emphasise this, Sam's own sight begins to fail due to the strain of serving as mediator in the communication of the family images to his mother. Moreover, the effect on his mother is not what he imagined it would be. Seeing the world again results for her not in demystification and emotional reconnection, but in radical disenchantment and an ultimate withdrawal from the world. The world is 'darker and uglier' than she had imagined it in her blindness; seeing her family for the first time since she was a child reminds her of their inevitable mortality; this knowledge estranges her from those closest to her and precipitates her death. In this respect, the evolution of seeing proves to be nothing more than a further stage in that modernising process of disenchantment of the world in which professionals are at the vanguard. Confined to the narrow spaces of bourgeois private life the insights produced by this new mode of seeing prove to be destructive.

Henry Farber's blindness is of the kind we have encountered in previous instances in this book – a devotion to the pursuit of technical expertise and professional recognition as ends in themselves to the detriment of other commitments and considerations. Despite his wife's death, he presses on with his research, seeking to perfect the process of image realisation using himself, Sam and Claire, and his aboriginal extended family as subjects. Professionalism is presented here not only as emotional blindness to family loyalties but also as ideological blindness to the broad social effects of technical rationality. Farber seeks to use the camera to produce visualisations of dreams and other unconscious processes. While this re-emphasises the disenchanting logic of technical rationality through the deployment of reproductive technologies, it also underlines the links between professionalism and the dynamics of colonialism and imperialism. As his aboriginal 'skin brother', Peter, reminds him, for Farber to abstract and reify images from the dreams of an aboriginal is not just to invade and demystify that person's unconscious, but to appropriate their – indeed the entire aboriginal culture's – 'secret knowledge' which is encoded in dreams.

This is to characterise professionals as colonisers and expropriators of the knowledges and cultures of communities less powerful, and less 'developed' in terms of so-called 'universal' standards of reason, than their own.[2] The village community disintegrates; thus, even as he 'excavate[s] nature for its principles', to use Burton Bledstein's definition of the professional's activity, Farber becomes increasingly alienated from it. Nature, envisaged as a refuge from the ideological and ethical tensions of professionalism and modernity, is nevertheless still rendered subservient to the professional will to power and knowledge.

Until the End of the World is therefore inhabited by an ambivalence towards the cosmopolitanism of professionals in the contemporary world system. On the one hand, it is credited with the potential for a principled resistance to multinational capital and for producing new kinds of visionary insight into the occluded dimensions of global space. On the other, it is presented as an aspect of the colonising logic of capitalist modernisation, of what Jameson calls the 'new and historically original penetration of Nature and the Unconscious' which reaches its highest point in late capitalism (Jameson, 1991: p. 36). It is also linked to a particular form of blindness to global questions which only serves to strengthen these negative associations. The Farbers's and Claire's pursuit of the technical logic of the camera in an exclusively inward direction, toward the recoding and visualisation of their dreamlife, is bound up with indifference to the global crisis that surrounds them, just as Axton's obsessive pursuit of the cult in *The Names* precluded an awareness of his own compromised insertion into the global networks of power.

In contrast to *The Names*, however, this ambivalence is ultimately resolved. Claire Tourneur, like her namesake Turner in Gibson's cyberspace trilogy, becomes the narrative pivot for the redemption of professionals as social agents. Her own and the Farbers's technological narcissism, their spectatorial addiction to dream images, is presented as both a retreat from public, worldly concerns and a kind of radical disorientation or unmapping. They had, remarks the film's narrator, 'wandered into a maze', becoming 'lost in the labyrinth' of the self. But this 'disease of images', as it is called, is cured by an encounter with narrative in a more traditional and public form, with what the narrator calls the 'magic and healing power of words and stories'. For Sam, this healing process is an effect of aboriginal oral culture as the village elders recount tribal myths that take his dreams away from him. For Claire, it is an effect of written narrative, as she reads the novel Eugene has written of her experience (this text also serves as a framing device for the film as a whole). This metafilmic critique of the cinematic apparatus is structured by a moral and ideological opposition between written and oral forms of telling on the one hand and visual forms on the other that recalls the tension between orality and literacy in *The Names*. But what particularly interests me here is the way that the critique of image obsession is used to stage a rehabilitation of the modes of seeing associated with professional rationality.

For it is Claire who, at the end of the film, assumes the burdens of an ethical and socially responsible professionalism at the service of the universal good to which both Sam and Henry Farber have proved unequal. When Claire recovers from her image obsession to become an astronaut working for 'Greenspace', monitoring the globe for 'pollution crimes', her own special powers of visualisation and the evolution of seeing produced by technical rationality at last find a public application that is universal (or at least planetary) in its scope. Claire's irresponsible, impassive cosmopolitanism is thus transformed into a publicly engaged but non-partisan global vision. In her case, the professional perspective provides a literal bird's-eye view of the planet by which the excesses of globalised capitalist modernisation can be monitored and regulated. The condition of professional estrangement is also recast in terms of analytical detachment and objective reason. Claire's location in orbit above the Earth signifies not so much alienation from the world and from nature, or a condition of being 'lost in space', as it does the critical distance necessary to perceive the world system in its totality and to protect nature from the ravages of an expansionist, multinational production system. In *Until the End of the World* outer space is a figure for that vantage point or 'high place' necessary for the exercise of professional vision, of what Bruce Robbins calls the 'longsightedness' more necessary than ever in a globalised world.

The film's affirmative shift from blindness to insight, however, is produced at the cost of considerable narrative incoherence. In particular, the question of the professional's uneasy relationship with power is avoided. The Farbers's initial political and ethical dilemma, their fears of corporate and state misuse of science, is not explored but displaced by the private, psychological dilemmas associated with the Oedipal structures of the bourgeois family. The ideological struggle for ownership of the new mode of seeing represented by the camera simply evaporates as the narrative's pretext. No explanation is given for how the camera eventually comes to be used for benign ecological purposes, commensurate with the non-sectarian rationality of professionals, rather than serving more powerful corporate or military interests. We are simply left to assume that the brush with nuclear annihilation represented by the rogue satellite has such a salutary effect upon the corporations and the state that they relinquish their claim to monopoly control of science, allowing a more rational, humane and universally beneficial disposal of its techniques through agencies of global regulation such as Greenspace. In this respect, the film reproduces some of the blindness of which it accuses its protagonists, dwelling on the self to the exclusion of the world, and culminating in a wishful redemption of professionalism which leaves in abeyance the hard political choices raised by the insertion of professionals into the global corporate web.

It is worth noting that the film reclaims professionalism through the discourse of ecology. As Alvin Gouldner has suggested, we can view ecology in its contemporary manifestations as an ideological inclination characteristic of the professional–managerial class. Ecology's global or planetary perspective expresses the cosmopolitanism and universalism of professional notions of reason, while what Gouldner calls its 'rejection of the idea of domination over nature' and its intimation of some kind of a 'return to nature' serve not only to criticise the irrationality of unregulated capitalist production but also to legitimate the notion of a holistic or 'green' science of social responsibility. This latter notion is particularly appealing to the humanistic fractions of the PMC whose thinking, Gouldner argues, is grounded in organic metaphors with romantic anti-capitalist antecedents. Ecology therefore is a vehicle of both professional–managerial class agency and solidarity, supporting PMC claims for its ability to manage the global system of production rationally, above the narrow sectionalism of naked class interests (Gouldner, 1979: pp. 42–3).

To characterise ecology in this way is not to diminish its importance or effectiveness as a critical or oppositional discourse. Rather, it is to seek to situate it in terms of what have been called antisystemic or new social movements. Theorists such as Immanuel Wallerstein, Giovanni Arrighi, Joachim Hirsch and Manuel Castells have demonstrated how such movements arise historically out of the crisis of the Fordist regime of accumulation and the reconfiguration of the world system with which Fordism was bound up (Arrighi, Hopkins and Wallerstein, 1988; Hirsch, 1983; Castells, 1997). In their impatience with what is denounced as the economistic politics of the 'old left', with its reliance on productivist thinking and the agency of the working class, these movements can be seen as both responses to and symptoms of the deterritorialisation of production and class relationships in the shift to post-Fordism (Wallerstein, 1991: pp. 72–4). Ecology in particular proposes a new relationship between the local and the global which reflects the ambiguity of the cosmopolitanism of the professional–managerial world view. It promotes a totalising and internationalist perspective on 'the planet' in which community is recast in increasingly universalist terms as humanity. But it is also inhabited by a secessionist impulse in which identification with the totality involves the partial repudiation of social groups whose position is ever more tenuous within that totality. For example, the ecological perspective involves a certain antagonism towards the metropolitan working class whose demands for reinvestment in productive industry and a return to full employment are perceived to be incompatible with sound ecological practice and the management of finite resources. Similarly, whether they are directly blamed for these things or not, the third-world poor's 'unsustainable' resource use and 'excessive' reproductive ratios are also objects for ecological disapproval, and the 'green' version of development ideology reiterates in some respects the old imperialist notion that it is the burden of the West to educate and enlighten the wretched of the earth.

Robert Reich has pointed to another aspect of the secessionist impulse of professional–managerial cosmopolitanism. Here identification with the global entails withdrawal from local sites of involvement and commitment. 'As borders become ever more meaningless in economic terms', he argues, 'those citizens best positioned to thrive in the world market are tempted to slip the bonds of national allegiance, and by doing so disengage themselves from their less favored fellows'. It is not difficult to detect that Reich is in fact describing here the terms of the dissolution of the Fordist class consensus which was secured by the linking of constant rises in productivity to proportionate increases in material standards of living within the bounds of the national economy. Now it is Reich's class of mobile and cosmopolitan symbolic analysts who reap the rewards of the new internationalism, while the working class remains tied to the declining and deterritorialised structures of domestic production. Reich notes that the professional–managerial class's preoccupation with the idea of community actually serves to mask or legitimate what he calls the 'politics of secession' by which its members progressively withdraw from public space into enclaves based on occupational similarity and high income, exposing other social groups to intensified hardship (Reich, 1991: pp. 3, 267–8).

We can read *Until the End of the World* as an exploration of the ambiguous political and ethical meanings of the cosmopolitanism of professionals. Claire's final location in orbit miles above the planet gives her the perspective necessary to see and act on a global level and in the universal interest. Yet it also signifies estrangement, separation, homelessness, as well as suggesting the kind of secession from more local and embedded forms of community discussed above. As we have seen, the motif of the professional in space is a recurrent one in stories that address the decomposition of Fordist patterns of social and economic organisation. This is a metaphorical register of the extent to which the social and political location of the professional–managerial class has become a central question in the construction and projection of post-Fordism.

Conclusion

Questioning Fordism and Post-Fordism

David Hounshell reminds us that the term 'Fordism' originated as a popular characterisation of the novel systems of industrial production introduced into the Ford automobile factories in the 1910s. But by the 1920s it had been displaced by the more technical-sounding term 'mass production', endorsed by Henry Ford's own entry under this heading in the 1925 edition of the *Encyclopaedia Britannica* (Hounshell, 1984: p. 1). At about the same time, however, the term Fordism was taken up by Antonio Gramsci who extended its earlier frame of reference from the factory floor to encompass what he saw as an epochal or historic shift in the social organisation of economic activity in its widest sense.

For Gramsci, Fordism described an emergent set of social and economic structures, particular to the United States, which represented a deliberate attempt to impose order upon the crisis-prone capitalism of unregulated, individualistic competition and open class conflict. This 'organisation of a planned economy' meant not just industrial reorganisation but social and cultural transformation too (Gramsci, 1971: p. 279). The technical and technological rationalisation of the labour process would necessarily entail the recomposition of class relationships and the revolutionising, in particular, of the wage earners' ways of life. New institutions, new forms of knowledge and legitimation, new social strata, even new modes of subjectivity and selfhood would arise out of and in response to this shift, Gramsci observed.

The revival of interest in Gramsci in the 1970s marked the next stage in the development of the notion of Fordism. Gramsci's suggestive notes were elaborated into a fully fledged and historically grounded theory of the development of American capitalism by the Marxist political economists of the regulation school. Fordism now described an historically specific regime of accumulation bound up with a constellation of social, political and cultural patterns and institutions through which the accumulation process was regulated and the conditions necessary for its reproduction stabilised. By placing the wage relation or the labour–capital contradiction at the heart of their theory, the regulationists paid due respect to the Gramscian notion of hegemony. Fordism was a specific, historically limited containment of class antagonisms that, while rooted in the disciplining machine logic of the capitalist production process, nevertheless entailed a high degree of qualified consent on the part of the wage earners themselves, embodied in the regime's institutions of regulation such as the apparatus of collective wage bargaining, the welfare system, and the culture of consumption.

This understanding of Fordism as a complex but always provisional institutionalisation of the class struggle which allowed accumulation to reach new heights during the three decades following the Second World War makes it a powerful alternative to other descriptions of the social and economic basis of the long boom in terms such as 'consensus capitalism' or 'postindustrial society'. These terms (and variants such as the 'affluent society' or the society of 'plenty' or 'abundance') rest on evolutionist assumptions about the elimination of economic crisis by ever-rising levels of productivity, the end of ideology, and the obsolescence of social class as a meaningful category.[1] As a result, they are incapable of explaining the the exhaustion of the long boom, the persistence of economic crisis, and the recrudescence of ideology and class conflict that accompanies it. In this respect, it is not surprising that the regulationist version of Fordism emerged at precisely that regime's moment of structural crisis in the mid-1970s, a crisis which other characterisations of postwar American capitalism had trouble explaining.[2]

But the notion of a Fordist regime of accumulation is not without its critics from within the field of Marxist political economy. Some have observed that it is 'difficult to discover any examples of "Fordism" in its pure form, even in the United States' (Clarke, S., 1988: p. 62). Others have questioned the extent to which so-called Fordist structural forms and practices were in fact characteristic of the post-1945 period at all; even if they were widely in place, it is suggested, this does not necessarily mean that they were responsible for the economic success of this period (Edwards, R., 1979: pp. 97–104; Sayer, 1989; Clarke, S., 1988 and 1990). It might also be asked how far an explanation of contemporary capitalism based on an analysis of American history can serve as a general description. That is, is Fordism a strictly American phenomenon as it was for Gramsci; or was the American model adopted sufficiently across Western Europe and elsewhere for these societies also to be understood as Fordist?

While these reservations are apposite and important, and remind us that the Fordist paradigm is not without its conceptual difficulties, I would argue that they do not seriously compromise its usefulness as an explanatory term. This is reflected in the fact that the term's critics themselves continue to deploy it even as they take issue with some of its implications, finding no other adequate way to describe and understand the peculiar forms of post-1945 capital accumulation throughout the industrialised West (Davis, 1978 and 1986; Clarke, S., 1988 and 1990).

Fordism, then should not be thought of as an essence which must map directly on to a complex and shifting social and historical reality; nor should it be seen as a monocausal model for which the empirical absence of any one of its principal conditions is sufficient to discredit the whole idea. Rather, Fordism serves as a broad theoretical framework for seeking an understanding of the relationship between economy, society and culture in the advanced industrialised West, particularly the United States, in the period from the Second World War (though its origins must be traced back to the Progressive era), and for producing an account of crisis and structural change in this period. It is thus its explanatory power which makes the concept of Fordism an important tool for the analysis of contemporary culture and society.

Yet if the notion of Fordism is in some respects problematic then the notion of post-Fordism is more so. I have been wary throughout this book about making substantial claims for the nature of post-Fordism, even of suggesting that such an entity is with us in anything like achieved and coherent form. As my title implies, post-Fordism is still perhaps best seen as a 'project' yet to emerge fully or independently from the crisis of Fordist structural forms. Like Fordism, though, post-Fordism will be a contingent and historically limited outcome of the contest between capital and labour – mediated by institutions, ideologies, discourses, social groups and the application of technologies – that has no predetermined result or final shape. This is to say that, like Fordism, it will not entirely be the result of the intentionality either of capital or labour, or of any other social group for that matter, nor should it be conceived in functionalist terms as a transformation somehow 'designed' from on high to safeguard capital accumulation or perpetuate certain forms of class and institutional power, though it certainly may have these effects. As Alain Lipietz has argued, regimes of accumulation and modes of regulation are best understood as provisional and contingent institutionalisations of class conflict whose features and effects are largely accidental and always historically circumscribed (Lipietz, 1987a: Chapter 1).

The post-Fordist hypothesis is, though, based on a detailed historical analysis of the crisis of Western capitalism in the 1970s and '80s. From this point onward the central features of Fordist regulation – collective wage bargaining, universal welfare provision, mass Taylorist work organisation and so on – have come indisputably under pressure. While the exact 'content' of post-Fordism cannot as yet be precisely specified, the hypothesis is nonetheless 'the nearest thing we have to a paradigm which can link widespread changes in forms of production to changes in class relations, state forms and individual identities' (Rustin, 1989b: p. 303). The Fordism/post-Fordism model therefore serves as an interpretive device for framing questions about the nature and direction of change in contemporary Western societies and cultures. In this respect it is similar to the notion of postmodernism, which I also see as another conceptual tool for questioning social and cultural processes rather than as a stable and definitive description of empirical reality. Post-Fordism and postmodernism, therefore, might best be understood in terms of Louis Althusser's adaptation of Thomas Kuhn's notion of a 'problematic' – as concepts which do not so much specify answers as map out broad fields of investigation and posit key questions for contestation and argument (Kuhn, 1970; Althusser and Balibar, 1979: pp. 154–5).

The kinds of questions posed by the post-Fordist problematic are precisely those addressed by the stories discussed in this book. In this respect, attending to narrative representations of social and economic change can illuminate and bring together debates that are too often conducted largely in the separate fields of political economy, social theory and cultural criticism. In particular, it can provide for an exploration of the ways in which crisis, change and conflict are shaped into narrative patterns of significance for broad public consumption at a symbolic level. We have seen how microelectronic technologies have provoked a variety of cultural anxieties about changing patterns of work, class, community and identity which have been expressed and resolved in stories that dramatise such changes and reflect on their implications through style, structure and plot. We have seen how the cosmopolitan processes of globalisation have raised questions about the range and adequacy of individual cognitive capacities and how these, too, have been addressed and worked through by stories that try to represent, explore and come to terms with the new worldspace of multinational capital and communications.

The questions posed by the shift to post-Fordism rehearse in many ways, then, the problems raised by the notion of postmodernism. Do grand narratives of collective progress and liberation still carry any weight in an increasingly fragmented and differentiated economic and social scene? What is the status of the self as it is increasingly penetrated by and bound into microelectronic technologies and cybernetic systems and models? What happens to traditional connections with nature and the material world via work and production when mediation and simulation become the dominant processes of social, economic and cultural life? This is not to suggest that post-Fordism and postmodernism are equivalent but rather to suggest that there are insights to be derived from considering postmodernism in conjunction with the Fordist/post-Fordist paradigm.

Several commentators have tried to tie postmodernism as a concept and as a cultural style or attitude down to a particular social group or class, broadly speaking to what I have been calling the professional–managerial class (Lash and Urry, 1987: pp. 285–300; Callinicos, 1989: pp. 162–71; Pfeil, 1990: pp. 107–18; Jameson, 1991: p. 407; Frow, 1993: pp. 272–4). I have tried to suggest that many of the concerns raised by the disarticulation of Fordism are bound up with the anxieties, values and outlooks of this class. To read postmodern culture through the framework of the Fordist/post-Fordist paradigm helps us to understand it not just as the 'expression' of a privileged social group or generational class fraction, but as a contradictory discourse through which this class negotiates its ambivalent and ambiguous insertion into the class struggle as the capital–labour relationship is recomposed. The contradiction between different kinds of postmodernism – what have been called by Hal Foster a subversive, critical postmodernism of 'resistance' and a blithe and accommodatory postmodernism of 'reaction' (Foster, H., 1985: p. xii), or what we might want to describe as the contradictory dynamic of resistance and reaction *within* many different instances of postmodern cultural forms – might then be traced to the historical conditions that structure the PMC's contradictory social location.

This is to argue, in a slightly circuitous way, for the continued importance of class analysis and class-based readings of cultural texts in spite of the postmodernist turn away from class in favour of the categories of gender, race, ethnicity, sexuality and region as organising concepts. If there is one thing that this study of narratives of social and cultural change through the framework of regulation theory has suggested, it is the extent to which issues of class, class experience, and class identity are thrown to the fore in stories which attempt to register, understand and negotiate such change. In particular, as we have repeatedly seen, the much contested idea of professionalism serves as a key vehicle through which many of these issues of change are explored. This reiterates my claim that the agency of the professional–managerial class is a particularly important feature of contemporary capitalist society and culture with respect to both post-Fordism and postmodernism alike. Thus these latter formulations should be stimuli to the extension and revitalisation of class analysis. They should not be bywords for its abandonment.

Notes

Introduction

1. This conceptual distinction follows Marshall Berman's formulation of the terms modernism and modernity (Berman, 1983: pp. 15–16).
2. The re-examination of Marxism via the question of postmodernism can be followed in Laclau and Mouffe (1985), Hall (1986), Nelson and Grossberg (1988), Ross (1989b), Kellner (1989) and Aronowitz (1990).
3. Harvey (1989) generally identifies Fordism with the institutionalisation of modernist precepts and experiences in culture and social life. The breakdown of Fordist structures and the turn towards what he calls 'flexible specialisation' in the organisation of production and markets is seen to correspond with the rise to cultural dominance of postmodernist features in social and cultural life.
4. Accounts of the development of mass consumption which situate its first flowering in the late nineteenth and early twentieth centuries can be found in Ewen (1976 and 1988), Ewen and Ewen (1982), Fox and Lears (1983), Leach (1993), Lears (1994), May (1983) and Marchand (1985).
5. See for example Norman Mailer's 'A Note on Comparative Pornography' and 'From Surplus Value to the Mass Media', both written during the mid-1950s. These are acute theorisations of what have come to be seen as themes central to postmodernity – the commodification of desire and the invasion of the psyche by the signifying apparatus of the media (Mailer 1968a and 1968b). Daniel Boorstin's *The Image* (1961) is likewise what we might call a Fordist statement of a postmodern theme – the displacement of reality by images.
6. This sense of detachment from material engagement with the world is in many ways related to the individual's position within the productive system, that is, arguably, to class position. Jackson Lears identifies a postmodern sense of empty selfhood and disconnectedness from reality amongst an early twentieth-century American middle class for whom direct material production was giving way to consumption and involvement with the media and technologies of communication (Lears, 1983). The same sense is strongly registered in the cultural and social criticism of 1950s' America where it becomes a central concern of analysts of the historical emergence of what is seen as a new middle class of bureaucratic administrators and service workers more than ever removed from any direct involvement in industrial production (see Bell, 1988; Mills, 1951; Riesman, 1961; Whyte, 1960).
7. David Montgomery (1987) and Richard Edwards (1979) describe the ways in which F.W. Taylor's principles of scientific management were widely presented by supporters during the 1910s and '20s as means for factoring class grievances, class consciousness and, hence, class itself as a meaningful category, out of the organisation of production and out of social relations altogether. Writing in the 1950s, Bell, Riesman and Mills all tended to assume that the prodigious expansion of the white-collar occupational sector and the new middle class of service workers spelled the extinction of the working class as a collective social force. In a piece first published in 1956, Bell, for example, argued that the automation of the production process was 'chang[ing] the basic composition of the labour force, creating a new *salariat* instead of a *proletariat*' (Bell, 1988: p. 268, author's emphasis). This led him to challenge, in the epilogue to *The End of Ideology* (1960), the usefulness of class as a social category.
8. Again, Bell, Riesman and Mills all expressed such revised conceptions of power. For Bell, power was so dispersed in Fordist America that radicals no longer found it possible to define an enemy in the absence of any clearly identifiable class of capitalists or *bourgeoises* (Bell, 1988: p. 312). Riesman likewise identified a shift from what were relatively clearcut images of social power in the productive capitalism of nineteenth-century America to 'an amorphous power structure'

in the bureaucratic consumer capitalism of the 1940s and '50s (Riesman: p. 206). Mills, too, declared that in a bureaucratic, corporate world 'dominated by a vast system of abstractions ... power shifts from the visible to the invisible, from the known to the anonymous, so that one cannot locate the enemy and declare war upon him' (Mills, 1951: p. 110).

9. Differing accounts of the crisis of liberal democracy in relation to the collapse of the Fordist growth formula can be found in Habermas (1975), Bell (1976), Wolfe (1981), Bowles and Gintis (1982), S. Clarke (1990) and Woodiwiss (1993).

10. The key statements of end-of-ideology thinking of the 1950s are contained in the introduction and epilogue to Bell (1988). The debate provoked by Bell's hypothesis can be followed in the collection edited by Waxman (1968). Richard Pells (1989) provides a good account of the wider social and cultural context of end-of-ideology thinking in the 1950s.

11. On the links between narrative and historical understanding I'm thinking especially of the work of Hayden White (1976, 1978 and 1987) on modes of history writing, and of Jameson (1981) on narrative as a cognitive form.

Chapter 1

1. For other theorisations of this process which is the subject of Part 4 of this book, see Smith (1984), Harris (1987), Lipietz (1987a) and Chase-Dunn (1989).

2. Mike Davis argues that the crystallisation of the structural forms of the Fordist class compromise came in 1950 with the 'Treaty of Detroit' between the United Auto Workers union and General Motors (Davis, 1986: p. 52).

3. On the legitimation crisis of liberal democracy see in particular O'Connor (1973), Habermas (1975), Bowles and Gintis (1982) and Woodiwiss (1993).

4. The unsettling consequences of stagflation for the dominant postwar paradigm in economic thought – variants of Keynesian demand-side theory – are outlined in Rowthorn (1980) and Bell and Kristol (1981). Alongside a return to militant free-market ideology and a shift in emphasis from the manipulation of demand to control of the money supply, there arose in response to the collapse of consensus in economic thinking attempts to adapt Keynesian precepts to the new situation in the form of a 'post-Keynesian' economics (Galbraith, 1978).

5. The labour theory of value has come under increasing scrutiny in recent years, especially from proponents of the so-called 'knowledge' or 'information' society who locate the source of value in science and knowledge rather than human labour (Bell, 1973; Naisbitt, 1982; Stonier, 1983; Poster, 1990; Drucker, 1993; Gates, 1996). Within Marxist political economy there has also been some debate about the labour theory of value (Steedman et al., 1981; Bowles and Gintis, 1981).

6. Jameson's essay 'Periodising the '60s' has some fascinating suggestions about the links between the slump of the 1970s and developments in American society and culture that are surprisingly absent from his extended work on postmodernism. Anthony Woodiwiss's provocative *Postmodernity USA* argues that postmodernity can entirely be accounted for by the economic and political crisis of the United States in the late 1960s and '70s (Jameson, 1988c; Woodiwiss, 1993).

7. Regulation theory is a branch of Marxist or neo-Marxist political economy developed in Europe, largely France, during the 1970s and '80s. It is based in Gramsci's original insights into the connections between the forms of industrial organisation pioneered by Ford and wider shifts in the organisation of the social, cultural and even subjective lives of workers. The regulation theorists generalised Gramsci's concerns, arguing that specific forms of industrial organisation were bound up with particular processes and institutions of social, political and cultural regulation. Together these could be understood to constitute a particular regime of accumulation through which the mode of production is reproduced. Though formulated in Europe, regulation theory, like Gramsci's observations, is based in an analysis of the historical development of American capitalism since the American Civil War. The principal statement of regulation theory is Aglietta (1979). Lipietz (1985 and 1987a) has developed regulation theory with respect to the international economy, while Castells (1980) and Davis (1986) draw heavily on the regulation approach in their accounts of the crisis of American capitalism in the 1970s and '80s.

Chapter 2

1. Weinstein notes, too, that the spectre of social revolution and socialism also motivated business leaders in their acceptance of the need for, and vocabulary of, reform (Weinstein, 1969: p. x).
2. This refers us to the idea that Progressivism was a major factor in inhibiting the growth of a genuinely socialist working-class movement in the United States. Weinstein suggests that Progressivism was a movement wherein business leaders hijacked and diverted the American labour movement from the path of radical reform (Weinstein, 1969: p. xiii). Lash and Urry argue that it was rather the emergence of a powerful professional–managerial class in the Progressive era that blocked the development of a radical labour movement (Lash and Urry, 1987: p. 10). The Ehrenreichs similarly attribute the fact that the American left has been predominantly middle class rather than working class to the early influence of the PMC and its links with Progressive ideologies (B. and J. Ehrenreich, 1979: p. 45).
3. As Daniel Bell wrote approvingly in 1953, consensus became the operative notion through which 'the intellectual rehabilitation of American capitalism [was] completed' after the crises and ideological onslaughts upon it of the 1930s (Bell, 1988: p. 94).
4. This is not just a matter of deskilling as a result of the imposition of scientific management techniques and the rationalisation of the labour process. It also involves professional intervention into the social, cultural and even subjective life of working-class communities by groups of 'experts' who would come to constitute what are commonly called the caring professions (J. Ehrenreich, 1985). Such experts or humanistic professionals mediate not so much between capital and labour at the point of production as they do between the 'people' and the state, with the focus on the domestic conditions of existence of the working-class family. Some commentators have seen in this process the destruction of an autonomous working-class culture and the replacement of genuinely communal, *gemeinschaft*-style social relations by therapeutic, bureaucratised and ultimately authoritarian client relationships which create dependency and extend the power of expert elites (Lasch, 1977a, 1977b, 1996). Thus the emergence of the professional–managerial class weakened labour not merely in spheres of work, but within most areas of social, cultural and political life (Urry, 1986: p. 52).
5. The emergence of a culture of professionalism in late nineteenth- and early twentieth-century America is traced in Bledstein (1976), Haskell (1977) and J. Ehrenreich (1985). Harold Perkin (1990) has powerfully argued for professionalism to be seen as *the* shaping influence on British social organisation since 1880.
6. Pfeil records that in 1980, 59 per cent of all 25–35-year-olds and 82 per cent of all *employed* 25–35-year-olds (22.2 million out of 37.4 million American citizens) could be designated by occupation as members of the professional–managerial class (Pfeil, 1990: pp. 98–9).
7. See also Wilkinson (1984 and 1988), Baritz (1989) and B. Ehrenreich (1989) for accounts of this conflation of the notion of American social character with the middle-class professional.
8. James Carey (1989) discusses technology in this expanded sense.
9. Frederick Winslow Taylor, leader of the movement for scientific management and author of *Principles of Scientific Management* (1911), wrote that his techniques for the rational organisation of the workplace could 'be applied with equal force to all social activities: to the management of our tradesmen ... of our churches, our philanthropic institutions, our universities, and our governmental departments ... What other reforms could do as much toward promoting prosperity, toward the diminution of poverty and the alleviation of suffering?' (quoted in B. and J. Ehrenreich, 1979: pp. 22–3). On the pervasiveness of Taylorist ideas in American society see Banta (1993).
10. The technocratic critique of capitalism focused on what was seen as the contradiction between 'business' on the one hand and 'industry' on the other (M. White, 1976: p. 155). 'Business' (taken to mean the owners of property and capital) sought only profit and was thus uninterested in enabling 'industry' (taken to mean the forces and techniques of production) to be organised for maximum efficiency and the collective good. Only the engineers, technicians and professional managers who understood the technical operations of the industrial system were disposed – and, moreover, competent – to organise production on such a rational basis. But, as Thorstein Veblen observed in *The Engineers and the Price System* (1921), to do so would bring them into conflict with their employers, revealing the fact that business (the capitalist class) stood in the way of the full, socially beneficial development of industrial production (Veblen, 1965: pp. 61 and 67–9).

Chapter 3

1. Dennis Hayes has noted that 'For volatility and permanent innovation, the electronics industry simply has no parallel in the history of American manufacturing ... A Silicon Valley building architect explained: "Product life-cycle averages only two years. The shortened cycle of concept/R&D/producing/marketing demands continual changes in managing, manufacturing, warehousing etc. ...The shortened time periods create explosive demands for change"' (Hayes, 1990: p. 162).

2. This is not to imply that Lyotard is a technological determinist. For him, the corrosive effect of modern technologies and techniques on the credibility of grand narratives stems from their subordination to the demands of a specifically *capitalist* conception of efficiency or 'performativity'. Yet in stressing the determining role of efficiency in the development of techniques of production over, say, capital's need to secure *control* over the labour process, Lyotard could be accused of holding an overly technicist view of capital as a social relation. Both Braverman (1974) and Noble (1979, 1984) persuasively argue for the primacy, in the scientific development of productive technology, of capital's drive to secure and extend domination over labour, rather than of any narrow criterion of purely technical efficiency.

3. Like Lyotard, Bellah *et al.* conceive of the decline of grand narratives in linguistic terms. But for them, the erosion of traditionally unifying and legitimating public discourse, rooted in the erstwhile primary communal linguistic traditions of biblical and republican expression, is a consequence of the rise of modern private languages of the self, of individualism. They follow their precursors, Riesman and Rieff, in situating this decline of community within the wider turn towards consumption and its attendant cultural ethos of therapeutic well-being. Fredric Jameson notes, however, that from a left or Marxist perspective the very notion of community is a slippery one, often used with the intention or effect of masking issues of difference, be they of class, race or gender (Jameson, 1988b). Interestingly, in *The Good Society* (1992), their follow-up to *Habits of the Heart*, Bellah and his co-authors distance themselves from overtly nostalgic, anti-statist versions of communitarianism that, they argue, tend to identify community solely with 'face-to-face groups'. They invoke an expanded notion of citizenship as a counterbalance to such nostalgia (Bellah *et al.*, 1992: p. 6).

4. These and other costs of the privilege of working in the computer industry are detailed by Dennis Hayes (1990). Hayes's book is in the tradition of American community studies, being a deconstruction of the myth of California's Silicon Valley as a model post-Fordist community.

5. For an account of Innis's work and context see James Carey's essay, 'Space, Time and Communications' (Carey, 1989: pp. 142–72).

6. I use the term 'ascetic Fordist' on the basis of Packard's opposition of pink dinosaurism to the straightforwardly honest virtues of the Model-A Ford, 'perhaps the most rugged motor car ever built' (Packard, 1960: p. 99). In Veblen's case, it is ironic that the very social group in which he invested his hopes for the rational and moral reorganisation of production, the engineers in whom the 'instinct of workmanship' yet withstood the degradations of the 'price system' and pecuniary emulation, should turn out to be central to the construction of the consumption-based monopoly capitalism that he most dreaded (Veblen, 1965; Fox and Lears, 1983: p. ix; Noble, 1979).

7. Famously, Michel Foucault has named such undecidable or 'heteroclite' spaces 'heterotopias'. These are 'disturbing' spaces characterised by the 'linking together of things that are inappropriate ... so very different from each other that it is impossible ... to define a common locus beneath them all' (Foucault, 1970: pp. xvii–xviii). Pynchon's 1966 version of an 'other', repressed America, co-present with the high-tech consumer paradise of Southern California, draws on the title and substance of Michael Harrington's *exposé* of the persistence of poverty within the high-Fordist culture of abundance, *The Other America* (1963).

8. The notion of deterritorialisation is drawn from the work of Gilles Deleuze and Félix Guattari for whom this process is the principal feature of capitalism as a system (Deleuze and Guattari, 1984 and 1987; Heffernan, 1994).

9. A key statement of Marxist revisionism for the post-Fordist period is Laclau and Mouffe (1985). The 'New Times' project of the British *Marxism Today* group represents a more policy-oriented response to the conditions of post-Fordism (Hall and Jacques, 1988). On class, see the collections edited by Lee and Turner (1996) and John R. Hall (1997).

10. Mike Davis has commented on the remarkable 'hypertrophy of occupational positions in the United States associated with the supervision of labour, the organisation of capital and the implementation of the sales effort'. Davis argues that compared with Europe and Japan, American capitalism is vastly overburdened with managers, salespeople and lawyers, and that this non-productive layer is rapidly squeezing out productive labour from the economy, even in times of recession (Davis, 1986: p. 213).

11. C. Wright Mills (1951) and Daniel Bell (1973) both offer different versions of this 'service class exceptionalism' of American capitalism.

12. Hayes records that in 1982–3, Apple's Macintosh development team wore t-shirts that proclaimed 'working 90 hours a week and loving every minute of it' (Hayes, 1990: p. 116).

13. The Cotton Mather quote is from his *Bonifacius or Essays to do Good* (1710), reprinted in Perry Miller's anthology of Puritan writing (Miller, 1956: pp. 216–21). Interestingly in this context, Miller notes that Mather departed from founding father John Winthrop's totalising religious vision of community by acknowledging the pressures of secularisation. Instead of being formed out of 'one fabric of mutual dependence', society was increasingly fragmented into a series of communities of interest. Accordingly, Mather sought to 'form the righteous into *societies* instead of into *a* society', and he took the secular unit of the profession or 'specialised calling' as the basis for this revised vision of community (Miller, 1956: p. 216, emphasis added).

14. The notion of 'postmaterialism' derives from the work of political theorist Ronald Ingelhart who posits the emergence of a new set of values and attitudes influencing political behaviour in the West in the wake of economic affluence and world peace since 1945. The decline of class alignments and the rise of expressive concerns of identity and lifestyle are central to his thesis. Ingelhart's ideas are debated in Gibbins (1989).

15. The historical links between the computer and the processes of militarisation and bureaucratisation are strong. ENIAC, the first computer ever built, was sponsored by the Ballistics Research Laboratory in the United States and installed on completion in 1945 at the US Army's Aberdeen Proving Ground for weapons research and testing. UNIVAC, America's second major computer design project, went on completion to the US Census Bureau (Schiller, 1984: p. 17).

16. An early version of this thesis was James Burnham's *The Managerial Revolution* (1941). C. Wright Mills dubbed Burnham 'a Marx for the Managers' (Mills, 1963). See Hitchens (1990: pp. 243–50) for an account of the way in which Burnham's ideas became influential in the formation of American Cold War ideology.

17. Interestingly enough, the origins of the personal or minicomputer lie in the decentralising, anti-corporate, utopian techno-pastoralism of the 1960s' counterculture (Levy, 1984; Roszak, 1986). The very first publicly available personal computer was a self-assembly model marketed through that handbook of hippy anti-materialism, *The Whole Earth Catalog*. The Catalog's founder-editor, Stewart Brand, along with other notable denizens of the counterculture (Merry Prankster Ken Kesey, Grateful Dead lyricist Robert Hunter, LSD guru the late Timothy Leary) became in the 1980s a powerful advocate of microelectronic technology, the internet and virtual reality as technological realisations of hippy ideals and philosophies. In a similar countercultural vein, Apple's co-founder, Steve Wozniak, dropped out of his own phenomenally successful corporation to plough his personal fortune into restaging the 1969 Woodstock rock festival.

18. The *kudoka* interpretation of the crisis of Fordism derives from the Japanese International Trade Institute's 1987 report, *Outlook and the Problems of International Trade and Industry of the United States* (Tokyo: Japan Foreign Trade Council, Inc.).

Chapter 4

1. This post-1945 expansion of the professional–managerial class made the late 1950s and early 1960s, according to Barbara and John Ehrenreich, a golden age for the PMC whose growth was so rapid that extensive recruitment from the working class became necessary to fill the job openings. This kind of mass upward social mobility leads them to reject the arguments of C. Wright Mills (1951) and Harry Braverman (1974) that proletarianisation is a consequence of the massification of the white-collar strata. As I argue in Part 3 of this book, massification and proletarianisation are not identical processes, nor does the latter automatically follow

from the former. However, the Ehrenreichs's description of a partial *embourgeoisement* of the American working class is seen to be consistent with the increased radicalism of the 1960s which, they claim, in part reflected the rising confidence of the professional–managerial class (B. and J. Ehrenreich, 1979: pp. 30–31).

2. Section 14(b) of the 1947 Taft-Hartley amendments to the Wagner Act or National Labour Relations Act (1935) provides for individual states to draft and enact their own legislation to regulate union shop agreements. However, such legislation can only work in one direction, so to speak: that is, *for* capital and *against* labour. On enactment, Taft-Hartley itself became the furthest limit of union security and precluded the passage of legislation that could in any way extend the sphere in which organised labour could freely operate. Of those states that have since introduced what is known as right-to-work (RTW) legislation under the aegis of section 14(b), the vast majority are in the South and West. By 1986 (the year *True Stories* was released) 14 out of 17 states in the South/Southwest region had RTW status; seven out of 14 states in the West/Mountain region had RTW status; and, out of 19 states in the North/Midwest region, only one was RTW. The Southern Democratic veto has successfully thwarted several attempts by House Democratic majorities to repeal section 14(b) and re-establish a national basis for labour relations (G. Clark, 1989: pp. 196, 224–5). The Southern states' willingness to exploit RTW legislation has clearly been instrumental in undermining what Michel Aglietta identified as one of the key structural forms of the Fordist regime of accumulation – the nationally operative system of collective bargaining (Aglietta, 1979: pp. 190–7).

3. From the mid-1950s to the mid-1980s the Sunbelt states' share of Defense Department expenditure more than doubled, to over 60 per cent of the $260 billion awarded in defence contracts in 1985. Of that share California received nearly half – a quarter of the entire Pentagon budget. Correspondingly, since the mid-1950s the Midwest's share of military spending has shrunk from a third to a tenth, much of which now consists in jobs subcontracted by overburdened Sunbelt companies (Roszak, 1986: p. 41).

4. This curious lack of parodic or satiric resonance in *True Stories* refers us to Jameson's contention that postmodern artefacts (of which Byrne's film is a fine example) are essentially vehicles for pastiche or 'blank irony' rather than social or cultural criticism or direct engagement with historical forces. This reduction to pastiche is for Jameson a consequence of those same developments cited by Lyotard – the linguistic fragmentation of social life and 'the absence of any great collective project' or grand narrative (political emancipation from the capitalist mode of production through the agency of the working class), conditions which, as I try to show, are thematised in *True Stories*. Needless to say, the conclusions Jameson draws from this situation for both cultural production and society significantly differ from Lyotard's (Jameson, 1991: p. 17; 1984c).

5. Overall, Riesman's attitude toward this shift was one of ambivalence tending towards affirmation. His central notion of other-direction was not intended to carry the connotations of a crippling mass conformity that other commentators read out of it. Rieff's (1966), Lasch's (1979, 1984) and Bell's (1976) pessimism and hostility to therapeutic consumer culture exhibit degrees of mandarin contempt for consumerism and mass culture alike that Riesman did not share. Lears's (1983) Gramscian view of the shift from production to consumption in American culture is more politically critical and less weighted with moral pessimism, though there is a strong element of nostalgia for an assumed pre-consumerist golden age of integrated selfhood and popular autonomy in culture underlying his argument.

6. Rieff and Bellah both work with an implied conception of substantive, real community and hark back to a golden age of binding common faith and overarching religious collective values. As a result, they overlook the utopian aspects of therapeutic individualism and its collective forms, such as lifestyle enclaves and style subcultures. For an antidote to this tendency see Hebdige (1979) and Fitzgerald (1987).

7. Such early Talking Heads' songs as 'Don't Worry About the Government', 'Tentative Decisions' and 'Uh-Oh, Love Comes to Town' (from *Talking Heads 77*, 1977), and 'Found a Job' (*More Songs About Buildings and Food*, 1978) are brilliant microcosms of PMC experience, but, as Fred Pfeil points out (Pfeil, 1990: p. 111), the classic distillation of weightless professional–managerial angst has to be 'Once In a Lifetime' (*Remain in Light*, 1980).

8. This scene from *True Stories* should alert us to the fact that the shift to high-tech, post-Fordist structures of accumulation does not entail the disappearance of Taylorised patterns of work organisation. Indeed, for non-professional workers at the lower end of the IT industries, this

shift often means a return with a vengeance of such work practices. See Davis (1985), Morgan and Sayer (1988) and Tomaney (1994), as well as the discussion of combined and uneven development in Part 4 of this book.

9. See Andreas Huyssen's 'Mass Culture as Woman: Modernism's Other' (1986: pp. 44–62) for an exploration of how male anxieties about the encroachments of the marketplace into the autonomous realm of art were expressed in the sexist identification of indiscriminate consumerism with the category of the feminine. For an account of how the rise of a therapeutic cultural ethos in late nineteenth-century America was similarly linked to pejorative notions of femininity and was bound up with male fears about the growing cultural influence of women, see Ann Douglas (1977).

Chapter 5

1. Philip K. Dick's novel *Time Out of Joint* (1959) brilliantly dramatises this notion of mass culture as a compensation for and refuge from the stresses of adult social life. As long as his protagonist, Ragle Gumm, unquestioningly inhabits the 'unreal' world constructed especially for him out of the everyday materials of consumer culture, and centred on the neighbourhood supermarket, he continues to perform – unwittingly – an 'expert' service only he can provide that is essential to the security and survival of the state. Interestingly, this illusory world is both a projection of Ragle's internal psychic need for a habitat of remembered childhood security and material comfort and a fabrication imposed and maintained by the state employees and agents who masquerade as Ragle's neighbours and fellow citizens. Significantly, it is not through outright rejection of the 'illusory' nature of mass culture, but by embracing and analysing its elements critically – against the grain of their 'official' purpose, so to speak – that Ragle emancipates himself and comes into fully conscious opposition to the state he had previously 'unconsciously' served.

2. Jerry Rubin, 1960s' revolutionary and leader of the Youth International Party or 'Yippies', who became, by way of the various 'human potential' therapies of the 1970s, a successful 1980s' entrepreneur organising corporate hospitality for Wall Street finance houses, is frequently offered as the outstanding instance of what Todd Gitlin has called 'the cultural archetype of the Yippie-turned-Yuppie' (Gitlin, 1993: p. xxi). The PMC wrestled publicly with the moral and social consequences of this shift in numerous popular culture texts of the 1980s and early '90s, not least among them Lawrence Kasdan's film, *The Big Chill* (1983), and Ed Zwick's TV series, *thirtysomething*.

3. Robert Brenner suggests that whereas real wages increased by 2.6 per cent between 1960 and 1973 they rose by only 0.3 per cent between 1973 and 1996 (Brenner, 1998: Table 17). However, economist John Schmitt has more recently argued that despite 107 months of uninterrupted economic growth from February 1991 to January 2000 – the longest boom in American history since records began, longer even than the postwar boom – real wages are still one per cent *below* their 1973 level ('The Old Business Cycle Has Not Yet Been Licked', *Guardian*, 12 February, 2000: p. 18).

4. Lead or Leave's anxious emphasis on generational disadvantage contrasts interestingly with the sense of generational privilege central to one of the baby-boom PMC's major expressions of political consciousness, the Port Huron Statement issued by Students for a Democratic Society (SDS) in 1962. That document famously began, 'We are people of this generation, bred in at least modest comfort, housed now in universities, looking uncomfortably to the world we inherit' (Albert and Albert, 1984: p. 176).

5. For example, at the end of his memoir-cum-analysis of 1960s' radicalism, baby-boomer Todd Gitlin laments the fact that 'my generation numbers teachers more activist ... than their students, rock stars more antiestablishment than their audiences: this is mind-boggling for a generation who believed that youth had the privilege of vision' (Gitlin, 1993: p. 438).

Chapter 6

1. Thus in his technical introduction to cybernetics, Wiener concluded his opening chapter with the claim that cybernetic theory and the advent of modern automata had 'relegated the whole

mechanist–vitalist controversy to the limbo of badly posed questions' (Wiener, 1961: p. 44). In his wake, philosophers such as Richard Rorty and Daniel Dennett have adopted the general AI position on the formal continuity between reasoning machines and human consciousness in order to argue for the rejection of essentialist conceptions of the 'irreducibility' of mind. These essentialist conceptions, they claim, have preoccupied philosophy for too long and to little purpose, obstructing the development of either a 'mature psychology' (Dennett, 1981: p. xx) or 'self-images worthy of our species' (Rorty, no date: p. 35). Neither of these things, it is argued, need be grounded in a notion of what is irreducibly or essentially 'human' about mental activity.

2. Von Bertalanffy's originating notion of living systems (formulated in the 1930s) stressed their 'openness'. Yet when Wiener, von Neumann and Ashby adapted his biological model into formal mathematics this notion of openness was lost. The tension within cybernetics between openness and closure reflects the one already mentioned between communication and control. The fact that notions of closure and control prevailed within the science is, apart from the ideological and institutional context in which cybernetics developed, in some senses linked with the shift from biology to mathematics. There have continued to be adherents of the biological notion of cybernetics, Gregory Bateson especially, who argue strongly against the control, closure and manipulation model (Bateson, 1973).

3. David Noble records that 'between 1945 and 1955, there were over 43,000 strikes, idling some 27 million workers' and notes that automated machinery was from the first seen by management as a weapon for winning the struggle over 'who's running the shop' (Noble, 1984: p. 25).

4. Steve Heims regards this integration of science and power according to the imperatives of the United States' new position of global hegemony as 'the cardinal cultural transformation of the second half of the twentieth century' (Heims, 1980).

5. In January 1947 Wiener published an open letter in *Atlantic Monthly* headed 'A Scientist Rebels' in which he announced his refusal to yield scientific information for military purposes and called upon other scientists to do the same. In 1950 he spoke out against the institutionalisation of the Cold War through the cybernetic paradigm, warning that 'a sort of *machine à gouverner* is ... now essentially in operation on both sides of the world conflict' in which 'a mechanistic technique ... is adapted to the exigencies of a machine-like group of men devoted to the formation of policy' (Wiener, 1989: p. 189). In the same year Wiener initiated discussions with Walter Reuther, president of the United Auto Workers labour union, about the impact of automation on the labour process, believing that workers should be kept as informed as possible about the uses to which capital could (and, Wiener had no doubt, would) put cybernetic technology. Steve Heims (1980) gives a good account of Wiener's career and political development which he compares favourably with that of another founder of cybernetic discourse, John von Neumann, whose romance with power typifies, for Heims, the scientific establishment's wholesale incorporation into the military, state and business apparatus in the postwar period.

6. Parsons's sociological method pre-dated cybernetics, emerging in the context of the economic and social crises of the 1930s. Yet in the postwar period he incorporated the language and concepts of cybernetics so thoroughly into his work that it became another branch of systems thinking, and it was from this point on that he achieved his greatest influence.

7. This thesis was first proposed by Adolph Berle and Gardiner Means in 1932 and was widely used by end-of-ideology theorists in the postwar period (Berle and Means, 1932; Bell, 1988: Chapters 1 and 2).

8. Nor, strangely enough, did the belief of many of the system's critics. The personal computer that rejuvenated the microelectronics industry in the 1970s emerged out of the 1960s' counterculture and its hostility to the monopolisation of technology by the state, the military and the corporations. In this sense, the personal computer was designed as a practical critique of the 'totalitarian' nature of capitalist scientific rationality. It was promoted by sectors of the counterculture as an instrument of liberation and anti-authoritarian decentralisation. The conviction that American society could be redeemed by deepening the process of cybernation thus characterised managerial elites and elements of the counterculture alike (see Roszak, 1986).

Chapter 7

1. Hereafter referred to in the text as N, CZ and MLO respectively.

2. See Jameson (1991: pp. 260–78 and 1994: p. 60) for an analysis of the market as a utopian element of the capitalist imagination.

3. As I have suggested, Jameson's critique of Gibson conjures up the ghost of Georg Lukács, in particular the latter's dismissal of modernism. Modernism's stylistic radicalism reflected the surface characteristics of capitalist social reality well enough, but was so mesmerised by their volatility and intensity that, in contrast to his favoured form of bourgeois social realism, it capitulated to their mystifying logic and thus failed to reveal the underlying movement of historical (i.e. class) forces that ultimately, for Lukács, determined this reality (Lukács, 1977: pp. 36–9). It is evident from his remarks on SF in general and cyberpunk in particular that Jameson vacillates between viewing SF as the formal successor to Lukácsian bourgeois realism on the one hand and, in the case of cyberpunk at least, as a kind of 'modernist' deviation from it on the other.

4. Again Jameson vacillates here. He seems unwilling to decide whether a practice of cognitive mapping should rest on aesthetic–political principles drawn from Georg Lukács or from Theodor Adorno. That is, should it be ideologically progressive, affirmative and 'popular' in the manner of Lukács's didactic bourgeois realism; or should it be hermetic, renunciatory and unassimilable in the manner of Adorno's 'autonomous', anti-political modernism? In a fascinating discussion of Lukács and Adorno, Jameson attempted a dialectical resolution of their positions in which he arrived at the notion of a 'new realism' – clearly an early formulation of his notion of cognitive mapping (Jameson, 1977: p. 212). Yet, as his resistance to Gibson's representational strategies illustrates, cognitive mapping remains an imperative without substance, an aesthetic–cognitive void or, as Jameson put it in *The Political Unconscious*, 'an empty chair reserved for some as yet unrealised, collective and decentred cultural production of the future, beyond realism and modernism alike' (Jameson, 1981: p. 11).

5. Suvin is reluctant to get beyond an either–or conception of the cognitive value of a literary text, seen purely in terms of the dualities of complicity versus oppositionality, or ideology versus utopia. I try to suggest that it is precisely its ambivalences and contradictions that provide the clue to cyberpunk's historical significance.

6. A look at the history of SF would bear this claim out. SF's emergence as a distinct genre towards the end of the nineteenth century coincided with the birth of the PMC and its assumption of a central role in making the transition from unregulated *laissez-faire* to organised monopoly capitalism. SF henceforth developed into an important vehicle for the class's self-understanding, as well as for the expression of its ideologies and anxieties.

7. Klein here combines the insights of Claude Lévi-Strauss, Lucien Goldmann and Louis Althusser. For Lévi-Strauss, narrative is a variant of myth whose function is to provide imaginary or symbolic resolutions to real social contradictions. For Goldmann, such symbolic resolutions are to be seen as the responses of particular social groups or classes to crises in their understanding of their position and relative social power. Althusser generalised Lévi-Strauss's conception of myth to arrive at a definition of ideology as 'a representation of the imaginary relationship of individuals to their real conditions of existence', thus closing the circle between representation, narrative and ideology (Althusser, 1971: p. 162).

8. See H. Bruce Franklin (1980) and Andrew Ross, 'Getting Out of the Gernsback Continuum' (1991: pp. 101–35).

9. Klein here adapts Braverman's thesis about the inevitable proletarianisation of the middle class in monopoly capitalism.

10. Mellor draws attention to Albert Berger's important evidence of a fundamental shift in the composition of the SF audience beginning in the mid-1950s. Surveys of SF magazine readers and convention-goers from 1958 to 1975 revealed a decisive swing from an overwhelmingly science-oriented SF fandom to one in which those educated in the humanities and social sciences were preponderant. The significant expansion of the SF market in this period, as well as other forms of evidence such as SF's entry into university literature programs and the adoption of SF writers and texts as 'cults' by middle-class youth, also support these claims.

11. The outstanding exemplars of this mode would be Kurt Vonnegut and J. G. Ballard.

12. The question of biological reproduction is also what distinguishes the professional–managerial class from the working class 'below' it. The word 'proletarian' derives from the Latin *proletarius* – one whose only contribution to the state was his offspring.

13. This interest in and valorisation of non- or precapitalist enclaves is most fully developed in Gibson's portrayal of the Golden Gate Bridge community in *Virtual Light* (1993).

14. The social upheaval of the 1960s prompted a generally leftward shift in the still expanding and therefore relatively socially confident PMC. This confident radicalism is not inconsistent with the disillusionment Klein attributes to the class in the same period; it took the extreme compromise of its historic aspirations to reveal to the PMC the extent of its subordination to the imperatives of capital, producing a surge of resistance to incorporation. The economic crises of the 1970s and '80s, however, produced a rightward shift within the professional middle class – the yuppiefication scenario. But many neo-conservative commentators of the period continued to berate the PMC – for what they saw as its corrosive cultural libertarianism – under the heading of the 'new class'. See B. Ehrenreich (1989) and B. Bruce Biggs (1979).

15. The term 'jacking in' of course satirises the professional obsession with the technical high, suggesting its masturbatory and masculinist aspects. Interestingly, *Jacking In* was Gibson's preferred title for what was eventually published as *Neuromancer*, the original title being rejected by his publishers for predictable reasons of 'taste'.

16. Bruce Robbins observes how professionalism 'confers ... a version of immortality' on its holders, and he goes on usefully to explore the political tensions in professionalism's negotiation of a path between the opposing poles of individualism and collectivism (Robbins, 1993: p. 30).

17. For explorations of Gibson's and cyberpunk's masculinist bias see Ross (1991: Chapter 4), Springer (1991), and Wolmark (1994: pp. 109–21).

18. Father–daughter incest is a familiar metaphorical device for signalling the old, patriarchal capitalist class's desire to keep accumulation and ownership 'all in the family'. F. Scott Fitzgerald's *Tender is the Night* (1934), Norman Mailer's *An American Dream* (1966), and Roman Polanski's film, *Chinatown* (1974) are fine examples of its effectiveness in this regard. Interestingly, all these narratives are told from the viewpoint of would-be independent professionals each of whom engages in a struggle with a capitalist patriarch for sexual possession of the patriarch's daughter. It is not too hard to see here an allegory of the professional–managerial class's desire to assume social leadership from what it regards as an irrational and even corrupt ruling class. That in each of the above tales the professional hero fails to secure possession of the daughter and loses his integrity and independence in the process reflects darkly on the class's prospects for success in this venture.

Chapter 8

1. Discussion of *Blade Runner* is complicated somewhat by the existence of two officially released versions of the film. The version originally delivered to the studio by director Ridley Scott was deemed too bleak and ambiguous for commercial release, especially as it was scheduled to open alongside that most affirmative of SF blockbusters, Spielberg's *ET*. Warners ordered Scott to reshoot and re-edit parts of the film and alter the ending. The film's cult reputation grew over the decade after its first (and commercially undistinguished) screenings and Scott's original version was given an official release in 1992 as *Blade Runner: The Director's Cut*. See Bukatman (1997) for a detailed discussion of the film's production and release history.

2. The lines from Blake's poem spoken by Roy Batty are these from 'America: A Prophecy': 'Fiery the angels rose; deep thunder rolled/Around their shores, burning with the fires of Orc'. But Batty misquotes them, substituting 'fell' for 'rose'. Robin Wood suggests that this signifies the film's dramatisation of the failure and reversal of the political ideals associated with the American Revolution. We can also interpret the use of Blake's poem as an immanent critique of the American principle of revolutionary democracy itself. The replicants' slave status reminds us that slavery survived the American Revolution to become a central institution of the new Republic.

3. Lasch cites Elton Mayo's famous programme of experiments on the workforce of Western Electric's Hawthorne plant as a quintessential instance of the professional invasion and manipulation of popular or working-class experience on behalf of capitalist conceptions of productivity and order. Another pertinent example would of course be Henry Ford's sociology

department at his Detroit factories which sent out experts into the homes of Ford workers to supervise and regulate their domestic and family lives.

4. Paradoxically, this final sequence in its entirety actually unsettles the very idea of the 'natural' that it was intended to reinforce. Imposed by the studio which demanded a reassuring ending, Scott pieced together its montage of nature scenes using outtakes from Stanley Kubrick's recently completed film *The Shining* (Bukatman, 1997: p. 33). The effect of this is to further drive home the film's disturbing blurring of the boundary between the natural and the simulated in late capitalist culture.

5. I'm not suggesting here that these stereotyped gender positions bear any close relation to actual social reality; they are, rather, symbolic positions constructed within the film narrative for the production of meaning.

6. This scene is also of course a parody of and homage to Humphrey Bogart's famous bookstore scene as Philip Marlowe in Howard Hawks's *The Big Sleep* (1946).

7. Claudia Springer (1991) usefully discusses the ways in which cyborg imagery mediates wider cultural anxieties about masculinity and its responses to the claims of feminism and the bodily invasions of technology. Anne Balsamo (1988) has explored the implications of female cyborg images and their relation to science fiction's treatment of questions of human reproduction.

Chapter 9

1. The subtitle of Rostow's book, *A Non-Communist Manifesto*, indicates how far the theory of global Fordism was a key ideological tool in the struggle to resist the expansion of non-capitalist worldspace as more and more decolonising countries adopted the Soviet road to development. As John McClure points out, the foreign policy rhetoric of the Kennedy administration was consciously structured as a 'romance of development' aimed precisely at countering the 'romance of liberation' by which many decolonising nations sought to define the latest stage of their history (McClure, 1994: pp. 30–55).

2. By 'less uneven' I mean that the spatial differences between core and periphery became de-emphasised and even deliberately overlooked by the promoters of the 'romance of development' and the exporters of global Fordism. On the question of the human costs of neocolonialism, Fred Halliday suggests that the postwar peace and prosperity of the West was underpinned by the displacement of crisis and conflict into the third world which may have cost the lives of over 20 million people (Halliday, 1990: p. 6).

3. For an account of this spatial process in nineteenth-century imperialism see Glenn Morgan (1985).

4. McClure (1994) groups some of these narratives – including DeLillo's *The Names* – together under the heading of 'late imperial romance'. Other noteworthy texts dealing with the respatialisations bound up with the crisis of Fordism and American global hegemony would include William Gaddis, *J. R.* (1976) and *Carpenter's Gothic* (1985); John Updike, *The Coup* (1978); Tim O'Brien, *Going After Cacciato* (1978) and *The Things They Carried* (1990); Jayne Anne Phillips, *Machine Dreams* (1984); Toni Morrison, *Tar Baby* (1981); Joan Didion, *Democracy* (1984); Dennis Johnson, *Fiskadoro* (1986); and E. L. Doctorow, *Lives of the Poets* (1984). Current science fiction writing is dedicated virtually entirely to exploring the capitalist production of worldspace through transplanetary metaphors.

Chapter 10

1. As Robert Young notes, terms such as 'third world', 'first world', 'centre' and 'periphery' are unsatisfactory in so far as they offer a 'univocal description of an extremely heterogeneous section of the world'. However, as Young also notes, this means that 'suitable alternative general categor[ies] cannot by definition be produced' (Young, 1990: p. 11). I use them here as heuristic devices, acknowledging the problems that surround them.

2. A few examples of contemporary American magic realism would include John Nichols's New Mexico trilogy, *The Milagro Beanfield War* (1974), *The Magic Journey* (1978), and *The Nirvana Blues* (1981); Tim O'Brien's *Going After Cacciato* (1978); Toni Morrison's *Beloved* (1987); and Louise Erdrich's *The Beet Queen* (1987).

3. That Doctorow's narrator is also a writer suggests that, in terms of narrative itself, some kind of global perspective and internationalist commitment is necessary to resolve the crisis of the bourgeois novel of manners and private life, the moribund condition of which, at one level, 'Lives of the Poets' sets out to anatomise.

4. See Nadel (1992) for an account of this aspect of *Democracy*.

5. In *Players* (1977) and *Running Dog* (1978) DeLillo is interested in exactly the nature of the relationship between personal investment in a particular action or quest and the wider political or historical consequences of such investments. The same concern animates *The Names*.

6. Jameson's route from Weberian ideas of rationalisation to the notion of reification outlined in *The Political Unconscious* proceeds through Georg Lukács's *History and Class Consciousness* (1923).

7. For an exploration of these themes with relation to the process of commodification see Godden (1990: Chapter 2).

8. Eliades himself is mistaken in his exchange with Axton, believing him to be the banker, David Keller. This theme of mistaken identity runs through the novel and causes Axton to wonder if he himself is actually the intended victim of the act of anti-American violence in which Keller is shot. The suggestion here is that Eliades is, in some respects, as 'blind' as Axton, that binary modes of perception structured around 'us' and 'them', be they pro- or anti-imperialist, are inherently faulty. This failure properly to 'see' the other links Axton and Eliades together.

9. On the historical connections between cartography, imperialism and the rise of capitalism, see Harvey (1989: pp. 240–59).

10. This is perhaps the classic theme of imperial romance inherited from the epoch of nineteenth-century empire. As Charlie Marlow says of his African voyage in Joseph Conrad's *Heart of Darkness* (1902), 'Going up that river was like travelling back to the earliest beginnings of the world' (Conrad, 1972: p. 48). John McClure has noted the connections between DeLillo's character Owen Brademas in *The Names* and Conrad's Mr Kurtz (McClure, 1994: p. 134).

11. Geertz implies that a special kind of cosmopolitanism is required to overcome this antinomy. The ideal anthropological field worker, he tells us, should be 'perfectly self-tuned to his surroundings, a walking miracle of empathy, tact, patience and cosmopolitanism' (Geertz, 1993: p. 56). Yet, given the impossibility of attaining this, Geertz suggests that a highly developed and self-reflexive form of professionalism might just suffice. Thus a higher or 'meta' professionalism is offered as an antidote to the blindnesses and colonising impulses of ordinary, fallible professionals.

12. It was Benjamin Disraeli who wrote, during the period of high nineteenth-century imperialism, that 'the East is a career'. Edward Said, whose classic analysis of cultural imperialism *Orientalism* uses Disraeli's remark as an epigraph, also highlights the connections between professionalism and imperialism. Indeed, Said's study manifests its own peculiar form of nostalgia for a bygone era of European Orientalists whose professionalism was of the gentlemanly, scholarly and patrician sort. This is contrasted favourably to the nakedly instrumental, policy-driven and social science-based approach of modern American Orientalists (Said, 1978: p. 290–3). The link between professionalism and imperialism is also strongly made in *Heart of Darkness*. Marlow and the select audience to which he relates his imperial romance are all presented in terms of their professional identities. Marlow is 'the seaman' narrating his tale to 'The Director', 'The Lawyer' and 'The Accountant', each abstract and capitalised persona embodying the rationalising discourses of modernisation. In the end, for Marlow, it is precisely professionalism which can be invoked to legitimate the dirty business of colonisation and economic plunder. 'What saves us', he tells his audience of professionals, 'is efficiency, the devotion to efficiency' (Conrad, 1972: pp. 5–6, 10).

13. Reich claims that by the late 1980s symbolic-analytic activities occupied up to 20 per cent of the American work force. Workers involved in 'routine productive services' have been displaced from economic and political centrality because the bulk of production costs in the advanced capitalist countries are not now taken up by labour and investment but by the solving of technical problems and the manipulation of data. As an example Reich cites the microchip in which over 85 per cent of the production cost goes to design, engineering, patents and copyright, and less that 13 per cent to labour and investment (Reich, 1991: pp. 174, 103–4).

14. See Johnson (1972) and Bledstein (1976) for theoretical and historical discussions of this aspect of professionalism.

15. Robbins also observes that the view of the premodern, precapitalist past as 'rich in genuine relationships, organic community [and] cultural vitality' is one that is particularly self-serving for professionals in the humanities, in as much as this narrative of a 'fall' into modernity legitimates their role as guardians and interpreters of this lost past (Robbins, 1993: pp. 172–3).

16. There are further parallels with *Heart of Darkness* here. The whole of Conrad's tale is told at a double remove through both Marlow and the unnamed frame narrator who introduces us to Marlow. And within the narrative, the colonising missions of Kurtz and Marlow alike are driven by discourse. As Marlow says of Kurtz, 'I had never imagined him as doing, you know, but as discoursing'. It is through this capacity for discourse, associated with his ambiguous professional identity, that Kurtz has 'kicked himself loose of the earth', causing Marlow to suffer similar sensations of free-floating estrangement and disconnectedness. 'Before him', Marlow confesses, 'I did not know whether I stood upon the ground or floated in the air'. Ultimately, both figures are reduced to disembodied instances of discourse. What remains of Kurtz are 'his words' alone; while Marlow becomes to his interlocutors 'no more than a voice' (Conrad, 1972: pp. 67, 103, 95, 109, 39). A similar reduction to discourse occurs to Brademas in *The Names*. Listening to his account of his final encounter with the cult, Axton notes that 'the only strength was in his voice' (*Names*: p. 289).

17. Jacques Derrida has perhaps done most to suggest that the opposition between speech and writing is ultimately an unstable, as well as an ideological, one (Derrida, 1973). DeLillo performs a very Derridean operation of deconstruction on the speech/writing opposition in *The Names*, though for him the unavailability of origins and pure presence is the effect of certain specific cultural, historical and class conditions not, as it is for Derrida, of some ahistorical essence of language itself.

18. McClure reads this ambivalence about speech through an opposition between 'good' heteroglossic discourse and 'bad' monological discourse. DeLillo, he claims, is guilty of 'postmodern orientalism' in as much as heteroglossic speech is identified in *The Names* with the Western cultural and political tradition symbolised by the Acropolis. Monological speech is, on the other hand, projected on to what are presented as the anti-democratic and totalitarian cultures and polities of the Islamic Middle East. These are constructed as the dark 'other' of the Enlightenment heritage of Western democracy (McClure, 1994: pp. 133, 140). While persuasive to a degree (Axton and Brademas both betray a kind of repulsed fascination with what they imagine to be the monolithic nature of Islam), McClure's reading does not account for the degree to which DeLillo finds many kinds of linguistic and cultural totalitarianism in the discourses of the West itself, especially in the ideolects of the professions.

19. Roland Robertson (1990) has argued for a causal link between nostalgia and the process of globalisation.

Chapter 11

1. Wenders is in many respects the cinematic laureate of estrangement and deracination, a condition he renders with particular intensity in his dramatisations of the clash between European sensibilities and those American social and cultural forms which, as one of the characters in *Kings of the Road* puts it, have 'colonised our unconscious'. The condition of globalised estrangement expressed in *Until the End of the World* merely takes to new levels the themes of earlier films such as *Alice in the Cities* (1974), *Kings of the Road* (1976), *Paris, Texas* (1982), and *Wings of Desire* (1989). Each of these narratives details various forms of emotional and geographical homelessness, conditions which are bound up with mobility in both its social and spatial aspects and with the technologies of reproduction, in particular with variants of the cinematic apparatus itself.

2. As we have seen, this has both a racial and class dimension. Anthropology and ethnology can in some respects be understood as professional discourses which construct racially defined 'others' whose cultures and knowledges become available for invasion, appropriation and abstraction as a consequence of the simultaneous globalisation of capitalism and scientific rationality. Medical, sociological and managerial discourses can be seen as imposing similar kinds of colonisation and discipline upon what Christopher Lasch calls the 'popular' – by which he means essentially working-class – lifeworld of the core capitalist countries themselves (Lasch, 1984: p. 42).

Conclusion

1. There is, it should be noted, a neo-Marxist version of 'postindustrial' theory which, unlike Daniel Bell's (1973) and even 'left' versions such as Touraine's (1971) and Gorz's (1982), is not evolutionist in its assumptions and attends to the currents of power and class conflict that structure contemporary capitalist societies. This is Larry Hirschhorn's notion of postindustrial society as a projected, potentially socialist stage of social development beyond capitalism whose realisation depends precisely upon the struggles of workers and other marginal social groups to redefine the nature and meaning of production, work and technology in terms radically different from those of the prevailing market-based norms (Hirschhorn, 1984). This socialist postindustrialism derives from the utopian theories of the liberatory potential of modern technologies developed by the New Left and the counterculture of the 1960s (Brick, 1992: pp. 353–5). More recently, Fred Block has attempted to revive this oppositional and utopian notion of postindustrial society and, following André Gorz, link it to a humanist and ecological critique of the economics and politics of permanent growth (Block, 1990).

2. Hence Bell's sharp turn, after the optimism of *The Coming of Postindustrial Society* (1973), to the arena of culture and character in order to attempt an explanation of the economic crisis in *The Cultural Contradictions of Capitalism* (1976). Bell's theory of postindustrial society, based as it is on evolutionist and technological determinist notions of the redundancy of classes and class conflict, and the obsolescence of the labour theory of value in contemporary capitalism, simply cannot account for a crisis in the rate of accumulation. The cause of economic crisis is therefore sought 'outside' the economic apparatus in a crisis of the cultural system of motivations and legitimations which, according to Bell, no longer can persuade individuals of the righteousness and necessity of hard work and self-denial, qualities crucial in his view to economic success (see Heffernan, 1996).

Bibliography

Abercrombie, N. and Urry, J. (1983), *Capital, Labour and the Middle Class* (London: Allen and Unwin).

Abercrombie, N., Hill, S. and Turner, B. (1986), *Sovereign Individuals of Capitalism* (London: Allen and Unwin).

Adorno, T. W. (1977), 'Reconciliation Under Duress' in Ernst Bloch *et al.*, *Aesthetics and Politics* (London: Verso), pp. 151–76.

Adorno, T. W. and Horkheimer, M. (1979), *Dialectic of Enlightenment* (London: Verso).

Aglietta, M. (1979), *A Theory of Capitalist Regulation: The US Experience* (London: Verso).

——. (1982), 'World Capitalism in the Eighties', *New Left Review*, no. 136, pp. 5–41.

Ahmad, A. (1987), 'Jameson's Rhetoric of Otherness and the National Allegory', *Social Text*, no. 17, pp. 3–25.

Albert, J. and Albert, B. eds (1984), *The Sixties Papers: Documents of a Rebellious Decade* (New York: Praeger).

Albrow, M. and King, E. eds (1990), *Globalization, Knowledge and Society* (London: Sage).

Althusser, L. (1971), *Lenin and Philosophy and Other Essays* (New York: Monthly Review Press).

Althusser, L. and Balibar, E. (1979), *Reading Capital* (London: Verso).

Amin, A. ed. (1994), *Post-Fordism: A Reader* (Oxford: Blackwell).

Anderson, P. (1998), *The Origins of Postmodernity* (London: Verso).

Andersen, U. S. (1975), *Success Cybernetics: Practical Applications of Human Cybernetics* (West Nyack, N.J.: Parker).

Appadurai, A. (1990), 'Disjunction and Difference in the Global Cultural Economy', *Public Culture*, vol. 2, no. 2, pp. 1–24.

Aronowitz, S. (1990), *The Crisis in Historical Materialism: Class, Politics and Culture in Marxist Theory* (London: Macmillan).

Arrighi, G., Hopkins, T. and Wallerstein, I. eds (1988), *Antisystemic Movements* (London: Verso).

Ballard, J. G. *et al.* (1988), Cyberpunk Forum/Symposium, *Mississippi Review*, nos. 47/48, pp. 16–65.

Balsamo, A. (1988), 'Reading Cyborgs Writing Feminism', *Communication*, no. 10, pp. 331–44.

Banta, M. (1993), *Taylored Lives: Narrative Productions in the Age of Taylor, Veblen and Ford* (Chicago: University of Chicago Press).

Baran, P. and Sweezy, P. (1966), *Monopoly Capital: An Essay on the American Economic and Social Order* (Harmondsworth: Penguin).

Baritz, L. (1989), *The Good Life: The Meaning of Success For the American Middle Class* (New York: Knopf).

Barbrook, R. (1990), 'Two Souls of Post-Fordism', *Catalyst*, no. 3, pp. 28–9.

Barnet, R. J. and Muller, R. E. (1975), *Global Reach: The Power of the Multinational Corporations* (London: Jonathan Cape).

Barthes, R. (1982), *Empire of Signs* (London: Jonathan Cape).

Bateson, G. (1973), *Steps to an Ecology of Mind* (London: Paladin).

Baudrillard, J. (1975), *The Mirror of Production* (St Louis: Telos).

——. (1981), *For a Critique of the Political Economy of the Sign* (St Louis: Telos).

——. (1983), *Simulations* (New York: Semiotexte).

Bell, D. (1949), 'America's Un-Marxist Revolution', *Commentary*, no. 7, pp. 207–15.

——. (1973), *The Coming of Postindustrial Society: An Exercise in Social Forecasting* (New York: Basic Books).

——. (1976), *The Cultural Contradictions of Capitalism* (London: Heinemann).

——. (1980a), 'The Social Context of the Information Society' in T. Forrester (ed.), *The Microelectronics Revolution* (Oxford: Blackwell), pp. 500–51.

——. (1980b), 'Teletext and Technology: The New Networks of Knowledge and Information in Postindustrial Society' in *The Winding Passage: Essays and Sociological Journeys 1960–1980* (New York: Basic Books), pp. 34–65.

——. (1980c), 'The New Class: A Muddled Concept' in *The Winding Passage*, pp. 144–64.

——. (1988), *The End of Ideology: On the Exhaustion of Political Ideas in the Fifties* (Cambridge: CUP).

Bell, D. and Kristol, I. eds (1971), *Capitalism Today* (New York: Mentor).

—— eds (1981), *The Crisis in Economic Theory* (New York: Basic Books).

Bell, D., (1993), *Communitarianism and Its Critics* (New York: OUP).

Bellah, R., Madsen, R., Sullivan, W., Swidler, A. and Tipton, S. (1985), *Habits of the Heart: Middle America Observed* (London: Hutchinson).

——. (1992), *The Good Society* (New York: Vintage).

Bergesen, A. (1980), 'Cycles of Formal Colonial Rule' in Hopkins and Wallerstein (eds), *Processes of the World System*, pp. 119–80.

Berle, A. (1955), *The Twentieth-Century Capitalist Revolution* (London: Macmillan).

Berle, A. and Means, G. (1932), *The Modern Corporation and Private Property* (New York: Macmillan).

Berman, M. (1983), *All That Is Solid Melts Into Air: The Experience of Modernity* (London: Verso).

Biggs, B. B. ed. (1979), *The New Class?* (New York: McGraw-Hill).

Biskind, P. and Ehrenreich, B. (1987), 'Machismo and Hollywood's Working Class' in D. Lazere (ed.), *American Media and Mass Culture: Left Perspectives* (Berkeley: University of California Press), pp. 201–15.

Bledstein, B. (1976), *The Culture of Professionalism: The Middle Class and the Development of Higher Education in America* (New York: Norton).

Block, F. (1977), *The Origins of International Economic Disorder* (Los Angeles: University of California Press).

——. (1990), *Postindustrial Possibilities: A Critique of Economic Discourse* (Berkeley: University of California Press).

Bluestone, B. and Harrison, B. (1982), *The Deindustrialization of America: Plant Closures, Community Abandonment, and Dismantling of Basic Industry* (New York: Basic Books).

Blumin, S. M. (1985), 'The Hypothesis of Middle-Class Formation in Nineteenth-Century America: A Critique and Some Proposals', *American Historical Review*, no. 90, pp. 299–338.

——. (1989), *The Emergence of the Middle Class: Social Experience in the American City 1760–1900* (Cambridge: CUP).

Boden, M. A. (1987), *Artificial Intelligence and Natural Man* (London: MIT Press).

Bolter, J. D. (1986), *Turing's Man: Western Culture in the Computer Age* (Harmondsworth: Penguin).

Bonefeld, W. and Holloway, J. eds (1991), *Post-Fordism and Social Form: A Marxist Debate on the Post-Fordist State* (London: Macmillan).

Boorstin, D. (1963), *The Image, Or What Happened to the American Dream?* (Harmondsworth: Penguin).

Bosquet, N. (1980), 'From Hegemony to Competition: Cycles of the Core?' in Hopkins and Wallerstein (eds), *Processes of the World System*, pp. 46–83.

Bowles, S. and Gintis, H. (1981), 'Structure and Practice in the Labor Theory of Value', *Review of Radical Political Economics*, vol. 12, no. 4, pp. 1–26.

——. (1982), 'The Crisis of Liberal Democratic Capitalism: The Case of the United States', *Politics and Society*, vol. 11, no. 1, pp. 51–93.

Braverman, H. (1974), *Labor and Monopoly Capital: The Degradation of Work in the Twentieth Century* (New York: Monthly Review Press).

Brenner, R. (1998), 'The Economics of Global Turbulence: A Special Report on the World Economy 1950–98', *New Left Review*, no. 229, special issue.

Brenner, R. and Glick, M. (1991), 'The Regulation Approach: Theory and History', *New Left Review*, no. 188, pp. 45–119.

Brick, H. (1992), 'Optimism of the Mind: Imagining Postindustrial Society in the 1960s and 1970s', *American Quarterly*, vol. 44, no. 3, pp. 348–80.

Bronfenbrenner, M. (1971), 'Japan's Galbraithian Economy' in Bell and Kristol (eds), *Capitalism Today*, pp. 175–86.

Bruno, G. (1990), 'Ramble City: Postmodernism and *Blade Runner*' in Kuhn (ed.), *Alien Zone* (London: Verso), pp. 183–95.

Bukatman, S. (1993), *Terminal Identity: The Virtual Subject in Postmodern Science Fiction* (Durham, N.C.: Duke University Press).

——. (1997), *Blade Runner* (London: BFI).

Bukharin, N. (1975), 'World Economy and National Economy' in Radice (ed.), *International Firms and Modern Imperialism*, pp. 23–34.

Burawoy, M. (1985), *The Politics of Production: Factory Regimes Under Capitalism and Socialism* (London: Verso).

Burnham, J. (1962), *The Managerial Revolution* (Harmondsworth: Penguin).

Byrne, D. (1986), *True Stories* (London: Faber).

Calleo, D. P. (1982), *The Imperious Economy* (Cambridge, Mass.: Harvard University Press).

——. (1984), 'Since 1961: American Power in a New World Economy' in W. Becker and S. Wells Jr. (eds), *Economics and World Power* (New York: Columbia University Press), pp. 391–457.

Callinicos, A. (1989), *Postmodernism: A Marxist Critique* (Cambridge: Polity).

Carey, J. W. (1989), *Communication as Culture: Essays on Media and Society* (London: Unwin Hyman).

Castells, M. (1980), *The Economic Crisis and American Society* (Oxford: Blackwell).

——. (1997), *The Power of Identity: The Information Age, Economy Society and Culture*, vol. 2, (Oxford: Blackwell).

Chandler, A. D. (1962), *Strategy and Structure: Chapters in the History of the American Industrial Enterprise* (Cambridge, Mass.: MIT Press).

——. (1990), *Scale and Scope: The Dynamics of Industrial Capitalism* (Cambridge, Mass.: Harvard University Press).

Charrier, Y. (1984), '*Blade Runner*: Or, the Sociology of Anticipation', *Science Fiction Studies*, vol. 11, no. 1, pp. 50–60.

Chase-Dunn, C. (1989), *Global Formation: Structures of the World Economy* (Oxford: Blackwell).

Chomsky, N. (1969), *American Power and the New Mandarins* (Harmondsworth: Penguin).

Clark, G. L. (1989), *Unions and Communities Under Siege: American Communities and the Crisis of Organized Labor* (Cambridge: CUP).

Clarke, J. (1991), *New Times and Old Enemies: Essays on Cultural Studies and America* (London: HarperCollins).

Clarke, S. (1988), 'Overaccumulation, Class Struggle and the Regulation Approach', *Capital and Class*, no. 36, pp. 59–92.

——. (1990), 'The Crisis of Fordism or the Crisis of Social Democracy?' *Telos*, no. 83, pp. 71–98.

Clecak, P. (1983), *America's Quest for the Ideal Self: Dissent and Fulfilment in the '60s and '70s* (New York: OUP).

Clinton, H. R. (1996), *It Takes a Village: And Other Lessons Children Teach Us* (New York: Touchstone).

Conrad, J. (1972), *Heart of Darkness* (Harmondsworth: Penguin).

Cooke, P. (1988), 'Modernity, Postmodernity and the City', *Theory, Culture and Society*, no. 5, pp. 475–92.

Cooper, R. and Burrell, G. (1988), 'Modernism, Postmodernism and Organizational Analysis', *Sociological Perspectives*, vol. 9, no. 1, pp. 91–112.

Coupland, D. (1992), *Generation X* (London: Abacus).

——. (1994), 'Dutch Reformation', Douglas Coupland Homepage, http://www.coupland.com

——. (1995), 'The Past Sucks', Douglas Coupland Homepage, http://www.coupland.com

——. (1996), *Microserfs* (London: Flamingo).

——. (1997), *Polaroids From the Dead* (London: Flamingo).

Cronin, J. E. (1980), 'Stages, Cycles and Insurgencies: The Economics of Unrest' in Hopkins and Wallerstein (eds), *Processes of the World System*, pp. 101–17.

Crook, S., Pakulski, J. and Waters, M. (1992), *Postmodernization: Change in Advanced Society* (London: Sage).

Csicsery-Ronay, I. (1988), 'Cyberpunk and Neuromanticism', *Mississippi Review*, vol. 16, nos. 2–3, pp. 266–78.

——. (1992), 'The Sentimental Futurist: Cybernetics and Art in William Gibson's *Neuromancer*', *Critique*, vol. 33, no. 3, pp. 221–40.

Czitrom, D. J. (1982), *Media and the American Mind: From Morse to McLuhan* (Chapel Hill: University of North Carolina Press).

D'Amico, R. (1978), 'Desire and the Commodity Form', *Telos*, no. 35, pp. 88–122.

Davenport, C. (1990), 'The Changing Wealth of the US Ruling Class', *Monthly Review*, no. 42, pp. 33–8.

Davenport, R. W. and the editors of *Fortune* magazine (1952), *USA: The Permanent Revolution* (London: Heinemann).

Davidow, W. and Malone, M. (1992), *The Virtual Corporation: Structuring and Revitalizing the Corporation for the 21st Century* (New York: HarperCollins).

Davis, M. (1978), 'Fordism in Crisis: A Review of Michel Aglietta's *Régulation et Crises: L'Expérience des Etats-Unis*', *Review*, vol. 2, no. 2, pp. 207–69.

——. (1985), 'Urban Renaissance and the Spirit of Postmodernism', *New Left Review*, no.151, pp. 106–13.

——. (1986), *Prisoners of the American Dream: Politics and Economy in the History of the US Working Class* (London: Verso).

——. (1990), *City of Quartz: Excavating the Future in Los Angeles* (London: Verso).

Dawley, A. (1976), *Class and Community: The Industrial Revolution in Lynn* (Cambridge, Mass.: Harvard University Press).

Dean, J. W. (1981), 'The Dissolution of the Keynesian Consensus' in Bell and Kristol (eds) *The Crisis in Economic Theory*, pp. 27–34.

Deleuze, G. and Guattari, F. (1984), *Anti-Oedipus: Capitalism and Schizophrenia* (London: Athlone Press).

——. (1987), *A Thousand Plateaus: Capitalism and Schizophrenia* (Minneapolis: University of Minnesota Press).

DeLillo, D. (1987), *The Names* (London: Vintage).

——. (1991), *Players* (London: Vintage).

——. (1992), *Running Dog* (London: Vintage).

Dennett, D. C. (1981), *Brainstorms: Philosophical Essays on Mind and Psychology* (Brighton: Harvester).

Derrida, J. (1973), 'Differance' in *Speech and Phenomena and Other Essays on Husserl's Theory of Signs* (Evanston: Northwestern University Press), pp. 129–60.

——. (1976), *Of Grammatology* (Baltimore: Johns Hopkins University Press).

Didion, J. (1979), 'On the Mall' in *The White Album* (Harmondsworth: Penguin), pp. 180–6.

——. (1987), *Democracy* (London: Pan).

Doctorow, E. L. (1986), *Lives of the Poets: A Novella and Six Stories* (London: Pan).

Doll, S. and Faller, G., '*Blade Runner* and Genre: Film Noir and Science Fiction', *Literature Film Quarterly*, vol. 14, no. 2, pp. 89–100.

Douglas, A. (1977), *The Feminization of American Culture* (New York: Avon).

Dowd, D. (1974), *The Twisted Dream: Capitalist Development in the United States Since 1776* (Cambridge, Mass.: Winthrop).

Drucker, P. F. (1971), 'The New Markets and the New Capitalism' in Bell and Kristol (eds) *Capitalism Today*, pp. 58–97.

——. (1981), *Towards the Next Economics and Other Essays* (London: Heinemann).

——. (1993), *Post-Capitalist Society* (Oxford: Butterworth).

Eagleton, T. (1990), 'The Politics of Postmodernism' in D. Zadworna-Fjellstad and L. Bjork (eds) *Criticism in the Twilight Zone: Postmodern Perspectives on Literature and Politics* (Stockholm: Almquist and Wiskell), pp. 21–8.

Edwards, P. (1989), 'The Closed World: Systems Discourse, Military Policy and Post-World War II US Historical Consciousness', in Levidow and Roberts (eds), *Cyborg Worlds*, pp. 135–58.

Edwards, R. (1979), *Contested Terrain: The Transformation of the Workplace in the Twentieth Century* (London: Heinemann).

Ehrenreich, B. (1989), *Fear of Falling: The Inner Life of the Middle Class* (New York: Pantheon)

Ehrenreich, B. and Ehrenreich, J. (1979), 'The Professional–Managerial Class' in P. Walker (ed.) *Between Labor and Capital* (Boston: South End Press), pp. 5–45.

Ehrenreich, B. and English, D. (1979), *For Her Own Good: 150 Years of the Experts' Advice to Women* (London: Pluto Press).

Ehrenreich, J. (1985), *The Altruistic Imagination* (Ithaca: Cornell University Press).

Etzioni, A. (1994), *The Spirit of Community: The Reinvention of American Society* (New York: Touchstone).

Ewen, S. (1976), *Captains of Consciousness: Advertising and the Social Roots of the Consumer Culture* (New York: McGraw-Hill).

——. (1988), *All Consuming Images: The Politics of Style in Contemporary Culture* (New York: Basic Books).

Ewen, S. and Ewen, E. (1982), *Channels of Desire: Mass Images and the Shaping of American Consciousness* (Minneapolis: University of Minnesota Press).

Fanon, F. (1967), *The Wretched of the Earth* (Harmondsworth: Penguin).

Featherstone, M. (1989), 'Postmodernism, Cultural Change and Social Practice' in Kellner (ed.) *Postmodernism, Jameson, Critique*, pp. 117–38.

——. (1991), *Consumer Culture and Postmodernism* (London: Sage).

Feenberg, A. (1990a), 'Postindustrial Discourses', *Theory and Society*, pp. 709–33.

——. (1990b), 'The Ambivalence of Technology', *Sociological Perspectives*, vol. 33, no. 1, pp. 35–50.

Finnegan, R., Salaman, G. and Thompson, K. eds (1987), *Information Technology: Social Issues* (London: Hodder and Stoughton).

Fitting, P. (1987), 'Futurecop: The Neutralization of Revolt in *Blade Runner*', *Science Fiction Studies*, no. 14, pp. 340–54.

——. (1991), 'The Lessons of Cyberpunk' in Penley and Ross (eds) *Technoculture*, pp. 295–315.

Fitzgerald, F. (1987), *Cities on a Hill: A Journey Through Contemporary American Cultures* (London: Pan).

Foster, D. A. (1991), 'Alphabetic Pleasures: *The Names*' in Lentricchia (ed.) *Introducing Don DeLillo*, pp. 157–74.

Foster, H. ed. (1985), *Postmodern Culture* (London: Pluto).

Foucault, M. (1970), *The Order of Things: An Archaeology of the Human Sciences* (London: Tavistock).

——. (1979), *The History of Sexuality, Volume 1: An Introduction* (Harmondsworth: Penguin).

Fox, R. W. and Lears, T. J. eds (1983), *The Culture of Consumption: Critical Essays in American History 1880–1980* (New York: Pantheon).

Franklin, H. B. (1980), *Robert A. Heinlein: America as Science Fiction* (New York: Oxford University Press).

——. (1983), 'America as Science Fiction: 1939' in G. E. Slusser *et al.* (eds) *Coordinates: Placing Science Fiction and Fantasy* (Carbondale: Southern Illinois University Press), pp. 107–23.

——. (1985), 'Don't Look Where We're Going: Visions of the Future in Science Fiction Films 1970–1982' in G. E. Slusser *et al.* (eds) *Shadows of the Magic Lamp: Fantasy and Science Fiction in Film* (Carbondale: Southern Illinois University Press), pp. 73–88.

Frow, J. (1993), 'Knowledge and Class', *Cultural Studies*, vol. 7, no. 2, pp. 240–81.

Fry, T. (1990), 'Art Byting the Dust: Some Considerations on Time, Economy and Cultural Practices of Postmodernity' in P. Hayward (ed.) *Culture, Technology and Creativity in the Late Twentieth Century* (London: John Libbey), pp. 163–72.

Fukuyama, F. (1989), 'The End of History?' *The National Interest*, no. 16, pp. 3–18.

——. (1992), *The End of History and the Last Man* (Harmondsworth: Penguin).

Gaddis, W. (1987), *Carpenter's Gothic* (London: Picador).

Galbraith, J. K. (1963), *American Capitalism: The Concept of Countervailing Power* (Harmondsworth: Penguin).

——. (1967), *The New Industrial State* (Harmondsworth: Penguin).

——. (1969), *The Affluent Society* (Harmondsworth: Penguin).

——. (1978), 'On Post-Keynesian Economics', *Journal of Post-Keynesian Economics*, vol. 1, no. 1, pp. 8–11.

Gates, B. (1996), *The Road Ahead* (Harmondsworth: Penguin).

Geertz, C. (1993), *Local Knowledge: Further Essays in Interpretive Anthropology* (London: Fontana).

Gibbins, J. R. ed. (1989), *Contemporary Political Culture: Politics in a Postmodern Age* (London: Sage).

Gibson, W. (1986), *Neuromancer* (London: Grafton).

——. (1987), *Count Zero* (London: Grafton).

——. (1988a), *Mona Lisa Overdrive* (London: Grafton).

——. (1988b), *Burning Chrome* (London: Grafton).

——. (1993), *Virtual Light* (Harmondsworth: Penguin).

Giddens, A. (1984), *The Constitution of Society* (Cambridge: Polity).

Gitlin, T. (1993), *The Sixties: Years of Hope, Days of Rage* (New York: Bantam).

Glass, F. (1989), 'The New Bad Future: *Robocop* and Sci-Fi Films', *Science as Culture*, no. 5, pp. 7–45.

Godden, R. (1990), *Fictions of Capital: The American Novel From James to Mailer* (Cambridge: CUP).

Gordon, D. M. (1980), 'Stages of Accumulation and Long Economic Cycles' in Hopkins and Wallerstein (eds) *Processes of the World System*, pp. 9–45.

Gordon, D. M., Edwards, R. and Reich, M. (1982), *Segmented Work, Divided Workers: The Historical Transformation of Labour in the United States* (Cambridge: CUP).

Gorz, A. ed. (1978), *The Division of Labour: The Labour Process and the Class Struggle in Modern Capitalism* (Brighton: Harvester).

——. (1982), *Farewell to the Working Class: An Essay on Postindustrial Socialism* (London: Pluto).

Gottdiener, M. and Kominos, N. eds (1989), *Capitalist Development and Crisis Theory: Accumulation, Regulation and Spatial Restructuring* (New York: St Martin's).

Gouldner, A.W. (1970), *The Coming Crisis of Western Sociology* (London: Heinemann).

——. (1976), *The Dialectic of Ideology and Technology: The Origins, Grammar and Future of Ideology* (New York: The Seabury Press).

——. (1979), *The Future of Intellectuals and the Rise of the New Class* (New York: OUP).

Gramsci, A. (1971), *Selections From the Prison Notebooks* (London: Lawrence and Wishart).

Gross, D. S. (1989), 'Marxism and Resistance: Fredric Jameson and the Moment of Postmodernism' in Kellner (ed.) *Postmodernism, Jameson, Critique*, pp. 96–116.

Habermas, J. (1975), *Legitimation Crisis* (Boston: Beacon Press).

Hall, J. R. ed. (1997), *Rethinking Class* (Ithaca: Cornell University Press).

Hall, S. (1986), 'The Problem of Ideology: Marxism Without Guarantees', *Journal of Communication Inquiry*, vol. 10, no. 2, pp. 28–44.

——. (1988), 'Gramsci and Us' in *The Hard Road to Renewal* (London: Verso), pp. 161–73.

——. (1989), 'The Meaning of New Times' in Hall and Jacques (eds) *New Times*, pp. 116–34.

——. (1991), 'Brave New World', *Socialist Review*, vol. 21, no. 1, pp. 57–64.

Hall, S. and Jacques, M. eds (1989), *New Times: The Changing Face of Politics in the 1990s* (London: Lawrence and Wishart).

Halliday, F. (1990), 'The Ends of the Cold War', *New Left Review*, no. 180, pp. 5–24.

Handy, C. (1990), *The Age of Unreason* (London: Arrow).

Haraway, D. (1985), 'A Manifesto For Cyborgs: Science, Technology and Socialist Feminism in the 1980s', *Socialist Review*, no. 80, pp. 65–107.

——. (1991a), 'Cyborgs at Large: Interview with Donna Haraway' in Penley and Ross (eds) *Technoculture*, pp. 1–20.

——. (1991b), 'The Actors are Cyborg, Nature is Coyote, and the Geography is Elsewhere' in Penley and Ross (eds) *Technoculture*, pp. 21–6.

——. (1993), 'The Biopolitics of Postmodern Bodies' in L. S. Kaufman (ed) *American Feminist Thought at Century's End* (Cambridge, Mass.: Blackwell).

Harrington, M. (1963), *The Other America: Poverty in the United States* (Harmondsworth: Penguin).

——. (1977), *The Twilight of Capitalism* (London: Macmillan).

——. (1987), *The Next Left: The History of a Future* (London: I. B. Tauris).

Harris, N. (1987), *The End of the Third World: Newly Industrialising Countries and the Decline of an Ideology* (Harmondsworth: Penguin).

Harvey, D. (1982), *The Limits to Capital* (Oxford: Blackwell).

——. (1989), *The Condition of Postmodernity: An Enquiry into the Origins of Cultural Change* (Oxford: Blackwell).

——. (1991), 'Flexibility: Threat or Opportunity?' *Socialist Review*, vol. 21, no. 1, pp. 65–76.

Haskell, T. L. (1977), *The Emergence of Professional Social Science in America: The American Social Science Association and the Nineteenth-Century Crisis of Authority* (Urbana: University of Illinois Press).

Hayes, D. (1990), *Behind the Silicon Curtain: The Seductions of Work in a Lonely Era* (Montreal: Black Rose Books).

Hebdige, D. (1979), *Subculture: The Meaning of Style* (London: Methuen).

——. (1986), 'A Report on the Western Front: Postmodernism and the Politics of Style', *Block*, no. 12, pp. 4–26.

Heffernan, N. (1994), 'Oedipus Wrecks, or, Whatever Happened to Deleuze and Guattari? Re-reading *Capitalism and Schizophrenia*' in B. McGuirk (ed.) *Redirections in Critical Theory: Truth, Self, Action, History* (London: Routledge), pp. 110–65.

——. (1996), 'Culture at Modernity's End: Daniel Bell and Fredric Jameson' in D. Murray (ed.) *American Cultural Critics* (Exeter: University of Exeter Press), pp. 270–94.

Heims, S. J. (1980), *John Von Neumann and Norbert Wiener: From Mathematics to the Technologies of Life and Death* (Cambridge, Mass.: MIT Press).

Henderson, J. (1991), *The Globalisation of High Technology Production* (London: Routledge).

Hirsch, J. (1983), 'The Fordist Security State and New Social Movements', *Kapitalistate*, vol. 10, no. 11, pp. 75–87.

——. (1991), 'Fordism and Post-Fordism: The Present Social Crisis and Its Consequences' in Bonefeld and Holloway (eds) *Post-Fordism and Social Form*, pp. 8–34.

Hirschhorn, L. (1984), *Beyond Mechanisation* (Cambridge, Mass.: MIT Press).

——. (1988), *The Workplace Within: Psychodynamics of Organisational Life* (Cambridge, Mass: MIT Press).

Hitchens, C. (1990), *Blood, Class and Nostalgia: Anglo-American Ironies* (London: Vintage).

Hofstadter, R. (1955), *The Age of Reform* (New York: Knopf).

Hopkins, T. and Wallerstein, I. eds (1980), *Processes of the World System* (London: Sage).

Hounshell, D. A. (1984), *From the American System to Mass Production, 1800–1932* (Baltimore: Johns Hopkins University Press).

Howe, I. (1963), 'Mass Society and Post-Modern Fiction' in *A World More Attractive* (New York: Horizon), pp. 77–97.

Hutcheon, L. (1988), *A Poetics of Postmodernism: History, Theory, Fiction* (London: Routledge).

Huyssen, A. (1986), 'Mass Culture as Woman: Modernism's Other' in *After the Great Divide: Modernism, Mass Culture, Postmodernism* (Bloomington: Indiana University Press).

Hymer, S. (1975), 'The Multinational Corporation and the Law of Uneven Development' in Radice (ed.) *International Firms and Modern Imperialism*, pp. 37–62.

Innis, H. (1950), *Empire and Communication* (Oxford: OUP).

Jackall, R. (1988), *Moral Mazes: The World of Corporate Managers* (New York: OUP).

Jacoby, R. (1987), *The Last Intellectuals: American Culture in the Age of Academe* (New York: Farrar, Straus & Giroux).

Jameson, F. (1972), *The Prison House of Language* (Princeton: Princeton University Press).

——. (1974), 'Change, SF, and Marxism', *Science Fiction Studies*, vol. 1, no. 4, pp. 272–6.

——. (1977), 'Reflections in Conclusion' in *Aesthetics and Politics* (London: Verso), pp. 196–213.

——. (1979), 'Reification and Utopia in Mass Culture', *Social Text*, no. 1, pp. 130–48.

——. (1980), 'SF Novel/SF Film', *Science Fiction Studies*, no. 22, pp. 319–22.

——. (1981), *The Political Unconscious: Narrative as a Socially Symbolic Act* (London: Methuen).

——. (1982), 'Progress versus Utopia, or, Can We Imagine the Future?' *Science Fiction Studies*, no. 27, pp. 147–58.

——. (1984a), 'Postmodernism, or The Cultural Logic of Late Capitalism', *New Left Review*, no. 146, pp. 53–92.

——. (1984b), 'Review of Don DeLillo, *The Names* and Sol Yurick, *Richard A.*', *Minnesota Review*, no. 22, pp. 116–22.

——. (1984c), 'Foreword' to J. F. Lyotard, *The Postmodern Condition: A Report on Knowledge* (Manchester: Manchester University Press), pp. vii–xxv.

——. (1986a), 'On Magic Realism in Film', *Critical Inquiry*, no. 12, pp. 301–25.

——. (1986b), 'Third World Literature in the Era of Multinational Capitalism', *Social Text*, no. 15, pp. 65–88.

——. (1988a), 'Cognitive Mapping' in Nelson and Grossberg (eds) *Marxism and the Interpretation of Culture*, pp. 347–57.

——. (1988b), 'On *Habits of the Heart*' in Reynolds and Norman (eds) *Community in America*, pp. 97–112.

——. (1988c), 'Periodising the '60s' in *The Ideologies of Theory, Essays 1971–86, Volume 2: Syntax of History* (London: Routledge), pp. 178–208.

——. (1991), *Postmodernism, or, The Cultural Logic of Late Capitalism* (London: Verso).

——. (1994), *The Seeds of Time* (New York: Columbia University Press).

——. (1998), 'Culture and Finance Capital' in *The Cultural Turn: Selected Writings on the Postmodern, 1983–1998* (London: Verso), pp. 136–61.

Johnson, T. J. (1972), *Professions and Power* (London: Macmillan).

Kanter, R. M. (1977), *Men and Women of the Corporation* (New York: Basic Books).

Keegan, V. (1993), 'Has Work Reached the End of the Line?', *Guardian* section 2, 28 September, pp. 2–3.

Kellner, D. ed. (1989), *Postmodernism, Jameson, Critique* (Washington D.C.: Maisonneuve Press).

Kellner, D., Liebowitz, F. and Ryan, M. (1982), '*Blade Runner*: A Diagnostic Critique', *Jump Cut*, no. 29, pp. 6–8.

Kern, S. (1983), *The Culture of Time and Space* (London: Weidenfeld and Nicholson).

Kester, G. H. (1993), 'Out of Sight is Out of Mind: The Imaginary Space of Postindustrial Culture', *Social Text*, no. 35, pp. 72–92.

Kidder, T. (1981), *The Soul of a New Machine* (New York: Avon).

King, R. H. (1976), 'From Creeds to Therapies: Philip Rieff's Work in Perspective', *Reviews in American History* (June), pp. 291–6.

Klein, G. (1977), 'Discontent in American Science Fiction', *Science Fiction Studies*, vol. 4, no. 11, pp. 3–13.

Kolko, J. (1988), *Restructuring the World Economy* (New York: Pantheon).

Kuhn, A. ed. (1990), *Alien Zone: Cultural Theory and Contemporary Science Fiction Cinema* (London: Verso).

Kuhn, T. S. (1970), *The Structure of Scientific Revolutions* (Chicago: University of Chicago Press).

Kuhns, W. (1971), *The Postindustrial Prophets: Interpretations of Technology* (New York: Weybright and Talley).

Kumar, K. (1995), *From Post-Industrial to Post-Modern Society: New Theories of the Contemporary World* (Oxford: Blackwell).

Laclau, E. and Mouffe, C. (1985), *Hegemony and Socialist Strategy: Towards a Radical Democratic Politics* (London: Verso).

Lasch, C. (1977a), *Haven in a Heartless World: The Family Besieged* (New York: Norton).

——. (1977b), 'The Siege of the Family', *New York Review of Books*, vol. 24, pp. 15–18.

——. (1979), *The Culture of Narcissism: American Life in an Age of Diminishing Expectations* (London: Abacus).

——. (1984), *The Minimal Self: Psychic Survival in Troubled Times* (New York: Norton).

——. (1986), *The New Radicalism in America, 1889–1963: The Intellectual as Social Type* (New York: Norton).

——. (1988), 'The Communitarian Critique of Liberalism' in Reynolds and Norman (eds) *Community in America*, pp. 173–84.

——. (1991), *The True and Only Heaven: Progress and Its Critics* (New York: Norton).

——. (1996), *The Revolt of the Elites and the Betrayal of Democracy* (New York: Norton).

Lash, S. (1990), *Sociology of Postmodernism* (London: Routledge).

Lash, S. and Urry, J. (1987), *The End of Organised Capitalism* (Cambridge: Polity).

Leach, W. (1993), *Land of Desire: Merchants, Power, and the Rise of a New American Culture* (New York: Vintage).

Lears, T. J. (1983), 'From Salvation to Self-Realisation: Advertising and the Therapeutic Roots of the Consumer Culture, 1880–1930' in Fox and Lears (eds) *The Culture of Consumption*, pp. 1–37.

——. (1994), *Fables of Abundance: A Cultural History of Advertising in America* (New York: Basic Books).

Leary, T. (1992), 'The Cyberpunk: The Individual as Reality Pilot' in McCaffery (ed.) *Storming the Reality Studio*, pp. 245–58.

LeClair, T. (1987), *In The Loop: Don DeLillo and the Systems Novel* (Urbana: University of Illinois Press).

Lee, D. J. and Turner, B. S. eds (1996), *Conflicts About Class: Debating Inequality in Late Industrialism* (London: Longman).

Lefebvre, H. (1971), *Everyday Life in the Modern World* (London: Allen Lane).

——. (1976), *The Survival of Capitalism: Reproduction of the Relations of Production* (London: Allison and Busby).

Lenin, V.I. (1939), *Imperialism: The Highest Stage of Capitalism* (New York: International Publishers).

Lentricchia, F. ed. (1991), *Introducing Don DeLillo* (Durham, N.C.: Duke University Press).

Levidow, L. and Roberts, R. (1989a), Introduction to Levidow and Roberts (eds) *Cyborg Worlds: The Military Information Society* (London: Free Association Books), pp. 7–9.

——. (1989b), 'Towards a Military Information Society' in Levidow and Roberts (eds) *Cyborg Worlds*, pp. 159–77.

Lévi-Strauss, C. (1972), *The Savage Mind* (London: Weidenfeld and Nicholson).

Levy, S. (1984), *Hackers: Heroes of the Computer Revolution* (New York: Doubleday Anchor).

Lilienfeld, R. (1978), *The Rise of Systems Theory: An Ideological Analysis* (New York: John Wiley).

Lipietz, A. (1985), *The Enchanted World: Inflation, Credit and the World Crisis* (London: Verso).

——. (1986a), 'Behind the Crisis: The Exhaustion of a Regime of Accumulation – A Regulation School Perspective', *Review of Radical Political Economics*, no. 18, pp. 13–32.

——. (1986b), 'New Tendencies in the International Division of Labour: Regimes of Accumulation and Modes of Regulation' in Storper and Scott (eds) *Production, Work, Territory*, pp. 14–40.

——. (1987a), *Mirages and Miracles: The Crises of Global Fordism* (London: Verso).

——. (1987b), 'Rebel Sons: The Regulation School', an interview by Jane Jenson, *French Politics and Society*, vol. 5, no. 4, pp. 17–26.

——. (1989), 'The Debt Problem: European Integration and the New Phase of World Crisis', *New Left Review*, no. 178, pp. 37–50.

Lukács, G. (1969), *The Historical Novel* (Harmondsworth: Penguin).

——. (1977), 'Realism in the Balance' in *Aesthetics and Politics* (London: Verso), pp. 28–59.

Lyon, D. (1988), *The Information Society: Issues and Illusions* (Cambridge: Polity).

Lyotard, J.-F. (1984), *The Postmodern Condition: A Report on Knowledge* (Manchester: Manchester University Press).

Lyotard, J.-F. and Thebaud, J.-L. (1985), *Just Gaming* (Manchester: Manchester University Press).

Maccoby, M. (1976), *The Gamesman: The New Corporate Leaders* (New York: Simon & Schuster).

Mailer, N. (1968a), 'A Note on Comparative Pornography' in *Advertisements for Myself* (London: Panther), pp. 350–3.

——. (1968b), 'From Surplus Value to the Mass Media' in *Advertisements for Myself*, pp. 353–6.

Mandel, E. (1978), *Late Capitalism* (London: Verso).

——. (1980), *The Second Slump: A Marxist Analysis of Recession in the Seventies* (London: Verso).

——. (1989), 'Theories of Crisis: An Explanation of the 1974–82 Cycle' in Gottdiener and Kominos (eds) *Capitalist Development and Crisis Theory*, pp. 30–46.

Mann, M. (1973), *Consciousness and Action Among the Western Working Class* (London: Macmillan).

Marchand, R. (1985), *Advertising the American Dream: Making Way for Modernity, 1920–1940* (Berkeley: University of California Press).

Marcuse, H. (1972), *One-Dimensional Man* (London: Abacus).

Marglin, S. (1978), 'What Do Bosses Do? The Origins and Functions of Hierarchy in Capitalist Production' in Gorz (ed) *The Division of Labour*, pp. 13–54.

Marx, K. (1977), *Economic and Philosophical Manuscripts of 1844* (London: Lawrence and Wishart).

——. (1970), *Wages, Price and Profit* (Peking: Foreign Languages Press).

——. (1972), *Theories of Surplus Value* (London: Lawrence and Wishart).

——. (1976), *Capital* vol. 1 (Harmondsworth: Penguin).

——. (1967), *Capital* vol. 3 (New York: International Publishers).

Marx, K. and Engels, F. (1973), *Manifesto of the Communist Party* (Peking: Foreign Languages Press).

Marx, L. (1964), *The Machine in the Garden: Technology and the Pastoral Ideal in America* (New York: OUP).

Matusow, A. J. (1984), *The Unravelling of America: A History of Liberalism in the Sixties* (New York: Harper and Row).

May, L. (1983), *Screening Out the Past: The Birth of Mass Culture and the Motion Picture Industry* (Chicago: University of Chicago Press).

McCaffery, L. ed. (1990), *Across the Wounded Galaxies: Interviews with Contemporary American Science Fiction Writers* (Urbana: University of Illinois Press).

—— ed. (1992), *Storming the Reality Studio: A Casebook of Cyberpunk and Postmodern Science Fiction* (Durham, N.C.: Duke University Press).

McCannell, D. (1992), *Empty Meeting Grounds: The Tourist Papers* (London: Routledge).

McClure, J. A. (1991), 'Postmodern Romance: Don DeLillo and the Age of Conspiracy' in Lentricchia (ed) *Introducing Don DeLillo*, pp. 99–116.

——. (1994), *Late Imperial Romance* (London: Verso).

McHale, B. (1987), *Postmodernist Fiction* (London: Methuen).

——. (1992), 'Elements of a Poetics of Cyberpunk', *Critique*, vol. 33, no. 3, pp. 149–75.

McLuhan, M. (1964), *Understanding Media: The Extensions of Man* (New York: Signet).

Mellor, A. (1984), 'Science Fiction and the Crisis of the Educated Middle Class' in C. Pawling (ed.) *Popular Fiction and Social Change* (Basingstoke: Macmillan), pp. 20–49.

Melman, S. (1970), *Pentagon Capitalism: The Political Economy of War* (New York: McGraw-Hill).

Meyerowitz, J. (1985), *No Sense of Place: The Impact of Electronic Media on Social Behavior* (New York: OUP).

Michaels, W. B. (1987), *The Gold Standard and the Logic of Naturalism* (Berkeley: University of California Press).

Miller, J. D. (1990), 'Neuroscience Fiction: The Roman à Synaptic Cleft' in G. E. Slusser and E. Rabkin (eds) *Mindscapes: The Geographies of Imagined Worlds* (Carbondale: Southern Illinois University Press), pp. 195–207.

Miller, P. ed. (1956), *The American Puritans: Their Prose and Poetry* (New York: Doubleday Anchor).

Mills, C.W. (1951), *White Collar: The American Middle Classes* (New York: OUP).

——. (1956), *The Power Elite* (New York: OUP).

——. (1963), 'A Marx for the Managers' in I. L. Horowitz (ed.) *Power, Politics and People: Collected Essays of C. Wright Mills* (New York: OUP), pp. 53–71.

——. (1983), *The Sociological Imagination* (Harmondsworth: Penguin).

Minkenberg, M. and Ingelhart, R. (1989), 'Neoconservatism and Value Change in the USA: Tendencies in the Mass Public of a Postindustrial Society' in Gibbins (ed.) *Contemporary Political Culture*, pp. 81–109.

Montgomery, D. (1980), *Workers' Control in America: Studies in the History of Work, Technology and Labor Struggles* (Cambridge: CUP).

——. (1987), *The Fall of the House of Labor* (Cambridge: CUP).

Moravec, H. (1988), *Mind Children: The Future of Robot and Human Intelligence* (Cambridge, Mass.: Harvard University Press).

Morgan, G. (1985), 'From West to East and Back Again: Capitalist Expansion and Class Formation in the Nineteenth Century' in H. Newby *et al.* (eds) *Restructuring Capital: Recession and Reorganisation in Industrial Society* (Basingstoke: Macmillan), pp. 124–55.

Morgan, K. and Sayer, A. (1988), *Microcircuits of Capital: 'Sunrise' Industry and Uneven Development* (Cambridge: Polity).

Murray, F. (1983), 'The Decentralisation of Production: The Decline of the Mass Collective Worker?' *Capital and Class*, no. 19, pp. 74–99.

Nadel, A. (1992), 'Failed Cultural Narratives: America in the Postwar Era and the Story of Democracy', *boundary 2*, vol. 19, no. 1, pp. 95–120.

Naisbitt, J. (1982), *Megatrends: Ten New Directions Transforming Our Lives* (New York: Warner).

Neale, S. (1989), 'Issues of Difference: *Alien* and *Blade Runner*' in J. Donald (ed.) *Fantasy and the Cinema* (London: BFI), pp. 213–23.

Neef, D. ed. (1998), *The Knowledge Economy* (Boston: Butterworth-Heinemann).

Nelson, C. and Grossberg, L. eds (1988), *Marxism and the Interpretation of Culture* (Basingstoke: Macmillan).

Nichols, B. (1988), 'The Work of Art in the Age of Cybernetic Systems', *Screen*, vol. 29, no. 1, pp. 22–46.

Noble, D. F. (1979), *American By Design: Science, Technology and the Rise of Corporate Capitalism* (New York: Knopf).

——. (1984), *Forces of Production: A Social History of Industrial Automation* (New York: OUP).

——. (1995), *Progress Without People: New Technology, Unemployment and the Message of Resistance* (Toronto: Between the Lines).

Nye, D. E. (1994), *American Technological Sublime* (Cambridge, Mass.: MIT Press).

O'Connor, J. (1966), 'Monopoly Capital', *New Left Review*, no. 40, pp. 38–50.

——. (1973), *The Fiscal Crisis of the State* (New York: St Martin's).

——. (1975), 'Productive and Unproductive Labor', *Politics and Society*, vol. 5, no. 3, pp. 297–336.

——. (1986), *Accumulation Crisis* (Oxford: Blackwell).

——. (1987), *The Meaning of Crisis: A Theoretical Introduction* (Oxford: Blackwell).

——. (1989), 'An Introduction to a Theory of Crisis Theories' in Gottdiener and Kominos (eds) *Capitalist Development and Crisis Theory*, pp. 21–9.

Ong, W. J. (1983), *Orality and Literacy: The Technologising of the Word* (London: Methuen).

Packard, V. (1960), *The Waste Makers* (Harmondsworth: Penguin).

——. (1965), *The Pyramid Climbers* (Harmondsworth: Penguin).

Palloix, C. (1977), 'The Self-Expansion of Capital on a World Scale', *Review of Radical Political Economics*, vol. 9, no. 2, pp. 1–28.

——. (1978), 'The Labour Process: From Fordism to Neo-Fordism' in Gorz (ed.) *The Division of Labour*, pp. 46–67.

Parrinder, P. (1977), 'The Black Wave: Science and Social Consciousness in Modern Science Fiction', *Radical Science Journal*, no. 5, pp. 37–61.

Parsons, T. (1954), 'The Professions and Social Structure' in *Essays in Sociological Theory* (New York: The Free Press).

——. (1966), *Societies: Evolutionary and Comparative Perspectives* (Englewood Cliffs, N.J.: Prentice-Hall).

——. (1968), 'Systems Analysis: Social Systems' in David L. Sills (ed.) *International Encyclopedia of the Social Sciences* XV, pp. 458–73.

Pells, R. (1989), *The Liberal Mind in a Conservative Age: American Intellectuals in the 1940s and '50s* (Middletown, Conn: Wesleyan University Press).

Penley, C. (1990), 'Time Travel, Primal Scene and the Critical Dystopia' in Kuhn (ed.) *Alien Zone*, pp. 116–27.

Penley, C. and Ross, A. eds (1991), *Technoculture* (Minneapolis: University of Minnesota Press).

Perkin, H. (1990), *The Rise of Professional Society: England Since 1880* (London: Routledge).

Petras, J. and Davenport, C. (1990), 'The Changing Wealth of the US Ruling Class', *Monthly Review*, vol. 42, pp. 33–38.

Pfeil, F. (1990), 'Makin' Flippy-Floppy: Postmodernism and the Baby-Boom PMC' in *Another Tale to Tell: Politics and Narrative in Postmodern Culture* (London: Verso), pp. 97–125.

Polan, D. (1988), 'Postmodernism and Cultural Analysis Today' in E. A. Kaplan (ed.) *Postmodernism and Its Discontents: Theories, Practices* (London: Verso), pp. 45–58.

Porush, D. (1985), *The Soft Machine: Cybernetic Fiction* (London: Methuen).

Poster, M. (1990), *The Mode of Information: Poststructuralism and Social Context* (Cambridge: Polity).

Poulantzas, N. (1975), *Classes in Contemporary Capitalism* (London: New Left Books).

——. (1978), *Political Power and Social Classes* (London: Verso).

Przeworski, A. (1980), 'Material Bases of Consent: Economics and Politics in a Hegemonic System', *Political Power and Social Theory*, no. 1, pp. 21–66.

Pynchon, T. (1966), *The Crying of Lot 49* (London: Pan).

Radice, H. ed. (1975), *International Firms and Modern Imperialism* (Harmondsworth: Penguin).

Rapoport, A. (1968), 'Systems Analysis: General Systems Theory' in David L. Sills (ed.) *International Encyclopedia of the Social Sciences* XV, pp. 452–8.

Reich, R. B. (1991), *The Work of Nations: Preparing Ourselves for Twenty-First Century Capitalism* (New York: Knopf).

Renshaw, P. (1992), *American Labour and Consensus Capitalism, 1935–1990* (London: Macmillan).

Reynolds, C. H. and Norman, R.V. eds (1988), *Community in America: The Challenge of 'Habits of the Heart'* (Berkeley: University of California Press).

Rieff, P. (1966), *The Triumph of the Therapeutic: Uses of Faith After Freud* (Harmondsworth: Penguin).

Riesman, D. *et al.* (1961), *The Lonely Crowd: A Study of the Changing American Character* (New Haven: Yale University Press).

Robbins, B. (1993), *Secular Vocations: Intellectuals, Professionalism, Culture* (London: Verso).

Robertson, R. (1990), 'After Nostalgia: Wilful Nostalgia and the Phases of Globalisation' in Turner (ed.) *Theories of Modernity and Postmodernity*, pp. 45–61.

——. (1992), *Globalisation: Social Theory And Global Culture* (London: Sage).

Roediger, D. R. (1991), *The Wages of Whiteness: Race and the Making of the American Working Class* (London: Verso).

Rorty, R. (no date), 'Mind's Place in Nature' (undated typescript).

Rosenthal, P. (1991), 'Jacked In: Fordism, Cyberpunk, Marxism', *Socialist Review* (Spring), pp. 79–103.

Ross, A. (1989a), *No Respect: Intellectuals and Popular Culture* (London: Routledge).

——. ed. (1989b), *Universal Abandon? The Politics of Postmodernism* (Edinburgh: Edinburgh University Press).

——. (1991), *Strange Weather: Culture, Science and Technology in the Age of Limits* (London: Verso).

Rostow, W. W. (1960), *Stages of Capitalist Development: A Non-Communist Manifesto* (Cambridge: CUP).

Roszak, T. (1986), *The Cult of Information: The Folklore of Computers and the True Art of Thinking* (London: Paladin).

Rowthorn, R. (1980), *Capitalism, Conflict and Inflation* (London: Macmillan).

Rushkoff, D. ed. (1994), *The GenX Reader* (New York: Ballantine).

Rustin, M. (1989a), 'The Trouble with "New Times"' in Hall and Jacques (eds) *New Times*, pp. 303–20.

——. (1989b), 'The Politics of Post-Fordism, or The Trouble with "New Times"', *New Left Review*, no. 175, pp. 54–77.

Ryan, M. and Kellner, D. (1990), *Camera Politica: The Politics and Ideology of Contemporary Hollywood Film* (Bloomington: Indiana University Press).

Said, E. (1978), *Orientalism* (London: Routledge and Kegan Paul).

Sayer, A. (1989), 'Postfordism in Question', *International Journal of Urban and Regional Research*, vol. 13, no. 4, pp. 666–95.

Schiller, H. (1984), *Information and the Crisis Economy* (Norwood, N.J.: Ablex).

Schwab, G. (1989), 'Cyborgs and Cybernetic Intertexts: On Postmodern Phantasms of Body and Mind' in P. O'Connell and R. Con Davis (eds) *Intertextuality and Contemporary American Fiction* (Baltimore: Johns Hopkins University Press), pp. 191–213.

Seltzer, M. (1992), *Bodies and Machines* (London: Routledge).

Sennett, R. (1986), *The Fall of Public Man* (London: Faber and Faber).

——. (1999), *The Corrosion of Character: The Personal Consequences of Work in the New Capitalism* (New York: Norton).

Sennett, R. and Cobb, J. (1972), *The Hidden Injuries of Class* (Cambridge: CUP).

Sklar, M. J. (1988), *The Corporate Reconstruction of American Capitalism 1890–1916: The Market, the Law, and Politics* (Cambridge: CUP).

Smart, B. (1992), *Modern Conditions, Postmodern Controversies* (London: Routledge).

Smith, N. (1984), *Uneven Development: Nature, Capital and the Production of Space* (Oxford: Blackwell).

Sobchack, V. (1987), *Screening Space: The American Science Fiction Film* (New York: Ungar).

Sohn-Rethel, A. (1978), *Intellectual and Manual Labour: A Critique of Epistemology* (London: Macmillan).

Soja, E. (1989), *Postmodern Geographies: The Reassertion of Space in Critical Social Theory* (London: Verso).

Spindler, M. (1983), *American Literature and Social Change: William Dean Howells to Arthur Miller* (London: Macmillan).

Spivak, G. (1988a), *In Other Worlds: Essays in Cultural Politics* (London: Routledge).

——. (1988b), 'Can the Subaltern Speak?' in Nelson and Grossberg (eds) *Marxism and the Interpretation of Culture*, pp. 271–313.

Springer, C. (1991), 'The Pleasure of the Interface', *Screen*, vol. 32, no. 3, pp. 303–23.

Stark, E. (1991), 'The Cybernetic Psyche', *Socialist Review*, vol. 89, no. 4, pp. 155–61.

Steedman, I. *et al.* (1981), *The Value Controversy* (London: Verso).

Stephanson, A. (1989), 'A Conversation with Fredric Jameson: Regarding Postmodernism' in Ross (ed.) *Universal Abandon?* pp. 3–30.

Sterling, B. ed. (1988), *Mirrorshades: The Cyberpunk Anthology* (London: Paladin).

Stivale, C. (1991), 'Mille/Punks/Cyber/Plateaus: Science Fiction and Deleuzo-Guattarian "Becomings"', *SubStance*, no. 66, pp. 66–93.

Stonier, T. (1983), *The Wealth of Information: A Profile of the Post-Industrial Economy* (London: Thames-Methuen).

Storper, M. (1989), 'The Transition to Flexible Specialisation in the US Film Industry', *Cambridge Journal of Economics*, vol. 13, pp. 273–305.

Storper, M. and Scott, A. J. (1986a), 'Production, Work, Territory: Contemporary Realities and Theoretical Tasks' in Storper and Scott (eds) *Production, Work, Territory*, pp. 3–66.

—— eds (1986b), *Production, Work, Territory: The Geographical Anatomy of Industrial Capitalism* (Boston: Allen and Unwin).

Susman, W. I. (1984), *Culture as History: The Transformation of American Society in the Twentieth Century* (New York: Pantheon).

Suvin, D. (1988), *Positions and Presuppositions in Science Fiction* (London: Macmillan).

——. (1992), 'On Gibson and Cyberpunk SF' in McCaffery (ed.) *Storming the Reality Studio*, pp. 349–65.

Tallack, D. (1991), *Twentieth-Century America: The Intellectual and Cultural Context* (London: Longman).

Tam, H. B. (1998), *Communitarianism: A New Agenda for Politics and Citizenship* (London: Macmillan).

Telotte, J. P. (1995), *Replications: A Robotic History of Science Fiction Film* (Urbana: University of Illinois Press).

Tomaney, J. (1994), 'A New Paradigm of Work Organisation and Technology?' in Amin (ed.) *Post-Fordism: A Reader*, pp. 157–94.

Touraine, A. (1971), *The Postindustrial Society* (New York: Harcourt-Brace).

Trachtenberg, A. (1982), *The Incorporation of America: Culture and Society in the Gilded Age* (New York: Hill and Wang).

Trilling, L. (1966), *Beyond Culture: Essays on Life and Literature* (London: Secker and Warburg).

Tronti, M. (1976), 'Workers and Capital' in Conference of Socialist Economists Pamphlet no. 1, *The Labour Process and Class Struggles* (London: CSE), pp. 92–129.

Tugendhat, C. (1975), *The Multinationals* (London: Eyre and Spottiswoode).

Turkle, S. (1984), *The Second Self: Computers and the Human Spirit* (London: Granada).

——. (1995), *Life On the Screen: Identity in the Age of the Internet* (New York: Simon & Schuster).
Turner, B. S. (1989), 'From Postindustrial Society to Postmodern Politics: The Political Sociology of Daniel Bell' in Gibbins (ed.) *Contemporary Political Culture*, pp. 199–217.
—— ed. (1990), *Theories of Modernity and Postmodernity* (London: Sage).
Turner, L. (1971), *Invisible Empires: Multinational Companies and the Modern World* (New York: Harcourt, Brace, Jovanovich).
Urry, J. (1986), 'Capitalist Production, Scientific Management and the Service Class' in Storper and Scott (eds) *Production, Work, Territory*, pp. 43–66.
——. (1990), *The Tourist Gaze: Leisure and Travel in Contemporary Societies* (London: Sage).
Veblen, T. (1932), *The Theory of the Business Enterprise* (New York: Scribners).
——. (1953), *The Theory of the Leisure Class: An Economic Study of Institutions* (New York: Mentor).
——. (1965), *The Engineers and the Price System* (New York: Kelley).
Walker, P. ed. (1979), *Between Labor and Capital* (Boston: South End Press).
Wallerstein, I. (1979), *The Capitalist World Economy* (Cambridge: CUP).
——. (1984), *The Politics of the World Economy* (Cambridge: CUP).
——. (1990), 'Societal Development or Development of the World System?' in Albrow and King (eds) *Globalisation, Knowledge and Society*, pp. 157–72.
——. (1991), *Geopolitics and Geoculture: Essays on the Changing World System* (Cambridge: CUP).
Waxman, C. I. ed. (1968), *The End of Ideology Debate* (New York: Simon & Schuster).
Weber, M. (1985), *The Protestant Ethic and the Spirit of Capitalism* (London: Allen and Unwin).
——. (1991), 'Science as a Vocation' in H. H. Gerth and C. Wright Mills (eds) *From Max Weber: Essays in Sociology* (London: Routledge), pp. 129–56.
Webster, F. (1995), *Theories of the Information Society* (London: Routledge).
Weinstein, J. (1969), *The Corporate Ideal in the Liberal State 1900–1918* (Boston: Beacon Press).
Wexler, P. (1990), 'Citizenship in the Semiotic Society' in Turner (ed.) *Theories of Modernity and Postmodernity*, pp. 164–75.
White, H. (1976), *Metahistory: The Historical Imagination in Nineteenth-Century Europe* (Baltimore: Johns Hopkins University Press).
——. (1978), *Tropics of Discourse: Essays in Cultural Criticism* (Baltimore: Johns Hopkins University Press).
——. (1987), *The Content of the Form: Narrative Discourse and Historical Representation* (Baltimore: Johns Hopkins University Press).
White, M. (1976), *Social Thought in America: The Revolt Against Formalism* (New York: OUP).
Whyte, W. H. (1960), *The Organisation Man* (Harmondsworth: Penguin).
Wiebe, R. H. (1967), *The Search for Order 1877–1920* (New York: Hill and Wang).
Wiener, N. (1960), 'Some Moral and Technical Consequences of Automation', *Science*, vol. 131, pp. 1355–8.
——. (1961), *Cybernetics: or Control and Communication in the Animal and the Machine* (Cambridge, Mass.: MIT Press).
——. (1964), *God and Golem Inc.: A Comment on Certain Points Where Cybernetics Impinges on Religion* (London: Chapman and Hall).
——. (1989), *The Human Use of Human Beings: Cybernetics and Society* (London: Free Association Books).
Wilkins, M. (1970), *The Emergence of Multinational Enterprise: American Business Abroad from the Colonial Era to 1914* (Cambridge, Mass.: Harvard University Press).
——. (1974), *The Maturing of Multinational Enterprise: American Business Abroad 1914–1970* (Cambridge, Mass.: Harvard University Press).
Wilkinson, R. (1984), *American Tough: The Tough-Guy Tradition and American Character* (Westport: Greenwood Press).
—— ed. (1988), *The Pursuit of American Character* (New York: Harper and Row).
Williams, W. A. (1961), *The Contours of American History* (Chicago: Quadrangle Books).
Wilson, H. T. (1977), *The American Ideology: Science, Technology and Organisation as Modes of Rationality in Advanced Industrial Societies* (London: Routledge).
Wilson, R. (1992), 'Techno-Euphoria and the Discourse of the American Sublime', *boundary 2*, vol. 19, no. 1, pp. 205–29.
Wolfe, A. (1981), *America's Impasse: The Rise and Fall of the Politics of Growth* (New York: Pantheon).

Wollen, P. (1991), 'Cinema/Americanism/The Robot' in J. Naremore and P. Brantlinger (eds) *Modernity and Mass Culture* (Bloomington: Indiana University Press), pp. 42–69.

Wolmark, J. (1994), *Aliens and Others: Science Fiction, Feminism and Postmodernism* (Hemel Hempstead: Harvester-Wheatsheaf).

Wood, R. (1986), *Hollywood From Vietnam to Reagan* (New York: Columbia University Press).

Woodiwiss, A. (1993), *Postmodernity USA: The Crisis of Social Modernism in Postwar America* (London: Sage).

Wright, E. O. (1985), *Classes* (London: Verso).

Young, R. (1990), *White Mythologies: Writing History and the West* (London: Routledge).

Zuboff, S. (1988), *In the Age of the Smart Machine: The Future of Work and Power* (London: Heinemann).

Index

Abercrombie, Nicholas, 145
Adorno, Theodor, 224
Affluent Society, The (Galbraith), 35
Aglietta, Michel, 20, 25, 28, 40, 44, 58, 115, 169, 217, 221
Ahmad, Aijaz, 166
Alice in the Cities (film), 228
Althusser, Louis, 214, 224
American Dream, An (Mailer), 225
American Revolution, 153, 225
American social character, 57–67, 70, 100–1, 218
Anderson, Perry, 2
Apple (corporation), 60, 220
Aronowitz, Stanley, 55, 62, 216
Arrighi, Giovanni, 210
Artificial intelligence, 9, 45, 105, 118, 148–61, 223
Ashby, W. Ross, 106–7, 223
Automation, 4, 68, 109–10, 113–18

Baby-boomers, 72, 88–91, 95
Ballard, J. G., 224
Balsamo, Anne, 226
Barthes, Roland, 70
Baran, Paul, 133–4
Bateson, Gregory, 122, 223
Baudrillard, Jean, 2, 15, 52, 105, 116–17, 151
Beet Queen, The (Erdrich), 226
Bell, Daniel, 2, 30, 32, 34, 40, 62, 70, 89, 113–14, 129, 216–17, 218, 221, 229
Bellah, Robert, 34, 46–7, 57, 59–62, 78–81, 133, 219
Bellamy, Edward, 45
Beloved (Morrison), 226
Benjamin, Walter, 152
Berger, Albert, 224
Berle, Adolph, 31, 32, 119, 133, 223
Berman, Marshall, 168, 216
Bertalanffy, Ludwig von, 107, 122, 223
Big Chill, The (film), 222
Big Sleep, The (film), 226
Biskind, Peter, 85
Blade Runner (film), 9, 118, 138, 148–61, 167, 201, 225

Blake, William, 153, 225
Bledstein, Burton, 34, 205, 206, 208
Block, Fred, 229
Boorstin, Daniel, 216
Brand, Stewart, 220
Braudel, Fernand, 168, 172
Braverman, Harry, 58–9, 66, 154, 219, 220, 224
Brenner, Robert, 222
Bretton Woods monetary agreement, 23, 173, 174, 176
Bruno, Giuliana, 151
Bukharin, Mikhail, 168–9
Burnham, James, 220
'Burning Chrome' (Gibson), 123–4
Byrne, David, 47, 71, 72–87

Callinicos, Alex, 89
Capitalist class, 26, 113; in Gibson's cyberspace trilogy, 132–4
Capital-labour accord, 3, 6, 27, 30, 173, 175
Carey, James, 39, 78
Carpenter's Gothic (Gaddis), 181, 226
Castells, Manuel, 20, 25, 210, 217
Chandler, Alfred D., 44, 165, 166, 177
Chaplin, Charlie, 45
Charlie's Angels (TV show), 98
Chase-Dunn, Christopher, 174, 176
Chinatown (film), 225
City of Quartz (Davis), 15
Clark, Gordon L., 87
Class, 3–4, 6, 9, 22, 26, 55, 113, 116, 215, 216; in *True Stories*, 82–7; in *Microserfs*, 88–96; in Gibson's cyberspace trilogy, 131–47; in *Blade Runner*, 148–61; in *The Names*, 192–204; *see also* Capitalist class; Professional-managerial class; Working class
Clinton, Bill, 46
Club of Rome, 107
Cobb, Jonathan, 82, 84–6, 152
Cold War, 7, 111, 127, 220, 223
Coming of Postindustrial Society, The (Bell), 229
Communication as Culture (Carey), 39
Communitarianism, 46, 62, 99, 219

Community, 46–9, 60–63, 70, 75–81, 87, 97–100, 219
Conrad, Joseph, 227, 228
Consensus, 30–31, 41, 84, 130–31, 218
Consumerism, 19–20, 26, 52, 97, 117, 166
Consumption, 2, 6–7, 18, 20, 21, 25–7, 55, 68–9, 77, 79, 90, 92, 193, 216
Corporations, 19, 21, 29, 44–6, 59, 69–70, 133–4, 202–3
Counterculture, 64, 220, 223, 229
Count Zero (Gibson), 118, 123, 131–47; see also Cyberspace trilogy
Coup, The (Updike), 226
Coupland, Douglas, 42, 47, 62, 70–1, 88–102
Crisis, 3, 18–25, 27–8, 42–3, 175, 181–3, 213, 229
Croly, Herbert, 149
Crying of Lot 49, The (Pynchon), 51–4
Cultural Contradictions of Capitalism, The (Bell), 89, 229
Culture of Professionalism, The (Bledstein), 205
Cybernetics, 9, 18, 45, 105–18, 129, 146, 149–50, 222–3
Cybernetics (Wiener), 105, 148
Cyberpunk, 124–6, 224, 225
Cyberspace, 123–47
Cyberspace trilogy (Gibson), 118, 123, 131–47, 148–9, 152, 154, 156, 161, 167, 177, 208
Cyborg, 26, 107, 118, 149–61, 226

Data General (corporation), 42–71
Davidow, William H., 88, 100
Davis, Mike, 2, 14–15, 19, 21, 23, 28, 34, 41, 44, 51, 72, 90, 175, 193, 217, 220
Dawley, Alan, 84–5
Deindustrialisation, 69–70
Deleuze, Gilles, 171, 219
DeLillo, Don, 178, 179–204, 205, 227, 228
Democracy (Didion), 181–2, 226, 227
Dennett, Daniel, 223
Derrida, Jacques, 200, 228
Design for a Brain (Ashby), 106
Deskilling, 57–8
Dick, Philip K., 222
Didion, Joan, 83, 181–2, 226
Doctorow, E. L., 181, 226, 227

Edwards, Richard, 27, 216
Ehrenreich, Barbara, 32–4, 35, 59, 65–6, 83, 85, 88–9, 91, 145, 156, 157–8, 159, 203, 218, 220–1
Ehrenreich, John, 32–4, 59, 65–6, 83, 88–9, 156, 218, 220–1
Eisenhower, Dwight D., 110
'End of History?, The' (Fukuyama), 117–18

End-of-ideology, 7, 31, 96, 112–18, 217
Engels, Frederick, 167–8, 202
Engineers and the Price System (Veblen), 63, 218
English, Deirdre, 157–8
Erdrich, Louise, 226
ET: The Extra Terrestrial (film), 225
Ewen, Stuart, 56, 216

Fanon, Frantz, 179, 196
Fear of Falling (Ehrenreich), 35, 159
Featherstone, Mike, 166
First World War, 171
Fiskadoro (Johnson), 226
Fitting, Peter, 124
Fitzgerald, F. Scott, 225
Flexible accumulation, 41–2
Ford, Henry, 24, 26, 57, 212, 225–6
Ford Foundation, 109
Fordism, 3–10, 24–8, 29–36, 49, 72–3,130–1, 146–7, 212–15; and American social character, 57–60, 64–7, 76; and baby-boom, 88–90; and globalisation, 165–78; and systems theory, 111, 114
Forrester, Jay, 107
Fortune (magazine), 30, 31
Foster, Hal, 215
Foucault, Michel, 175–6, 219
Fox, Richard W., 79–80, 86, 216
'Fragments of a Hologram Rose' (Gibson), 119–23, 125, 149
Frankfurt School, 26
Fukuyama, Francis, 7, 117–18, 119
Future of Intellectuals and the Rise of the New Class, The (Gouldner), 119

Galbraith, J. K., 35, 114, 145, 159
Gaddis, William, 181, 226
Gates, Bill, 49, 60, 94–5
Geertz, Clifford, 192–3, 227
Gender, 47, 98, 222; in Gibson's cyberspace trilogy, 142–3, 225; in Blade Runner, 156–9
General Electric (corporation), 110
General Motors (corporation), 30, 217
Generation X, 90–2, 97–9
Generation X (Coupland), 91–2
Gibson, William, 9, 57, 71, 93, 118, 119–47, 148–9, 152, 156, 159, 161, 167, 177, 208, 224, 225
Giddens, Anthony, 7
Gingrich, Newt, 73
Gitlin, Todd, 222
Glass, Fred, 161

Globalisation, 7–8, 19, 69–70, 118, 165–78, 205–11
Global village, 49
Going After Cacciato (O'Brien), 226
Goldmann, Lucien, 224
Good Society, The (Bellah), 133, 219
Gordon, David, 27, 175
Gorz, Andre, 229
Gouldner, Alvin, 34, 112, 119, 129, 137, 141, 145, 159, 194, 210
Gramsci, Antonio, 24–5, 29, 58, 212, 213, 217
Grand narrative, 7, 46, 77, 214, 219
Grateful Dead, The, 220
Great Depression, 3, 7, 18, 112
Green movement, 161
Grossberg, Lawrence, 216
Guattari, Felix, 171, 219

Habermas, Jürgen, 41
Habits of the Heart (Bellah), 34, 46, 219
Hall, Stuart, 2, 5
Halliday, Fred, 226
Haraway, Donna, 159–60, 176
Harrington, Michael, 219
Harris, Nigel, 175–6
Harvey, David, 19, 41, 43, 50, 62, 150–1, 153, 166, 170, 172, 173, 175, 185, 186, 206, 216
Hayes, Dennis, 48, 60, 61–3, 70–1, 219
Heart of Darkness (Conrad), 227, 228
Heims, Steve, 223
Hemingway, Ernest, 184
Henderson, Jeffrey, 176
High-tech ideology, 42, 115
Hirsch, Joachim, 210
Hirschhorn, Larry, 229
Hofstadter, Richard, 31
Hounshell, David, 212
Howe, Irving, 1
Human Use of Human Beings, The (Wiener), 108, 129
Hunter, Robert, 220
Huyssen, Andreas, 88, 222
Hymer, Stephen, 202

IBM (corporation), 44, 99, 101
Imperialism, 169, 171
Individualism, 61, 78, 80
Inflation, 21, 27
Information technology (IT), 9, 40–71, 74–87, 88–102, 166–7, 176–8
Innis, Harold, 49–50
International Monetary Fund, 173
Internet, 49

Iranian Revolution, 182
Iran–Iraq War, 182

James, Henry, 184
Jameson, Fredric, 1–2, 9, 13–15, 19, 51, 53–5, 62, 76, 80, 89, 96, 117, 119–21, 124–5, 138, 159–60, 166–7, 176, 177–8, 179–80, 184, 185, 197, 208, 217, 219, 221, 224, 227
Jobs, Steve, 60
Johnson, Dennis, 226
Johnson, Philip, 15
Johnson, Terence, 34
J.R. (Gaddis), 226

Kellner, Douglas, 156, 216
Kesey, Ken, 220
Keynesianism, 72, 217
Kondratieff, N. D., 16
Kemp, Jack, 73
Kidder, Tracy, 42–71, 73
Kings of the Road (film), 228
Klein, Gerard, 126–8, 131, 135, 145–6, 154, 224, 225
Kolko, Joyce, 174
Kubrick, Stanley, 226
Kuhn, Thomas, 214
Kuhns, William, 45, 67

Labor and Monopoly Capital (Braverman), 154
Labour theory of value, 22, 116, 217
Labour unions, 26, 30, 109–11, 221
Laclau, Ernesto, 216, 219
Language games, 46–7, 76
Lasch, Christopher, 7, 57, 62, 70, 155, 221, 228
Lash, Scott, 2, 29, 70, 218
Late Capitalism (Mandel), 13–14, 15–24
Lead or Leave (campaign network), 91, 222
Lears, Jackson, 55–6, 65, 79–80, 86, 216, 221
Leary, Timothy, 220
Lefebvre, Henri, 170–71
Lenin, Vladimir Ilyich, 16, 97, 168–9, 171
Levidow, Les, 146, 149–50
Lévi-Strauss, Claude, 224
Liebowitz, Fran, 156
Lilienfeld, Robert, 107, 109, 113
Lipietz, Alain, 70, 172, 174, 214, 217
'Lives of the Poets' (Doctorow), 181, 226
Long boom (1945–73), 3, 6, 39, 128
Long waves of accumulation, 16–18, 23
Lonely Crowd, The (Riesman), 34
Looking Backward (Bellamy), 45
Lukács, Georg, 124, 224, 227

Lyotard, Jean-François, 2, 41, 46–8, 76–7, 81, 116, 166, 204, 219

Machine Dreams (Phillips), 226
Magic realism, 180
Mailer, Norman, 216, 225
Malone, Michael S., 88, 100
Managerial Revolution, The (Burnham), 220
Mandel, Ernest, 2, 13, 15–24, 39, 170, 171
Manifesto of the Communist Party (Marx and Engels), 167–9
Mann, Michael, 83
Marcuse, Herbert, 114–15
Marshall aid, 4, 172
'Mass Society and Post-Modern Fiction' (Howe), 1
Marx, Karl, 5, 15, 17, 19, 22, 29, 31, 116, 167–9, 170, 171, 173, 187, 202
Marxism, 1, 16, 24, 55, 97, 113, 116, 168–9, 213, 216, 217, 219
Marxism Today (magazine), 219
Mather, Cotton, 59–61, 220
Mayo, Elton, 225
McClure, John, 226, 227, 228
McHale, Brian, 51
McLuhan, Marshall, 45, 49
McNamara, Robert, 111
Means, Gardiner, 32, 133, 223
Mellor, Adrian, 128, 224
Meyerowitz, Joshua, 50
Michaels, Walter Benn, 133
Microserfs (Coupland), 42, 47, 62, 66, 71, 88–102, 135, 152, 154, 167
Microsoft (corporation), 49, 93–5
Military expenditure, 21, 72–3, 221
Military-industrial complex, 110–11, 127
Mill, John Stuart, 165, 167
Mills, C. Wright, 1, 34, 127, 196, 216–17, 220
Modern Times (film), 45
Mona Lisa Overdrive (Gibson), 118, 123, 131–47; *see also* Cyberspace trilogy
Montgomery, David, 149, 216
Morgan, Kevin, 176, 177
Morgenstern, Oskar, 107, 109, 111
Morrison, Toni, 226
Mouffe, Chantal, 216, 219

Narrative, 8–9, 224
Names, The (DeLillo), 178, 179–204, 205, 208, 209, 227, 228
Nelson, Carey, 216
Neocolonialism, 173
Neumann, John von, 107, 109, 223
Neuromancer (Gibson), 118, 123, 131–47; *see also* Cyberspace trilogy

New Deal, 127
New Industrial State, The (Galbraith), 145
New Left, 33, 88, 115, 229
New Mexico trilogy (Nichols), 226
New Right, 73
Nichols, Bill, 148, 152–3
Nichols, John, 226
Nixon, Richard Milhous, 174
Noble, David, 26, 36, 59, 110, 219, 223
Nye, David, 56–7

O'Brien, Tim, 226
O'Connor, James, 21, 33, 73, 115, 181
One Dimensional Man (Marcuse), 114–15
Ong, Walter, 197–8
Organisation Man, The (Whyte), 34
Other America, The (Harrington), 219

Packard, Vance, 34, 52, 161, 219
Paris, Texas (film), 228
Parsons, Talcott, 111–12, 223
Pells, Richard, 217
'Periodising the 60s' (Jameson), 217
Pfeil, Fred, 72, 88–9, 145, 156, 203, 218
Phillips, Jayne Anne, 226
Players (DeLillo), 187–8, 227
Polanski, Roman, 225
Political Economy (Mill), 165, 167
Port Huron Statement, 222
Poster, Mark, 44–5
Post-Fordism, 3–10, 27–8, 69–71, 87, 89–90, 99–100, 130–1, 146–7, 213–15; and globalisation, 176–8; and technology, 40, 48, 115–18
Postindustrial society, 2, 6, 19, 40, 114–16, 212
Postmaterialism, 63, 220
Postmodern Condition, The (Lyotard), 46–8, 78
Postmodernism, 1–2, 5, 6, 8, 13, 14–15, 19, 23, 41, 44, 46–9, 51, 66, 70, 89–91, 138, 151, 165–6, 177–8, 179, 214–15, 221
Postmodernity, 1–2, 5, 6, 13, 41, 44, 138, 165–6
Principles of Scientific Management (Taylor), 218
Professionalism, 33–4, 63, 86, 139–44, 154–9, 206–11, 218
Professional-managerial class (PMC), 9, 10, 30–6, 59, 63, 65–6, 72, 80–2, 88–92, 94–7, 99–102, 112, 134–5, 210–11, 215, 218, 220, 225; and globalisation, 177; and science fiction, 126–31; in Gibson's cyberspace trilogy, 137–47; in *Blade Runner*, 155–61; in *The Names*, 192–204; *see also* Professionalism
Progressive era, 29–33, 34, 35, 218

Promise of American Life, The (Croly), 149
Protestant ethic, 57, 60, 77, 89
Pynchon, Thomas, 51–4, 219
Pyramid Climbers, The (Packard), 34

RAND Corporation, 109, 111, 117–18, 174
Reaganomics, 14, 182
Regulation theory, 24–8, 31, 212–13, 217
Reich, Michael, 27
Reich, Robert, 193–4, 204, 210–11, 227
Republican Party, 73
Reuther, Walter, 223
Rieff, Philip, 47, 57, 78–9, 221
Riesman, David, 34, 44, 47, 57–60, 64–8, 76, 216–17, 221
Right to work legislation, 72, 221
Robbins, Bruce, 142, 192, 196, 200–1, 203, 209, 225, 227
Roberts, Kevin, 146, 149–50
Robertson, Roland, 228
Rorty, Richard, 223
Ross, Andrew, 86, 87, 216, 224
Rostow, W. W., 173, 226
Roszak, Theodore, 72–3, 78
Rubin, Jerry, 222
Running Dog (DeLillo), 227
Rushkoff, Douglas, 91
Rustin, Michael, 24
Ryan, Michael, 156

Said, Edward, 227
Sayer, Andrew, 176, 177
Schiller, Herbert, 41, 71, 166
Science fiction, 119–21, 124–31, 224, 226
Scientific management, 3, 24, 26, 36, 57–8, 110
Scott, Ridley, 9, 118, 225
SDS (Students for a Democratic Society), 222
Second World War, 4, 7, 105–7, 109, 165
Sennett, Richard, 57, 62, 82, 84–6, 99–101, 152
Shannon, Claude, 107
Shining, The (film), 226
Shopping malls, 80, 82–3
Shostack, Arthur B., 110
Silicon Valley, 39, 61, 102
Sklar, Martin, 29, 31
Smart, Barry, 7
Smith, Adam, 31, 101
Smith, Neil, 170, 185, 190, 196
Socialism, 59, 113
Sociological Imagination, The (Mills), 1
Sohn-Rethel, Alfred, 186
Soja, Ed, 51, 175, 176
Soul of a New Machine, The (Kidder), 42–71, 73, 75, 85, 152, 167
Space, 50–1, 87, 165–78, 185–92

Springer, Claudia, 226
Stages of Economic Growth, The (Rostow), 173
Stagflation, 22, 217
Star Trek (TV show), 96
Sublime, 56–7
Sunbelt region, 72–3, 87, 221
Surplus value, 17, 19–20, 21–2, 23, 25, 97, 170
Supreme Court, 80
Susman, Warren, 24
Suvin, Darko, 125–6, 224
Sweezy, Paul, 133–4
Symbolic analysts, 193, 204, 211, 227
Systems theory, 107–18, 122

Taft-Hartley amendments, 221
Talking Heads, 72, 73, 81, 221
Tar Baby (Morrison), 226
Taylor, F. W., 26, 218
Technological revolutions, 17, 20, 22, 39, 106, 131
Tender is the Night (Fitzgerald), 225
Theory of the Leisure Class, The (Veblen), 52
Things They Carried, The (O'Brien), 226
Third world, 19, 173, 175–6, 179–80
thirtysomething (TV show), 222
Thompson, E. P., 32
Time Out of Joint (Dick), 222
Touraine, Alain, 229
Trilling, Lionel, 130
True Stories (film), 42, 47, 66, 71, 72–87, 152, 154, 159, 221
Turkle, Sherry, 44, 51
Turner, Louis, 203
Twentieth Century Capitalist Revolution, The (Berle), 119

Uneven development, 169–70, 177–8, 201–4
United Auto Workers, 30, 173, 217, 223
Until the End of the World (Film), 178, 205–11, 228
Updike, John, 226
Urry, John, 2, 29, 36, 70, 145, 184, 218

Veblen, Thorstein, 36, 52, 63, 161, 218, 219
Vietnam War, 8, 114, 174, 181, 202
Virtual Corporation, The (Davidow and Malone), 88, 100
Virtual Light (Gibson), 225
Vonnegut, Kurt, 224

Wage relation, 25–7, 40
Wagner Act, 221
Wallerstein, Immanuel, 8, 168, 172, 175, 176, 191, 210
Weaver, Warren, 107

Weber, Max, 184
Weinstein, James, 30, 218
Wenders, Wim, 178, 205, 228
White, Hayden, 217
Whole Earth Catalog, The, 220
Whyte, William H., 34, 44
Wiebe, Robert, 30, 32
Wiener, Norbert, 67, 105–8, 110–11, 127, 129, 136, 148, 150, 222–3
Wilson, Charles E., 110
Wings of Desire (film), 228
Wollen, Peter, 40
Women's Liberation Movement, 98
Wood, Robin, 153–4
Woodiwiss, Anthony, 40, 217
World Bank, 173

Woodstock Rock Festival, 220
Working class, 6, 17, 18, 24, 26, 34, 57–8, 64, 83, 86, 113, 218, 225; and globalisation, 176, 193; in True Stories, 82–7; in Gibson's cyberspace trilogy, 138–9; in Blade Runner, 159–61
'Work of Art in the Age of Mechanical Reproduction, The' (Benjamin), 152
Wozniak, Steve, 60, 220
Wretched of the Earth, The (Fanon), 179, 196
Wriston, Walter, 176

Young, Robert, 166, 226
Yuppies, 89, 90, 203, 222

Zuboff, Shoshana, 56, 65